The Bodyguard's Bible
THE DEFINITIVE GUIDE TO CLOSE PROTECTION

Bible Publications First Edition 2007

ISBN 978-0-9554523-0-7

Designed and typeset by Bible Publications. All photos by author unless otherwise stated

Printed and bound in great Britain by The Bath Press, Bath

The Bodyguard's Bible
THE DEFINITIVE GUIDE TO CLOSE PROTECTION

James Brown BEM

BIBLE
PUBLICATIONS

The author is a licensed Close Protection Officer who has over 25 years experience as a bodyguard. He has protected a vast range of clients from page 3 girls to Royalty, as well as super rich businessmen and the rich and famous.

In 1988 he founded a very successful close protection agency and training school in Europe that continues to this day. He has trained bodyguards that have gone on to look after members of the British Royal Family and the rich and famous all over the world.

This book has a companion web site which can be found at:
www.bodyguards-bible.com

Contents

Close Protection an Introduction

As any sensible person will know, reading a book on martial arts will not make you a competent martial artist. Likewise, this book will not turn you into a Close Protection officer. To become a professional Close Protection officer you need to attend a formal course in Close Protection from a recognised provider, pass examinations and then gain valuable on the job experience. Experience is impossible for a book to provide, but this book allows you to benefit from the vast experience of its contributing authors and it contains everything you need to know to pass a course. It will also serve as a reference book for those that have qualified and are already working in the industry.

A Book of facts and expert opinion

This is a book of facts, information and expert opinion. It is not an exposé of Bodyguard's secrets. There are no 'professional secrets' in the Bodyguard industry; anyone that tells you that there are such secrets is probably a Walter Mitty type. (Walter Mitty is a fictional meek, mild man with a vivid fantasy life.) Good Close Protection is achieved through the application of a few ground rules, hard work and copious amounts of common sense, which in my experience is certainly not common! Unfortunately, neither this book nor the very best course can teach common sense! This is an attribute that a candidate must turn up with.

In recent years, there has been a bit of snobbery in the Close Protection industry. Operators who called themselves Bodyguards were looked down upon as if they were in some way inferior or unprofessional. Plenty of Bodyguards when getting married have probably recorded any number of job titles under the 'occupation column' such as Close Protection Officer (CPO), Executive Protection Officer (EPO), Personal Protection Specialist (PPS), Personal Protection Professional (PPP) or Personal Protection Officer (PPO). Any name except Bodyguard.

In This Chapter

An Introduction to the Close Protection Industry

How to use this book to become a professional

In this book we use the terms 'Close Protection' (CP) and talk about Close Protection Officers (CPOs), but we will also use the word Bodyguard – and why not? Bodyguards have been called Bodyguards for over a thousand years, so why stop now?

Many people, if you asked them to describe a Bodyguard, will conjure up an image of that large gorilla/gangster-like character, with fat fingers festooned with heavy gold rings. An intimidating figure that speaks in words of one syllable, clearing people out of the path of his client with a grunt and an elbow rather than an 'excuse me', and looking like he couldn't run twenty yards without stopping to catch breath.

In addition, many people think that the security staff that they see at music or boxing events are Bodyguards. These people are not Bodyguards; they may well be trained in crowd management functions and may work part-time as bouncers in bars and clubs, but they are not Bodyguards. Others might think that Bodyguards are secret service or 007 types in expensive suits with gadgets and guns galore. They would also be wrong. The reasons for people having these popular misconceptions are not hard to find. The heavies employed in advertising, exhibitions and soap style television are purposely easy to spot. Their already high profile is often over emphasised.

The man in the street 'sees' real Bodyguards working every day, if not in the flesh then on the television news. Seeing them is one thing but realising that they are security professionals is another. They are seen but not noticed because they strive to maintain a low profile. Not only do they look normal, their suit fits and their knuckles don't drag along the ground! The reasons that professionals can go unnoticed is discussed elsewhere in this book, but suffice it to say, they do not look like the public's idea of a Bodyguard and this actually helps them as they go about their days work.

Because people generally expect the gorilla type of Bodyguard, it is not uncommon for professional Close Protection officers to be told "you're too nice, too small, too tall, too short, or even too pretty to be a Bodyguard". (The author has never been called pretty!) Very often, the Bodyguard blends into the background of his client's business and social schedule, and he is always trying not to draw any undue attention to himself or his client. Being of normal build and stature can help in this situation.

> SOME THINK THAT ALL BODYGUARDS ARE SECRET SERVICE OR 007 TYPES IN EXPENSIVE SUITS WITH GADGETS AND GUNS GALORE.

Sometimes, a low profile is not as important and I have known some excellent Bodyguards who look exactly like the stereotypical Bodyguard – big, menacing guys (and a few girls) whose presence screams, "Do not mess with me or mine!" The reason, though, that these people were excellent professionals is because they have intelligence to match their stature.

So, who are these modern Bodyguards that we generally do not notice, and what makes them so special? The twenty-first century Bodyguard is often found in a smart but neutrally toned business suit, presenting a discreet and subdued image to the outside world. He is a highly skilled and motivated individual, constantly assessing potential risks and weighing these against his skills and the measures he must take to minimise them. He is fit, not overweight, and an expert in first aid, fire fighting, defensive driving, weapon systems, unarmed combat and communication skills. He will be well trained in all of the skills and drills that he uses daily to safeguard the peace of mind and maybe the life of his principal.

The traditional Bodyguard look.

Condoleezza Rice seems to be well protected by these Bodyguards who I hope are a little fitter than they look!

Picture EMPICS

One could be forgiven for thinking that there are jobs everywhere for this new breed of Bodyguard and everyone who is only a little bit rich or famous uses them. The truth is that there are not enough good Bodyguard jobs out there for all the 'Bodyguards' that want to be one. In contrast, there are not enough 'good' Bodyguards out there for all of the jobs that need doing! It is rare for a team leader of a CP operation to be one hundred percent happy with all of his team; there are always members that are close to losing their jobs. The team leader is always getting rid of poor performers and people who do not 'gel' with the team, or at least confining them to night shifts 'in the garden'. There are just not enough good Bodyguards to go around, and who really wants to hire a bad or indifferent one?

The Bodyguard is concerned with all aspects of security throughout his working day. By contrast, his client will hardly devote any time to security at all. At the highest level, the client is at best only dimly aware that the service is being provided, let alone that they are the entire focus of it. Flexibility and quick thinking, along with good advance work and lots of common sense all play their part.

There is something about the way a good Bodyguard will position himself, his presence, his demeanour, the eye contact and positive movement, these are all extremely reassuring to his clients. Clients that are confident in the ability of the Bodyguard are a pleasure to work with. A professional relationship develops and both Bodyguard and client go about their business, neither interfering with the other's function. They become a team.

In an ideal situation, whether working 'one on one' or as part of a team, everyone will be at the right place at the right time. No one will ever lose the keys to the client's car, the car will never break down, it won't rain when you've forgotten the umbrella and the principal won't oversleep. You'll never get lost en route, you'll never get unexpected visitors, the battery on your mobile phone will never die and you'll never

> THE MARK OF A GOOD BODYGUARD IS THAT HE KEEPS A LEVEL HEAD IN A CRISIS, REASSESSES THE SITUATION AND THEN EMBARKS ON THE CORRECT NEXT COURSE OF ACTION.

hit fog when you're late. The hotel will always be expecting you, your driver won't oversleep, you'll always have the right map, the radio range will be miles, you'll never bleed on your clean shirt and the principal will never change his mind. The plane won't be early or late, you'll eat three meals a day, customs won't stop the team and wave the principal through and you'll always know what's happening next. Ideal situations do happen, but not by accident. They must be made to happen. The Bodyguard makes good things happen and stops bad things happening.

Even with the best planning things can go wrong, and it is the mark of a good Bodyguard that he keeps a level head in a crisis, reassesses the situation and then embarks on the correct next course of action. It's not easy but that's what the training is for and every assignment you complete builds experience and confidence until getting it right becomes the norm.

This book will show you exactly what you need to do to become a first class Close Protection Officer. It will point you towards and show you how to select the very best training and provide you with the knowledge you need to pass your course with distinction. Even after your training, this book becomes the bible for all your subsequent assignments and will be a constant reference companion.

Who Uses Bodyguards

People who are rich can worry that others might steal their riches from them, kidnap their loved ones for ransom, or attack them out of jealousy. They may well think that they need a Bodyguard to allay their fears. But you do need to be very rich to employ a Bodyguard. If a client wants just one person on duty at any time, 'twenty-four-seven', that equates to two or three men working shifts. This is going to cost over of $300,000 a year, which is a considerable sum even if they are filthy rich. If, as many do, they use a whole team of security personnel then a sum akin to a major lottery win is required every year. So the Bodyguard might well be a necessity but he could also be described as a 'luxury item' that only a few can afford. There is a bit of irony here: the rich and famous feel that they need Bodyguards because they are rich and famous, but it is only they that can afford them anyway!

A team of Bodyguards working hard to keep their principal safe. Picture EMPICS

The main function of a Close Protection Officer is in essence quite simple. Officers are employed to defend their clients from all forms of attack, on them, their loved ones and their property. They are also employed to deal with accidents and emergencies. Close Protection Officers ensure that the Principal can get on with his life without worrying too much about their security. If only it were that simple!

It must be said that there are vast numbers of extremely rich and sometimes famous people who never feel the need to employ Bodyguards. They get by with the judicious use of locks, alarms and copious amounts of common sense. Most of these people live long and happy lives, never regretting the decision not to employ a Bodyguard. In contrast, there are others who have used Bodyguards most of their lives. They may have had a Bodyguard with them on their very first trip to nursery school and cannot imagine going through life without a person nearby to protect them. They can be utterly dependent on a Bodyguard for every security-related aspect of there lives.

The different users of Bodyguards

Some people employ Bodyguards for no other reason than it's fashionable to do so, and the more Bodyguards they have somehow makes them appear more important. In some circles, a large Bodyguard team can be as impressive a success symbol as the £200,000 car that only gets used to go to the odd party, or the yacht that only gets used for three weeks a year. This type of principal can be a pain, because you really are a 'designer accessory' rather than the security professional you aspire to be. But the money is good and, as long as you don't mind carrying the odd bag or walking the dog, the job is as secure as they come. What's more, because the risks are slight, there are no shortage of takers for this type of position.

Some users of Close P rotection have a very real (or sometimes imagined) reason for protection. They see the use of a Bodyguard as an absolute necessity (sometimes a necessary evil). Moreover, they take you and their security very seriously. This type of principal is employing protection for all the right reasons. Apart from the obvious risk to you when working with a client with 'real' threats present, this is the very best type of principal to work for.

The aforementioned are of course not the only users (or abusers) of protection. There are those that have protection thrust upon them; sometimes it is not the end user that is paying for it and in some cases would rather not have it at all. Generally, this type of principal is, for example, sons, daughter and wives. Another group is company executives or representatives, where the company perceives a threat and pays for the protection. Depending upon the threat, this type of protective effort may be very welcome or frowned upon by the protected.

As a private Close Protection Officer you will not be involved with public figures that require protection such as members of government. This protection is more often than not provided by the State. There may be some overlap from time to time and private contractors might find themselves helping on the fringes of what is clearly a government area of responsibility. Rarely, however, is there enough work of this kind around which to build a business. There is one other type of person who comes to you in need of protection; the one that needs your protection but cannot afford your fee. You'll have to

> THE BEST PRINCIPAL TO WORK FOR IS ONE THAT
> TAKES THE THREATS SERIOUSLY

make a decision on that one but it shouldn't be too difficult!

One thing that can be said is that once a principal has used the services of a good protection team then they are very reluctant to dismiss it and go unprotected. It's like a belief in 'Sod's Law'. (Anything that can go wrong will do so.) The day that the protection is not there, will be the very day that they really need it. It's unfortunate for the Bodyguard when a principal starts to think (even for a moment) that he can do without the protection. He might be reluctant to dismiss the team in case he needs them for some unseen or unanticipated danger, but this is where the rot can set in. The client may start to ignore some or all of the advice you give him; he may start to resent the inconvenience of having a Bodyguard with him 24 hours a day; he may start leaving you or your team behind when doing things which he considers are 'safe'; he may start cutting down on team numbers or not renewing security equipment.

> THE RICH AND FAMOUS FEEL THAT THEY NEED BODYGUARDS BECAUSE THEY ARE RICH AND FAMOUS, BUT IT IS ONLY THEY THAT CAN AFFORD THEM ANYWAY!

Then there follows the danger that the Principal decides to 'get his money's worth' from the team and starts putting them to work in other areas such as in the garden. This is very short-sighted on the part of the Principal and it makes no sense to employ a well-trained professional Bodyguard to do anything other than Bodyguard. At this point, the Bodyguard has to make some decisions. It's not an issue of dignity (I don't weed gardens.), rather it is one of function. A Bodyguard is employed on the calculated assumption that his services as a Bodyguard will be at some time needed. 'Sod's Law' will again dictate that when you are needed you will be walking the dog or collecting some groceries, instead of being alongside the person you have been paid all this time to protect. Do you want this job or not?

Summary

There are many different users of protection, just as there are many different types of Bodyguard. Between the extremes of being a fashion accessory to a superstar or working with very real threats in a war zone there is plenty of work for professional Close Protection Officers.

Once you are working your employer must be made acutely aware of your function; to him it may appear that you are doing nothing all day long. You must educate your Principal as to what your function is. To do your job properly you must have the trust and complete co-operation of your principal or you may as well not be there. Communicating with your principal is of extreme importance. He or she is paying for the kind of protection that will enable them to go about their business and social schedules with the confidence that you are doing your job and with as little inconvenience to them as possible.

Personal Security

Like the landscape gardener who's grass at home always needs cutting, and the painter's house in dire need of decorating, the security operative should never be guilty of neglecting the security of his most important asset, himself. Being an expert in security and security systems is how a Close Protection Officer earns a living, but 'personal security' has nothing to do with making a living; it's about 'living' and about how you live. A part of us has to be given up entirely to monitor our personal security. We should not do anything in life without considering what impact our actions or surroundings will have on our security.

On many occasions, operators who are the most diligent persons at work are sometimes the same ones that do not check under their own vehicles, and let strangers, such as meter readers, into their own home without scrutinising identity cards. They would never be this negligent during their 'working day', but allow themselves to switch off at home.

When a Close Protection Officer takes on an assignment, he or she can place him/herself in the very same danger that their client faces. In fact, their very association with their new client can make the Close Protection Officer a legitimate target in their own right. Targeting members of the security team to 'get at' the Principal is not uncommon. Officers may be followed home and then put under duress with threats to their family if they do not give away information. They might simply be captured and tortured for the information that they have, or they could be harmed just to send a 'message' to the Principal. This means that the protection officer must make every effort to ensure his personal security procedures are effective.

In This Chapter

The Three Principles of Personal Security

Coopers Colour Codes

Learn how to look after your Principal by looking after yourself

Understand the link between Adrenalin and Awareness

To ensure our personal security, many of the security measures that we carry out on a daily basis for our client must be carried over into our private lives, ensuring that we, and our families, are never followed, that our houses are secure, and that we have laid down procedures for action to be taken in the event of attacks. These attacks might include shooting, bombs, telephone threats, kidnap attempts, etc. Not forgetting fire, flood, earthquake and tidal waves and the hundred and one other things that may have an impact on our personal security.

Much of the time, most Close Protection Officers are working away from home. So it's even more important that their families are security conscious and exercise good personal security. The Close Protection Officer's family might be inclined to leave all the security planning to the Close Protection officer in the family! Nevertheless, as we will learn later, they are ultimately responsible for their own security and should be one hundred percent involved in it. Criminal and terrorist organisations have used families of the security officer to put pressure on him or her to assist them in their objective(s). Do not let it be you or yours.

The Three Principles of Personal Security

The personal security issues we deal with from here onwards apply to everyone, no matter what their occupation. You have a moral duty to ensure that anyone important to you is at least made to understand the principles of personal security. There are only three of them. These three Principals should form the basis of your personal security whether you are working as a BG or not. They are principles that you live by in your normal daily life. It is difficult – if not impossible – to put the three principles of personal security into an order of importance as they are equally important.

1. **Everyone is Responsible for their own Security.**

2. **Security should be Commensurate with the Threat.**

3. **Constant Awareness is the basis of Good Security**

Everyone is responsible for their own security

This means you! And it means your Principal, and for that matter your wife or your husband; all of these people are responsible for their own security. No adult can entirely hand over the responsibility for their security to another. When we go shopping, do we hand over all of our own security responsibility to the security officer at the entrance with the blazer and two-way radio? If we are walking alone at night, are we relaxed about our own security just because there are some closed circuit TV cameras in the area? Of course not! We are ultimately responsible for our own safety and security. It is when we take our own or our family's security for granted that we will be taken by surprise when our security is breached. Also, as we will learn later, it is when we are surprised, that we are at our weakest.

A VIP might be rich enough to go some way to discharging his responsibility by employing a Close Protection team, e.g. hiring a security consultant and buying the latest security equipment for his home, car and workplace. But if the VIP chooses the wrong equipment or the wrong security team or employs a dodgy consultant, and if

APPLYING TOO MUCH OR TOO LITTLE
SECURITY CAN COST YOU YOUR JOB

any of these things cause a security meltdown, it is not the fault of the kit or the team. The responsibility for the security failure is ultimately the responsible of the VIP. No matter how many experts the VIP hires, he is still ultimately responsible for his own security. He should have bought the right equipment, sought advice which was more professional and employed someone who wasn't going to let him down! Your Principal is responsible for his own security, even if he passes some or even all of that responsibility to you.

If your Principal ignores the good security advice you give him, he is being responsible for his own security (you might say irresponsible!). Suppose you allow the Principal to ignore your advice, fro example to go to a particular venue without backup, and you go with him. When some incident happens and you get hurt trying to deal with the problem without the backup you asked for, whose fault is that? YOURS. It's not his fault that you got hurt, it's YOURS; you are responsible for your own security. YOU made a decision to go without backup. Neither you nor anyone else can shirk this responsibility or delegate it to someone else. EVERYONE IS RESPONSIBLE FOR HIS OR HER OWN SECURITY.

Security should be Commensurate with the Threat

Security at most international airports is very thorough these days. We have to turn up three hours before takeoff. We cannot check-in the Principal's bags any more; he has to stand in line like the rest of us. Even though the first or business class check-in lines are much smaller than economy, it's still a queue, and our Principal is asked the same questions, as the economy class passengers. Do you have any banned articles? Have you packed your bag yourself?

All this additional security before flying is a major inconvenience, for short flights it might even be quicker to drive! But is all this extra security resented? No, not really. Most responsible people actually like the fact that everyone on the plane has undergone a strict security check before boarding. They feel so much safer because of it. Many people won't fly anywhere if there's no security at the airport.

Imagine if people could buy a ticket and then just queue to catch a plane with no real security checks at all. Not so long ago, domestic flights in many countries used to be just like that. Even if the law allowed it, an airline with no security checks would very quickly go bust through lack of customers. So, even though people are really inconvenienced with three hour check-in times and lots of searches, they don't really resent the security measures. Essentially then, you can inconvenience people a lot with your security measures, and, as long as they think it's necessary, they will put up with the inconvenience.

All security is inconvenient. How convenient would it be to be able to leave our cars unlocked in the car park when we go shopping, no fumbling on our return with locks, alarms and shopping? How much more convenient would it be, to be able not only to leave the car unlocked but the keys in the ignition? We could just get in and drive away. Except that in real life and in most places in the world today, when we got back to the car park the car would not be there, it would be stolen. So we go through the inconvenience of choosing a well lit car park, preferably one that is manned or is at least covered by a camera. We park where we can be seen by the guard or the camera, ensuring that no valuables are visible, locking the car, ensuring that it is alarmed and the keys are kept secure. We accept this inconvenience because we know that we will lose our car if we do not.

If you take a set of scales and load one side with your security measures, convenience, which is on the opposite side of the scales, will always suffer as a result. Security is inconvenient. This inconvenience will only be tolerated if people think it is a necessary inconvenience. Always try to keep the scales of security and convenience in balance. Remember that people will not consider a high level of security to be too inconvenient if they understand the threat. If they don't understand the threat then you are not doing your job. Everyone involved must understand why your precautionary security measures are in place. If they don't, you will be labelled as an over-zealous 'jobsworth'. It can be difficult to keep these things in balance but normally your job will depend on it. Too much or too little security are each a sacking offence.

Constant Awareness is the Basis of Good Security

How long can you remain constantly aware? Let's say you have just secured a three week job looking after someone. Could you remain constantly aware for the full three weeks? Or would your awareness drop within a couple of hours as soon as you 'relaxed' into the job?

How can you remain constantly aware? If you are working as a Close Protection Officer then your client is paying you to be constantly aware. What about your family? Are you going to be constantly aware with regard to their safety and security? Of course you are! Constant awareness means just that: constant, continual, complete.

Some people seem to be naturally more aware than others, noticing everything and never being taken by surprise. Trust me when I say there is nothing natural about it. It's a skill that you must learn. Some people learn quicker than others, but this is a skill that is hard to master and takes many months to acquire. Even then, considerable practice is required to keep you truly constantly aware. This skill is so important that we will now cover it in some detail.

The reason that you must remain constantly aware might appear to be obvious. Yes, you need to be acutely aware of your surroundings if you have any chance of doing your Close Protection job properly or making it to your 21st birthday. But, if you are aware, then you are much less likely to be taken by surprise. Essentially this is the reason why being aware is so important: when we are taken by surprise we are next to useless, as will see later. It is very easy to 'switch-on' and become aware. The hard work is to stay there. It takes a conscious act to switch on but switching off is normally an unconscious act. You've got the very best intentions; you switch yourself on and then before you know it something happens to show you that you have drifted in to an 'unaware' state.

A classic example of drifting into an unaware state can happen when driving on the motorway. We know it is dangerous and we try to stay alert, but it is difficult. It's boring, there isn't a lot to stimulate us. We should be stimulated, travelling at 80 mph in a tin box, surrounded by concrete and in many cases having idiots doing their very best to kill us. That should be stimulus enough! But before we know it our eyes close and we sleep. It might only be for a second, or a split second, but we switch off totally and become as unaware as it's possible to be. We're asleep! We then wake; maybe we were drifting across a lane, or woken by the shudder of the vibration-line at the side of the carriageway. We are now wide awake and alert. But for how long? Soon, we will be drifting off again. Coffee and fresh air may help in this instance but we cannot go through life high on caffeine with our window down!

> WE CANNOT GO THROUGH LIFE HIGH ON CAFFIENE WITH OUR WINDOW DOWN

Cooper's Colour Codes

For reasons that we will learn in the next chapter, if we are switched off, unaware and ignorant or oblivious to our surroundings, then when we are inevitably taken by surprise, our reactions will be poor. In situations where lives can depend upon good reactions, we have to be aware. Many people owe there life to one Jeff Cooper for keeping them alert and alive.

Who was Jeff Cooper

Jeff Cooper was born John Dean Cooper on May 10, 1920, and known all over the world as 'Jeff'. He is a former Marine Lt Colonel, who served in WWII and Korea. He is recognised as the father of what is commonly referred to as 'the modern techniques of shooting'. This modern technique deals with 'practical' shooting. That is the use of firearms in their intended roles as *tools* for personal protection rather than sport or recreation. Whilst his skill with firearms is almost legendary, he is best known for his colour codes, which depict levels of awareness. While teaching law enforcement he devised the colour codes so that police officers wouldn't get taken by surprise when finding themselves in life-threatening situations. Such situations might require their having to think about what to do while under pressure and the effects of adrenalin, when they really should be already doing it! Cooper chose four codes or levels of awareness: WHITE, YELLOW, ORANGE, and RED. These are explained below:

Code White

RELAXED, unaware and completely unprepared. This is where it is said that 95 percent of people spend 95 percent of their time. Totally switched off. If he is attacked in this state, his attacker has everything on his side, that is, surprise and everything that goes with it. If we get an adrenal dump when in Code White it will be a big one. An attack will be over before we were aware it was even underway.

You can see people in Code White all of the time. Just look around you; it's rare that anyone will notice you looking. Anyone who has worked in surveillance, following people, will know just how oblivious people can be of the people around them. Code White is no place to be!| We should always make the conscious decision to move our level of awareness to Code Yellow.

Code Yellow

RELAXED ALERTNESS. Running scenarios through your mind, and thinking of ways to overcome them while remaining switched on. Your mindset is: "Today could well be the day I have to defend myself." There is no specific threat, but you are aware that anything could happen and bad things happen when you are not expecting it! You are bristling with anticipation; you use your eyes and ears, and your carriage says "I am alert." You need to concentrate to stay in Code Yellow. It is a conscious decision to move from white to yellow but if you don't maintain your awareness you will drift back to Code White without realising it. With a little practice, however, you can live in Code Yellow indefinitely.

> WE DRIFT UNCONSCIOUSLY INTO CODE WHITE BUT IT REQUIRES A CONSCIOUS THOUGHT TO PUTS US BACK INTO CODE YELLOW

Code Orange

SPECIFIC ALERT. Because you are alert in Code Yellow you will often see or hear things that push you to Code Orange. You shift your primary focus to whatever your alert mind has noticed. This is an evaluation stage, in which you start making decisions on the situation. You will be getting adrenalin. Your mindset is: "If this situation develops as I think it might, I may have to fight or run away." What is that? What I am going to do about it?" You can maintain this heightened state of awareness for several hours.

Code Red

FIGHT TRIGGER. "We See Red." When we were in Code Orange we made decisions, or if time hasn't allowed at least started to make decisions about what we might do if this or that happened. Well, it's HAPPENED. Now we are ready, we have had a massive dose of adrenalin but because we were already receiving it, via a tiny drip feed in Code Yellow and then another larger doses in Code Orange, the adrenalin doesn't have as many of the debilitating effects. It's our friend, we're harder, smarter and more likely to win.

Adrenalin

We learned in the chapter on personal security that to maintain our awareness we have to be continually assessing situations for threats and then planning our responses to them. When something unexpected happens that requires a positive response from you, that moment is not the time to begin planning what you are going to do about it. If you weren't expecting it then you were probably surprised by it and when you are surprised, your reactions will be poor. This is due to a failure to understand the effects of adrenalin on our bodies. Not only that, if we are continually exposed to adrenalin, unless you know how to cope with it you can become seriously ill. Understanding and managing our adrenalin is a skill so fundamental to our industry that it requires us to look into it further.

Adrenalin and Our Reactions

Think of the times that you have been surprised, when someone 'made you jump', perhaps on purpose. Maybe they shouted 'Boo!' or possibly you were just 'switched off' and then saw or heard someone in your space. This type of surprise has happened to most people at some time. When it did happen, you were lucky the person that made you jump wasn't holding a video-camera. If they had of been, the camera would have recorded your surprise as your 'emotional mind' tried to work out what was happening; the silly face you pulled, the colour draining from your face, the jerk away from the noise, arms flailing, your mouth open as if to say something but merely emitting a small scream or grunt. The camera would record your un-focussed eyes, and then the sudden realisation as your 'rational mind' took over from its emotional counterpart.

It would highlight your realisation that you are in no danger, just the subject of a prank. The camera would make good, but rather embarrassing, TV.

A Positive Reaction

When things go wrong, Close Protection Officers are expected to react positively to the situation, making lightening fast decisions and taking the correct actions. We must ALWAYS be expecting someone to metaphorically say boo because when we are expecting it, there is no shock value or at least the shock is minimised. Because our anticipation/expectation has caused us to release small amounts of adrenalin into our bodies, it 'charges our system' and makes it much more difficult for us to be surprised.

Mother Nature was not in an optimistic mood when she endowed early man and of course, women, with the capacity to make good judgments about how to survive in a life-threatening situation. To counter this she made our stress reaction and survival system work with lightening speed. Millions of years of evolution have endowed us with a set of automatic weapons, which take over in the event of an emergency. The hypothalamus, which is a part of the brain, sends a message to the amygdalae, which recognise the data and immediately associates it with danger.

So at the sight of a sabre-toothed tiger or a charging rhino, our amygdalae – which are basically almond shaped masses of grey matter, found deep inside each of the hemispheres of our brain, and which can be thought of as the 'alarm company', which handles all our body's emergency alarms – sends out messages to alert the body of the impending danger.

The amygdalae send messages to every major part of the brain and triggers secretions of hormones such as adrenalin, which mobilises our centres of movement, makes us almost impervious to pain and activates the cardiovascular system, along with the muscles and the gut. Within seconds we can run faster, hit harder and with more accuracy, see better, hear more acutely, think faster and jump higher than we could just seconds earlier.

I can testify that under the effects of a lot of adrenalin, the body just doesn't feel pain. I once witnessed a novice skydiver leave half a little finger trapped in a plane as he leapt out; the finger was literally torn off. He didn't notice it during the one minute of freefall but in the second or two after the parachute opened, the pain became apparent as the adrenalin left.

We have all heard stories of adrenalin-charged mothers lifting heavy objects, such as cars – which they couldn't ordinarily lift – to save a child. These women might say afterwards that they 'don't know where they found the strength'. We know that the adrenalin provided it.

These are all good things. They can help us do our job, but some effects can be detrimental. For instance, while we might be able to see better, we might also develop 'tunnel vision' and only see the main danger while missing others. We might also suffer auditory exclusion, reducing our hearing capacity, and, worst of all, we could lose fine motor co-ordination and manual dexterity. Some might even 'freeze' under its effects, suffering a complete sensory overload, known affectionately in skydiving circles as 'brain fade'. These effects are not so helpful in an emergency situation.

Adrenalin is an exceedingly quick-acting hormone. Our body produces it from two glands sitting just above each kidney. When we are faced with an emergency, the subsequent dump of adrenalin will cause our heart to start pumping at two or three times its normal resting rate. This increase in pumping frequency and power is required so that our major muscles, such as the legs, the arms and even the heart itself, which is also a muscle, get all of the oxygen and other nutrients they need to enable them to function at a heightened 'life-saving' level. The tiny blood capillaries under the skin will tighten so as to restrict the flow of blood to its surface. This not only puts the blood to work on the vital organs, it allows us to sustain small surface wounds without bleeding to death. This loss of blood to the skin's surface explains why some people might be described as 'white as a sheet' when they are scared.

EVERONE GETS ADRENALIN. WE ARE HARD-WIRED TO RELEASE IT WHEN WE ARE FACED WITH DANGER

Sensory Overload

Each bodily function that the body decides is not needed for the fight or flight process will be shut down. This will include sexual function, which will stop immediately, and digestion. Even our immune system may be turned off. Some of the blood that normally feeds our brain is no longer sent to support its cognition (thinking), so what is left is referred to by some people as the 'frog brain', This is a primitive and totally reactive brain that does not have much access to our training, such as our action-on drills and pre-learned techniques. We get what is called sensory overload; so much is going on in such a short time that we cannot take it all in. Total 'brain fade' ensues.

In addition, adrenalin will often cause someone to instantly urinate, defecate, or both. The body knows that it can run faster or fight more effectively with an empty bladder and bowel. Accompanying all of these physical reactions, we have a very real compression of time, during which our perception of events leads us to feel that things are happening in slow motion. After an adrenal 'dump' it can be very difficult to remember all the details of an event. Which is why police get so many different stories from adrenalin-charged witnesses after an incident.

Putting Adrenalin to work

As far as the Close Protection Officer is concerned, most of the effects of adrenalin are positive but only if they understand them. When the body is suddenly startled by all those feelings and chemicals it can have very negative results. We can avoid these things by never moving from Code White to Code Red in one moment. YELLOW THROUGH ORANGE AND THEN RED IS THE IDEAL BUT YELLOW TO RED IS INFINITELY BETTER THAN WHITE TO RED.

Fear

The effects of adrenalin on the body are normal; they are a normal bodily function designed to help us to survive life-threatening situations. But when the effects occur in people who do not understand what is happening to their bodies, they mistake these preparations for fight or flight as unbridled fear or 'a panic attack'. In quieter moments they will convince themselves that they can't handle pressure situations and that they are cowards. They will see FEAR as a mnemonic of "Forget Everything And Run". Once a person has convinced him/herself that he/she is spineless, any subsequent release of adrenalin to the system is associated with fear and then continues to reinforce that misconception. What must be understood is that everyone gets adrenalin; we cannot stop our body from producing it. We are 'hard wired' to release it when we are faced with danger.

In some hazardous sports, such as caving, climbing, skydiving and motor sport, we can see and study the effects of adrenalin in a controlled environment. The effects of adrenalin on the body generated by an extreme sport are the same, or very similar, to those you might get as a Close Protection Officer when an incident occurs. Examining how adrenalin can affect sportsmen and women can give us a good idea about how it will affect us.

We know that once the body gets used to a dangerous situation it doesn't react so violently to it. Jumping out of an aeroplane at 14,000 feet would quite rightly be considered by many to be dangerous. They would be right; it is dangerous. Nevertheless, once the hypothalamus gets used to the unnatural act of leaping from an aircraft, it doesn't send the same signals it did the first time it saw that the ground was three miles below.

An experienced skydiver will often be laid back enough to catch up on some sleep on the slow aircraft ride to altitude; others might carry a book to pass away the 15 or 20 'boring' minutes. A first time-skydiver – or even someone who has done a hundred jumps – would not be able to relax enough to sleep on the climb to altitude, but somewhere between three and five hundred jumps, the hypothalamus relaxes us a little, and it would become possible. I have seen people fall into a deep sleep on the climb to altitude. Often, they are woken only by the movement of other jumpers moving to check pins and handles. Sometimes, the sleeper doesn't even realise he is on a plane. He wakes up a little startled and as consciousness grips him with the memory that he is skydiving, a little panic attack ensues, during which he realises that in a few seconds he is going to jump, and watching him start to check his kit can be quite amusing.

The experienced skydiver still has adrenalin, enough to mobilise his muscle groups and aid his concentration, but doesn't have the massive adrenal dump that can be so debilitating. If we were working as an armed escort in Iraq, our initial duties would feel a little like the first-time skydiver, but with continued exposure the body receives just enough adrenalin to remain alert and ready for anything. In Iraq in 2006/7 you could be shot at or blown up at any moment. You didn't have to imagine what might happen as it was happening all the time. You just wondered when or if it was going to happen to you and did everything in your power to ensure it didn't.

The effects of an adrenalin dump are for immediate use; we cannot store them. Fight or flight is happening NOW, not in a minute or two's time. The massive adrenal dump that someone receives when leaving an aircraft for the first time may make them kick and thrash wildly. This is exactly what shouldn't be done if a successful parachute deployment is to be achieved, but the effect only lasts for a few seconds. The mind quickly grabs back some consciousness, blood flow starts returning to the thinking part of the brain and he or she starts to carry out what they know to be the best thing to do, which is to arch hard, belly to earth. This gives them stability and gives the parachute space to deploy.

> THE EFFECTS OF ADRENALIN ARE FOR IMMEDIATE USE. WE CANNOT STORE IT

Many first time skydivers are strapped to the front of an experienced jumper. When they exit the aircraft a camera jumper is right there with them with the camera strapped to their head and recording everything. As the first-timer moves toward the open door, the initial adrenalin dump occurs. There is a terrorised expression and sensory overload, with the eyes clamped shut. However, this reaction quickly passes. The skydiver can soon feel the airspeed building up and then, as they fully recover their senses, they realise the noise of the plane has given way to a new noise – that of the freefall wind. They feel the wind on their face as they speed up to around 120 miles an hour, the cognitive part of the brain is quickly restored and they start thinking clearly: "I'm alive, everything is going to plan." A pre-arranged tap on their shoulders to spread their arms, and they do it just as they were taught. They may even chance opening there eyes. If so, they will see the ground a long way down, and someone with a camera on his head flies right to within a foot from their face. The cameraman smiles, suddenly there is a big smile for the camera. The cameraman give a thumbs up sign and the first timer smiles even more as a he points his thumbs skyward.

The first-timer is relaxed and thinking, the emotional mind has retreated and his rational mind is now working. Suddenly, there is another tap on the arm. The freefall is going to end just as the first-timer had become accustomed to it. It's time to deploy the parachute. The emotional mind is back. Is it going to work? Is it going to hurt? I've never been here before. BANG! More adrenalin as they are jerked upward by the deploying canopy. The cameraman seems to be falling quickly and somehow crazily away from them. In just two seconds he is the size of a hamster. Quietly, the canopy is open, they are floating, turning, just hanging there 4,500 feet up. The adrenalin is almost gone and the jumpmaster talks to them. The thinking, rational brain is back. They enjoy the view; they can see the plane just landing, far below them. They wonder how it has beaten them down and may search out their car in the car park, looking for familiar things on the ground below. But suddenly, they are not floating, they are falling. The ground seems to be rushing up to meet them at a speed that will break every bone in their body. More adrenalin is released making it difficult for

This first time skydiver can't bring himself to look down. Many first timers have a complete sensory overload and can remember nothing about the first part of the skydive. Only after they realise that they are still alive does the rational brain kick back in and then they open their eyes and start to enjoy the skydive.

them to concentrate – sensory overload. The jumpmaster flares the canopy and the ground suddenly slows its rush, as they land gently. The first-timer is unaware that the jumpmaster had to shout at him three times to bend his knees; the adrenalin had stolen his hearing again. A soft landing! He is still alive! There is the cameraman again, right in his face. Most of the adrenalin is immediately gone. There is a smile for the camera, though it's impossible to undo the chest strap because the fingers and arms are still shaking quite violently. Usually, the first words muttered are, 'Let's do it again!' and another adrenalin junkie is born. But before this person can jump alone, to enjoy the adrenalin adventures, they need to be able to handle the effects of the adrenalin. This is done by plenty more jumping starting with relatively undemanding jumps. Then, as the student progresses, things become a little harder, getting the body used to the experience so that not quite so much adrenalin is released and what is released is used to good effect.

The WOW Factor

On Close Protection courses in the 1980s we started to measure student's reaction times, both with and without adrenalin. Typically, the reaction time might be measured in response to a particular incident, such as a gun firing or an attack of some kind. We called this time the 'WOW FACTOR', the state of frozen confusion that occurs at the moment of shock. The measurements were really only made for fun, but did go someway to explaining the effects of adrenalin to our students.

The faster you reacted, the lower your wow factor. We would have great fun with a video and a stopwatch timing the students', and quite often, the instructors' reactions. I remember that some students' Wow Factor would have been better measured not with a stopwatch but with a calendar! Apart from the odd student almost everyone could improve their Wow Factor with practice at applying the techniques that are outlined here.

In a Close Protection role the wow factor can be made worse (longer reaction time) by the very nature of our work. Close Protection is not a daily routine loaded with exciting, dangerous and stimulating events. Rather, it is a day in, day out routine, often unexciting and familiar work, where the greatest battle is that against mind-numbing boredom. This is a dangerous situation, because when we are bored we are most likely to switch off and move to Code White , and it is then that our wow factor will be measured in long seconds rather that bits of a second.

Muscle Memory

We have stated that we cannot really control the release of adrenalin but we can deal with it a little better. However, we do know that if we repeat actions enough times and commit them to 'muscle memory', we will do those things 'on autopilot', even when we are suffering from the initial shock of a large adrenal dump. A good example of this is when we are driving. For example, let's say that we are driving a car, performing an overtaking manoeuvre on a large truck. Suddenly, an oncoming car appears 'from nowhere' and it looks like a head-on crash is imminent. We instantly get adrenalin – lots of it – but we have to make a decision. In this situation we have to very quickly choose between three courses of action: brake and pull back in behind the truck; accelerate past and squeeze in front of the truck; or see if we can pull off somewhere on the wrong side of the road out of harm's way. Many people who drive in Code White don't get past the first option, they BRAKE AND HOPE.

If we were driving in Code Yellow, the adrenalin helps rather than hinders: time slows down for us and we choose the best option, based upon the razor-sharp thinking, that the adrenalin has given us. We assess our speed and both that of the oncoming car and the truck, we take into account the road conditions and width before instantly choosing our best option. Let's say that in this situation the decision was to accelerate hard and complete the overtake. Muscle memory now takes over, we

> OUR ACTION-ON-DRILLS NEED TO BECOME AS INSTINCTIVE AS BLINKING AND DUCKING

dip the clutch and go down a gear. Then, releasing the clutch while feeding back in the power, we accelerate to safety. We didn't fumble the gear change and everything was smooth – the adrenalin saw to that. You might say that if the driver was in Code Yellow, he wouldn't be in that position, and you would of course be right. But, as the saying goes, 'Shit happens', so let's be in Code Yellow when it does.

It is a physiological fact that if we repeat an action enough times in a certain set of circumstances it will become habit forming. Indeed, the resultant muscle memory will ensure that when we don't have time to think, the muscles will carry out what they have practised automatically. An example of this is the one just given, when we used the clutch, throttle and gear lever smoothly, positively and in the correct sequence. So on those rare occasions, when, in real life, an event occurs, the correct habitual response should occur instantly. If it does not, then the physical things have not been practised enough. It may take thousands of times to commit something to muscle memory, but the result is obviously worth it. When we are in Code Red the time for decision-making has passed. There is no time for weighing the pros and cons of various alternative courses of action. It is a time for action/reaction, but reaction based on appropriate and correct responses. A reaction which is based on panic and confusion is simply an illustration of an incorrect attitude and understanding of what training is designed to achieve. Practise for when things go wrong and you'll be rewarded when they do.

Things committed to muscle memory become as instinctive as blinking and ducking; we do them quickly and without thinking. Take someone who is looking out of a closed window, if you surprise them by throwing a bucket of water at the window from outside, they will instinctively blink and duck out of its path. Then, moments later, they will realise how silly they look because they were in no danger at all of getting wet. Throw another bucketful at the window and, even though they are ready for it, they will still probably blink and have to consciously work at resisting the urge to duck again. The brain knows that you are not going to get wet behind the glass, but blinking and ducking are instinctive and when something has become instinctive it becomes hard not to do it.

Practise a physical action/reaction enough and muscle memory will make it instinctive. Instinctive things are those we do without thinking. This ability is very important to the Bodyguard; it is essential that he carry out some of the immediate-action drills enough times to commit them to muscle memory and make them instinctive. When we find ourselves in Code Red with a massive release of adrenalin, in the time it takes our mind to grasp and take control of the situation our unconscious mind is already carrying out some things instinctively. Muscle memory is strong enough to override your thinking; the following examples will explain this.

Driving in a car with a colleague, I notice that he turns his radio off as soon as his mobile phone rings so the noise of the radio doesn't interfere with the call. His phone rings many times a day. Sometimes the radio is not on when the phone rings, but his left hand still reaches to turn the radio off. The radio isn't on, so the brain hasn't asked for the radio to be turned off. Why does he try to turn it off? Muscle memory has taken over and the hand moves instinctively.

When training takes over

When adrenalin is involved, which we know can have some initial debilitating effects, it is good that we have committed things to memory so that they might become instinctive. One personal experience of when muscle memory has been used while under the extreme effects of a lot of adrenalin occurred during a sky dive over Florida when a main parachute malfunctioned. You can imagine that at the point of realising that you have a malfunction a massive adrenal dump occurs. Many years of practising the emergency reserve parachute drills had involved peeling a Velcro pad off the chest harness on the right side of the harness and then pulling this pad to 'cut away' the bad parachute and then one second or so later, pulling a metal handle on the left of the harness to activate the reserve. Because the malfunction was at high speed, the parachute was out but was in a condition technically known as a 'bag of washing'. It was just a tangled mess. This mess still catches some air and I found myself being spun violently around.

My emotional brain, which had taken over when I first noticed that something was wrong ("Shit, that doesn't look good!"), quickly gave way to my rational brain and I could think clearly. I knew I had plenty of height to allow a longer than normal one-second delay between cutting the bad parachute away and deploying the reserve. This extra height/delay would absolutely ensure that my deploying reserve would not get tangled with the bad canopy, which was pretty unlikely but I wanted to be sure. I pulled the pad and released the bad canopy; I counted (at the top of my voice) three full seconds before pulling the other handle to activate the reserve. But by the time I had counted to three I discovered that I had pulled the reserve handle already. By the time I got to three I was already safely under an open reserve. Muscle memory had taken over, just one second after I had cut away. I deployed the reserve, just as I had practised countless thousands of times. Muscle memory ignored my brain's request to wait for three seconds. I had practised this emergency procedure as one movement for years, and, when I was full of adrenalin, the muscle memory just took over. My reserve drills had become just as instinctive as blinking and ducking.

Armed with this knowledge we can practise, practise and practise. This will commit our responses to particular situations, to muscle memory. A Close Protection officer, who continually practises his responses to attacks on his client when walking or driving will, after a short time, start to commit things to muscle memory. Drills like parrying a knife thrust, J-turning a car, punching to buy time, drawing a pistol, or taking hold and control of the Principal. These must be committed to muscle memory if we have any hope of doing them under pressure and the effects of adrenalin.

For example, we might be when walking with the client when an adrenalin-inducing event occurs; our left hand takes hold and control of the client before the Bodyguard is even aware of what is happening.

Adrenalin and Stress

We learned in the chapter on personal security that to stay constantly alert we must inject a healthy dose of paranoia into our daily routine. Always expecting the worst to happen at any moment, and then working out what we might do about it. All of this "anticipation" introduces adrenalin into our bodies. Once the adrenalin is produced the body expects and needs to use it. The only way that it can be used effectively is to use it as it was intended that is to fight your way out of the situation or run away, you should note that both of these actions are physical rather than mental.

IN TODAY'S SOCIETY SOME PEOPLE CAN GET ADRENALIN JUST BY WATCHING TELEVISION,

You may get "adrenalised" lots of times in a single day. You might see a suspicious face in a crowd near your Principal, or hear a shout or loud noise. You might also get more into your system if your Principal is in a demanding mood, putting you on the spot or asking difficult or even potentially dangerous things of you. Adrenalin was meant to save us in life-threatening situations, but in today's society some people can get the adrenalin just by watching something on television, or asking their boss for a raise. Continual exposure of this cocktail of drugs is not good for our bodies in the long term.

A Stressful Environment

Close Protection can be a very stressful environment to work in, this stress can be compounded by other things such as:

- ☑ Working long hours, and a lack of sleep.
- ☑ Being away from home for long periods, especially if you have family problems
- ☑ Fear of letting the team or Principal down.
- ☑ Not getting on with the team leader or team member
- ☑ Not being in the best physical shape

Stress is a very serious issue and one that must be addressed as soon as you consider you may be suffering from it some symptoms of stress are shown below:

- ☑ Loss of appetite
- ☑ Unable to sleep properly.
- ☑ An increase in alcohol and tobacco consumption
- ☑ Poor concentration and irritability with team-mates
- ☑ The loss of sex drive
- ☑ Diarrhoea
- ☑ Feeling fatigued all of the time.

All of these symptoms are very general and any or all of them could point to conditions that are not stress-related. If you suffer from any of the symptoms above you may well be suffering from stress and should seek professional help. In my experience there are two things that keep Close Protection Officers stress free whilst at work, these are regular exercise and diet.

Exercise

Exercise is a fantastic way to relieve you of the stress after an eventful day. Put on some gloves and very aggressively attack a punch-bag. Not worrying too much about technique but just hitting that bag for all your worth. Go all out for at least 90 seconds, (it will hurt) having one minutes rest followed by another minute of continual hard-hitting. Get on a bike, run on the road or swim for at least 30 minutes every day. You may have noticed that we are fighting and running. This way we are using that adrenalin just as nature intended.

Diet

We know that adrenalin and the cocktail of drugs that are deployed into our bloodstream when we are stressed, are there to assist us in our fight or flight. Whoever designed our bodily functions did not expect us to feel hungry whilst we were fighting an enemy or running away from one. In the presence of adrenalin things like appetite are suppressed. You must eat even when you do not feel hungry. Force yourself to eat at mealtimes. If you let your appetite dictate whether you eat or not you will soon succumb to the stress. You will not have the energy to do your job properly or to exercise and get rid of the adrenalin at the end of the day.

Summary

Whenever you find yourself in Code White , put yourself back into yellow. Remember that we drift unconsciously into Code White , but it's a conscious thought that switches us back on.

You must understand that colour codes are not used like the military levels of alertness. They do represent the level of danger of some threat or other happening. Do not get confused; THE COLOURS REPRESENT THE LEVEL OF YOUR AWARENESS AND NOT THE AMOUNT OF DANGER YOU MIGHT BE IN.

To maintain our awareness, we have to be continually assessing situations for threats and then planning our responses to them. When something untowards happens, which requires an immediate response, then is not the ideal time to begin planning what to do about it. If you aren't expecting it then you're probably going to be surprised by it. When you're surprised, your reactions will be poor. Don't be surprised, think yellow.

Taken by surprise, the massive adrenal dump can put us in a state of shock, which will not only make our reaction time slower; we are more likely to make a wrong reaction or decision.

We cannot stop our bodies producing the adrenalin (nor would we want to); we are hard-wired to produce it. However, we can condition our body and mind to get used to the effects of adrenalin by creating opportunities in training that expose us to adrenalin.

By constantly anticipating the worst to happen and questioning what our response would be, we give ourselves a little adrenal drip which can assist us to control our thinking and reactions when we do get an adrenal dump.

During the initial shock phase of an adrenalin dump, we will carry out drills that we have committed to muscle memory and made instinctive.

If we are working in dangerous places or on assignments where the threats we face are considerable, it is all too easy to deteriorate because of stress. A proper diet coupled with a vigorous exercise goes a long way to avoiding stress. Look out for signs of stress in yourself and your colleagues and seek professional help immediately that you think you may be suffering from the debilitating condition.

Putting the Principal into code yellow

Your Principal employs you so that he can hand over the responsibility for his security to you. It is important therefore that the Principal is made aware of the first principle of personal security. It does not matter how much he pays you or how well you do your job. He is still ultimately responsible for his own security. He should be encouraged to mention anything at all that he feels will have an impact, however slight, on the security operation. In addition the Principal's family needs the same advice to stay safe. Some Principals will welcome your security briefing other will not. However it is unprofessional not to offer it.

There are very many users of Bodyguards who do not have the protection with them 24/7. Some users may stand their security down when they are at work, others stand the Bodyguard down in the evening when they home "safe" and can rely on the security provided by the Resident Security Team. Many Principals often carry out business and social functions with out their protection team; this will almost always be against the advice of the Bodyguard. This is often the case when the Principal feels that the protection team will get in the way. This is especially so when it comes to the early stages of sexual relationships when many Principals are guilty of sneaking off without their protection team.

In situations like this it is worth reminding the Principal that you can make the profile very low or even drop it completely out of sight while still providing adequate protection. Your advice and assistance may be accepted or rejected out of hand, but as a professional you have a duty to at least offer it. The best way to protect the Principal even when you are not there is to ensure that you instruct him on some basic security procedures and encourage him to follow them.

In This Chapter

Give your Principal an effective security brief for when you are not there.

Security tips for the home, office and when on the road.

General Security Briefing

The Principal must understand that a period of surveillance will always precede a planned attack. He is to look for surveillance and should tell you of anything suspicious, no matter how seemingly insignificant.

1. The Principal should be informed of the most effective means of contacting the Bodyguard. Pre-programming phone numbers into the Principals of phone so that he can operate the speed dial is to be recommended. But the Bodyguard's number on 'speed dial 9'

2. Establish a duress code, this code will let you know if something is wrong.

3. Never travel to the same place twice at the same time. Vary the timings of regular journeys as well as the route taken is much as possible.

4. He should not be predictable using the same car parking bay or newsagent can be very dangerous

5. Use different vehicles whenever possible, swap their use randomly.

6. Use a strict need to know policy with regard to the travel arrangements. Encourage the Principal to make his own travel arrangements or only use a trusted employee.

7. Sign up the Principals mobile phone for tracking. Don't forget to do the same for the spouse and children.

8. Your Principal needs to be aware that information in 'Who's Who' or 'Debretts Peerage' should not any include personal information that could be of use to any criminal or terrorist.

9. You must educate your Principal to always choose meeting locations himself especially when meeting strangers, or persons, he does not know very well.

10. Impress upon your Principal the importance of being unpredictable. Having a favourite table in the hotel coffee lounge or restaurant makes it much easier to locate you, or record your conversations.

11. If your Principal is rich and famous, then many people will recognise them in the street. But if they are just rich they should restrict the number of photographs in the public domain. Some of the richest people in the world go unrecognised because they very sensibly restrict the issue of photographs as much as possible.

On the road

Whenever the Principal drives without a Bodyguard or an escort section then he should be educated to do so safely. This can be difficult task because while some people will let you get away with insulting their spouse or mother. All people, male or female will hate you if you insult their car or question their driving ability!

1. When entering the vehicle the Principal should always have his keys in hand and ready for use.

2. After entering vehicle immediately lock the doors. Do this before anything else.

3. Avoid driving at night whenever possible. Ambushes and attacks are so much easier to facilitate under the cover of darkness.

4. Make sure the Principal understands the 2/30 rule

5. Always keep plenty of distance between him and the vehicle in front. This is applicable when moving as well as being stationary. You should always have enough room to stop or to evade the vehicle in front.

6. If something is not right with the vehicle, as long as you can still drive; continue to a place of safety before you investigate what is wrong. Run-flat tires should always be fitted

7. Whenever possible the Principal should change vehicles. Using pool cars is to be encouraged. The more nondescript the car is the better.

8. Encourage the Principal to vary his route to and from work as much as possible.

9. Remind him of the importance to always keep the vehicle's fuel tank is full as possible at all times.

10. The Principal should be aware that attackers will use places where the vehicle slows or comes to a halt to mount their ambushes. Whenever he is forced to stop such as at traffic lights or railway crossings he should look for escape routes in anticipation of being attacked. He should also time his approach toward these hazards, pacing the vehicle to avoid having to stop completely at the obstacle.

11. Never, ever stop for stranded motorists, if they need help use a mobile telephone and call the police but do not stop.

12. Never 'Nosey Park' Teach you Principal that he should never be a nosy parker, he should always reverse into parking bays so that he can drive out.

13. When travelling he should use his mirrors effectively to monitor for surveillance. Basic anti-surveillance drills should be encouraged.

14. The Principal must understand that if he is ever attacked he should never leave the vehicle unless absolutely necessary. He should be reminded that the vehicle can be an effective weapon in its own right.

15. If the Principal feels that he is being followed at any time he should immediately drive toward the nearest police station, army barracks or other safe haven in the area. He should call the police and describe his followers.

16. The Principal should never routinely use the same petrol filling station. It is a good idea for the Principal to arrange for others to fill the car.

17. The Principal should be taught how to carry out a cursory search of the vehicle and encourage carrying out the search regularly.

18. Advise the Principal to always leave the vehicle secured. A locked and alarmed the garage is best, but if the vehicle must be left alone then ensure that this is in a well lit area and make sure that he has a good look around the vehicle on his return. The Principal should ensure that he always uses the alarm when he leaves the vehicle.

At the residence.

1. At night in home and office locations remind the Principal that curtains should be drawn early and before the lights are turned on.

2. Never leave the home completely empty, at least one residential security team member or household staff should be left behind. If this is not practical then everything should be done to make sure that the residence looks occupied. This may well include the use of lights on a timer, sound files of dogs barking etc. Do not forget to cancel deliveries such as newspapers and milk.

3. If the residence does not have a safe room then one room, preferably an upstairs one should be made as safe as possible with a lock on the inside. Ensure that the mobile phone is upstairs at all times.

4. The Principal must be educated to call the police immediately something is not right. It is much better to be safe than sorry.

5. A list of emergency telephone numbers should always be near to the telephone.

6. Make sure that all everyone is aware of the importance of not opening a door without knowing exactly who is on the other side. Children of the home especially should be educated not to open the door.

7. The intelligent use of outside lights is to be encouraged.

8. If the Principal is a dog lover then one of the large guarding breeds such as the German shepherd, Rottweiler or Doberman can be used to good effect as many terrorists and criminals may well be scared of such animals and the noise that they make.

9. The house alarm should have a panic button attached, ideally in the alarm will call the police or a central station who will call the police.

10. All doors and windows should be protected against attack this may be in physical protection such as hinge bolts or overt protection such as bars and shutters.

The CP Team

A protective effort is always a team effort, even when working in a 'one on one' situation (one Bodyguard and one Principal). The team is a team of two; the Bodyguard and the Principal. One on one situations are commonplace for many reasons, the most common being that this is all the security that is deemed necessary (by the Principal). The one Bodyguard will wear many hats as well as being the Bodyguard. For instance, the chauffeur, the advance party, the personal assistant, a medic, a mechanic, a washer of cars and security consultant.

Some people will say that you cannot be a good Bodyguard if you have to worry about other things not directly related to security. For example, washing the car or doing the garden. However, generally speaking, if you want the 'one on one' job then these things will more than likely have to be done. It is not an ideal situation but you can balance them with a little application and common sense, and don't forget that in 'one on one' situations it is more than likely (but not always) that the threat is quite low. Also, it may be that the Principal's finances do not stretch to having more employees. The decision to take the job is yours, just as is it your right to leave if you are not happy.

Large teams

When there is a high threat, it is common to have teams of over 30 members spread over a couple of different residences and looking after all members of a large family. All teams, regardless of their size or purpose for being there, must function well. All members of the team need to be disciplined and have the ability to work well with different groups of people in widely varied settings. As a team member you must have the attitude and willingness to get along with people. You must come to work with the right attitude. There might be someone you dislike on a team, but you should be the only person that knows it!

In This Chapter

Understand the organisational make up of a CP Team

Learn the functions of team members

Although different companies and organisations will have different operating procedures the general breakdown of a large team is as follows. The following descriptions are brief and a more detailed discussion of the different elements and their function will be discussed later.

The Team Leader

This person may or may not be the Bodyguard to the main Principal as well as being in overall charge of the protective operation. The Team Leader's job is to ensure that everyone has all of the information that they need to enable them to carry out their function; he is usually the one that liaises with the Principal and the contracting security company if there is one. On most assignments, the Team Leader has the authority to hire and fire team personnel.

The Bodyguard (BG)

Usually abbreviated to BG, he is a member of the PES (discussed below). However, his role is quite different; while everyone on a team is in theory a Bodyguard, i.e. their function, whether they are drivers or they guard the garden gate, is that of guarding the Principal. There is only one BG per Principal. There may be a day BG and a night BG but generally there is only one BG on one Principal at any one time.

Areas of responsibilty. The Bodyguard looks after the immediate area around the Principal whilst the Personal Escort Section guard the outer cordon

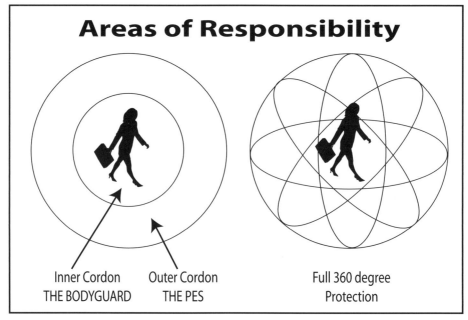

Areas of Responsibility

Inner Cordon
THE BODYGUARD

Outer Cordon
THE PES

Full 360 degree
Protection

The other 'Bodyguards' are referred to as the PES. The BG is the person that will be in close contact with the Principal at all times. His job is to shield the Principal from any danger, and ACE which is a acronym for Assess, Cover and control and Evacuate. The BG forms the inner cordon of defence and is responsible for seeing that no threat gets past him and to the Principal. When working as part of the PES, the BG is the one that never stands and fights. He runs away (with the Principal of course), giving body cover as he does so. This role can be (dependant upon the situation) in complete contrast to that of the PES.

The Bodyguard is the 'main man' or woman; he is the one with the ultimate responsibility for the welfare of his charge. He and the Principal are at the centre of concentric circles of protection (concentric circles have the same centre). He is the last piece of protection and he puts himself between every conceivable threat and the Principal. The other circles are made up of the PES and the RST, which we will learn about below.

The Personal Escort Section (PES)

The PES can have different functions depending on the situation in which they find themselves. Generally speaking, they provide an outer cordon of defence as opposed to the BG's inner cordon. In some situations their function may be the same as the BGs, that is, give body cover and get away from the danger. In other situations, their function may be to attack the threat and give the BG time to get the Principal away from the danger.

Again, depending upon the situation, the PES may be as close to the Principal as the BG; in others, they may be much further away. For instance, outside a venue in a car ready to be called upon if needed.

The Security Advance Party (SAP)

The makeup of the SAP will vary from one assignment to another; some may have one or two members that are dedicated to advance work and do nothing else. Others may only use an SAP when they have a particular need. Basically, the function of the SAP is to ensure that their are no surprises for the Principal while he is out and about on his social and business schedule. The SAP will travel in advance of the Principal, checking that routes and venues are OK. They may do this months in advance and it may include, for example, the planning of an overseas trip, or they might be just minutes in advance (it may be that the Principal wants an impromptu trip to a local restaurant with which the team are not familiar). The SAP carries out an important function; it needs to have excellent communication skills, exercise good personal security and be trained in all aspects of search.

The Residence Security Team (RST)

The RST, as the name suggests, look after the physical security of anywhere that the Principal is resident. This could be a house, a hotel, or a yacht. Many Principals secure all of their residences with an RST, even if they are only resident for a few weeks of the year. This is where most fledgling Bodyguards will serve their Bodyguard apprenticeship. The RST will need to have the skills to use the modern equipment that is now used to assist in the security of premises. They need to work hard and hope that they are 'noticed' and eventually move on to better things. Members of the RST will often be required to carry out route reconnaissance or to do some SAP work. Mess these tasks up and you are destined to 'stay in the garden'. Do a good job and the next time someone in the PES has a day off you might get to stand in and impress.

Drivers

While all members of the team should be able to drive, often the role of driver is a dedicated one. That is, someone is employed solely as a driver. This driver may or may not be trained in Close Protection. When they are not, it is a crime, because sometimes the most effective weapon that a Close Protection team has is the vehicle that they are in. In an emergency situation, it is much better to have a Close Protection trained driver that can work with the team rather than some fat chauffeur who is only employed because the Principal likes the way he wears his peaked cap and keeps the car clean!

Driving is a specialist role and if someone on the team is a dedicated driver then those drivers need also to be dedicated to building the defensive and evasive driving skills that a team may one day need. Of course, a smooth drive and a clean car are also important.

Some teams consist of just one person, others can be much larger. This chart shows how a small team might be organised

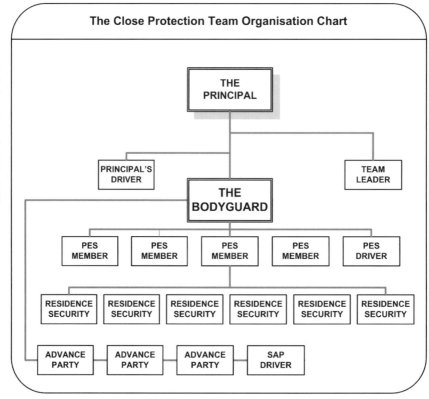

The Close Protection Team Organisation Chart

- THE PRINCIPAL
  - PRINCIPAL'S DRIVER
  - TEAM LEADER
  - THE BODYGUARD
    - PES MEMBER
    - PES MEMBER
    - PES MEMBER
    - PES MEMBER
    - PES DRIVER
    - RESIDENCE SECURITY
    - RESIDENCE SECURITY
    - RESIDENCE SECURITY
    - RESIDENCE SECURITY
    - RESIDENCE SECURITY
    - RESIDENCE SECURITY
    - ADVANCE PARTY
    - ADVANCE PARTY
    - ADVANCE PARTY
    - SAP DRIVER

Bodyguard Skills

It never ceases to amaze me how some people turn up on Close Protection courses and expect to be turned into Bodyguards just by paying a fee. Very often this is impossible. Even the very best trainers need people made of the 'right stuff' to start with. While many people are able to learn the basics, not everyone can apply themselves to the demanding role of the Close Protection Officer. While many skills can be learnt, practised and honed to perfection, the Bodyguard candidate should turn up with some essential skills. Many of these skills you will have spent your whole life learning, such as communication skills. If you haven't got them right in 25 years why do you think that a training course of 25 days can make any difference?

A good brain with lots of common sense

For most of the time, a Close Protection Officer has to 'think on his feet' and make decisions based upon information that he continually and constantly analyses. At the same time, he must at all times provide the very best protection to his client. He does this by applying skills that he has been taught, but, and it's a big but, he also has to apply copious amounts of common sense to the problems of the day and unfortunately no one can teach common sense. Either you have it or you haven't. Anyone who is a bit slow and not razor sharp in their thinking is never going to be a good Close Protection Officer no matter how much training they have had. The best Bodyguards also develop a sort of sixth sense; it seems as though they are able to foresee problems long before they occur.

A professional attitude

A good Close Protection Officer displays a good attitude towards others. He is never too important to speak to lowlier members of the team, even the toilet cleaner, while he's in the hotel. I have seen whole operations come undone because the CP team has breezed into a hotel and 'larged it', giving it the big 'I am' and giving no one any courtesy or respect.

The more important the VIP the more important and puffed up the security can become, alienating the very people that can help

In This Chapter

The skills that you need to before you commit yourself to training as a Bodyguard them do their job. House cleaners will go out of their way to clean or indeed not clean rooms outside of their normal schedules. This might allow you to enter areas such as laundry rooms or similar, providing you with better surveillance and security for your Principal. They may do this because of the relationship that a good attitude builds; talking down to them or displaying a superior attitude will not help your case. Security officers and managers in a hotel might be earning a lot less than you, but they will bend over backwards, giving you not only additional, valuable manpower or camera monitoring, but the building and area knowledge that they have taken months to learn. A bad attitude displayed towards these guys and girls will deny you this valuable resource. The hotel security will resent you and make your job as difficult as they can. If the doorman or concierge respect and like you, then they can be a great help. If they think that you are an 'arsehole', then favours like parking permits will not be available, no matter how important your Principal is. The head waiter can do you and your Principal lots of favours, serving you quickly and looking after the rest of the team. So you can see that even in a hotel the attitude displayed by the team is of immeasurable importance. An old saying goes something like

> I HAVE LOST COUNT OF THE NUMBER OF CLOSE PROTECTION 'PRIMA DONNAS', WHO THINK THAT THE SECURITY OPERATION REVOLVES AROUND THEM

"Try to treat others as you would have them treat you." I would like to offer the following saying: "A good Close Protection Officer treats everyone that he meets with genuine courtesy and respect and as a possible resource."

I have lost count of the number of Close Protection 'prima donnas', who think that the security operation revolves around them rather than the Principal. They treat anyone below them like dirt on a shoe, and are full of their own importance. These people do not last long, and any respect they do receive is false and disappears as soon as their backs are turned.

A good appearance

Looking the part is not as important as many might think, but only because they have a wrong idea about the part. The Close Protection Officer frequently needs to be synonymous with the Principal. Of course, Principals come in all shapes and sizes and if keeping a low profile is important to the Principal then a Close Protection Officer who doesn't look like one is an advantage. Size can be a deterrent to fans of pop stars and the bigger and uglier this type of officer appears can help him do his job.

Confidence

Close Protection Officers come in all shapes and sizes, but they have to exude confidence in their own ability. A Bodyguard might be a little apprehensive when he meets a Principal for the first time, but should he appear nervous? The words nervous and Bodyguard should not really be mentioned in the same sentence. You will always appear to be confident, even when you aren't.

Your appearance, as you will learn later, has to fit in with the Principal's lifestyle somewhat. You may be looking after someone who is covered in tattoos, but if you are also covered in tattoos you are limiting your job prospects by restricting yourself to work in an environment where such tattoos are accepted.

Being a team player

Teamwork is fundamental to Close Protection. People who work together as a team are effective and can accomplish more. In order to work successfully within a Close Protection team it is important to become a team player. A team player works well with other people on the job, even if they do not like them. In order to be a good team player, one must be willing to compromise, think of ways to solve problems, and not demand that their ideas are used. Loyalty and commitment to the team are essential qualities of a team player. Good team players are continually thinking of ways to meet the goals and objectives of their team. They will not let personal issues, or likes and dislikes get in the way or upset the balance and spirit of the team. They are adaptable, flexible, and willing to work in different conditions and environments for the good and benefit of the team.

Honesty

It should go without saying that Bodyguards should be honest but I know of a Close Protection company that employs a Bodyguard called 'Bobby the Thief.' Your Principal will expect everyone in the team to be honest; if he or she catches you out in the tiniest, whitest, single solitary lie then this will bring your whole integrity into question. Close Protection Officers must never be less than honest. Dishonest Bodyguards can end up in jail. I heard about two guys in London who thought they might be able to blackmail their Principal by taking a story to a newspaper about an alleged animal fetish. They underestimated the Principal, who went straight to the police. It really is a pre-requisite; you need to be honest and able to prove it with criminal record checks and references. In the UK and in many states of the USA you will not get a licence if you have a criminal record.

Punctuality

Being late more than once will almost always cost you your job and sometimes even before you get the job. I have told otherwise ideal candidates in an interview that they won't be getting the job because they turned up late for an interview! In a job as important as Close Protection, being where you're supposed to be and being there on time is essential.

Second language

The benefits of learning a second language are enormous for the Close Protection Officer; he can often double his employment prospects if he can speak a second language.

Most English and Americans expect others to speak English. 'No one speaks English in this place' and 'Why don't they speak English?' are statements made many times by frustrated Close Protection Officers trying to work in a foreign country. Normally, they don't speak English for the same reason that we don't speak Bengali or French. Unless we are taught very young, languages can be hard to master and you need to be well motivated to learn another language as an adult.

Surprisingly, however, people do speak a second or even third language. Many continental Europeans are fluent in two or three languages. Millions of Africans speak not only their own language, but often the language of the country or empire that used to colonise them, such as French, English or Portuguese. But these same people will also speak a couple of different tribal dialects. Many Japanese people speak a minimum of two languages

Communication Skills is much more that just your ability to talk into a mobile phone or two-way radio

Middle Eastern Royal families and many successful business people (often the very people we are looking after) can shift effortlessly between their native tongue to French. Many could embarrass some BBC news presenters with their excellent grasp and pronunciation of Oxford English. So while millions of others speak second languages, the vast majority of the English speaking world is as monolingual as an English pirate's parrot.

Therefore, you should learn a second or third language. Which language you choose to learn is up to you, but you should choose wisely. Also think about where the work is and where you would like to work. Russian, Mandarin, Arabic and Japanese would be good choices. More people speak Spanish than English and there are almost four times as many people that speak Mandarin than Arabic.

Learning Welsh might increase your chances of working in Aberystwyth and Patagonia. However if you want to broaden your horizons to take in Venezuela, Uruguay, Peru, Panama, Argentina, Mexico, Cuba, Chile, or any of at least a dozen other countries where Spanish is the primary language, learning Spanish would be very beneficial or even essential.

You do not need to be fluent in a language to get the benefit. Having a basic collo-quial grasp of a language and having the confidence to have a go at using it will reap rewards. Any assistance or cooperation that you need in the course of your work (or recreation) will be much more forthcoming if you at least try to make yourself understood in the local lingo. This is infinitely better than the normal English speak-ers' practice of just speaking English s-l-o-w-e-r and LOUDER until they are under-stood! Learning a new language is a must, but why stop there? Once you have learnt one, learn other! It not only gets easier, you make yourself even more employable.

Communication skills

One of the most important skills, the one that lets many would-be Bodyguards down badly, is so completely fundamental to our role that its importance cannot be over-emphasised here. That skill is communication.

The Close Protection Officer has to have complete mastery of communication skills; they have to communicate in many different ways and at all levels. I have seen many men who thought that they were born to be Bodyguards; guys who were masters of this or that martial art. They had spent their whole life in either the dojo or the gym. They thought that they only had to turn up for a couple of weeks and then pick up a certificate, making them a Close Protection expert. These same men, some of whom looked as though they were incapable of being scared of anything, froze when asked to stand up at the front of the class and introduce themselves to the rest of the candi-dates. Maybe they thought that throughout their Close Protection career they would be the 'strong and silent type', having no idea of the importance of communication skills in this industry. When these peo-ple are told quietly during the first tea break that they are wasting there time and are being sent home, more than one of them has been stuck for words and tried to resort to violence. This, of course, reinforces our point! Essentially, there are three basic channels of communication and the Close Protection Officer needs to be a master of each.

> COMMUNICATIONS SKILL IS THE MOST IMPORTANT SKILL THAT WE CAN POSSESS

1. **Words**

2. **Tone**

3. **Non-Verbal Communication**

The correct choice of words used in the right context is obviously essential. The tone used is more important than the words and the non-verbal channels of communica-tion (tone, gestures, facial expressions, stance and clothes, etc) are a vital ingredient of any communication. Some studies suggest that these non-verbal channels make up over 65 percent of our communication. Imagine someone calling you on the telephone and saying, 'You are in big trouble'. You have heard the words but the tone is important. It is the tone in which the words are said that will tell you whether you are in big trouble. Now imagine that it is a video phone and you can see the person who is threatening the trouble smile and wink at you. The words now mean nothing. The non-verbal communication has told you that you are not really in trouble.

Without good communication skills, everything else is a waste of time. You might be an excellent driver, a crack shot and martial artist, well trained in First Aid and look the part. But everyone in the industry knows that the ability to communicate is one of the most important skills that you can possess and if you haven't got it then you will never get a chance to show off your shooting or driving skills because you will never get past the job interview.

What are good communication skills?

The ability to communicate is not merely radio communication (although that is important), but the day-to-day communication with other team members, the Principal, visitors, contractors, etc. Far too often mistakes occur, accidents happen and human relationships fail because of a lack of communication skills. When you meet your Principal or team leader for the first time, you must be able to communicate well. Remember, your non-verbal communication will always be 'talking', even when

Communication skills is not just about what comes out of your mouth. You communicate in lots of ways, such as how you wear your hair, the clothes you wear, the way you stand, the way you walk. All of this is communication. Look at the difference in the way the guy is communicating. A simple smile or a frown can communicate much.

your mouth is not! The clothes you wear, the way you stand, your hairstyle, your clean or dirty shoes, your deportment. Each of these things has to communicate the right message. If any of these things are neglected, then you will not last long and will probably not get a job in the first place.

> # "I KNOW YOU BELIEVE THAT YOU UNDERSTAND WHAT YOU THINK I SAID, BUT I AM NOT SURE YOU REALISE THAT WHAT YOU HEARD IS NOT WHAT I MEANT."

Communication, whether spoken or written, is simply a way of passing ideas, thoughts, instructions and reasons from one person to another. In the written form, we refer to them as reports and these are covered later in these pages. For now, concentrate on the spoken word. The inflection in the voice frequently signals aggression and that is a root cause of misunderstanding. The way a sentence is phrased can often make a lot of difference – the difference between an order and a request, for example.

1. **You will come this way.**

2. **Will you come this way?**

Misunderstandings happen because of accent. Thus, a man from Tyneside and a man from Cornwall both speak English but with sufficient regional accent to cause an enormous amount of confusion. Another source of communication breakdown is due to differences of interpretation or meaning of words. What may be acceptable to one group can be totally offensive to another. To be referred to as a 'fag' at Eton is acceptable, but the same expression used in the USA would not. Many other instances can be found and it is a truism that England and America are two countries divided by a common language. Incomplete understanding of a language is another cause of communication breakdown. Many types of nationality of a Principal are encountered whose command of the English language is incomplete and care must be exercised to ensure misunderstandings do not arise through this cause.

Communications and professional relations

Regardless of the scope of the Close Protection operation, the officer will have cause to interact with various elements of society. On a daily basis, a Close Protection Officer will communicate not only with his Principal but also colleagues up and down the command chain. Situations both routine and extraordinary might mean communicating with the police, emergency services, contractors, security consultants and gardeners. The Close Protection Officer must be able to communicate with these people in a manner that reflects the professionalism of the security team and the position of the Principal. A hallmark of the Close Protection Officer's professionalism is the way that he can communicate with an attitude of calm confidence.

Avoiding communication breakdowns

Listen to what is being said, not what you think was said or expect to be said.

If you're not sure what was meant by any communication, ask for clarification. It might be a bit embarrassing to ask for clarification, but far less embarrassing than getting a simple instruction wrong or messing up in front of your Principal.

- ☑ Do not adopt an aggressive tone. Remember, the tone of how you say something can be more important than the words. It doesn't make you sound tough and will invariably get an aggressive or unwanted response

- ☑ Do not use slang or jargon. This could be misinterpreted; it is not appreciated by most people

- ☑ Be firm but without being demanding. This is not a contradiction.

- ☑ 'Sir' or 'Madam' are easy words that will smooth the way in most situations.

- ☑ Above all, whenever you want to communicate, put the brain into gear before taking the brake off the tongue!

- ☑ Always be polite, but do not confuse this with servility. You are not a servant, you're a Close Protection Officer!

First Aid

First Aid skills are important in any walk of life, but being skilled in First Aid is absolutely fundamental to being a protection professional. Some schoolchildren are now taught very basic First Aid. This is a good thing. First Aid should be on everybody's curriculum. Over the years, I have seen and been amazed at the number of Bodyguards' CV/resumes that make no mention of First Aid. When questioned in interview, these candidates mention that yes, they have done First Aid in the Army: 'about ten years ago' or 'I did a lifesaving course, "a while ago"'.

This is simply not good enough. I can guarantee with some certainty that First Aid skills will be needed in a career of Close Protection. You may never need that bootleg turn that you practise over and over in the car or the quick draw and chair roll that you have perfected for hotel corridors; but you will need your knowledge of First Aid.

First Aid is a skill like any other; it needs constant practice to remain effective. Techniques and ideas change so it is imperative that you carry out continual training and remain up to date. Most books on 'Close Protection' include a chapter on First Aid but this is a token gesture and often used only to pad out the book. Authors tend to stick to sexy First Aid like suckling chest wounds, tracheotomies and gunshot wounds. They ignore the simple facts, such as their Principal is hundreds of times more likely to die choking on a pretzel than be shot in the chest. First Aid needs its own book, and cannot be covered in a single chapter. You will need to undertake a course in First Aid.

In the UK when the Security Industry Authority (SIA) commissioned the key skills or core competencies, the draft documents included just sexy First Aid. Some sensible folk lobbied to get this taken out and be replaced by a formal qualification in First Aid. Eventually, the SIA chose the Health and Safety Executive's 'First Aid at Work' course, which is run over four days and which is accompanied by written and practical exams. In the UK, therefore, you will need this First Aid qualification to get a licence to operate as a Close Protection Officer. The course covers much more than tracheotomies and for those that really want to know, yes, they do teach you about suckling chest wounds. The course will cover the following:

> HOW CAN SOMEONE BE A BODYGUARD WHO IS NOT WELL TRAINED IN FIRST AID? THEY CANT.

☑ Introduction to first aid

☑ Personal hygiene

☑ Circulation

☑ Resuscitation

☑ Dressings and bandages

☑ Wounds and bleeding

☑ Circulatory disorders

☑ Duties of a First Aider

☑ The skeleton

☑ Fractures

☑ Unconsciousness

☑ Burns and scalding

☑ Handling and transport

This course certificate is valid for three years; thereafter, before your certificate runs out, you must undertake a two day refresher course. Go over three years and you will have to do the whole course again to get re-certificated.

Further first aid courses

While the basic First Aid course above is enough to get you a licence to operate in the UK you should consider at least two other First Aid qualifications, which are essential if you are to become a protection professional.

Automated External Defibrillator Course

This short course teaches you how to use an Automated External Defibrillator (AED). This device can be used to administer measured electric shocks to people in the throes of cardiac arrest and is the best way of increasing their chance of survival. Many Close Protection teams routinely carry AEDs and you must be trained in their use. The course content would include:

- ☑ Personal safety, assessing the incident
- ☑ Priorities: DRAB checking and sending for help
- ☑ Unconscious casualty
- ☑ Breathing and circulation
- ☑ Resuscitation: adults
- ☑ Choking
- ☑ Assessment of basic life support skills
- ☑ Basic information about the heart, and how defibrillation works
- ☑ Chain of survival
- ☑ Defibrillation (recognition of heart rhythms)
- ☑ Introduction to the machine, including care and maintenance
- ☑ Practical use of machine and application of pads
- ☑ Voice prompts and appropriate responses
- ☑ CPR and use of AED on casualty
- ☑ General guidelines for using a defibrillator
- ☑ Protocols and candidate practice
- ☑ Special circumstances
- ☑ Handing over to emergency services
- ☑ Practical exercises

Normally, 'de-fib' courses last around one day and the course certificate must be renewed every six months.

First Aid for children

All of the skills that you will learn on the above courses are aimed at giving first aid to adults. First aid techniques for children differ in some crucial areas. Participants learn about techniques for resuscitating children and infants, conducting risk assessments and how to deal with choking, burns, scalds and seizures. In a career in Close Protection, you will find that you work for Principals that have families that include young children. You will often be charged with their care. You need to know what to do in the event of an accident or illness. If you are working in an environment that includes children, you cannot be a Bodyguard without these skills.

These courses can be hard to find, but some organisations in the UK and USA run courses aimed at the childcare sector, nursery schools, etc. The child First Aid courses are normally run over one or two days and are valid for three years.

If you are not trained in First Aid then you are not a Bodyguard. You must obtain the minimum requirement then add the other courses such as de-fib and child first aid as soon as you can. Make sure that you remain current, read your course notes regularly

First Aid is a Skill that once learned need to be refreshed on a regular basis

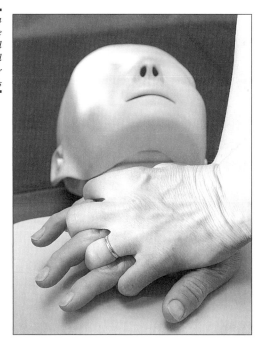

and do not forget to book your refresher courses in advance so you are not forced to do the training in full all over again. That said, I know an operator that never does refreshers; he always does the courses in full every three years or so. He says that his client pays and he learns a lot and retains his skills much better.

Summary

There are many skills that we can learn on our journey to become a Close Protection Officer other than attributes such as honesty, integrity and loyalty. These were best learnt at our mother's knee! The skills that can be learnt from a course in Close Protection or from reading this book, such as communication skills, First Aid, surveillance detection and driving must complement other basic skills and attributes. Close Protection Officers must also be punctual, honest, fiercely loyal, well groomed, and trustworthy, with lots of integrity. They must be a good team player and have lots of self discipline. A good listener and confidant, they must also ooze confidence in all that they do.

High & Low Profile Protection

The are two very different ways of providing Close Protection. We can either provide it with a high-profile, which leaves no one in any doubt that we are Bodyguards and why we are there. Secondly, we can provide protection with the emphasis on maintaining a low profile so that we do not attract any undue attention. Most of your assignments will probably be a mixture of the two profiles, with only a few being one hundred percent high or low profile

High Profile Protection

This type of protection is the one that most people see, they see it because it's meant to be seen, it is supposed to have a very high deterring factor and it does. Many of the most controversial and flamboyant rock and pop stars use high profile protection, there is nothing discreet about this protection, the Bodyguards are usually huge and the way that that they position themselves around or in front of their Principal leaves everyone in no doubt about what they are there for.

In many cases the reason for the high profile is to deter fans from getting too close. Fans can be very dangerous; Principals could easily be crushed and hurt by the very people who love them. There is also always the chance that the psychopath is out there posing as a fan and waiting his chance to pounce. Many stars today get the odd dodgy fan; these people seem to turn up for every concert, talk or book-signing. Sometimes one of these fans will cross the line and start stalking the star. Many stars these days want to foster a good relationship with there fans, but there are plenty of others that want to keep fans at a distance, so that a smile or handshake isn't misinterpreted and turns a fan into a deluded stalker.

In This Chapter

Understand the difference between different profiles.

Why profile is so important

The pros and cons of the different profiles

Subtle security is not what this type of Principal needs, the security has got to be seen and feared for it to be effective. In this type of scenario the BG's must have knowledge of working with large crowds, they must be able to plan effectively to get the Principal in and out of 'hot' venues, they have to be trained in how to deal with the press that will never be too far away.

On some occasions these 'stars' use their high profile Bodyguards to get them the publicity that they always crave. In showbiz, publicity normally always equates to

It would be very hard for this Bodyguard to adopt a low profile. He has a high profile image and is employed as a deterrent. Everyone can see what he is there for and you can guess the response if you approach them.

Picture EMPICS

dollars. Let's say that the Principal wants to go jogging in a public park early in the morning, there is minimum risk if no one knows of the intended jog. They probably will not be recognised, especially if they wear a baggy sweat suit and woollen hat and just have a Bodyguard or two jog with them, and maybe a couple more at a discreet distance behind or strategically placed

> **BIG BODYGUARDS ON HIGH PROFILE ASSIGNMENTS DO PROVIDE PLENTY OF DETERRENT VALUE. HOWEVER, POUND FOR POUND, FAT ONES DO NOT**

within the park. But if they want to be recognised they will take a whole protection team out jogging. They will be noisy and they will manhandle anyone who gets in their way. Someone will have invariably leaked it to the press that xyz superstar is jogging in Hyde Park at 7am. This of course increases the risk of anything happening, letting people know where you are going to be is never a good idea. But many Principals are prepared to take on this additional risk, especially those that trust their security team to sort out any trouble.

I recall an incident about a female pop star staying in a very exclusive hotel in the South of France. She enjoyed using her high profile security team to assist in keeping her profile high. This star worked hard at staying fit and decided early one morning she would like a swim in the hotel pool. She dispatched her minders to the pool who found a couple of other hotel (paying) guests enjoying a swim. In a typically aggressive high profile way they asked these people to leave the pool as their client wanted to train alone, after a heated debate the people left the pool but not I hope before they urinated in it! High profile protection does not give you a license to assault or be rude to people. You can be a deterrent and stay within the law, it just requires a little training and professionalism.

Another type of high profile protection can often be seen on our television news. An ambassador or similarly important person visiting a dangerous place is seen surrounded by officers bristling with weapons. They are screaming (metaphorically) "do not mess with us." In similar high profile assignments the Bodyguards whilst not showing there weapons all have a hand inside a jacket or have bulges in their clothing giving the high-profile impression that they have weapons and are ready for anything.

High profile protection can be much easier to learn than low profile, many high profile protection assignments on the C and D list celebrities are carried out by doormen, bodybuilders and ninja types with no training whatsoever and they cope quite well (as long as nothing goes wrong!) Generally if you are big and ugly enough look the part and have a bit of common sense, high profile protection will come much easier than low profile. Many untrained officers work on high profile assignments, and a lot of these will have drifted into the industry from working the doors as a bouncer. However these people will almost always be found wanting just when their Principal needs them most.

Low Profile Protection

Good low profile protection is almost an art form, you have to apply good training with copious amounts of common sense, it is not just a matter of being there and looking "Well Hard" as in most cases of high profile.

You probably see Bodyguards working all the time, almost on every news bulletin if you know what to look for you can see these ordinary looking boys and girls doing there job. Many will 'see' them but do not necessarily 'notice' them. Once you are in the business you will see Bodyguards working everywhere. A good Close Protection Officer maintaining a low profile will be synonymous with his Principal and the situ-

You do not have to be a six foot seven inch salad dodger to provide high profile protection. These two Bodyguards protecting The Israeli Prime Minister are only slight in build. However they are a High profile deterrent because everyone knows that they wouldn't be there if they weren't experts with the concealed weapons they are carrying.

EMPICS

ation they are in. They will always be in the right place at the right time. They will not be 'showing out' or giving anyone any menacing stares, but they will be providing just as much protection than their high-profile counterpart.

Outside of the ranks of the famous film TV and rock personalities most people require their security to be a little more subtle. They do not want any lesser protection in fact in most cases they require rather more protection, as their threats may be more real. However they realise that they may well bring unwelcome attention upon themselves if they go everywhere with a big wall of muscle, dark-glasses and gun.

A considerable number of film, rock and pop stars will always require protection and as luck would have it they can afford it. There are many Close Protection Officers, the world over, that would do anything to get on the security detail of any of the Hollywood A list; far too many than there are jobs for. However you should realise that for every famous user of Close Protection there are hundreds of other users. Most of these are not famous at all outside of there own business environments or community. Importantly most of these people do not want high profile showbiz style protection. They want low profile professionals.

Summary

You should really only adopt a high profile went absolutely necessary. In many countries of the world you are much safer when you keep a low profile and go about your business unnoticed. Sometimes the decision is not easily reached. Let's say that you are working in a country with a high risk of a kidnap. You need to decide whether the best way to avoid being kidnapped is for the Personal Escort Section to look well armed and ready. Or should you and your Principal adopt such a low profile that you would not be considered as being a kidnap target. Experience has shown is that very often the best way in a situation such as this is to adopt a position between the two profile extremes? There is far more work available outside of celebrities and show business and it is here where most people will work.

Threat Assessment

I n the Close Protection environment and in most books on the subject, the terms 'threat assessment' and 'risk assessment' are commonly used indiscriminately and often to mean the same thing. This usage is incorrect. Another equally wrong interpretation I have seen in a recently published Close Protection book is that threats are those things that you have no control over and risks are those things that you have. If we could 'control risk' then nothing would ever go wrong. The best we can do is minimise risk whilst trying to negate it completely. To enable you formulate a plan of action to protect a client, you should understand that these terms mean two very different things. However, I do acknowledge that sometimes the difference between the two can become blurred.

Essentially, a threat is something that your or your client may have to deal with: the threat of a kidnap, a car crash, identity theft or an earthquake. Risk represents the likelihood of these threats happening. The threat of an earthquake in the United Kingdom, for example, is not much of a threat because the likelihood (risk) of a dangerous earthquake in the UK is remote. Risk is used to describe the possibility and probability (the likelihood) of a threat happening.

When people sit down to write what is commonly called a 'risk assessment', they write a list of things that they call 'risks'. They are in fact building a list of threats; a risk assessment is assessing the likelihood of those threats happening. A definition of threat assessment for Close Protection could read as follows:

> **DETERMINE THE RISKS ASSOCIATED WITH ALL POTENTIAL THREATS AND THEN BALANCE THESE WITH THE SECURITY MEASURES WE CAN TAKE TO NEGATE THEM.**

Don't be confused. In Close Protection, threats are the danger and risks are the likelihood of the threat happening. The threat when we cross a road is that we might be hit by a car. What is the risk of that happening when a, we cross without looking left or right or b, we stop at the kerb, assess the traffic, its direction and speed and then make a decision about when it is safe to cross? By doing this we reduce the risk of the threat happening. Simple.

In This Chapter

The difference between threat and risk

How to 'profile' your Principal

Understand Dynamic Threat Assesssment

Threat Assessment; why we do it

The bedrock of personal protection is based upon an accurate threat assessment. It is impossible to determine the correct type and amount of security measures we may need to protect someone unless the type of threat and the risk of it occurring have been established. While you might think it reasonable that we strive to protect our client from each and every threat, it's important to understand that you cannot protect someone from every threat, all of the time. Nor would we want to, firstly because it's practically impossible to do so and secondly because to strive to do so is neither efficient nor effective.

The two big C's that should be employed when formulating responses to risk are COMPROMISE AND CONVENIENCE. All security is based on a compromise and this is always being balanced with convenience. These two Cs seriously erode security. Let's say that your task was to protect the British Prime Minister. It would be easy to install him in a specially constructed bunker in the Tower of London and lock him in there. Here he could easily run the country and all his other affairs by email and videophone. The security would be excellent, he would be safe. However, this would not be convenient for him. He would want to be out and about all over Westminster and the world. When the Prime Minister leaves the foolproof security we have designed for him at the Tower, his perfect security is now compromised and is much less effective. We have to COMPROMISE our security for the sake of the Prime Minister's lifestyle and CONVENIENCE.

The best protection operation then is the one that affords the correct and appropriate level of protection with the minimum intrusion into the Principal's normal lifestyle. The key to establishing this level of protection is to perform a threat assessment. Once the potential for harm has been evaluated, you must then determine the risks of the event happening and then assess what security measures must be put into place to control that threat. Where possible, threats and their associated risks should be avoided all together; where this isn't possible you must focus your efforts on minimising the risk or the consequences of it.

Salting the Step

It's very easy when carrying out a threat assessment to focus only on major things such as terrorist attacks, kidnaps and other such threats. You will remember that in the definition of threat assessment you are asked to assess ALL potential threats. 'Salting the Step' was a term used in our company with regard to threat assessment. Occasionally you might be asked, "Have you salted the step?" The questioner was asking you if you had looked at all the other maybe less glamorous threats, whose associated risks could prove to be as damaging as any terrorist attack. The saying originates from an assignment back in the nineteen eighties when a team were looking after a very elderly Middle Eastern royal, headed up by a very enthusiastic Bodyguard/team leader, who was always stressing to his team the importance of threat assessment, continuation training and practising the team in their emergency drills. The team and the team leader were always 'ready for anything', well, anything except the ice that formed overnight on their Principal's front doorstep! The resulting slip on the ice led to a broken hip and a lengthy stay in hospital for the Principal, and left a team leader looking for work!

So salting the step came to mean assessing all of those other, seemingly 'lesser' threats, which could be easily overlooked, the little things that at the time maybe seemed less important than working on the safe room and emergency evacuations. Things like fire and trip hazards are often forgotten. Unless you have been told otherwise, we are looking after a Principal's complete physical well being, his peace of mind and his privacy. Anything that intrudes even slightly into these must be considered a threat, which you will include in your assessment.

Types of Threat Assessment

There are different types of threat assessment. There are those associated with people, places and events, as well as dynamic assessments that we make on the move. Most assessments, apart from the dynamic ones, which we will discuss later, will be carried out by someone with experience, so that all of the threats associated with the person, place or event can be assessed. This assessment is written down so that others in the team are made aware of it. It is not a good idea for just one person, no matter how experienced that person is, to carry out a threat assessment on his own. The whole team, or, if the team is very large, then some key members from it, are in a much better position to ensure that no threat is overlooked. I have often heard the question, "If I am working in a one-on-one situation then must I do threat assessments on my own?" It would be rare for there to be no one to help. Don't forget the Principal – he or she is in a unique position to help. What about a trusted friend or family member? They may well be able to help. Sometimes someone not close to the protective operation can point you towards areas you might have overlooked. If you must do threat assessments on your own then do them very carefully and re-visit the assessment often. Any assessment, whether it's going to be delivered orally in a briefing or committed to paper and then distributed, must be CLEAR©. That is:

Comprehensive

Logical

Easy to Understand

Accurate

Relevant & Re-visited

How do we do it?

The first thing that we should do whenever we carry out a threat assessment on any trip or type of property, such as the Principal's home, office, boat or hotel is to compile a complete list of threats. The best way to do this, in a team, or on your own, is to use the process of brainstorming. This is an excellent tool for coming up with ideas as long as you stick to the rules.

Brainstorming Rules

Collect as many ideas of threats as possible from all participants, with absolutely no criticisms or judgments made while ideas are being generated.

- ☑ All ideas must be made welcome no matter how silly or far out they may seem. The more ideas you have the better. It's amazing how one small idea can develop and throw up threats that might otherwise have been missed.

- ☑ Absolutely no discussion takes place during the brainstorming activity. Talking about the ideas will take place after brainstorming is complete. Talking about them now will stem the flow of ideas.

- ☑ Whenever someone offers up a threat, do not criticise or judge. Don't even groan, frown, or laugh. All ideas must be treated equally valid at this point.

- ☑ Do not try to put the threats in any order of importance at this stage.

- ☑ Do build on others people's ideas.

- ☑ Do write all ideas on a flipchart or board so the whole team can easily see them. This should avoid any repeats.

The Brainstorming Sequence

One team member should review the topic of the brainstorm, i.e. security of the Principal's office, using 'why', 'how', or 'what' type questions.

Example:

Let's say that the topic for the brainstorm is assessing threats at the Principal's office environment. What threats might this area or office present us with?

Everyone should think about the question silently for a few moments. Each person might want to jot down his/her ideas on a sheet of paper. For example, someone might note:

1) Theft (2) Fire (3) Industrial Espionage (4) Flood (5) Surveillance (6) Business neighbours (7) Ramming the front gate, etc.

Everyone suggests ideas by calling them out. The team member in charge of the brainstorming session should be enforcing the rules. The rule that often needs reinforcing is the no criticism judgement rule. For best results, this rule needs to be applied rigidly. If people think they are going to be ridiculed they may well not mention something they think about which is important.

Sorting the list of threats

After the brainstorming session you will have a list of threats. Some will obviously be more important than others and they will be in no particular order. You must now methodically work through this list and apportion an amount of risk of the threat becoming a reality. The threats should then be placed in order with the threats carrying the most risk placed at the top of the list.

Decide on Security needed

You must go through your list of threats and decide what security measures you need to minimise or negate them. When working through this list and working out the security measures be careful to remember 'security/convenience'.

This is not as easy as it sounds as many factors now come into the equation. Okay, so we may have identified a particular threat; let's say it's an international terrorist organisation. But how is this threat going to manifest itself? To understand this, we must look into the threat even further, i.e., what are the particular aims of the terrorist group? What is their modus operandi? Do they shoot, bomb, kidnap, blackmail or are they capable of all these? If they shoot, is it short or long range? If they kidnap, do they have a history of killing the kidnapped anyway, whatever the outcome? All of these factors must be analysed before we decide on the type and amount of security required.

Profiling the Principal

No threat assessment can be complete without you having knowledge about the person you are protecting. What is he like? What does he do? These are basic questions that may be asked. However, although they do need to be answered, just knowing these two bits of information will not assist you much in your threat assessment. We do in fact need to know everything about our Principal – mostly we are told only what the Principal or one of his assistants thinks we need to know.

Threat assessment becomes easier, the more we know about our Principal. Consider the implications if our Principal was a skydiver or mountain climber. Surely this knowledge would have some impact on or threat assessment. Consider also the implications if we weren't aware of the Principal's religious beliefs and business interests! What if the Principal plays a lot of golf? (When did you last secure a golf course!) What if he just loves going to Indian restaurants? What if his younger brother despises him or his ex-mistress still loves him? The information that we can glean by profiling our Principal can be of great benefit and of the utmost importance. Some information, no matter how insignificant it might seem initially, could prove to be life saving. Some of these questions we may be able to ask directly. In fact, your Principal might think it odd if you didn't quiz him about some aspects of his life. Asking if he is married would be acceptable; asking if he has a mistress might not be!

Much of the profile will be built over time. I have seen some questionnaires that ask if Principal uses drugs or prostitutes. The answers to these potentially embarrassing questions will probably become all to apparent very early on in the assignment, so you can spare your Principal's blushes by not asking him to acknowledge his vices in writing! If the threats are sufficiently serious then you might dispense with the softly-softly approach and ask the embarrassing questions up front. This information once known can be very important and must be fed back into your threat assessments.

We developed the Seven P's©. Each P forms a heading for you to fill up with information from your initial briefings or in the first few weeks of the work commencing. We will discuss these in more detail below: The 7 P's©

The Seven P's of Principal Profiling

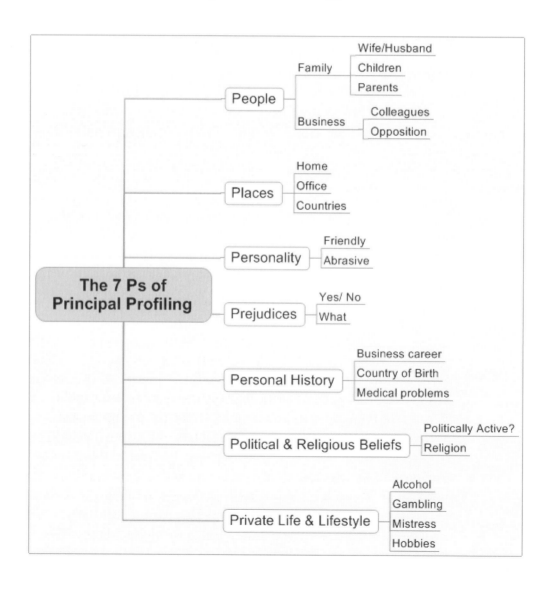

1. People

Our Principal can be related to many other people in many different ways: by blood, marriage, friendship, business, leisure, casually or intimately. Any of these relationships can be the cause of many problems. For instance, a dangerous amorous liaison, a jealous wife/girlfriend/boyfriend, an unscrupulous business associate, problem children, the list goes on. We must know (or get to know) the people that our Principal meets as well as his enemies.

2. Places

Where people are born, where they work and play. These are matters of importance to the threat assessment. Places that can be safe for some people can take on a dangerous aspect for others according to their relationship to that place. Had the danger to President Kennedy in travelling to Dallas in 1963 been correctly assessed and made known to him, the danger would have suggested special security measures. Those measures weren't taken and the rest, of course, is history. What threats do the places in your Principal's life present?

3. Personality

A certain kind of personality – abrasive, contentious – tends to attract trouble! If your Principal has this type of personality, you will probably be acutely aware of it. Many professional businessmen have combative personalities. They might make friends or enemies very quickly. You do not have to like the person that you work for. If he has the type of personality that makes people hate or dislike him, e.g., conceited, forceful, abrasive, rude or domineering. This knowledge should keep the Close Protection Officer on his toes!

4. Prejudices

Prejudices are particularly dangerous attitudes; they are often ingrained within the person. Prejudices can give rise to their mirror image, e.g., if someone is prejudiced against black people this normally gives rise to others who are just as prejudiced against the people who are prejudiced against black people. The good BG will carefully watch and be aware of his Principal's attitudes so that he can pre-empt or eliminate the special hazards that they might generate. People are prejudiced against lots of things, not just people. Your boss might be prejudiced against a particular brand of vehicle or chain of hotels, All this is good information to be aware of.

5. Personal history

This part of your profile should note things such as the Principal's medical history and current medication, names that he has been known by in the past, date and place of birth, past and present nationalities, family ties, marital status and history. This information should be accompanied by relevant dates, places of residence, mother tongues and other languages, honours and distinctions, military service, other public service, occupation and occupational history and titles. A note should be made of how much of this personal information can be obtained by the public, i.e., by referring to Who's Who, Burkes Peerage, etc. Any relevant medical history should also be noted, to include any medications, blood group, allergies, etc.

6. Political and religious persuasion

Obviously we need to know of the Principal's political standing. Is he an active member of any political party? Particular political persuasions could cause us problems, as could the Principal's religious beliefs. A good Close Protection Officer will be aware of both and will anticipate when these beliefs or ideals may cause problems.

7. Private life and lifestyle

Is the Principal a recluse? Does he drive his own cars? Does he use drugs or prostitutes? Does he play golf, skydive, rock climb or eat lots of Chinese food? Maybe he travels extensively, works long hours, doesn't drink, rides horses or watches a lot of TV. Does he travel nationally or internationally? Perhaps he has a mistress or commits adultery. Does he have a high or low profile? Is he a workaholic, an alcoholic or a kleptomaniac? Does he entertain a lot, at home or in hotels? The list of information that we can learn about the Principal is almost limitless and obviously the more we know the better our protective efforts can be.

Putting the threats and security measures together

Once we have completed our threat assessment, leaving no stone unturned and no question unanswered, we can start to put it together using the guidelines given above. It will be frustrating. Some of the points that we will make will be dismissed by the Principal, maybe because the security measure that we are proposing cramps his style, or, even more common, he can't afford to purchase the fleet of armour-plated vehicles that you are suggesting is necessary!

Good threat assessment comes with methodical planning, sound research and the ability to put it all together into a workable protection assignment. It's no good saying that the threat is from an extreme animal liberation organisation, so we are going to need six guys on him at any one time. Just think for a moment how these extremists could hurt your Principal. They might use bombs – mail bombs or car bombs. They might shoot – short range or long range. Perhaps they'll use poison – injecting into food or water. Maybe they'll ram his vehicle, commit arson or seek to achieve their objectives in any number of ways. You must be prepared for them, with security measures in place to counteract them all. Don't forget that they will have the element of surprise; they'll use subterfuge and treachery and probably won't worry about you or other bystanders. This is another good reason to make sure your assessment is good – it directly affects you!

Threat assessments must be revisited often. Do them again, go over every detail, especially the list of threats or possible threats. The threat assessment is never really complete; you are always revamping it and reassessing it.

Dynamic threat assessment

We can carry out vigorous threat assessments, on our Principal, his home and office, and his enemies. When completed, these assessments will form the basis of our whole protective effort. However, by themselves these assessments are only the start. The most important assessments are carried out every day 'on the fly'. 'Dynamic Threat Assessment' is a continual process, that helps you to effectively assess any situation that might affect you or your Principal's safety as it is unfolding. You are continuously assessing the circumstances you are in and must adjust your response to meet the threats presented as they appear.

It might sound a little complicated at first, but it is a simple process and you do it already. Almost everyone carries out a dynamic threat assessment continually, hardly giving it a thought. But before we discuss what a dynamic threat assessment is how we do it, it will pay us to look at the frequently used word 'dynamic' and see what it actually means. The Microsoft Encarta dictionary on my computer says that something or someone is dynamic when they are 'vigorous and purposeful, active and changing over time'. So dynamic is the very best way to describe the threat assessment that we carry out constantly throughout our whole waking day. Dynamic threat assessments must be vigorous and purposeful and it they are changing all of the time, then dynamic is the best word to describe the assessments that we continually carry out.

We carry out a dynamic threat assessment when we cross the road, when we stop at the kerb, and when we assess the situation. If it is safe to cross the road, we do so; if it is busy and dangerous we look for assistance in the form of a pedestrian crossing. While we cross the road we keep an eye open, looking for any danger that may suddenly appear. If a car appears and presents a danger to us we will be ready to take evasive action. Dynamic Threat Assessment is all about SAFETY© This is another acronym.

Stop and Think

Whenever we are presented with a situation that requires us to assess the threat, think 'stop'. I have seen hundreds of candidates on courses rush in to a situation without thinking; a fraction of a second is all that might be needed. Just saying 'Stop!' in your head can give you a vital second or so to think. Years ago on first-aid courses, some instructors would teach candidates that the first thing they should do when they came on to a scene that might present a danger to themselves was to thrust their hands in their pockets. This action was the 'Stop' or, in this case, 'Assess the situation, am I in danger?' The candidates were less likely to rush in because the hands in the pockets were the trigger to remind them to be safe. A Close Protection Officer does not want to be putting his hands in his pockets but when he comes across a situation that requires some action, he should stop for a split second and assess the situation. This will ensure that the response to the threat is appropriate and effective.

Stop and Think

Assess the Threat

Find Help

Evacuate the principal

Take Action

You are Responsible for your own Security

Assess the Threat

When dynamically assessing threat we should be applying the POPE© model. The model throws up four buzz-words that assist in assessing a situation in real time.

1. Person

Threats tend to come from people. What person are you assessing? What don't you like about him or her? You will be continually assessing people who come within a distance where they might harm you or your Principal. You are assessing to judge whether you may be at risk. Is the person a known enemy? Does he fit the profile of a known enemy? Have you met the person before? What do you know about him? Does he have a history of anger or aggression? Is he a known criminal? If you don't know him, what can you judge from his appearance and behaviour? How does he appear? Is he looking at you and/or your Principal? How is he dressed? Is he clean and tidy, dishevelled, dirty or unshaven? Is he suffering from the effects of drink or drugs? Does he look as though he has criminal intent?

2. Objects

Objects within the POPE model are the objects that affect you and your Principal's safety. You assess a situation with regard to the threats presented by the person and/or any objects. An object might mean the knife in the assailant's hand, the bomb under your car, but it could also mean apparently innocent objects such as drinking glasses. Even a pool cue could be used against you. Does the junkie you want to move away from your Principal's car have an object like a needle in his hand?

3. Principal

What is the threat against your Principal? If he has threats against him that might involve a bomb under his car, then an object under or near his car will take on a more serious meaning than if he did not. When carrying out a Dynamic Threat Assessment the profile of the Principal must always be at the forefront of the Protection Officer's mind.

4. Environment

Assess the situation with regard to where you are, including the time of day, other people around, lighting, etc. Where are you – in Iraq or Ipswich? Are you on the street or in a relatively safe area? Who knows you are there? Is it public knowledge that you were going to be there? Are you in a bar with no security or a casino with lots of it? The environment that you are in is critical to your assessments.

Some types of threat assessment are best approached in a methodical way. Dynamic Threat Assessment is not methodical. The last thing you are going to do while as-

```
Person
Objects
Principal
Environment
```

sessing threat on a minute-by-minute basis is to work through a POPE threat list. POPE is an acronym to help candidates in a classroom remember the type of things that they should consider when carrying out a dynamic assessment in real time. The information from POPE, coupled with the judicious use of lots of common sense, should ensure that threats are noticed and reacted to accordingly. Dynamic Threat Assessment needs to be practised continually if you are to become accomplished at it. Those of you that have read about personal security earlier in the book will realise that Dynamic Threat Assessment will help us immensely with the third principle – 'constant awareness'.

Find Help

Common sense will decide if you need to spend time finding help. If your Principal's home appears to be under attack in the middle of the night, then calling the police before you take other action could well be the right thing to do. In a street encounter then looking for help might be wasting time that could be used evading or attacking the threat, but if help can be summoned by a simple push of a button on your two–way radio then it might me stupid not to summon it. Note the use of 'might be' and 'could be'. That is because every incident is going to be different and it's your call. If you are going to summon help do it early. Give them the time they need to respond so that they can be there when you need them.

Evacuate the Principal

A threat is best tackled by not tackling it. Avoidance is always the best option. If you can evacuate the Principal from the danger then do so. Do it fast and ideally it's best if it's done to a plan. But if you don't have a plan it doesn't matter, just get out of there and remember to take your client with you! There might well be situations where escape appears to be impossible; if this is the case then we must still do something!

Take action

If escape is impossible then you must take action. What action you take and how you take it will, of course, depend on the situation you are in. What you must remember is that the whole purpose of any action you take has only one purpose and that is to escape with your Principal. So whether you are punching, shooting, ramming, or stamping you are only doing enough to make good your escape.

You are Responsible for your own Security

It should go without saying that the first Principal of personal security should never be ignored, but when presented with a situation many people rush right in without it would seem a care for there own safety. Remember that if you are hurt then who is going to do your job and look after the Principal.

The Category System

In the Police or the Army, where resources are almost unlimited and sometimes the actual VIP doesn't get much say in the protective effort, the category system is a well proven method of putting a label on a threat assessment. In addition, many private companies and organisations like to put their VIPs into one of as many as seven categories of risk. Each category represents a level of threat/risk and the counter measures (number of men and equipment) required. You should not use a category system if you have a choice. The two main reasons why you should not use a category system are as follows:

1. Let's say that a category system states that a 'level two VIP' requires a team of X

number of men and X type of equipment. It is very rare in the commercial world that we can just slot someone into a category and expect him to employ that amount of men and equipment; it just doesn't work. Normally, if the threat to a VIP is real he will employ however many he feels is necessary or how many he can afford. He may not want an armoured car even if the category he is in stipulates he should have one.

2. Slotting VIPs into categories, especially low ones, tends to switch the protection team off. In an ideal world, we know it shouldn't but in the real world it does. Rather than working from the threat assessment directly, people seem to have the attitude of "Oh, he's only a Cat 4, why should anyone be following us?"

There is absolutely no reason why you should want to put your Principal in a category threat. If you want to use a category system or you work for a company that uses one, then I suggest that you use a very simple three category system that we used for many years.

Category One

Here, the threat is very real, and it is not IF IT WILL HAPPEN, it is WHEN IT WILL HAPPEN. Possibly, the only thing stopping the threats manifesting themselves is the protective efforts of the security team. A good test to decide if a person is in category one is to imagine what would happen if the security team weren't there. If you think that without security your Principal would be murdered, then he is probably category one. A classic example of a category one would be Mr Salman Rushdie, who has a death threat on his head. This man could not walk freely where there was a high Muslim population without fearing for his life. A category one VIP would have as much security as was necessary or as much as he could afford.

> **Category 1 When it happens**
>
> **2 If it happens**
>
> **3 Everyone Else!**

Category Two

The subtle difference between one and two is the transposing of the words WHEN and IF. In category two, we are saying if it happens, it might happen, it could conceivably happen. This category includes most MPs, pop stars and well-known personalities, etc. A politician or rock star could walk freely in most UK/USA cities. He may draw a crowd but the chances of living to tell about it are much greater than a category one threat. Again, category twos have as much security as they need or can afford.

Category Three

It is in this category that we place everyone who does not fall into category one or two. It contains a lot of people. These are businessmen and other not-so-prominent people, who have only general or very low threats against them. Typically, many of these people can afford to employ a permanent protection team only at times of a heightened threat. Very often, they employ just one person, who acts as Bodyguard, chauffeur, gardener and bag carrier!

Keeping abreast of current world affairs

Close Protection Officers must ensure that they know a little about what is going on in the world. This business can quickly take you from an environment that you know well and are comfortable with to another continent with a hundred and one problems that you should be aware of if you are to do your job properly.

Just reading a quality newspaper daily is a start. But while you might find the tabloids a little more interesting, knowing who is dating who is not as much help as knowing that the country you planned to stop over at has just undergone a coup d'état!

Modern technology can push news to your laptop computer, or even your mobile phone. There are lots of 'news clipping services', many of which are free. You supply keywords such as Bodyguard, Sri Lanka, Animal Liberation, etc., and whenever any of those words appear in a news story anywhere in the world you get it emailed to you. If you are looking after a Principal that makes the news, putting their name in a news clipping service as a keyword is a good idea. You can then keep abreast of anything said about your Principal in any publication or other media anywhere in the world. This type of information is invaluable when working on your threat assessments.

Knowing the enemy

Crime and Terrorism touches everyone. You do not have to be a VIP or work in the Close Protection industry to be exposed to the dangers of crime or terrorism. A few different types of terrorists or criminals are outlined below:

Anarchists

Anarchist terrorists oppose all forms of government or any type of authority. They advocate a society based free association of individuals. Anarchists are very often allied with Leftist groups.

Anti-Abortionists

Anti-abortion terrorists commit acts of terrorism against abortion providers and supporters of the "pro-choice" movement. Typically motivated by religion in their opposition to abortion, these terrorists frequently target abortion clinics and doctors. America is one of the main sufferers of the Anti-Abortionists.

Anti-Globalisation:

Anti-globalisation terrorists oppose the integration of the world into a single free market. They believe global capitalism negatively impacts both individuals and indigenous cultures. Anti-globalisation attacks often focus on multinational corporate and trade targets such as McDonalds Restaurants, Starbucks and some international banks. Regular demonstrations in the worlds capitals and at meetings like the G8 summit are often a cover fro the Anti-Globalisation terrorist.

Communist/Socialist:

Communist/socialist terrorists commit acts of terrorism to pressure their government to redistribute wealth or to change ownership of industrial means of production. They often attack in opposition to such government policies as the privatisation of state industry and resources or the reduction of entitlement programs such as pensions or welfare. Examples in this category include Túpac Amaru Revolutionary Movement of Peru.

Environmental/Animal Rights Extremists:

Environmental/Animal Rights terrorists commit acts of terrorism to influence their government's environmental policy or to stop/bankrupt private companies that are perceived to be harmful to animals or the environment. Examples in this category include the Animal Liberation Front and The Earth Liberation Front

Nationalist/Separatist:

Nationalist terrorists commit acts of terrorism to defend what they believe to be the interests of their national group or in reaction to colonialism. Nationalist terrorist groups often seek autonomy or statehood on behalf of a minority ethnic or religious population that resides within a larger state, in which case the terrorists are separatists as well as nationalists. Examples in this category include ETA (Basque Fatherland and Liberty) from Northern Spain and Liberation Tigers of Tamil Eelam.

Racists:

Racist terrorists include all groups that select targets based on their ethnicity. One of the most famous being the Klu Klux Klan and the White Aryan Resistance.

Religious:

Religious terrorists commit acts of terrorism in order to comply with a religious mandate or to force other to follow that mandate. These groups tend to be less interested in achieving policy change and less amenable to political concessions or negotiations. Examples in this category include Christian terrorists such as the Lord's Resistance Army in Uganda. Islamist such as Al-Qaeda and the Armed Islamic Group in Algeria.

Stalkers

Celebrity stalking is a fast-growing phenomenon. If your Principal is the subject of a stalker then you have to work exceptionally hard to ensure that the stalker does no harm to the Principal. This is because some stalkers will do absolutely anything to get close to their target. Most people became aware of celebrity stalking in the 1980s. Many will remember some of the high-profile stalking tragedies that ended in death. John Lennon was shot in December 1980 by Mark Chapman. Nine years later Rebecca Schaefer, who was a rising TV personality, was shot dead outside her home. Her killer had been infatuated by Rebecca since seeing her in a commercial for her TV show My Sister Sam.

The vast majotity of stalking is carried out by males and involve a sexual element

Brad Pitt, Meg Ryan, Gwyneth Paltrow, Madonna and Stephen Spielberg are all big name stars that have been stalked. There have also been stalkers among high-profile sports stars, the most famous being Monica Seles.

While celebrity stalking always grabs the headlines, 'ordinary' people are being stalked more and more. Some recent studies in America have shown that around 12 percent of women have had some experience of being stalked.

There are many motivations for stalking; obvious ones such as infatuation and obsession have seemingly become commonplace. Much of the stalking is centered on a sexual element. Jealousy and anger and the wish for contact and control may or may not be sexual motivated. This stalking may start from a simple rejection or a perceived rejection. Indeed, many stalking dramas start at the end of relationships.

These relationships might have been long engagements or marriages or may have just been a one-night-stand. Equally, the relationship might never have existed outside of the stalker's mind. Many celebrity stalkers will have only seen their targets on the television or in their mind's eye. Because stalking is such a common crime, the Close Protection Officer needs to know a little about this phenomenon and how to deal with it properly.

Definition of stalking

Stalking is a repetitive pattern of unwanted harassment or threatening behaviour committed by one person upon another. This harassment can take many forms: it may be carried out by email or telephone; the target may be followed on foot or in vehicles; residences or places of work may be overtly monitored by the stalker; letters and gifts may be sent to the home or office.

Mostly a male thing?

Stalking is mostly carried out by men on women. However, there are plenty of men stalked by women as there are men stalked by men. When Jonathan Norman was arrested for stalking Steven Spielberg, a police detective testified at the time that Norman was obsessed with Spielberg and wanted to rape him. When he was arrested he was carrying handcuffs, duct tape and razor blades!

What can we do?

Firstly we should never ignore a stalker hoping that he will go away. Most of the time things get worse until they are actually stopped by the police and imprisoned. And in many cases, even imprisonment of the stalker does not end the harassment as they will continue their campaign from within the jail.

Some Principals that you might work for may have a particularly obsessive or fanatical fan base. These fans may do anything to get an autograph, a handshake, a kiss or a smile. They might camp outside your Principal's hotel room for hours on end, but they are not stalkers. As soon as a fans' actions causes your Principal to feel harassed or threatened in anyway, and this action is then repeated, then such a situation may be defined as one person stalking another.

The longer the stalking goes on, the more obsessed or fanatical the stalker can become, so it is imperative that we try to get the stalker stopped as soon as possible. For the police to be able to act you will need to collect evidence that shows the wilful, malicious and repeated harassment of your Principal and also that it threatens his or her safety.

You must carefully keep all of the evidence that you can. This might include letters or answer machine recordings, video footage from closed-circuit television or hand-held cameras, still photographs, voice recordings as well as gifts and cards, etc. Items that have been handled by the stalker, such as cards letters and gifts should not be handled excessively by anyone. If you know that the letter is from the stalker, because you recognise the handwriting or style of envelope, then do not even open it. Leave this to the police who will be anxious to prove ownership of the writing, the letter, the postage stamp and envelope, all of which may hold vital evidence. You must also record in a log all sightings of the stalker.

Lots of different actions have been tried in the past to put a stop to stalking. Stalking the stalker is one option, and it may work, but giving the stalker a taste of his own medicine is against the law. So is 'making him an offer that he cannot refuse'. The best way forward in any stalker situation is to involve the police as soon as possible. Gather as much evidence as you can, and while you are waiting for the police to do their work you should ensure that the protection you are providing is completely effective.

Summary

Generic threat assessments are done on places and jobs. You might do a threat assessment on travelling to a particular country, or the job or position that your Principal holds. These have to be thorough meticulous and CLEAR, assessing all potential threats and then putting the security measures in place to negate them. The threat assessment must be done with the cooperation of the Principal, and the Principal must be profiled by using the seven Ps. We carry out the dynamic threat assessment throughout our waking day, applying the POPE model.

You need to become an expert in terrorist groups and their methods of operation. There are terror groups in every country of the world, so being an expert on them all could be very difficult. You should though be an expert on every group operating in the country you live and work in. Also remember that many terrorist organisations pay no heed to country borders and are global in operation. You need to know all about these also. A good starting point is . http://www.tkb.org this is the Terrorism Knowledge Base and it offers in-depth information on terrorist incidents, groups, and trials

Over the years, I have come across people who couldn't even name the person that they were looking after; they knew nothing at all about them. "I'm just on the gate, I know my job and that's enough." It's NOT enough. Dynamic Threat Assessment is impossibly ineffective if you do not know who you are looking after and why. No assignment, no matter what the duration or the perceived threats against the Principal, should be started without an examination of the threats you might face. Anything less and you are just not doing your job.

Bomb Awareness and Recognition

The purpose of the information in this chapter is to give you a relatively simple understanding of the way that bombs work. It is hoped that this knowledge will assist you in making the right decision should you ever come across something of which you are suspicious. The best advice whenever you come across anything that you think is suspicious is always the same:

MOVE IN THE GENERAL DIRECTION OF – AWAY!

Improvised Explosive Device (IED)

The bomb is the most common form of weapon used by terrorists, though the use of improvised explosive devices is not just a weapon of the terrorist as many people, from the criminal to disgruntled employees, can and do use bombs to further their aims. A bomb can be hidden in a car or truck, strapped to the waist of a suicide bomber, delivered to your door by the postman or placed in the hold of a passenger aircraft.

Why are Bombs such a common Weapon?

An advantage of the bomb over other murderous weapons is that the bomber does not have to be there: he could be thousands of miles away when the bomb detonates. Compare that to using a knife or gun, where the perpetrator has to be there and the chances of his being captured or killed are quite high.

In many countries around the world, there is strict control of all lethal weapons. The illegal procurement of a gun to kill a particular person can in many countries prove quite difficult. By obtaining a gun from the underworld the terrorist or criminal is then involving other persons who could eventually testify or identify them should they ever be caught.

Almost Every Schoolboy can make a bomb

A few innocent items purchased from the hardware store or garden centre and with a small amount of easily obtainable knowledge (public libraries or the internet for instance) the average person can make an Improvised Explosive Device (IED) for a very small amount of money and with little or no risk of being discovered. It is this simplicity and anonymity that makes the bomb a favourite weapon for many criminals and terrorist organisations around the world.

The Components of a Bomb

A bomb can be broken down into five main components:

- 💣 **Time and Power Unit**
- 💣 **A Detonator or Igniter**
- 💣 **The Explosives or Incendiary Mix**
- 💣 **Arming Switch (Optional)**
- 💣 **Booby Trap (Optional)**

Time & Power Unit

Time and Power is to be discussed as one unit; however, they can be two distinct parts of the bomb in their own right. The time element in a bomb's make up is important to the terrorist in two ways. First, he needs time to escape the bomb's blast and make his getaway. Second, he may employ time to create the blast at an exact time of his choosing. He can create this time delay in a number of ways. For instance, chemical delays can start the explosion (acid takes a specific time to 'eat through' a wrapping and often the wrapping is made of condoms). Mechanical timers might be alarm clocks, watches, memo parking timers, kitchen timers, etc. Electronic timers include computer- controlled ones, such as those found in a home video or DVD recorder, etc. He can also detonate a bomb at a time of his choosing 'on command'. He might do this with remote control, or use command wires of the type you may have seen soldiers blow up bridges on TV. Not all bombs have a time element. However, they will all have a power unit of some description; the modern terrorist will invariably use electricity as the power to initiate his explosive device, and he will use batteries ninety-nine percent of the time to provide the small amount of electricity needed.

Battery technology has advanced leaps and bounds since the nineteen seventies and eighties. They have reduced in size considerably and will hold their power for a number of years. Most people have a small marvel of a 1.5 volt battery on the wrist, as quartz watches require this constant power. Meanwhile, many will be familiar with the very thin batteries that are placed inside Christmas cards that when opened will play the tune of 'jingle bells' quite happily until Easter! It is battery technology like this that makes it much easer for the terrorist to make letter bombs for instance.

The components of a bomb can clearly be seen. The Time & Power Unit, the Explosives and Detonator Wire. However If it is in a bag you wont see anything, but it is still a bomb, its just not obvious until its left some-place where suspicions are aroused

Detonator or Igniter

Detonators detonate explosives and igniters ignite incendiary mixes. Detonators are needed to provide the initial 'kick' that is required to set off a high explosive charge; they contain a small amount of explosives encased in a metal tube. Most modern explosives in good condition will not explode without one. Igniters are used to ignite incendiary mixes and can be as simple as a torch bulb that has had the glass broken, so that when a current passes through it, the filament glows hot and ignites the incendiary mixture. Incendiary mixes can be prepared from easily obtainable household items, such as weedkiller and sugar.

These devices are used as 'fire bombs' to destroy property rather than people. They are placed in buildings near combustible materials, timed to go off in the middle of the night, or when the fire is least likely to be detected. They can cause many thousands of pounds worth of damage. The devices themselves are small enough to fit into a cigarette packet.

The Explosives

The fundamental concept behind explosives is very simple. At the most basic level, an explosive is just something that burns or decomposes very quickly, producing a lot of heat and gas in a short amount of time.

Explosives come in many forms, from basic black powders (gunpowder) found in fireworks and shotgun propellants, to modern plastic explosives. The latter are used mainly by the military but now all too often fall into the hands of terrorists or criminals. In between these there are many commercially produced dynamites used for blasting in quarries and for underwater demolition, etc. Not only do the terrorists find the explosives easy to obtain, they can also make there own! But usually they prefer to use plastic explosives. For example, Plastic Bonded Explosive (PBX) is made by binding a substance like polyisobutylene with an explosive such as RDX cyclotri-methylenetrinitramine ($C_3H_6N_6O_6$), sometimes called cyclonite, or hexogen. The binder has two important jobs:

- ☄ It coats the RDX, so it's less sensitive to shock and heat. This makes it relatively safe to handle.

- ☄ It makes the explosive material highly malleable, much like children's play stuff. You can mould it into different shapes for cutting and changing the direction of the explosion.

High explosives need to receive a powerful boost to kick off the chemical reaction. Because of the stabiliser elements used in their makeup, it takes a considerable shock to set off this reaction; you can throw plastic explosives on a fire (if you feel the need to) and it will just burn, it will not detonate. Soldiers have been known to burn plastic explosives as an improvised cooking fire. Contrary to what Hollywood might have you believe, shooting at the plastic explosives, even with a high velocity weapon, will probably not detonate them. That is a job for the detonator.

When the detonator starts the chemical change in the explosives, it decomposes to release a variety of gases, such as nitrogen and carbon oxides. The gases initially expand at an incredible speed of more than five miles a second, applying a huge amount of force to everything and anyone in the surrounding area. In action movies, we often see our hero outrunning an explosion, but, in reality, no one can outrun an explosion. In one second everything is normal and in the very next second the explosive and everything around it is totally destroyed.

It is a tribute to the inventors that plastic explosives are so safe to handle and have remained stable for years. Indeed, the author has handled plastic explosives that was over 25 years old, and was as good as new.

Arming Switch

Arming switches are built into bombs so that they can be transported in relative safety. Then when the bomber is near the target, or places the bomb, the bomb can be activated. The switch can be as simple as just a break in the electrical circuit which is operated by a switch or as complex relays of barometric switches that can 'arm' the bomb at a preset height above sea level, should the bomb be on an aircraft.

Booby Traps

A bomb can be a booby trap in its own right, that is to say, it will not go off until the anti-handling device is activated. A bomb that is designed to be triggered by remote control or by time delay can also incorporate a booby trap. The terrorist's train of thought here is that should his bomb be discovered before, let's say, the timer activates it, he can booby trap it so that any attempt at moving or defusing the device will result in detonation, thereby going someway to achieving his main aim. It is for this reason that all suspect devices should be considered booby trapped. Booby traps are victim operated. Do not become a victim.

BOOBY TRAPS ARE VICTIM OPERATED

For a booby trap to achieve its aim, it obviously must not give the appearance of being booby trapped. IEDs can be booby trapped very easily, and ninety percent of the time, the more simple the trap the greater the chance of the bomber's success. To show this simplicity we will discuss a few easily obtained items that the bomber can use to construct booby traps. Booby traps that rely on pressure, either 'pressure on' or 'pressure off' are two of the most common and simplest to set up.

Pressure Mats, which keep two parts of the electronic circuit apart by foam or similar material are activated when trodden upon complete the circuit, these can be made quite simply or be purchased off the shelf as a component part of a 'do it yourself' burglar alarm.

Most people are familiar with the rather large micro switches that are used in fridges (to turn the light on and off) and cars (operating the courtesy light). However, as a trip to any high street electrical store will show, these switches come in very small sizes and for a few pence, you can purchase a tiny switch, which can be adapted to let an electric current pass through it when pressure is either applied or removed.

It is a simple operation to wire a photosensitive cell into a bomb's circuit and when light hits the cell, it allows the electrical current to pass through it thereby enabling the current to reach the detonator. Bombs of this type can be placed in a darkened garage and when the car headlights hit it, the bomb detonates. The light sensitive cell also has limited potential for triggering letter or parcel bombs when they are opened, allowing light to hit the cell.

The humble clothes peg can be adapted to the bomb maker's needs in a variety of ways. It can be turned into a reliable timer, and push or pull type of pressure off triggers. The mercury tilt switch, infamous for being used as the triggering system that killed MP Airey Neave at the House of Commons car park in 1979, can be easily incorporated into a bomb and costs only a few pence. The way they work is simplicity itself: the circuit is broken by two wires inside a glass vial; if the vial is tilted, mercury rolls to the circuit wire, bridges them and completes the circuit.

When something is suspicious - The 4C's

It doesn't matter whether we are suspicious of a suspect car, which could contain many hundreds of pounds of explosives, or a suspicious-looking letter that has been delivered by the postman. Our reactions and drills will always be the same. We follow the rule of the 4 Cs:

- 💣 **Confirm**
- 💣 **Clear**
- 💣 **Cordon**
- 💣 **Control**

CONFIRM

Firstly, we confirm our decisions. Are we suspicious? If so, carry on with the 4Cs. 'Confirm' does not mean, **go and get your boss so he can have a look!** Nor does it mean going nearer to the suspect item to see if you can see or hear one of the essential components, e.g. "It's not ticking"; "I can't smell anything!"; "I can't see a booby trap!" This is not what the confirm means.

Many people get this wrong! Over the years I have seen some ridiculous confirms. I have seen policemen kick an item to see if it's a bomb! Can you believe that! Well, it's true. I have also seen a policeman open the two locks on a large leather briefcase, which had been reported as suspect, near the vicinity of two British princesses at a charity fashion show in Chelsea. He lay down and faced the other way as he clicked open the locks. Maybe he thought that laying down and facing the other way would protect him if a couple of pounds of high explosives exploded inches from him. I was told about this by another policeman after the incident. Even though I was there, I had moved in the general direction of away as soon as someone shouted up the suspicious case, so I was well out of the way when those locks clicked open! I later asked the 'hero policeman' why he hadn't just arranged for the princesses to go out of the rear and called in the experts. His response was, "Why? It was only a briefcase." I wonder if that idiot is still around.

I witnessed another example of the wrong way to confirm while watching a TV documentary about a man from Liverpool, who was training some Bodyguards in the art of vehicle search. A young trainee had just noticed that in the foot-well of the car he was searching was a bomb. It looked like the type of bomb you would see on the set of a Mel Gibson movie – sticks of explosives, a clock and curly wires, etc. There was no way that it could be mistaken for anything else. The young guy did the right thing and ran away as fast as he could. He was then stopped by his instructor, who asked him what was happening. He replied by telling the instructor he had seen a bomb in the car. The instructor barked at him, "What are you going to do now?" The trainee declared he would run away. "No you won't," said the instructor, "you will carry out the 4Cs. What's the first C?" The trainee couldn't remember; the stress was too much for him. The instructor then reminded him that the first C was to confirm his suspicions. The trainee claimed that he didn't need to confirm anything and described the obvious bomb that he had seen. However, the instructor insisted that he go back to the vehicle and confirm. He did so under duress. This is absolutely wrong; it's exactly what you should not do.

CONFIRMING YOUR SUSPICIONS DOES NOT MEAN GOING BACK TO THE BOMB!

Confirming your suspicions needs a bit of thought. Why are you suspicious? Let's say that you are working as part of a security advance party, working half an hour ahead of your Principal, checking over a hotel in which the Principal has a one hour meeting. You notice in the large reception/meeting area of the hotel a small airline carry-on type bag that has been left unattended. Immediately, you are suspicious. There are lots of other bags in the reception but they are all accompanied. So how do you confirm your suspicions? Want you don't do is go anywhere near it (not even if you've seen on TV a guy from Liverpool urging someone to do the same). Try to confirm or allay your suspicions by being sensible. Turn off any mobile communications, speak to reception or the concierge. Do they know who the bag belongs to? Ask to speak to security, get them working on the problem. They may well just walk right up to it and move it for you (while you, of course, move in the general direction of away!). That would be most helpful. They may be complacent, seeing lots of unattended bags every day. They haven't been blown up yet, so why should today be any different? Once the case is moved and you're happy, the meeting your Principal has scheduled can go ahead.

If you cannot find the owner of the bag, you have decisions to make. You've confirmed your suspicions; the bag is a threat. Your threat assessment might have your Principal to be the last person that someone would want to blow up. Your Principal might not be the intended target, but this makes little difference, as bombs are indiscriminate killers. You have to get a message to the Principal or the Bodyguard, let them know you have a problem and what that problem is. The Bodyguard and the Principal will decide what to do next; more often than not they will move in the general direction of away. Ask yourself why you're suspicious. Depending upon the answers you come up with, you will dismiss it or move on to the second of the 4 Cs.

CLEAR

The 'Clear' procedure, the second of the 4 Cs, differs depending on whether you are in a public or private place when you discover something you think is suspicious.

Public Area

Clear means, CLEAR THE AREA OF PEOPLE, move them to a safe area so that no one will be killed or injured if your suspicious item turns out to be a bomb. However, common sense must prevail when we are in a public place. If we are back in that hotel with the suspect bag, we might well make the decision to stop the Principal from attending the hotel, but should we evacuate the whole hotel?

The chances of the bag being 'just a bag' are a lot higher than it being a bomb. Just because we are not prepared to take the risk and have our Principal anywhere near it does not mean that we should start shouting for everyone to leave the building. If the hotel staff evacuated every time there was a piece of unattended luggage in reception, they would spend a lot of time on the pavement/sidewalk. In this instance, it would be prudent to make sure that the hotel reception/security is made aware of your suspicions, before you and your team clear the area. It is not our job to be evacuating public places; get it right and you might be a hero but get it wrong, and you will probably be sued for loss of business and countless other claims for loss and stress. Let people know and then go.

Private Area

If we find something that we think could be a bomb and we are on private property, such as the Principal's residence, office or yacht, clear means exactly that. CLEAR THE AREA OF YOU AND EVERYONE ELSE, sound the alarm and carry out your previously planned and practised evacuation procedure to a safe area.

Evacuations should never be left to chance, especially in large houses, boats and offices. These drills must be practised. Maybe you can get the Principal to take part in your drills, but you probably will not. This doesn't really matter as long as everyone else knows what they're doing; they can ensure that the Principal gets to where he should be. Drills must be regular, practice makes perfect. In the heat of the moment it's very easy to carry out an evacuation and to forget someone. Your boss won't thank you for not evacuating one of his guests or a family pet.

When evacuating, remember that the biggest killer can be the blast wave and what's contained in it, such as glass and debris. You need to plan the safe area to evacuate to; this will probably not be the same area that you evacuate to in the event of fire. You may well need more than one evacuation plan. Your procedure might be completely different for a suspect bomb that's found in a car at the front of the building to the procedure you plan in the event of something being found in the post room inside the building.

CORDON

Place a cordon around the area at a safe distance to stop anyone inadvertently entering the danger area. This might be as simple as securing the post room after a dodgy item of mail has been discovered and not letting someone wander into the building

CONTROL

The last of the 4Cs is 'Control' and by this we mean control the whole situation. This will involve ensuring that the Principal gets to a place of safety, the cordon remains intact, that everyone is accounted for, and emergency services are called for. Always ensure, if possible, that the person who has seen or discovered the suspect item is available for the police or bomb squad to interview.

If the 4Cs are carried out promptly, we stand a good chance of saving life. The worst thing you can do is delay the implementation of the 4 Cs by getting a second opinion to confirm your suspicious, etc. Have the courage of your convictions; if your suspect package turns out to be something quite legitimate, don't worry. It's better to be safe than blown to bits!

Bombs in the Post

Letter bombs, which include parcels, packages and anything delivered by post or courier, have been a commonly used terrorist device.

Your risk assessment should give you a good idea of the likely threat to your Principal and indicate the precautions you need to take.

Letter bombs have traditionally been explosive or incendiary but these days they could conceivably be chemical, biological or radiological. When you receive a suspicious delivery you will have no idea what particular type it is, so your Action On Drills should be flexible enough to cover different eventualities.

If you are sure that a letter has been through the normal postal service then you can assume that the bomb will have received substantially rough handling in the post, so it's unlikely to detonate when being moved. As our postal services seem to get worse and it takes longer and longer to receive a letter, it is highly unlikely that a letter bomb will be programmed to explode at a particular time. Letter bombs are booby traps and as we now know, booby traps are victim operated and any attempt at opening them may set them off. However, if a suspect package was delivered by courier, then there may well be a timer involved as when sending things by courier the terrorist or criminal can be much more accurate with delivery times.

Letter bombs come in a variety of shapes and sizes; a well-made one will look innocuous, but there may be a number of tell-tale signs that can lead you to become suspicious of it. By themselves, these signs may be innocent, but a combination of a few and you will need a cautious approach. If you have access to equipment such as x-ray scanners and explosive detectors then use them to support or allay your fears.

The 7S's of Bombs in the Post

SIZE

Is the letter big enough to house a device without being obvious? A bomb-making expert could probably booby trap an airmail letter, but, generally speaking, the envelope has to be reasonably large to accommodate the components. Padded envelopes, or 'jiffy bags' are a popular choice. Does it seem unusually heavy for its size? Most regular letters weigh up to about 30g, whereas an effective letter bomb will have to weigh 50-100g and will probably be at least 5mm thick.

SHAPE

Is the package oddly shaped or lopsided? Are there lumps, denoting the possibility of batteries or a switching system? Tubes that are commonly used to protect documents through the post have been used as bombs.

SENDER

Do you recognise the handwriting? Is the writing in an unfamiliar foreign style? Check the postmark. Where did it come from? Does the label match the area from where it came? Is it unexpected, of unusual origin or from an unfamiliar sender? Is there no return address? Can you verify the address? Is it poorly or inaccurately addressed? For instance, incorrect title, spelt wrongly, title but no name or addressed to someone no longer associated with your Principal.

STAMP

Is there no stamp? Maybe it was hand-delivered or arrived by other means. Is the postmark blurred, or smudged or missing? Does it have more than the appropriate value of stamps for its size and weight? The terrorist may well put extra postage stamps on the bomb because the last thing he needs is for it to be returned to sender!

SEAL

Has the letter been sealed more securely denoting it is containing something that must be kept in – tape, staples, etc? Is the envelope flap stuck down completely (a normal letter usually has an ungummed gap of around 35mm at the corners)? Is the letter or parcel heavily sealed at one end, inviting you to open it from the other? Is there is a pin-sized hole in the envelope or package wrapping?

STAIN

Is there an oily stain showing through the envelope or oily fingerprints on the outside? Some explosives can weep small amounts of an oily type of liquid that will produce stains.

SMELL

Explosives can smell particularly the nitro glycerines and nitro toluenes. Is there a strange smell such as almonds or marzipan? If there is it could be a bomb, or then again it could be a cake!

Dealing with large amounts of mail

Although any suspect item should be treated seriously, remember that the great majority will be false alarms and depending upon who your Principal is, you may receive some hoaxes. You must ensure that your procedures for dealing with dodgy mail is effective and not needlessly disruptive. Remember the second Principal of personal security;

Study all mail carefully. There may well be some valuable clues there. You just have to look!

Security measures must be commensurate with the threat. Consider the following when planning for letter bombs.

1. Make sure that you are aware of the modus operandi of persons/organisations identified in your threat assessments. Seek advice from your local police, who may well have information that you can put to good use.

2. Process all incoming mail and deliveries at one point only. On high risk assignments this should ideally be off-site or in a separate building, or at least in an area that can easily be isolated and in which deliveries can be handled without taking them through other parts of the building.

3. Make sure that all staff who handle the mail at the central point are well briefed and properly trained.

4. Ensure that you have a designated safe area for placing suspect packages. Choose an area that does not hinder a safe evacuation. Ensure everyone knows where that safe area is, Ensure that the safe area is easily accessible to the police/bomb squad and their equipment.

5. Ensure that all sources of incoming mail (e.g. Royal Mail, couriers, and hand delivery) are included in your screening process.

6. Ideally, the designated post room should have independent air conditioning and alarm systems, as well as scanners and x-ray machines.

7. Your post room should have protective equipment, such as gloves, overalls and face masks.

8. The post room should be easy to evacuate; the staff that works there should practise the evacuation procedures and routes.

9. Once an evacuation has been made, ensure that no one can inadvertently wander near to the suspect package. Prepare signs to display to staff in the event of a suspected or actual attack.

Car Bombs

Vehicle bombs are fast becoming one of the most effective weapons in the terrorist's arsenal. They are capable of delivering massive amounts of explosives, driving the cars right up to their target area and causing a great deal of damage. There are three types of car bomb

Under vehicle improvised explosive device (UVIED)

A UVIED is a type of small victim-operated booby trap IED, placed in, on or under a vehicle. It is designed to explode when the vehicle moves, killing or injuring the occupants. Many people have been killed over the years with UVIEDs Many of the victims would have seen the IED if only they had bothered to look.

Vehicle-borne improvised explosive device (VBIED)

A VBIED is a car or van filled with explosive, driven to a target and then detonated. Rather than a bomb being attached to the car or van, the car is the bomb. VBIEDs can carry large amounts of explosives and are capable of killing large numbers of people and causing structural damage to buildings.

Large vehicle-borne improvised explosive device (LVBIED)

An LVBIED is usually a large lorry or truck filled with explosives. These vehicles enable the terrorist or criminal to carry several tonnes of high explosives right up to the intended target. They are capable of causing many casualties and major destruction of property, over a range that can be measured in thousands of square metres.

The bomb makers can make the bomb many miles away from the intended target. They can then drive the bomb to the target and detonate it by remote control or use a driver prepared to commit suicide.

UVIEDs can be thwarted by the regular use of cursory and systematic searches. But if your Principal is at risk from people who might use a VBIED or a LVBIED, then you need to have systems in place to combat them.

You should ensure that you have an effective access control system and that you employ sensible parking restrictions in vulnerable areas.

Wherever possible you should use physical barriers to keep all unauthorised vehicles at a safe distance.

Vehicles that are permitted to approach your building should ideally be authorised in advance and then searched on arrival. The identity of the driver should also be cleared in advance and then checked immediately on arrival.

Wherever there is a risk of VBIEDs you should ensure that you make your building as blast resistant as possible. This might include physical blast barriers and window film, etc.

Suicide Bombers

Close Protection Officers, along with everyone else in civilised society, are rightly scared of and not quite sure how to defend against the new phenomenon of the suicide bomber.

The concept of killing oneself while killing others is definitely not a new warfare tactic, nor is it confined to the Middle East. World War II Japanese Kamikaze pilots were suicide bombers as were the 9/11 hijackers.

This new era of suicide bombings was thrust upon the world by the Islamic terrorist movement Hezbollah. In 1983, Hezbollah suicide truck-bombers killed 64 U.S. embassy workers in Beirut. Later the same year, again using a suicide truck-bomber, Hezbollah killed 200+ people in a U.S. Marine compound near Beirut. These Lebanon attacks were so successful that terrorists began to adopt the suicide-bombing tactic worldwide.

How Would a Suicide Bomber Attack?

Though the 9/11 terrorists were, or course, suicide bombers, the most common forms of suicide attack will likely involve terrorists hiding explosives strapped onto their bodies, carrying bombs in bags or suitcases, or delivering explosives by a car, van or a truck. We can predict with some certainty the type of suicide attack we should expect in the West by looking at the long history of suicide attacks in the Middle East.

A suicide bomber in Europe or the US would more than likely be an Islamic fundamentalist, either from al-Qaeda or a Palestinian extremist group such as Hamas or Hezbollah.

The target of a suicide bomber would rarely be an individual and would almost certainly be a highly populated space and a well-known, public area. Whenever the Close Protection Officer is a prime target with his Principal (or without) he should be extra vigilant to spot suicide bombers. Prime targets include:

- Underground trains or buses and subways

- Restaurants, discos, nightclubs and casinos

- Shopping centres

- Train or bus stations

- Airport check-in lines

- Schools and universities

- Sports stadiums

- Cinemas and theatres

- Churches, temples and other religious gatherings

What can the Suicide Bomber Achieve?

A suicide bomber will try to place himself and his bomb wherever he thinks he will kill the most people. Just a single suicide bomber can carry enough explosive on his body to kill or seriously injure everyone onboard a train or bus. Or, if he is in an open area he could kill and maim anyone in a 50-foot radius and injure many more beyond that. A bomber driving a truck can carry hundreds of pounds of explosives and can devastate large areas of a city.

Surviving a Suicide Attack

To survive a suicide bomber and the inevitable pandemonium and disruptions that follow, your Action On Drills will depend upon your proximity to the bomber and your actual location.

The Principal's Residence or Office

If you are at the Principal's home or office when you learn of a suicide bombing in or near your city, you must take the Principal to your safe room. Gas masks should be worn until you are sure that the bomb was not a radiological dispersal device (dirty bomb). You should remain there, listening to radio and TV reports or other reliable media sources for at least two hours. There are often secondary follow-on bombings and you do not want to be on the roads.

If you are unlucky enough to be within one mile of any bang or explosion that sounds like a bomb, you must presume it was a dirty bomb. That is, until you hear otherwise from a reliable media source although this could take a couple of hours. Meanwhile, ensure that in the safe room all vents, air conditioners and windows are closed. Use gaffer tape and plastic sheeting on air vents and anywhere else where air pollutants may gain entry.

Public Transport

Suicide bombings on buses and trains such as those on 7/7 in London have been lethal. The safest spots may be near the back of the train carriage or bus, away from the entrance. On the underground, select a less-crowded carriage towards the rear of the train. Due to the confined nature of busses and trains it is likely that you will be killed or injured. If a bomb is detonated in another carriage and you and your Principal are survivors, then think ACE: Assess, Cover and Control and then Evacuate. You must be aware of other dangers – secondary bombs and live train rails.

Walking with the Principal outside a Public Venue

If you are walking or sitting outside and a suicide bomber strikes nearby: at the first flash or blast, take the Principal to ground immediately. Hit the ground hard and get as low as possible to avoid debris and smoke. If there is natural cover, use it as additional shelter. Expect a secondary device! *Think ACE!*

Beware of building collapse. Buildings in the vicinity of a bomb can suffer catastrophic damage and collapse. Once you've ACE'd out of the immediate area, get away from any other structures that are burning or damaged. ALWAYS assume until told otherwise that the bomb was 'dirty'.

Increasing your Chances of Surviving the Suicide Bomber

Avoid the bomber's likely target spots. If your Principal must visit these places then try not to do so at the busiest times. Experience tells us that suicide bombers use the busiest times to kill more people and use the cover of the crowds to remain undetected. Avoid queues, especially at airports and train stations. When entering and leaving such places let the main crowds disperse before you approach.

Always look for natural cover, and use it whenever you can. Look for things that can shield you from the blast. Assume that the blast may well come from the largest crowd or the main entrance to the airport or station, but keep away from large windows as the damage done by glass in an explosion is massive. Don't stand too close to large building walls as the bomb's shockwave can travel along walls and if the 'fast wind' doesn't get you then any shrapnel or debris in it will.

Identifying the suicide bombers

Most of the suicide bombers in Israel are Arab men aged 18 to 22 years old, but the Israelis have learned to their cost that anyone, young or old, can be a suicide bomber. Old women, young girls and men disguised as Israelis have all detonated bombs that they wore. A bomber carrying explosives on his body will need to disguise the bomb, so be suspicious if you see someone wearing a winter jacket on a hot day. Far less obvious are bombers that carry explosives in a bag or suitcase. Witnesses/survivors of attacks have said that they have seen the bombers messing/fiddling with the bags just prior to detonation. To ensure that their passage to martyrdom is complete, bombers have been seen to clutch the bags to their chests just before detonation. Studies of video tapes of suicide bombings show that many of the bombers appeared, understandably, to be very anxious and apprehensive, and that many appeared to be acting suspiciously and drenched in sweat.

You should remain alert to the following

- 💣 Persons wearing unseasonably warm clothing

- 💣 Anyone with protruding bulges under his or her clothing

- 💣 Persons who are sweating, mumbling, or fidgeting

- 💣 Persons that are trying to avoid security personnel

- 💣 Persons with a pale face from recently shaving off a beard.

- 💣 Persons that are trying to fit into crowds that they would not usually belong with

Anyone who is in a public place and appears to be in any way suspicious should set your internal alarm bells ringing. ACE out of there as quickly as you can.

There may well be occasions where you cannot evacuate. Passengers on the Air France flight had nowhere to run from Richard Reid, the so-called 'shoe bomber'; they had to tackle him there and then. Stopping the bomber from detonating the bomb is the only way. This might mean wrestling him to the ground and literally holding his arms. Some brave Israelis have rugby-tackled bombers from behind, anticipating that they will use their arms to instinctively break their fall rather than detonate the bomb. Others say that two well-placed bullets in the head will stop the bomber, but, of course, there is no fool- proof way to deter the suicide bomber. Just lots of vigilance, common sense and, I guess, a lot of luck.

Summary

It is said that "a little knowledge can be a dangerous" this is especially true when talking about bombs and improvised explosive devices. Bombs of any description should be treated with the utmost respect. You need to ensure that you are never in the vicinity of a bomb, but if you find that you are, then move the the general direction of.......... away. Never go near anything that you are suspicious of. Turn your radio and mobile phone off, then call in the experts. Watch how bomb disposal experts, with years of experience will do anything to avoid going anywhere near the bomb. Let us follow their example.

Kidnap For Ransom

The risk of kidnap can be high wherever you are in the world and the list of high-risk countries is constantly changing. Presently the threat is greatest in parts of Latin America, Asia and the Middle East. Kidnappers can act alone but are predominantly highly organised terrorist or criminal groups, motivated by political aims or, much more commonly, for cash. In many countries, employees of international organisations, even if the organisations are charities, are attractive targets due to the high profile of those organisations.

One of the main reasons that some people employ Bodyguards is because they have a very real fear of themselves or their loved ones being kidnapped. Anyone who is known to be rich is in danger of being kidnapped by criminals who want to extort money from their friends or family. Kidnapping for enrichment is an age old crime that today has matured into an established worldwide multi-million dollar business – for a business it is. There are other motives for kidnap and world leaders such as Saddam Hussein and Idi Amin have taken westerners as hostages for political motives. Presently in Iraq kidnapping is endemic. Statistically, kidnapping, in all its forms, all over the world is on the increase.

The actual offence of kidnapping became law in the UK as late as 1982 when the "Taking of Hostages" Act of 1982 received royal assent. The Act provides for a maximum sentence of life imprisonment on conviction. Briefly, the Act provides legislation where is becomes an offence to: "Detain any person in order to compel a state, International Government Organisation or person to do or abstain from doing any act, or threaten to kills, injure or continue the detention."

In This Chapter

Understand the motives behind most kidnaps.

Learn what you should do if your Principal is kidnapped

The Motives For Kidnap

There are three Principal motives for the taking of hostages:

1. **Criminal**
2. **Political**
3. **Emotional and Mental Illness**

Criminal motives

The taking of hostages in the act of other criminal offences, such as making a getaway from a bank robbery, is the most common cause of criminal kidnap in the UK. However, there are many recorded incidents in which persons have been held against a demand of payment. Figures supplied by Kroll Inc. a leading American risk consulting company, say that of the worldwide 15,000 reported kidnaps each year 75 percent of those are resolved by a ransom payment. Figures like this reinforce the feeling that kidnap is a business that is here to stay.

Political motives

Less common in the UK and European mainland but very common in some countries, the hostages are frequently taken and then held in the hope that some political advantage or concession may be gained. Often the hostage can be held against a demand for the release of prisoners. We have all been sickened by terrorists' home made videos of hostages admitting under duress to crimes, resulting in their being tortured and murdered. You do not have to be rich and have Bodyguards to be kidnapped by terrorists. Very often just the right skin colour or continent is enough to make a kidnapper choose you as a victim.

The emotional or mentally ill motive

Within this category fall the cases such as the abduction of children by estranged parents. Occasionally, cases are reported of mentally ill persons who abduct children for no other reason than a desire to satisfy an emotional need. In this category we can also place the sexual pervert who abducts children for no other reason than sexual, let's hope they rot in hell.

Reducing the risk of being kidnapped

For those criminals carrying out a kidnap for ransom it can be a difficult and complicated process, which requires careful planning and the close collaboration of around a dozen or more people. The primary objective for any kidnappers is to discover who is actually worth kidnapping, i.e. victims who can pay a ransom.

The kidnappers' team will carry out studies of the victims, their backgrounds, their business, properties, employers and of course, their financial status. The kidnappers also need people to locate and maintain a secure place to hold the victim until the ransom is paid. They need people to serve the victim food and drink. Importantly they need people to speak, usually on the telephone, with the victim's family or business in order to make the ransom demand and to agree on the arrangements for it to

It is rare for the Bodyguard to be kidnapped alongside the Principal, Bodyguards are normally killed. So If your Principal is kidnapped and survives the ordeal you are either dead or at best unemployed!

be paid. They need people to plan the delivery of the ransom and to serve as guards as the ransom is delivered. Clearly, kidnapping for ransom is not a one man crime and the gangs involved can be very large.

To be a success the kidnap they need to know exactly where that victim will be at a given moment. They must study their potential victims in order to make sure they or their loved ones or company bosses have sufficient money or have access to it. They will also study the routes and routines of their potential victims to see if that person will be in a particular place at a particular time. They will also be looking at the victim's security arrangement (if any) and look at where is at its weakest. To do all this work, the kidnapper requires competent people to work with and a considerable amount of time and effort. Kidnapping is a risky business to be in; kidnappers need to be very careful not to get caught planning or actually carrying out the kidnap.

The initial surveillance will usually occur at a known location. This will more than likely be the residence; however, it could obviously start from the office, airport or hotel, etc. They want to determine exactly where the victim will be at a given moment and what his security will be like at that time. If they can do this, their operation will more often than not be successful. By the time the kidnappers are ready to carry out the kidnap, they may well have studied the victim and his family for up to six weeks. They will have planned in detail the kidnap and the place where the victim will be held. They will have practised the operations a number of times right there in front of you. You just have to notice it!

There are statistics that say over 90 percent of kidnaps are successful. That means that in 90 percent of cases the victim, and the security team if they had one, missed a lot of surveillance. Over 80 percent of kidnaps take place on a weekday morning. Mornings are when routines are easy to establish and very hard to vary. The trip to work and the school run are the most likely time to be ambushed and kidnapped. To avoid being noticed you must not set patterns. School may start at 9am. Varying your times by 10 minutes is not enough; whole hours are needed.

> IF NINETY PERCENT OF KIDNAPS ARE SUCCESSFUL THEN A LOT OF SURVEILLANCE GOES UNNOTICED

If you are doing the school run in an area with a high risk of kidnap your travel must be unpredictable. Let's say school starts at 9am. On Monday, leave at 7am; on Tuesday, try 10am; Wednesday, arrange for 'home school'; on Thursday, go in for 9am and Friday, maybe 8am. Remember the message; varying a time by minutes is just not enough.

Some people might say that all we do by varying the times so much is to make the snatch squads' brief a little harder but still as easy. The kidnappers' view of such a routine might be: "The victim, along with one Bodyguard, leaves for school almost every weekday sometime between 6am and 10am." To a certain extent that is true but they would be missing the whole point, or should I say two points of varying routes and timings.

1. If we have an unpredictable travel pattern we have much less chance of being noticed and chosen as a victim in the first place. If we are not noticed than we are not going to be chosen as a victim.

2. When we vary our routes and timings we are sending a message to anyone that does have us under surveillance that we are 'doing our job'. This may well make them choose some other, softer target that has no security, or shows a complete lack of awareness and professionalism by not varying times and routes.

Surveillance, and especially good surveillance is hard to spot, but you can see it. You just have to look hard and look a lot. Surveillance detection is an extremely important part of the Close Protection Officer's function and is covered in another chapter.

Many countries have a high incidence of kidnap. You must do your homework when travelling abroad. If the kidnaps are carried out with criminal intentions, discuss with the client about keeping a low profile, maybe hiring a four-wheel drive rather than a stretch limo. If you think the boss stands out and might become a target for criminals you are not doing your job if you don't at least warn him of the possible consequences. If the risk is real then suggest kidnap insurance (insurance is only useful when the victim is kidnapped by criminals; however, the small print on the policies needs to be read (and understood) as this can minimise the potential loss. If the incident of kidnap has political motives, early research must be carried out. Maybe they are only kidnapping Americans, or it could be that they might be interested in any westerner. You must know whether your client would be a good target for them. If so, you must plan your trip carefully and employ as much security as necessary.

Kidnap and ransom insurance

Your threat assessment must be carried out thoroughly. If you deduct that there is even the slightest risk of kidnap for profit or otherwise then you should suggest to your client that they consult with a kidnap for ransom specialist. In the event of your client's kidnap, there may well be some very conflicting interests from the many different parties that might be involved, which might include you as the Bodyguard (if you weren't taken out at the time of the kidnap!), the client's family, friends, fellow employees or employers. There may well be involvement from local government and local indigenous law enforcement agencies and diplomats. The kidnap for ransom specialist would use their expertise and experience of countless other kidnap situations. These professionals will act as a central filtering point for all the people involved. Their experience in a situation can prove to be invaluable as they advise on how to work and deal with the authorities, how to handle the media and how to manage the family of the victim. Kidnap for ransom negotiations are for the experts and should never be attempted by you! As a Close Protection Officer you need to involve these experts as soon as possible.

YOU SHOULD COMPILE A 'KIDNAP FILE', WHICH WILL INCLUDE GOOD QUALITY RECENT PHOTOS OF YOUR CLIENT ALONG WITH ANY RELEVANT PERSONAL DETAILS,

Part of the service provided by kidnap for ransom consultants will be to provide detailed 'what if' information, that will not only prevent kidnap in the first place but advise on what to do if you are taken hostage and prepare you or your Principal for the physiological and psychological effects of the illegal captivity.

In the absence of this professional advice you should, at the very minimum advise your Principal that if he is kidnapped he should heed the following advice:

1. Try to control emotions (much easier said than done, but it must be said).
2. Do not offer resistance once it is clear that the kidnap has been successful.
3. Do attempt to build a relationship with the captors, but start very slowly.
4. Be prepared to accept isolation.
5. Do not do anything to antagonise the captors.
6. Follow all instructions implicitly.
7. Do not make threats or promises.

Whenever the risk of kidnap is anticipated you should compile a 'kidnap file', which will include good quality recent photos of your client along with any relevant personal details, e.g. medical history and current medication. You should set up a means of verifying whether the kidnap is genuine – a pre-arranged code given to the Principal so that he/she might relay back should the kidnap happen. You should know about any insurance, and have the emergency contact details of the kidnap consultants.

The most prominent kidnap for ransom specialists are, in no particular order:

Kroll Europe, Middle East & Africa
10 Fleet Place
London EC4M 7RB
United Kingdom
Phone: 44 (0) 207 029 5000
Fax: 44 (0) 207 029 5001
http://www.krollworldwide.com

Control Risks
Cottons Centre
Cottons Lane
London
SE1 2QG
United Kingdom
Tel: + 44 20 7970 2100
Fax: + 44 20 7970 2222
http://www.crg.com/

Bodycover

Bodycover, as the word suggests, means using your body as a shield to protect your Principal from an attack. The 'attack' might come from a bullet, an egg, a shout, a knife, or a punch. This is where the term 'bullet-catchers' originated. The Bodyguard, by placing himself between the attacker and his Principal will 'catch' the bullet meant for his boss. Well that's the theory anyway!

Assess Cover Evacuate ACE

There are three stages of providing 'bodycover'. The acronym, to remember the sequence, is ACE©

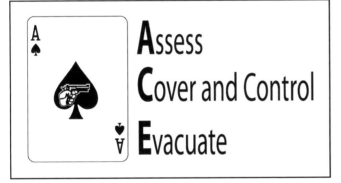

Assess

Throughout your working day as a Close Protection Officer you are constantly assessing situations, looking for possible threats. With regard to providing bodycover you might be reacting to a gun shot or a shout or even something that you have seen and don't like the look of, such as a suspect package or person. Before you can act you need to assess the situation. It's no good running away with the Principal if you are running in the wrong direction. Your actions might be different should a gun attack be short or long range, or whether it is a knife, a grenade or even a flour bomb. Assessing the situation might take you a nanosecond or ten seconds but providing good cover and evacuation depends upon the accuracy of your initial assessment.

In This Chapter

Learn how to provide bodycover to your Principal.

Long or short range attacks.

Understand the importance of ACE

Cover and control

Providing bodycover means placing your body between the danger and the Principal. You are providing cover to his head and vital organs. This action needs to be quick and instinctive. You must practise providing this cover from all sorts of positions. You may need to provide cover from any direction while walking, while driving or sitting down. While providing this cover you ensure you are able to control the Principal both physically and with your voice. You should be able to run (with your Principal) defend yourself, punch or shoot a weapon.

When working with a Personal Escort Section, at the 'cover' stage of your ACE, it might be that the best form of cover is one where everyone 'caves-in' on the Principal and protects him while the best method or direction of evacuation is decided upon. What type of cover you use will depend upon factors such as what is actually happening and whether you have an escort section

Evacuate

The best evacuations are planned for, but the next best thing is just to quickly remove the Principal away from the danger. Whenever possible, the bodycover remains on throughout the evacuation. Removing the Principal from danger while providing the bodycover is not easy. It is easier with the cooperation of the Principal, but must also be practised without that cooperation. Your Principal will also have a belly full of adrenalin and be experiencing 'fight or flight'. This could mean that the Principal is with you, or has brain fade, and you need to communicate through this to ensure that the Principal does not hamper the evacuation.

Getting the Principal out fast providing bodycover whilst doing so

Bodycover must be practised

Providing bodycover must be turned into muscle memory and become instinctive. Practising providing the cover from left, right, front, rear, and above will cover most situations. You do not have to practise giving cover from all points of the compass. Just by practising the main directions given above you will build enough instinctive muscle memory to react to an attack from any direction. The way that you position your body and move to execute the bodycover will differ slightly with attacks from each direction.

When you start giving bodycover it will feel slow and clumsy. Practice will make it slick

Responses to attacks are known as 'action on' drills or 'immediate action' drills. For clarity we will use just the one term 'action-on-drills' (AODs). Your AODs will vary depending upon lots of different factors, such as the type of attack, your location, whether you are working one-on-one or have an escort section. ACE will almost always apply, but there may be occasions where evacuation is simply impossible, or where the Close Protection Officer's best course of action is to stay and fight rather than run. Common sense and experience will be your only guide in such matters. But because most of the time ACE will apply, this is what we will practise over and over again and then some more. Our ACE will need to be as instinctive as ducking, and to get there means that we must practise a lot.

When practising bodycover, it is best to get the basics right from a static position before you start adding other elements such as movement or being in confined spaces such as vehicles or hotel corridors, etc. Your practice should not be with your Principal but with colleagues or a willing wife or husband, etc. When you are an expert, you could and should run your Principal through the drills, so that he knows what to expect, but do this only once or twice. Do not do your practice sessions on the Principal; it's not conducive to learning. Furthermore, unless your Principal is a rugby player type then he will find it all a little too hard and aggressive. The risk of injury is also too high.

Using weapons with bodycover

If you are on an assignment where you routinely carry weapons then the AODs must be practised with the weapon. Most of the drills described below can be used with or without a weapon. However, some of the training needs to be heavily supervised as some of the drills can be very dangerous, especially for those new to bodycover or weapons. All of the responses to attack below aim to provide bodycover but at the same time leave your strong arm free to punch, shoot or assist in the Principal's evacuation.

Training for attacks,

The following drills are for the Bodyguard, or the person that is nearest to the Principal at the time of attack. If you have an escort section then their drills will be different and are covered in detail later.

Start slow and stand still

Initially you should start from the classic position of behind and slightly to the right or left of the Principal. Starting from a static position is best. You will have enough to think about and coordinate without having movement to consider. Movement can be introduced gradually as muscle memory kicks in and the basics are mastered. When you learned to drive a car, remember how much easier it was to concentrate on driving safely when you weren't trying to remember which pedal to push, when to push it and how hard. Once you had committed the clutch, brake and accelerator function to muscle memory, you could then apply all of your attention to the road. If you practise taking hold of the Principal and effecting bodycover enough times it will become instinctive. You will then have more time to think about the right course of action.

Assess the situation; you need to be able to effect the bodycover without taking your eyes away from the threat. This will require you to step in between the threat and your Principal and get the bodycover applied. You should always take hold of and control the Principal; this will be done simultaneously, and can be both physically, by grabbing him, and by voice; "GET DOWN!" or "WITH ME!" His fight or flight mechanism may well choose flight, and you need to ensure that if you both decide on flight then you are both flying in the same direction while you are giving bodycover. The last thing you need is the Principal doing his own thing. When an attack is imminent or happening you become the boss, you are giving the orders. Your highest priority is to evacuate the Principal and remove him from the danger. It is imperative that you provide bodycover during those milliseconds of assessment. You will only be able to do this with copious amounts of practice.

> GET CONTROL OF THE PRINCIPAL PHYSICALLY AND WITH YOUR VOICE

Attacked from the front

When you are attacked from the front, it is almost as though the Principal is giving you the bodycover! Your positions must be reversed immediately. Keeping your head up towards the threat, you need to use the hand that is nearest the Principal. This

Effecting bodycover to a threat from the front. In the fraction of a second that the cover is effected the Bodyguard will be working on the most suitable response to the threat, shoot, punch, run etc.

should be your weak hand to take control, as you are stepping forward to put yourself between the Principal and the threat. Swing the Principal behind you – ideally, his back will be against yours – but as long as he is behind you the cover is on. From this position you should have the option of drawing and shooting a gun with your strong hand, punching or fending off or moving quickly away by turning so that you and the Principal are facing the same way. Then you can evacuate while you provide bodycover.

Attacks from the rear

By taking control of the Principal as you turn your head around (head-switch) to locate the threat, the Principal, who was slightly in front of you, should now be close behind you and receiving bodycover. You now have exactly the same options as attack from the front because the threat is now in front of you. The cover is on and you can shoot, punch and run, etc.

Attacks from the right

If you are right-handed this is the quickest move to effect the cover. You are already on the right. Your head-switch and turn is made at the same time you are taking control of the Principal with your weak hand. Pull him in close behind you. You are then providing effective cover and can shoot, punch or run in less than a second.

Attacks from the left

This one poses the most problems for right-handed protection officers. The weak hand reaches to take control, taking hold of the collar or shoulder of the Principal. With the weak hand, the protection officer must swing the Principal behind him as he moves towards the threat. As the Principal needs to move 180 degrees before the cover is on, this must be done quickly.

If the Principal is tall then a very fast variation can get the cover on much more quickly. As the head-switch is made, the control is taken with the weak arm, taking the Principal's collar; the protection officer then ducks under his own arm and the Principal ends up in cover behind the protection officer after travelling just 90 degrees. Doing it this way means that the weapon can be on target very quickly. The Principal should be very tight behind you. When practising this with live fire on the range, particular care has to be taken because the weapon is drawn and travels past the torso of the Principal as the protection officer goes under his arm. Only those very competent with weapons should practise this live.

When the threat is to the left you should still take hold of the Principal whilst you are getting between him and the threat

Effecting bodycover when the Principal is between you and the threat on your weak side is the most difficult cover to get right quickly enough. When you are learning this action it will feel slow and clumsy, but remember the old Excel ranges saying: 'slow is smooth and smooth is fast'. It will get quicker with practice. I have seen some organisations train for this situation by telling the Bodyguard not to take hold of the Principal, just move between the Principal and the threat. I suggest that this may be OK for some situations, but you should first train to take hold and to take control of the Principal. If you practise this enough it will become as fast and slick as any other method, with the advantage that the Principal is tight behind you and under your control, rather than succumbing to his own fight or flight dilemma and doing something foolish.

This is how you should end up. From this position you can engage with a weapon or your fists and you have the Principal under control. You can back up whilst you are shooting or just turn and run whilst still providing the cover

Attacks from Above

This type of attack could come from a sniper with a high firing position, mortar or grenades. ACE will still almost always apply except that sometimes finding hard cover or remaining on the ground providing bodycover may become a priority, depending upon the type of attack. A grenade-style attack can be better defended by remaining low and providing cover. Common sense and your wits being your very best weapon of defence from an attack from above.

If the protection officer is on his own then there may be times when the best way to protect the Principal is to ignore ACE and confront the threat head on. This is worst-case-scenario and normally short range situation where evacuation is just not possible, or the protection officer needs to 'punch-to-buy-time' that is, time to evacuate, but could be to buy time to draw and shoot.

Punching to buy time

'Punching-to-buy-time' should be practised often. You could try to buy time to draw a weapon, and this is practised on a range with a holstered weapon. Or you could be just buying time to enable to evacuate. When training with a weapon, the target is punched centre of mass with the weak hand or with both hands, the aim being to at worst unbalance them and at best send them sprawling and buy you time to draw your weapon. Realistic 'targets' that fall over or are spring loaded can be used, as can a regular fig 11 target on a knock down stand.

The punch to buy time coupled with the short draw takes a while to master and instructors need to ensure that trainees don't shoot a hole in their punching hand. It has happened!

Moving the Principal

Punching to buy time should not happen without first moving the Principal. This can be done by dropping him where he is and is easily done with a little practice. It does divert an imminent attack because the target (your Principal) has moved.

In this training scenario the bodycover and control of the Principal is initially applied whilst the situation is assessed

Dropping the Principal by pulling him backwards, away from the threat while at the same time kicking his leg(s) from under him, will get him down quickly, as will a scream from you to "GET DOWN!" An assailant with a knife, gun or fist, now has to look for his target, who will have moved quickly. This can buy you a precious bit of a second.

Moving the Principal violently sideways can with practise become a very good move. As you come forward to engage the threat, you use your body, but mostly your hip to force the Principal away, catch him right and you can push him several metres sideways. Where does the assailant look then? Does he look sideways for target acquisition or does he have to now focus on you, who will be already almost upon him. Putting the Principal on the floor or moving him sideways needs to be done aggressively if it is to work, but in a situation like this the aggression will be (or should be) there.

To be effective, training to provide bodycover must be carried out hard and aggressively. Sometimes there may well be slight injuries, but it should carry no more risk than a friendly game of rugby!

The Escort Section – engaging an attacker

If the protection officer comes under a short range attack when working with an escort section, it is their job to engage the threat aggressively while the protection officer employs ACE. There are no strict rules about who does what, because this must be decided upon at the time given the circumstances that you find yourself in.

The "Cave In". The Personal Escort section and the Bodyguard all cave in on the Principal to provide him with effective cover. When they evacuate they will all have a 'peice' of the Principal so that if anyone is shot or falls over the evacuation can continue.

Short range attacks

This could be with a knife, a handgun or a bag of flour, but immediately a team member sees anything that looks like an attack he will scream the threat and direction: "GUN-TWO-O-CLOCK!" Who does what next will depend upon where you are at the time. If you are between the threat and the Principal then you should engage the threat. If the Principal is between you and the threat you may have to decide whether to help with the evacuation of the Principal or to assist your colleagues in engaging the threat. Do not expect to be told what to do. Given the situation your common sense should tell you the right thing to do. At crunch time in a situation like this there is no time for a team leader to tell you what to do. Your actions need to be instinctive. Good Close Protection Officers are intelligent, they read situations correctly and react accordingly. There are hundreds of Close Protection Officers that think they are good, but they are only good until something goes wrong!

If you are engaging the threat then you should do so very aggressively and noisily. Engaging someone in this way cuts down their angles and they have to convert their attention from the Principal to you. This can buy your Principal the precious seconds needed to escape with a Bodyguard. Two or three members of the personal escort section charging aggressively and noisily at a lone gunman or knifeman would be enough to ruin the aim of even the coolest of attackers.

If you are evacuating the Principal then you should make sure that you remain as close to him as possible so that you are providing body cover but not so close that you hamper the Principal's running. Your escape will be much quicker if your Principal is able to run. The Bodyguard will have a hands-on hold of the Principal, but all members of the team should be close enough to take hold of him should the Bodyguard lose his grip for any reason.

Long-range attacks

In the event of you coming under a long-range attack the personal escort section is best employed providing full bodycover and evacuation to the Principal. Because the attacker is much further away, trying to engage him would be futile. So every attempt must be made to remove the Principal from the killing zone while providing full body cover for him. Some long-range attacks such as those with a mortar/grenade may require that you stay where you are and provide bodycover. If there is no natural cover you will have to cover the Principal with your body. Stay low and then move as soon as you feel it safe to do so.

Summary

You should be an expert at providing bodycover in any many given situations. From walking or sitting positions, whether you have a weapon or not. Bodycover should always be applied in the every first instance of something appearing wrong. If you need to fight your way out of a situation then to do so whilst still holding your Principal would be folly. If you need to use fists or feet then use your voice to control your Principal. Bodycover is a basic skill that you need to master. Sportsmen know that the basics always need to be practced. No matter how good a rugby player is, they always continually practice the basics such as passing and catching. No one is so good that they do not need to practice. You will get good only by lots of practice. But the only way to stay good is to practice whenever you can. Your aim is to practice enough that bodycover becomes as instinctive as blinking and ducking.

Cars & Drivers

C ar travel in most places in the world is inherently dangerous, especially and specifically if some terrorist or criminal is out there trying to kill you. But you do not need
to be the target of a criminal or terrorist gang. Some might say
that these days just being on the road is probably the most dangerous situation you can be in. In some cities, it seems like everyone
on the road is trying to kill you!

Close Protection Cars

It is a fact that a very large percentage of all attacks or kidnap attempts take place in or near the Principal's motor car. The reason
for this is clear. The criminal or terrorist will know that your
Principal will have lots security in place at his home and office.
But when their 'target' leaves all this security behind to travel in
a vehicle, even one with an escort, this is where he can be most
vulnerable. It's because of this vulnerability that we must practise
our vehicle drills until they become instinctive, why we try to stay
one jump ahead of an attacker and why we are always on the look
out for the surveillance that will invariably precede these attacks.

Driving Licences

An International Driving Permit (IDP) is an internationally recognised, low cost document which, when accompanied by your
driving licence, will allow you to drive a private motor vehicle in
a foreign country. An IDP is proof that you hold a valid driving
licence in your own country. It is not always necessary to have
one, since many countries recognise each other's licenses, but possessing an IDP has many advantages.

It is intended to overcome the difficulties drivers might have
while travelling in other countries, which may have widely varying
license requirements. Because the Close Protection

In This Chapter

**Choosing the right
vehicle**

**Learn all about armour
and protecting the car.**

**How to stay legal when
overseas**

Officer might find himself driving in another country at a moment's notice, the IDP is really a 'must have' document that can prove to be very useful. The IDP is printed in ten languages – the five United Nations official languages (English, French, Spanish, Russian and Chinese) plus German, Arabic, Italian, the Scandinavian languages and Portuguese. It can also prove to be a useful form of pictured ID in the case of a lost or stolen passport.

IDP's must be applied for in the country that the licence was issued. In the UK they can be obtained through all of the motoring organisations such as, the AA, RAC and Green Flag all of which can be found in any copy of the yellow pages. In the USA applications can be made to The American Automobile Association, 1000 AAA Drive, Mail Stop 28, Heathrow, Florida 32746-5063, Telephone number (407) 444-4240/700, fax: (407) 444-3780.

You should always take your original driving licence with you when driving abroad, even if you're a holder of an IDP. You may need to present it when hiring a car and might, if requested, have to show it to the local authorities.

This list of countries which require you to carry a permit is a quick reference guide only. You must refer to your IDP application form for a full listing and for any special conditions which may apply. If the country you are travelling to is not listed then we would still recommend that you contact an approved IDP outlet to check motoring regulations.

Afghanistan, Albania, Algeria, Angola, Argentina, Benin, Bhutan, Brazil, Bulgaria, Cayman Isles, Central African Rep., Chad, CIS, Colombia, Comoros, Curacao, Cote d'Ivoire (Ivory Coast), Czech Republic, Egypt, Equatorial Guinea, Guinea, Haiti, India, Indonesia, Iraq, Japan, Kampuchea, Korea (South), Kuwait, Leeward Islands, Macao, Nigeria, Pakistan, Philippines, Poland, Rwanda, Senegal, Slovenia, Somalia, Suriname, Swaziland, Syria, Taiwan, United Arab Emirates, Vietnam, Zaire, Zimbabwe. The Commonwealth of Independent States (CIS) comprises Armenia, Azerbaijan, Belarus, Kazakhstan, Moldova, Russia, Tajikistan, Turkmenistan, Ukraine and Uzbekistan. Leeward Islands are Antigua, Dominica, Montserrat, St Christopher, Nevis and Anguilla.

Insurance.

If you are driving then it is your responsibility to ensure that you are insured for the vehicle you are driving. You should have had sight of the insurance document, and either noted your name or more likely that it is an open policy that includes you. A common open policy will allow 'any driver with a clean licence and who is over twenty five'. "I thought I was insured" is not a defence in law. The best practise is to keep a copy of the insurance document in each vehicle.

Choosing the right vehicles.

On many occasions the vehicles that you use in Close Protection will be 'inherited'. By that I mean they will already be there at the assignment and you will have to make do with them. If you have the opportunity to specify vehicles for an assignment then there is plenty for you to consider. The basics will be obvious; you will of course need to know how many people will be travelling, including the escort section. Do you need vehicles for backup and luggage?

With these questions answered you should easily arrive at the number of vehicles you require. But what colour should you buy? Should they all be the same colour? If you want to maintain a high profile and show off the security as a deterrent then a convoy

Some Principals will own many different cars. A range of vehicles that can include stretch limousines, four wheel drives, luxury executive and super cars can be driven by the Bodyguard

of cars the same colour will do that for you. Even if the cars are nondescript and common, as soon as you put three of them the same colour on the same bit of road you will be noticed. Any team that has hired cars from an airport for a quick CP job and not specified different cars or at least different colours has felt pretty conspicuous as they left the airport. All cars, whenever possible, should have run flat tyres, or at the least have self healing tyres, by using a chemical that can be purchased at most good auto parts stores.

The Principal's car

Different colours, sizes and models will lower the profile. The Principal's vehicle may or may not be your choice, but this rarely matters as comfort, power and handling often do come together in the better vehicles. The top of the range cars such as Jaguars, BMWs Mercedes and Cadillacs are seen time and time again and are all excellent in a protection role.

If your Principal is one of those from the green camp and has invested in 'green' electric cars, then it is especially important that the escort vehicles are not green and they have some power to remove you from a situation at speed.

The Escort Vehicles

My absolute favourite escort vehicle is the Range Rover. This vehicle can fit in anywhere. It can sit outside the best hotels in London and New York, on the quay in the South of France or on the drive of your Principal's remote country residence and look as though its meant to be there The high seating gives superb visibility and enables you to get out of the vehicle at a run. It can easily jump kerbs, travel on verges or cross country; its ramming capability is also excellent. As long as you don't buy the diesel version, the Range Rover will keep up with all other vehicles, even powerful sports cars.

If your Principal's budget does not stretch to 4.6 litre Range Rovers, then any powerful four-door saloon will suffice. People carriers and Sports Utility Vehicles (SUVs) are good choices. Petrol or Turbo Diesel models are equally capable and it is rare that someone who employs a CP team worries about miles per gallon and running costs, but it has been known!

When choosing a vehicle you should be mindful of the profile that you wish to portray. It is difficult to maintain a low profile if your Principal insists on travelling in a gold Rolls Royce, with a private number plate and a flag flying on the bonnet. Clearly, in situations like these everyone is aware that the guys sat in the car behind, even if that car is nondescript, are members of the security team. If your Principal's car stands out, then nine times out of ten the escort should too. Even if your escort car is nondescript, a rifle barrel or two, sticking out the window, as can be seen in places like Iraq, certainly does increase the deterrent value

Hardening the vehicle

You might think that 'hardening the vehicle' means that we cover it in armour and, in some cases, you might be right. We will discuss armour later but meanwhile there is a lot more that you can do to harden your vehicle.

Tyres

'Run flat' tyres are almost a pre-requisite, even if you are not anticipating that your tyres are going to be shot out from under you. This is a simple device fitted to the wheel that stops the tyre from coming off the wheel. If you do ever suffer a puncture, imagine how much more convenient it is to continue your journey and get the tyre fixed later rather than have the Principal wait on the side of the road while you are messing about with the jack and a tyre lever! The second-best option is to use the widely available chemical compounds that can be purchased to make your regular tyres run flat. Early do-it-yourself kits were of dubious quality and best suited to bicycles and children's buggies. In contrast, the modern equivalents are much better. As long as the side wall remains intact and the tyre stays on the rim the tyres will run flat.

Fuel tanks

Fuel tanks need to be protected. Firstly you need to stop anyone contaminating your fuel. Vehicles will not travel far with contaminated fuel and you could easily be ambushed while you are 'broken down'. The locks on fuel filler caps are often poorly designed. Higher security caps are available so if any of your vehicles appears vulnerable in this area you should be able to rectify it.

Fuel tanks do not explode nearly as much as Hollywood might have us believe, and accidents, even high speed ones, rarely result in pyrotechnical displays. However if the vehicle does come under attack from bullets or bombs then the chances of the fuel tank exploding become very real. Anti-explosion tanks can be purchased or your original tank modified so that they are rendered very unlikely to explode.

Explosafe http://www.explosafe.ch is a leading manufacturer of explosion suppression systems; their system can prevent a fuel tank from exploding from various causes of ignition, including sparking, electrostatic discharge, external crash fires, gunfire, or terrorist activity. The explosafe system is based on a matrix of expanded aluminium alloy foil, slit and expanded to form a mesh of hexagonally-shaped openings. When layered, the mesh results in an open-celled bulk baffle, which can be cut to shapes and sizes to fit any container/fuel tank. How the system works is ingenious and it is worth a visit to their website to check out the product.

Auxiliary Tanks

Years ago, large cars often came with two tanks; some had manual switchovers that could embarrass you if you forgot to switch them over! These twin tanks are now rare and while you do not have to remember to switch tanks anymore, you could end up being stuck if the one tank that you do have to use loses its fuel. This is why some armoured car manufacturers build in a small auxiliary tank for use in an emergency; it may only have enough fuel for a few miles, but that should be enough to get you out of trouble.

Vehicle Alarms

Ideally all cars on the protection operation should be fitted with alarms. When working in a one-on-one situation this is an absolute must. Equally the alarms should text or page you when it is activated. While leaving a restaurant with the Principal it is nice to know that the car is there and hasn't been tampered with. You know it's okay because your pager would have told you if anything had happened. If your vehicle is locked and alarmed a bomb could still be placed underneath it or next to it. So a locked and alarmed vehicle in a locked and alarmed garage is ideal but not always practical. I know of a chauffer that locks and alarms his Bentley and then sprinkles talcum powder on the floor, to show up the footprints of anyone that has entered the locked and alarmed garage.

Armoured cars

One of the first armoured cars for a political leader is thought to have been a limousine built by the engineering firm O'Gara-Hess & Eisenhardt, for President Harry S. Truman in 1949.

Today, the technology has greatly moved on from these early tank-like vehicles that can save lives and do so even in the worst case scenarios. An excellent example of an armoured car saving its occupants is when Georgian President Eduard Shevardnadze survived an assassination attempt in 1998. A dozen heavily armed men ambushed his motorcade, opening fire on his vehicle with small arms, machine guns and rocket-propelled grenades. Three people were killed but thanks to the armour in his limousine, which had been a present from friendly governments in the West, the President survived the attack and is probably now a devoted fan of armoured cars. Armoured car manufactures work on protecting the car's occupants at three points:

☑ Protection at point of attack

☑ Provide the ability to evade and escape

☑ Allow the occupants to fight back with counter-measures

The car that saved Shevard-nadzes life. The armour stood up to a massive attack from machine guns and grenades

Protection at point of attack

The prime concern at the point of attack is the integrity of the passenger cabin; the occupants are surrounded by armour bullet-proof composites and bullet-resistant glass. In the most secure vehicles, the transparent side glass will be more than two inches thick and capable of withstanding direct arms fire. Today's top of the range cars can withstand sustained direct fire from AK-47 and other high velocity rifles, as well as the effects of grenade explosions.

Of great concern to the manufacturers and occupants is to defend an attack by a roadside bomb or mine. Today's cars are much more capable of doing so than they were in 1992 when the armoured car that Italy's top anti-mafia judge Giovanni Falcone was travelling in was blown up by a bomb that had been placed in trenches dug by the side of the road. The bomb was detonated as he passed. Even though he was travelling at around 100mph the car suffered severe damage and Falcone died along with his wife and three Bodyguards

All of the modern protection that the manufactures build in is designed to help the occupants of the armoured car withstand a serious assault until help arrives. However if even the defences of a military tank can be breached if it is a sitting target, so the next aim of the manufacturer is to give the vehicle the chance to evade its attackers.

Provide the ability to evade and escape

Standard on any good armoured car is top quality run-flat tyres. In the event of the armoured tyres disintegrating under attack (unlikely, as the tyres are designed to run if flat), the wide steel rims are strong enough for the vehicle to remain responsive and still enable a speedy escape. Outside of the passenger compartment, essential parts of the vehicle such as the battery, fuel tanks and engine block carry just as much armour. Some vehicles also have the radiator protected and use clever air ducting so that the radiator can still do its job. There are also systems to automatically seal the fuel tank to prevent explosions. Night vision systems can be incorporated so that when driving lights are shot out the driver can still see. Vehicles such as President Bush's Cadillac DeVille use an infrared camera to scan the road ahead. The heat signature of all objects ahead is converted into a view of the road which is projected onto the inside of the windscreen. Being stuck in a killing-zone is not conducive to long life. Evading an attack may often be the only way of surviving it.

Allow the occupants to fight back with counter measures

Gun ports give the occupants the ability to deliver counter attacks. An excellent counter measure for the Close Protection Officer is one-way bullet-resistant glass. This stops bullets from the outside but allows you to shoot at an attacker from the inside. This type of bullet-resistant glass is made by laminating a brittle sheet of material with a flexible material. When a person outside the car shoots a bullet into the window, the bullet strikes the brittle side first. This brittle material shatters around the point of impact and absorbs the energy over a large area. A bullet fired from inside the same car can easily pass through the glass because the bullet's force is concentrated on a small area, which causes the material to flex. This causes the brittle material to break outwards, allowing the bullet to pierce the flexible material and hopefully strike the assailant. While this tactic will probably be hard on the ear drums, it is one hundred times better to be able to return some fire and can easily make the difference between dying in or surviving an attack.

Armoured cars are mostly modified versions of normal cars, made by replacing the windows with bullet-proof glass and inserting layers of armour under the outer skin of the car. A quick glance and the car looks like any normal car, but closer inspection will turn up a few clues. The glass can be the biggest giveaway to the novice, especially when trying to read the tax disc or licence stuck on the inside, because it is then that the glass thickness is apparent.

A fully armoured car, one that withstands a sustained attack with high-velocity bullets, can be heavy. The manufacturers will, of course, upgrade the suspension and the brakes, but the vehicle's handling will be forever impaired. If you drive your Principal in an armoured car then practising defensive and evasive driving in a regular car is a waste of time; you must practise in the armoured car. Just make sure that you have plenty of space to train in! Some armoured cars drive terribly, with slow acceleration and handling. The worst ones corner and stop like a boat! There are exceptions of course, and things are getting better every year. Advances in new lightweight synthetic laminates and much improving ballistic glass with moulded door and window overlaps makes armoured car performance get better and better. It's not uncommon though for an armoured car to be ten or more years old and still in service. Just be aware of the car's capabilities and limitations and tailor your driving accordingly.

There are many makers of armoured cars and the cars that they armour are not all Bentleys and Rolls. Popular choices are the large BMW's, Range Rovers and Mercedes but many more common nondescript cars are armoured, such as Land Cruisers and BMW Saloons. Even cheap Skodas are armoured and can be used where a low profile needs to be maintained.

Summary
It does not matter how many vehicles your Principal owns, in fact using different vehicles is to be recommended as it makes it more difficult for anyone that may have you under surveillance. But every vehicle should be hardened as much as possible. While you would not expect the Principal owns a vintage car to get it armoured, you should convince him to at least put run flat tyres on it if he drives it on the public road. Always ensure that you are one hundred percent legal for the country you are operating in, this includes licences and insurance as well as the traffic laws.

Armoured Vests

The Bodyguard should make good use of armour whenever he can. The concealed vest he and his Principal might wear, the bullet-proof glass in the Principal's residence and the fully armoured vehicle that they might drive are all common uses of armour. A Close Protection Officer should have a good working knowledge of all types of armour, its capabilities and limitations and the pros and cons of its everyday use.

The history of body armour

Soldiers and civilians have been wearing body armour for thousands of years. As long ago as 3000BC ancient Egyptians were known to have draped themselves in thick animal hides to protect them in battle. Roman warriors covered their torsos with custom-made metal plates before going to war. By the 1400s, armour in the western world had become highly sophisticated allowing a warrior to fight effectively while being well protected. With the right armour an army became almost invincible.

When Berthold Schwarz, a German monk of the early 14th century, worked out how to use gunpowder to propel a projectile, the traditional armour makers' response was to make thicker and stronger armour. The projectiles initially only had enough energy to penetrate the thin layers of metal, but as weapons became more effective at piercing the armour and killing the wearer, the armour makers kept making the armour thicker, which of course meant heavier. The result was that to be effective at stopping a bullet the armour was too thick, heavy and cumbersome to wear.

In This Chapter

Learn about the skills
The different types of armour.

Understand armour's capabilities and limitations

Modern Armour

Today we have modern materials that can stop almost all bullets, even at point blank range. The person wearing the body armour will still feel the energy of a bullet's impact, but will feel it over the whole torso rather than in a specific area. If everything works correctly, the victim won't be seriously hurt.

Hard body armour

Today's hard armour is made out of thick ceramic or metal plates; it functions basically the same way as the iron suits worn by those medieval knights. It is so hard that a bullet or other weapon is deflected and just cannot penetrate. That means that the armour material meets the bullet with almost the same force with which the bullet pushes in, so the armour is not penetrated.

Police and military personnel in high-risk situations wear hard body armour. The bullet- proof plates are inserted into custom-made pockets in jackets and while modern ceramic plates are not as heavy as the armour worn by a knight of the round table, it is only just marginally more comfortable than that worn by our medieval cousins.

Typically hard body armour offers more protection than soft body armour, but, in a Close Protection role, it is much more cumbersome. This means that Close Protection Officers need compromise armour that is lighter and softer.

Soft body armour

It wasn't until the 1960s that engineers developed reliable bullet-resistant armour that a person could wear all day comfortably. Unlike traditional heavy, hard, metal armour, the armour developed was soft! It wasn't made out of pieces of metal but was formed from advanced woven fibres that were sewn into vests and other soft clothing. This is now known as soft body armour.

To most people the thought of 'soft body armour' doesn't quite make sense. How can a soft piece of clothing stop bullets? The principle at work is actually quite simple.

> SOFT BODY ARMOUR WILL NOT PROTECT YOU OR YOUR PRINCIPAL FROM HIGH VELOCITY RIFLES

A piece of bullet-proof material is just a very strong 'net' of fibres. This net of fibres 'catches' a bullet in a multilayer web of the woven fabrics. The engaged fibres absorb and disperse the energy of the impact to other fibres in the fabric weave. This transfer occurs at net 'cross-over points', where the fibres are interwoven. Additional energy is absorbed by the other layers in the body armour, reducing the amount of transferred energy that causes 'blunt trauma'. As unbelievable as it sounds, these woven fabrics are strong enough to perform, while offering the additional advantage of being more comfortable to wear, than traditional plastic or metal based shield products.

Choosing body armour for your client

The choice of armour that you and your client wear will of course be influenced by the threats and risks that you both face. If you base your day-to-day need on comfort then you will always choose to wear soft armour or be armour free. If you want the best available protection then you might opt for the heavier hard armour. There are

This table shows the different levels of armour and the type of ammunition that they can withstand

BALLISTIC LEVELS OF BODY ARMOUR		
Level	Weapon Calibre	Velocity (fps)
Level I	022 LRVH (40g) Load	1050 to 1100
	.38 Lead Round Nose	850 to 900
Level IIA	.357 Magnum (158g) Jacketed Soft Point	1250 to 1300
	9mm (124g) Full metal Jacket	1090 to 1140
Level II	.357 Magnum (158g) Jacketed Soft Point	1395 to 1445
	9mm (124g) Full Metal Jacket	1175 to 1225
Level IIIA	.44 Magnum (240g) Lead Semi -Woodcutter	1400 to 1450
	9mm (124g) Full Metal Jacket	1400 to 1450
Level III	7.62mm (150g) Full Metal Jacket	2750 to 2800
Level IV	30.06 (166g) .30 Calibre M2AP Armour Piercing	2850 to 2900

other things though to take into consideration. Bulky hard armour can impede your movement. In addition to this, being on your feet all day wearing hard body armour means you will lose a lot of body fluid, especially in a warm or humid environment. Soft, very concealable armour may not offer you or your client the protection you need.

Hard Armour might kill you!

Heavy body armour is difficult to disguise and anyone in close proximity will probably notice it. If it is obvious that ballistic plates are being worn, then an attacker may well be encouraged to go for a head shot to avoid the armour. A concealed vest of soft body armour might well make an attacker go for an easier body shot and the Principal could be saved by the vest. In this case, the heavy armour increases the risk rather than reduces it. The discomfort of wearing heavy armour makes it more likely that your Principal (and you) will avoid wearing it whenever possible, If the situation dictates that you must wear hard armour this can be made much more comfortable with well made vests and it pays to shop around to find the very best kit.

Bullet proof shields

It is a good idea to insert Level IIIA protection into a briefcase, or back pack. This will then transform an inconspicuous everyday object into a convenient ballistic shield for pistol and 9mm sub-machine-gun threats. these plates can also cover gaps in your body Armour when riding in un-armoured vehicles. The cover that a briefcase could give your Principal in a shooting situation could easily save his life.

The future of body armour

Recently there have been major advances in ballistic material, this is good news for the Close Protection Officer because new vests will have less bulk and be easily concealed whilst at the same time be more efficient. An interesting development is the use of nano technology. Nano technology is an umbrella term that covers many areas of research dealing with objects that are measured in nanometers. A nanometer (nm) is a billionth of a meter, or a millionth of a millimeter. American and Israeli companies say they are very near to building a super armour using this new science.

Summary

For the vest to work you have got wear it, and if you are going to wear it every day then it will need to be comfortable. If profile is an issue then a vest worn under street clothes can be used. For protection against rifles and high velocity weapons then the soft armour will have to be supplemented by armour plate. These hard slabs of armour come in many sizes but 10 in by 12 inch plates will fit in most vest pockets. Do not forget the assistance that a ballistic shield can give, in a car or disguised in a briefcase they can be invaluable.

There are a vast number of manufacturers and distributors of body armour. Google "body armor" and you will get over 46,000 links. So if you are shopping for it, get recommendations and look for references.

Vehicle Security and Search

While working as a Close Protection Officer you should carry out a search of all vehicles prior to using them. This search will be carried out whether or not the vehicle has been left unattended; however, if a vehicle has been left unattended then the search will be much more thoroughly and cautiously carried out. Essentially, there are two types of search cursory and full systematic.

Cursory searching

The cursory search should be carried out EVERY TIME you enter the vehicle. This is nothing more than a scan of the vehicle's surrounding area. You should examine the underside (which is best viewed from a distance), the wheel arches (which must be searched from a close point), along with the locks and windows to look for any evidence of tampering. Cursory searches are quick once you are experienced and can often be done with such a casual low profile hardly anyone will notice what you are doing.

Systematic searching

The full systematic search is a completely different matter: this is a thorough and methodical search that takes time and manpower. It is normally carried out only when the vehicle has been out of our care and control, e.g. away for servicing, or if it's a new car.

What are we searching for?

We are searching for any signs of tampering such as brake or fuel lines cut. The result of faulty brakes is obvious. A cut fuel line would make us break down as part of some kind of attack or robbery. A small amount of explosives could kill all of the occupants, a bug could transmit all of the occupant's conversations, and a small transmitter could give away the exact location of the vehicle at all times. Your full systematic search should take all of this into account.

In This Chapter

Learn about the different types of vehicle search.

Understand when you should search and why.

The Sequence of searching the vehicle

The search must be broken down into stages and each stage completed in order.

Surrounding Area

This might be for example, the car park or garage, the immediate area around the car, drains, freshly cultivated areas, hedges, culverts or dustbins. You are looking for wires, anything unusual at all. A bomb does not have to be in the car to kill or injure the vehicle's occupants.

Coachwork

Pay attention to the paintwork, chrome, mirrors, bumpers, hubcaps, windows, filler cap and number plates. You are looking for any signs of tampering, forced entry, fingerprints and smudge marks, etc.

Wheels and Arches

Check for cuts in tyres and brake pipes and ensure that no sharp objects have been inserted into the tyre. Make sure that wheel nuts have not been loosened. Also check inside the whole of the wheel arch; while doing so, make sure you look but don't touch because if a device was placed on the wheel, you could easily knock it off while feeling for it. Remember that bombs don't kill you but explosions do, so don't cause an explosion!

Underneath

Check the whole of the chassis, prop shaft, engine compartment, the whole length of the exhaust pipes, and the check inside the wheel area. Just underneath the sills is the common area for attaching small, improvised explosive devices; they can be attached by strong magnets. A small box half the size of this book, painted black and covered in road dirt could be hidden under a car and be overlooked if you don't know what the underneath of the vehicle looks like. You must be familiar so that little bit of box section that shouldn't be there is noticed!

Boot/trunk space

Remove all items from the boot, check all of the boot area, and check the spare for serviceability.

Interior

Open all doors after carefully observing through the windows for anything suspicious. Leave the doors open before conducting a thorough search of the whole interior. Start by searching the driver's seat, headrest and arm rests. Then you will be able to sit and kneel on this seat while you start to search the rest of the interior. The interior will take longer than you might imagine as there are many places that bugs or bombs can be hidden. Be systematic and methodical. Search everywhere, including the roof, floor, sides, front and rear.

Bonnet/hood

Check the release catch and then proceed with a full search of the whole engine compartment. If you are unfamiliar with the engine compartment then you will find it almost impossible to know whether something is a regular component or a bomb!

A mirror is an excellent tool for searching a vehicle. Do not keep your search kit in the boot of the car! Pocket mirrors are a good idea. A mirror without a light source shining on it is next to useless

Some operators take a digital photo of the engine compartment so they can refer back to it. Essentially if you check it properly and often enough, you will soon notice if something is not right. Only once the search of the engine compartment is complete should you turn your attention to the fluids and lubricant levels to check they are normal.

Final check

Leaving the doors open, start the engine, check all electrical equipment (lights, wipers, etc). Check gears, brakes and listen to the engine sound. Is it ok? Close the doors and drive, check the steering and the brakes. How does the engine sound? Are there any warning lights such as oil or ABS? What is the fuel state?

If you find something

If you find anything at all suspicious, DO NOT TOUCH. Use the 4Cs. (See chapter on Bomb Awareness).

Hooks & Lines

Beware the Close Protection book or training course that has you searching vehicles using hooks and lines to open the doors and the bonnet/hood from a safe distance. If you are so certain that there might be a bomb in the car that you are not prepared to open a door without being 50 yards away behind a wall, then call the bomb squad and let them remotely open the doors!

Make things easier for yourself.

Vehicles should never be left unattended but if this is impractical then they should only ever be parked in secure places. If the vehicle is left in an insecure environment, even for the shortest time, then a full systematic search must be carried out as soon as possible. Someone could attach a bumper-beeper (tracker) in seconds. Similarly, if a person had an illegitimate set of keys they could plant an effective bug or bomb inside the car in less than 45 seconds. You can make your searches quicker by using seals; if you use a unique seal to lock the vehicle's toolbox, just a glance will tell you if it has been tampered with. The same seals can be used on spare wheel storage areas. A subtle blob of paint or Tippex on screw heads will tell you immediately if a screwdriver has been used on them.

Under-Car Bomb Detectors

These are systems that will monitor the underside of the vehicle. They are fitted to the vehicle, look for magnets that might be attached and also monitor the noise

You must be familiar with your vehicle to have any chance of finding a transmitter or a bomb. If you know what it looks like, you may notice something out of place.

signature of the vehicle. A bomb attached to the car by any means will disrupt this signature and the alarm will activate. These systems are able to text or page you when they activate. Remember that even the most sophisticated under-car bomb detector will not let you know about the bomb that is near or next to the car!

Summary

Systematic searches take time and you should strive to avoid them at all costs. Avoid unattended parking whenever you can, but if you must leave the car then a manned car park is better than an unmanned one, and a car park with CCTV cameras everywhere must be better than one with none at all. Park near the attendant if there is one and avoid the quiet areas that are not overlooked, areas where someone could go to work on your car. Always carry out cursory searches and ensure that your systematic searches are methodical. Always get alarms fitted and if the threat warrants it then you should persuade the Principal to fit an under vehicle bomb detector.

Defensive and Evasive Driving

I have seen the disappointment on a student's face when he learns that defensive driving isn't throwing a car around and doing flip turns. It is in fact a style of road driving that keeps you away from other people's problems. It's an intelligent approach to driving that not only helps you keep your Principal alive, but ensures he arrives at a destination relaxed and having hardly noticed the journey. Not only that, defensive driving helps you save fuel, brakes, tyres and, if you drive for a living, your sanity! Defensive driving is what we do every time we travel upon the public roads; we 'defend' the space around our vehicle.

Basic driving skills

Most drivers think they are a better driver than everyone else, but if that is the case where did all those bad drivers come from! Almost all traffic accidents are entirely due to human error and are mostly due to unsafe driving practices or negligence.

Almost a third of all accidents are rear end shunts, and you wouldn't be the first escort driver to shunt the Principal during a moment's loss of concentration. Many accidents are the result of driving too close to the vehicle in front, which is a problem for us because very often while escorting a Principal a driver will remain quite close so that no other vehicle can jump in between the escort and the Principal.

In This Chapter

Where the Principal should sit in the vehicle, where his vehicle should be in a convoy

One car drills and convoy procedures

Vehicle ambushes and how to counter them

Carjacking

What makes you a good driver?

A good driver oozes confidence; he handles the vehicle efficiently and effectively. The ride is smooth, with the driver and vehicle operating as one, with skilful and effortless use of the controls.

The driver will have excellent observational skills coupled with the ability to remain alert throughout even the longest of drives.

He will be constantly and actively be scanning through 360 degrees, matching his vehicle's speed to the road conditions and the situation. He will have a highly developed sense of hazard awareness. He will display an excellent attitude to other road users.

Contrary to what we believe, we are not all good drivers. Some people are drawn into this aspect of Close Protection and they excel in it. However, ALL CLOSE PROTECTION OFFICERS SHOULD BE ABLE TO DRIVE, and officers without a driving licence should obtain one as soon as they can. All officers should know about the basics of defensive and evasive driving. You never know when you may have to take charge of a vehicle in an emergency. For example, maybe because of some administration mess up you're the only driver on shift today! So even if driving is not your strong point, learn the basics and practise them because you just don't know when you might need them.

Close Protection drivers

Very good Close Protection drivers are a rare breed. They need to have all the skills and attributes of a good Close Protection Officer, but they also need to be highly skilled drivers, capable of handling their vehicle right to the very limit of its performance and be safe and reliable, even when under extreme pressure. They need to make very quick decisions often under stress. They need to be cool and calm and not hesitate to show aggression should it become necessary. There is no room in Close Protection for a reckless or cavalier driver; the job is just too important. What makes these drivers so rare is that when someone has all of these attributes the very last thing they want is to be stuck behind the wheel of a car. They want to be out there with the Principal at the sharp end and the driving job be taken up by someone else, even though they might be less competent than they are.

Because the driving aspect of Close Protection is often ignored by the elite officers, this job is often taken up by less capable individuals. Some Principals have dedicated drivers that are not even Close Protection trained; they are employed purely because of their navigational knowledge of the city in which they are employed and that they do not mind wearing a grey peaked cap!

Many might look at a Close Protection driver and see a glorified taxi driver; this is especially so when the driver is 70 lbs overweight and seems to always be eating. I have come across quite a few of these. Often they are only still in the job because they have become a 'friend' to the Principal or his family. What is often not realised is that a fit and switched on driver really can save lives. They can use the vehicle to evade danger and use it as a weapon to attack a threat head on.

Driver training

Driver training is very important and ideally the training will be carried out in the regular vehicle, except of course, when this is impractical such as when ramming practice is taking place! However it cannot be stressed enough that a slick manoeuvre that you can do in an old Ford with a manual gearbox and bald tyres will be a lot harder to do in your regular car with tyres designed to hold the road and on regular road widths rather than airfield size training areas. Good driver training is hard to find. Ask around, someone who comes highly recommended by an independent referee has to better than a driving school even if it has got a flash web site.

Most people want to learn all of the fancy moves and turns, but they are much better employed learning how to become a good driver. You must be a good driver first. Advanced driving courses, e.g. those run by organisations like the Institute of Advanced Motorists are indispensable. Only when you are an advanced driver should your start practising all of the Close Protection modules such as evasive manoeuvres, ramming and high speed driving.

Where should the Principal sit in the car?

Some might say that he is at liberty to sit anywhere he likes, and some Principals do, ignoring all sensible advice. Some Principals may insist on driving themselves, and this is more common than you might imagine. While this is not the best situation you may well have to run with it and compromise. Ideally, when being driven, the Principal should sit in the rear seat behind the front passenger seat which will ideally be occupied by the Bodyguard. Though sometimes the Bodyguard is forced to travel in a backup car, all he can do then is to stay as close as is safe to be in a following vehicle. All doors should be locked immediately after the Principal is in the vehicle and strict observance of the '230' rule should be observed with regard to windows. The '2/30' rule states:

> **'No windows will be open more than two inches
> when the vehicle is travelling under 30mph.'**

If you are working with a threat level that demands an armoured car then open windows. Even if your AC isn't working your windows should remain closed at all times. If you were stopped suddenly in an ambush, even a window open one inch would render all that armour useless when the muzzle of a weapon is pushed through it!

Seat Belts.

There have always been two camps with regard to the wearing of seat belts. Both camps have always agreed that the Principal should always wear a seat belt; and this practise should be positively encouraged. Drivers are often briefed not to release the handbrake until the Principal has belted up.

Always wear your seat belt. The half second that it takes to undo it is worth the risk.

It has been the wearing of a belt by the Bodyguard that has always been a contentious issue, with one camp saying that the BG should always wear the belt, often quoting the first Principal of personal security, "Everyone is responsible for there own security" The other camp insists that because the Bodyguard may have to react very quickly and dive into the rear to give bodycover to the Principal, then the belt may well slow him down.

I must admit that over the years I have spent time in both camps and sometimes had a foot in each. However the death of the Princess of Wales who was not wearing a seat belt and the survival of her Bodyguard who was, should leave no-one in doubt that the Bodyguard should be belted in, as well as urging that the Principal is too. It is the law in many countries and states that belts must be worn, and this can help us when we have to gently insist that our Principal wears the belt.

One car drills

The Close Protection Officer will frequently find that he is on his own, sometimes even driving the vehicle. Having no backup to rely on means that your route planning, navigation, and timings must be meticulous. It is extremely important that the driver is extra vigilant at all times, as he can expect no assistance should he have a puncture, traffic accident or drive into an ambush. He should always observe the speed limit and never violate the local traffic laws. He should position himself at all times so that he is afforded the best view ahead and should use the rear view mirror extensively.

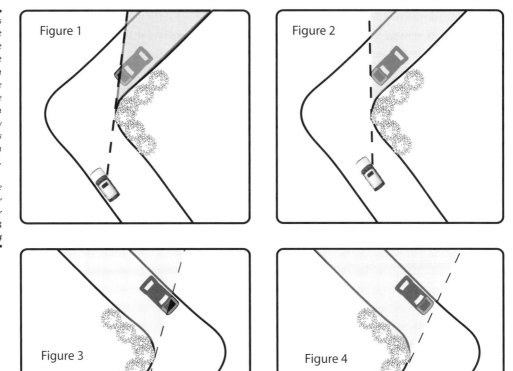

Figure 1 shows the correct road placement for a right hand bend in the UK. If the car stays on the centre line then the visibility suffers . This can be seen in figure 2.

This procedure is reversed for the left hander in figures 3 and 4

Convoy driving

Some convoys are seemingly ridiculous! A recent trip to the UK by President G. W. Bush resulted in a twenty-five vehicle convoy and this was not counting outriders! I doubt that many civilian protection officers get to ride in protective convoys that big. The convoy, even if it only consists of the Principal's vehicle and one escort vehicle, is the preferred way to travel. Not only are we safer when we are attacked, but things that might occur on our journey, such as engine failure, puncture or an accident are all better dealt with if we have an extra vehicle.

Where should the Principal be in the convoy?

If the Principal is employing a PES and they have a backup car they should always travel behind the Principal's car, as this is the best position to take defensive measures should the convoy come under attack. If attacked from the rear they are already there. If attacked from the flanks they can quickly overtake or undertake to place themselves between the threat and the Principal's car. If the attack comes from the front then they can overtake and take the threat on from the front. So, in a two vehicle convoy the Principal will always be in the front vehicle. Some might argue that he should travel in the rear every now and again to keep the bad guys guessing, but this is wrong. The escort vehicle is severely hampered in its responses to attacks should they come from anywhere other than the front. In a three-car convoy, the Principal can be in car 1 with the escort in 2 and 3, or position 2 with the escort in 1 and 3. In a four-car convoy, the Principal could be in any of the first three cars.

Two car drills

The most common protection convoy consists of just two vehicles. For the reasons stated earlier, the Principal will be in the lead vehicle with the escort section behind. The lead vehicle driver always has to be aware of the following escort vehicle. He will never pull into a line of traffic if there is not room for both him and his escort. Likewise, he will only cross lights when he is sure that there is enough time before the lights change for the escort to pass them.

When an escort vehicle driver trusts the lead vehicle driver, he will always follow. If the Principal's vehicle is turning right then the escort will always go with him, often only looking at the offside traffic, knowing that the other driver wouldn't have gone without it being clear on the nearside.

In this example the Principal's vehicle drives close to the nearside to give the escort a good view of the road ahead. If the escort can see an ambush just 3 seconds sooner then this could make all the difference

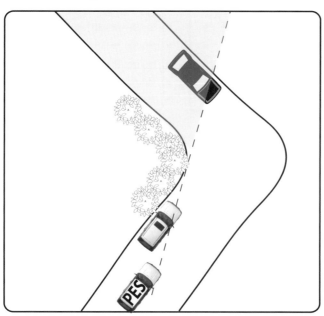

The lead vehicle must ensure that he positions himself with regard to giving the escort section good visibility of the road ahead. This means that he will be at a different position on bends and junctions to if he were a single vehicle with no escort. At junctions he will position himself so as to make it easier for the escort section to provide cover for them. This cover is both from live traffic or an attack of some kind.

Junction Drills

At junctions the Personal Escort Section provide bodycover. Whilst the escort will be constantly alert for surveillance and ambushes, their primary concern will be to protect the Principal from other road users. The risk of being hurt by Joe Public in a car is probably greater than any other threat. The risk of collision is greatest at junctions and it is here that the escort team will work hard to protect their charge. The diagrams that follow assume you are in the UK. If you are in a location where you drive on the 'wrong side' of the road then just reverse the instruction directions.

When turning left or right these are the positions you should adopt. You should be aware of vehicles coming up behind the Principal

Position prior to turning Left in UK

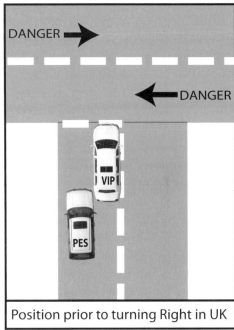

Position prior to turning Right in UK

Left Turns

The Principal's vehicle will pull over to the nearside as much as possible. The Escort vehicle will come up on the off-side, even if this does mean crossing the centre line.

The Principal's driver must drive for both vehicles, only pulling out into traffic when he is sure that there is enough room for both vehicles to effect their drills

Right Turns

To carry out the right turn effectively the Principal's vehicle will move to the centre line or may even straddle it if it is safe to do so. This will hopefully leave enough room for the escort vehicle to come through on the nearside to protect from the joining traffic which is now on the left. It is imperative that the Principal's driver anticipates how much space and time is needed for both vehicles to complete the turn.

When turning left the danger is from the right. The Escort vehicle will protect the Principal's vehicle throughout the manoeuvre. When turning right the opposite occurs

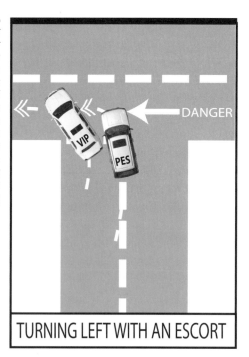

TURNING LEFT WITH AN ESCORT

TURNING RIGHT WITH AN ESCORT

Roundabout Drills

On large roundabouts these drills can be a little like ballroom dancing with all the lane changing. The aim is to keep the escorts bonnet/hood almost level with the Principals door, and then stay between him and the danger. This will mean changing lanes as the diagrams below show. On really busy roads these drills are all but impossible and the best thing to do is just stay as close to the Principal as possible

A left turn at a roundabout can be treated just like any other left turn

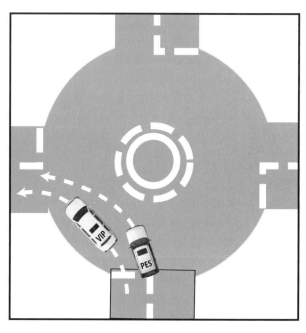

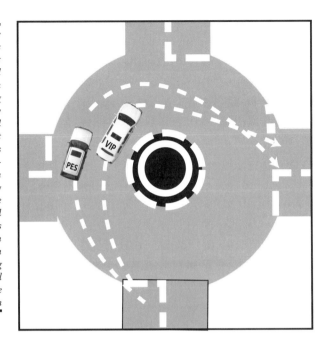

On large roundabouts the Escort vehicle will have to work hard providing cover. Firstly he will defend from the right as he enters the roundabout then immediately changing side to defend against others entering from the left then finally taking up the original position as the exit is taken

Motorway Driving

Motorways are relatively safe roads to travel on. The speeds can make it difficult to mount a rolling ambush and because all the vehicles are travelling in the same direction then the chances of collision are vastly reduced.

The main danger comes from erratic changes of lanes, and vehicles being too close. Because of the high speeds it is conceivable that if you were run off the road then the result could be catastrophic.

The 'On-Guard' position for motorways and dual carriageways. If the motorway is very busy or you want to maintain a low profile then sit back in behind the Principal

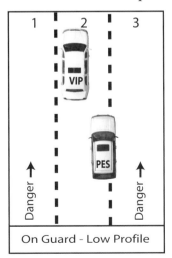

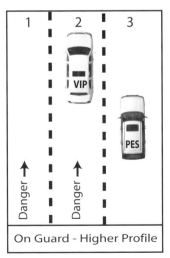

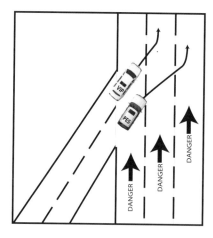

Entering the Motorway the Escort ensures that the traffic is kept away from the Principal

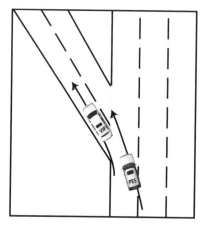

Leaving the motorway the Escort should stay behind the Principal until he is sure that there is no risk of anyone crashing into the rear. Once he is sure then he should assume his normal position

Depending on how busy the motorway is, the best way to travel is on or a fraction above the speed limit (road conditions permitting) with the Principal occupying the centre lane with the escort just behind in the fast lane. The escort vehicle will be stopping people overtaking long enough to check them out and satisfy themselves that the over taker is not about to commence a rolling ambush.

You need to be thick-skinned, slowing people up on the road will get a few fingers raised in your direction, and some people will undertake and come up on the inside of the Principal. If you want to keep the profile lower then you can just travel directly behind the Principal but still keep an eye on every over-taker.

Great care need to be taken when you enter the motorway, the escort section should provide cover to the Principal as he enters the first lane and then accelerates quickly into the centre lane..

Ambushes and attacks

If the solo vehicle or a convoy comes under attack then the priorities are the same as any other time we need to ACE it out of the danger area. There are a number of drills that we can practise for different situations. Practising for when you come under an attack is important, but it is paramount that the training is kept realistic. It is amazing how many people driver train by throwing a car around an old airfield or racetrack. The cars that the training is carried out in are usually old wrecks, normally with manual gearboxes, and almost always much smaller and lighter than the vehicle in which you would be driving with your Principal, which may come under attack. The tyres on the training vehicle may have no tread; the vehicle will probably not have ABS braking. The training areas will often be much, wider than the road that you will be ambushed.

ALWAYS EXPECT A SECONDARY ATTACK. WHATEVER EVASIVE ACTION YOU TAKE IN AN AMBUSH MAY HAVE BEEN SECOND-GUESSED BY YOUR ATTACKERS. YOU SHOULD ALWAYS EXPECT ANOTHER ATTACK IS IMMINENT.

All training must be realistic, so even though learning the basics in the old banger is sensible, as much as possible your training and all of your continuation training should be done in the vehicles that you will be using everyday on the job. I appreciate that you will not use your Principal's Bentley for ramming practice! But you should whenever possible practise things like emergency braking, high speed steering, and high speed reversing in the car your going to be in when you need the skills.

Different types of Ambush.

Of course not all ambushes are the same. There are different types of ambush for different targets, and the area will be a big factor when someone chooses to ambush you. But essentially the ambush will either be static or rolling.

Static ambush

This type of ambush relies on your stopping or moving very slowly through the killing zone, or the use of overwhelming fire power explosives from stationary positions as you pass through the killing zone. The attackers might create their own roadblock by placing a truck or cars across your path, or they might create other hazards such as attacking you where you naturally slow down or stop, such as level crossings, traffic lights and roundabouts. They could also use deception to halt or slow down your vehicle. Posing as police officers or feigning a road accident are both popular methods.

Rolling ambush

This is an ambush that happens on the move. It can be as simple as being overtaken by a motorcycle with a pillion passenger emptying a machine gun in your direction. You are unlikely to be attacked in this way if you are in an armoured car, as the small calibre machine gun fire will bounce off. However, the rocket-propelled grenades will have been fired from motorcycles and these may well defeat your armour. These drive-by shootings are fast and give you no time to react, but if you do get time then often the best weapon against a motorcycle is your car. Use it aggressively.

You could be hemmed in by ambusher's vehicles while they shoot at you. This could happen on any type of road from a country lane to a speeding autobahn. At high speed they will try to run you off the road as well as shoot at you. This rolling ambush will probably not cease if you stop the vehicle so you must stay mobile at all costs.

Surviving attacks

If the persons ambushing you are professionals with all the resources and time that they need, then surviving in the killing zone of this well-planned and executed ambush is going to be extremely difficult and highly unlikely. However, your attackers may have to compromise in many ways.

They may not have the required amount of men or weapons to make the ambush completely effective. They need committed men that are dedicated and disciplined to carry out the attack and they need overwhelming fire-power to ensure the success of the attack.

They may not have the time on the street that they would ideally need to set up the attack. This is especially true of back-stops that might stop you reversing out of the killing zone and cover all avenues of escape.

They might not be able to choose the ideal ambush site with care because it is difficult to pre-empt your movements as well as avoiding the attention of the police or other members of the public. The attackers will want to have an escape route for themselves; the route that they keep open for themselves might make an escape option for you.

Ambush basics

If you ever find yourself in an ambush situation then you need to exploit any weaknesses in the ambush and of course you need to do this very quickly. The protection of the Principal is of course your primary concern. At the first sign of anything hostile the Principal must be put into the footwell of the vehicle. You can put him there physically or just with your voice. If he has spotted the hostiles he might be there

AT THE FIRST SIGN OF SOMETHING BEING WRONG THEN THE BODYGUARD SHOULD IMMEDIATELY LEAVE HIS SEAT, DIVE INTO THE BACK AND COVER THE PRINCIPAL

already! The Bodyguard must get in the back of the vehicle. Some Close Protection training schools teach that if the vehicle is armoured then the Bodyguard does not have to get in the back with the Principal – this is wrong. The Bodyguard's job is to be in the back with the Principal. If you have to debus under fire, to escape on foot or

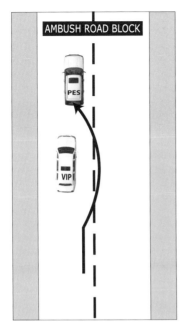

At the first sign of an ambush to the front the escort vehicle will provide bodycover by overtaking the Principals vehicle placing themselves between the ambush and the Principal. From this posi-tion they can reverse out of the ambush.

to change vehicles, you need to be as close to the Principal as possible. So at the first sign of anything happening get in the back with the Principal and get his head down.

There are three things that will assist you in surviving a roadside ambush.

    1. Spotting the Ambush Early

    2. Not Stopping in the Killing zone

    3. Using armoured vehicles

Spotting the ambush early

The earlier that we can spot an ambush, the more chance we have of carrying out any evasive action. Drivers and all team members must remain vigilant at all times, notic-ing the ambush just a few seconds earlier than the ambushers anticipate you might can make all of the difference.

Not stopping in the killing zone.

Standing and fighting is to be avoided at all costs. The attackers, even the most poorly trained ones, will ensure that they have better cover than you! You should always try to stay moving, that is, moving through or away from the killing zone.

Using Armoured Cars

Even in the most poorly planned and implemented ambush the odds are well stacked in the attackers' favour. The use of an armoured vehicle can most definitely be a life-saver.

This series of photographs shows how armoured cars save lives. It looks like the armour only just coped with the trauma, and you can see that the windscreen was almost blown out. All occupants survived the attack. Without the armour the occupants of this car would have died instantly

Counter ambush techniques

The only way to survive an attack is to get out of the killing zone. There is no right or wrong way; you have to base your decision on how you see the situation. Essentially, you will have just three options:

1. Continue moving forward to and through the ambush; you may have seen a way through or consider that ramming is an option (more on ramming later). You need to get the car moving and keep it going as long as you can. Your vehicle is the best weapon that you have. Many people when faced with a traumatic situation such as an ambush hit the brakes instinctively; even if this is the wrong thing to do.

2. Move left or right to avoid the ambush. Is there a way out by doing the unexpected, such as crossing a carriageway or driving off the road?

3. Reverse out of the killing zone or rapidly turn around and travel out the same way you came. This requires some skill and will depend upon how much room you have to manoeuvre. Even if there is no room to turn the vehicle, those that have practised their reversing skills will know that even going backwards cars can accelerate away at great speed. Some cars can go as fast in reverse as they can in second, but only if you have practised in them.

Principal's car out of action

If the ambush puts the Principal's car out of action, then a decision must be made quickly about evacuating him. Even if the Principal's car is armoured, the killing zone is no place to be unless you know that help is imminent. Moving the Principal is a difficult enough drill without being shot at. You will have to rely on the cover that your escort vehicle can provide; speed as well as returning as much fire as possible. All of the occupants of the Principal's car will get into the escort vehicle. If there is more than one escort vehicle then that is one more engine block between your Principal and his attackers.

Fighting your way out

As a last resort you may well have to abandon the vehicles and make a run for it. If the ambushers have done their job well you will probably not escape, but for the reasons mentioned earlier this may well be a way out. The team should use the vehicles to provide as much cover as possible. The car occupants should debus under this cover, provide bodycover for the Principal and get out of the killing zone as fast as possible, returning fire if possible. The conventional response to an ambush that you cannot get away from is to counter attack. The PES cannot effectively attack an ambush unless they have sufficient numbers and weapons. If they are forced to attack then it is at a time when the need for bodycover is paramount. For this reason if you are in a situation where an ambush is likely to occur then you should have extra personnel with you specifically tasked for counter ambush. These men will have their own vehicle and have suitable weapons. They will remain close behind the convoy but far enough away to not get caught in the ambush. This will allow the PES to do there job and provide bodycover and evacuate.

Ramming

The truth about ramming that no Close Protection school or book tells you is that you cannot ram effectively with today's modern cars fitted with airbags. If you ram the vehicle with sufficient force to move it then you run the risk of the airbags deploying which will immediately immobilise the vehicle. In the case of custom armoured vehicles you should consider disarming the airbags if you feel that you are more likely to ram your way out of a situation than need the bags for the protection they were designed for.

Ramming really is a life or death option. What you choose to ram must be movable. A large truck or a tree felled across a road cannot be rammed. You will just damage your vehicle and be a sitting duck right there in the killing zone. However, very often a roadblock is hastily put into place with perhaps one or two cars blocking the carriageway. A last resort action would be to ram your way through the makeshift barricade.

Slow down as if to stop, get in to first gear and then accelerate hard. Hold the vehicle in gear as when you make contact it may pop out of gear, which could be disastrous. Where you ram the other vehicle/s and with what part of your vehicle are critical. You need to ram the attackers' front or rear wheel. This is a solid area, which will give you the shove you need. If you are moving too slowly you risk not moving the vehicle, but if you are moving too quickly you risk damaging your vehicle. Do not forget that the car is an excellent weapon and if you can run down anyone on the way through an ambush then you should not waste this opportunity.

Ramming is something that you must practise; you must get a feel for it, learning the power and speed needed. You will probably find it easier than you imagine as well as being a lot of fun. During practice you will also notice how easy it is to get hooked up and trapped with the vehicle you are ramming, especially if you hit them broadside. Ramming will seem easy without all the adrenalin you will have in a real ambush situation. Modern cars with polystyrene and collapsible plastic bumpers make entanglement less likely, especially if you hit the target's wheel arches.

Dukes of Hazzard style driving away from an ambush

No Close Protection course would be complete without a day on the skidpan learning how to throw a vehicle around. The value of this training is suspect but can be great fun. To be of any real use the training should be carried out in the actual vehicles that you use on a daily basis. It really is no use practising your drills with slick tyres on a skid pan only to find out at the worst possible time that you or your car doesn't cope with the manoeuvre. But that said when 'learning' the skills you do not want to be using expensive vehicles unless you have hired them.

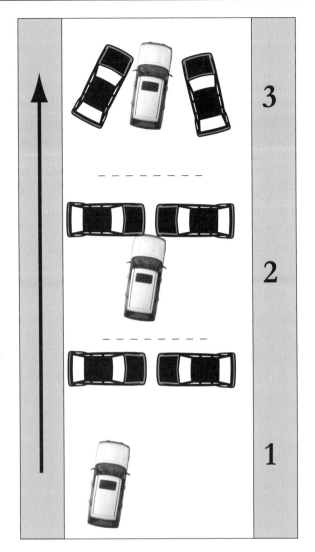

At Position 1. The vehicle slows as if to stop, engages first gear and then accelerates hard. At Position2. The vehicle makes impact on a solid part of the car, whilst being held in gear. At poistion 3. the car continues through and away as fast as possible. Ramming is a last resort. There are many things that can go wrong. The vehicles can lock up. If the vehicle is immobilised then you are trapped in the killing zone, so you must be ready to evacuate.

You can buy some scrap cars or better still hire some cars from the large car hire firms. You can easily trash tyres on these cars so if you are going to be doing a lot of learning then it is best to buy a cheap set of wheels and tyres and swap these as soon as you get to your training area. Learn the handbrake/bootleggers turn first this is the easiest to master and will give you the confidence to progress.

The Handbrake (Bootlegger's) Turn

If you are fortunate enough notice the ambush a few hundred yards ahead then a handbrake turn can quickly reverse your direction of travel away from the ambush. The turn is a controlled skid and the possibility of the turn going high is high. Lots of practice will enable you to recover quickly from the problems of poorly executed manoeuvres.

This can be done in both auto and manual vehicles, manual is easiest and your Principals car is very likely to be automatic rather than manual!

The vehicle needs to be travelling at around 25 to 30 mph

Come of the accelerator and positively turn the steering wheel to the right about half a full turn, at the same time as you turn the wheel apply the handbrake hard. If you are driving a manual you must depress the clutch now or you will stall, you need to also select 1st or 2nd (after a practice you will know what works best) gear but keep the clutch engaged.

When you are about 90 degrees into your turn release the handbrake and hit the accelerator and straighten out facing the way you came. If in a manual you will let out the clutch as soon as you hit the accelerator. If you get everything right you should enter a controlled skid and end up in the opposite lane. Steer away as fast as you can.

With some cars It is easier to initiate the turn by initially applying a flick of the steering wheel in the opposite direction, before violently turning it back into the required direction,

The 'J' (Moonshiner's)Turn

This looks like a handbrake turn in reverse, it allows you to quickly turn 180 degrees within the confines of a two lane road. If you find the road is blocked and you come to a stop, this reverse out when quickly engaged, can get you to safety fast.

Engage reverse and accelerate hard in a straight line, this is harder than it looks and must be practised. You will be surprised at how fast most cars can travel in reverse, but after around 4 seconds you will be flat out and to go faster you need to change direction so you can use the faster forward gears, so as the engine screams that it cant go faster prepare to do several things all at once.

While the car is still moving in reverse, turn the steering wheel hard to the right (or left if you drive on the right) while simultaneously engaging the handbrake. Do not touch the accelerator. The car should spin at least 90 to 180°.

You will find yourself facing either 90 or 180 degrees from the ambush. Release the handbrake and get in second gear (first is best for some cars) or get it into low drive if you are in an automatic. Then accelerate away.

Car-jacking

You might think that the last person a robber would steal a car from is a Bodyguard, but it happens, especially in one-on-one situations when the Bodyguard has no backup. The Bodyguard may well find himself driving a very desirable car and some people will go to great lengths to steal it. Carjacking is normally done at gunpoint or knife-point. It is a violent crime, very much on the increase in the USA and Europe.

The Hand-brake or Boot-leggers turn

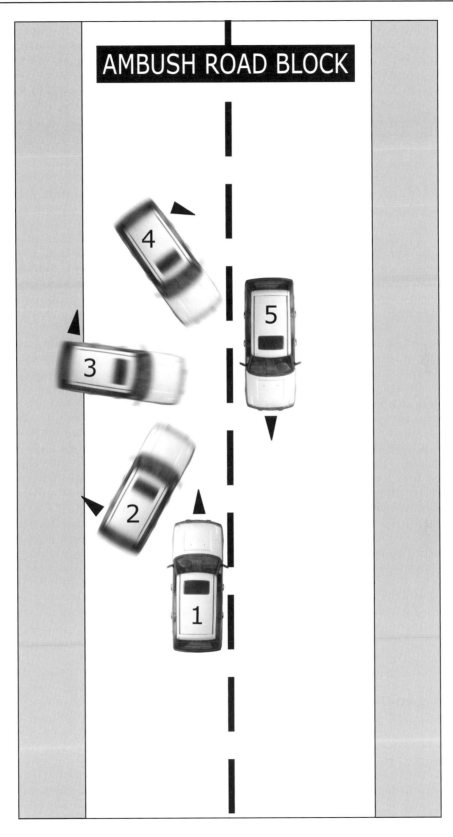

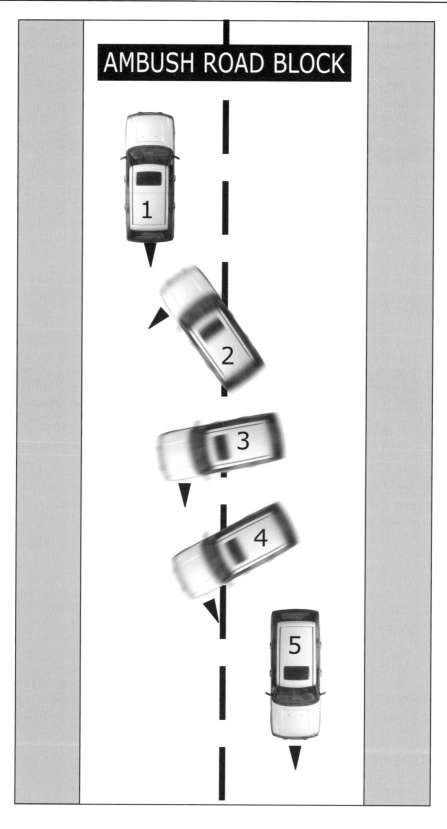

The reasons for the popularity of carjacking may well have something to do with the ever more sophisticated alarms and immobilisers that manufacturers install in their new luxury vehicles. This makes it harder for the crook to steal so when he does want to steal the car it is much better for him if he can steal the keys as well and carjacking achieves this aim.

While many luxury cars are stolen to order, some carjackers may well just do it for kicks: the nicer the car the more kudos the thief achieves. There is no set pattern to carjacks and while most will happen at night, they can occur at any time of day. Carjacked on the way to work is a common occurrence in some cities.

If drugs and weapons are involved in the carjack then there is a high chance of violence being used at the first sign of any resistance. Unless the attacker is heavily under the influence of drugs, then he will probably have as must adrenaline as the victim. However you feel, it is just not worth risking you or your Principal's life for a car that will be replaced by the insurance company anyway. As soon as you have given up the car get yourself and the Principal, if he is with you, away from the area as quickly as possible. You will feel bad about it and you might beat yourself up about it for a long time after but you must remind yourself that by not offering any resistance you were doing the right thing.

Mostly carjackers are opportunists; you just do not give them the opportunity to rob you of your vehicle. You are most vulnerable at traffic lights and stop signs as well as car parks and your own driveway.

The 'bump and rob'

A common carjack scenario starts with you being gently rear ended. If you are suckered into getting out of the vehicle, then you could be robbed at gunpoint or someone may just jump in the car and steal it. This would be a disaster if the Principal was still in it! If someone gives you a little shunt and you are going to get out make sure you know what you are getting out into. The best policy is to ignore small rear ends. Just try to get a note of the vehicle index. If they follow you then lead them straight into a populated area or better still a police station or military barracks.

Getting in the car

If the vehicle has been parked where the public can see it then it may well have been targeted by carjackers. As you approach the vehicle make sure you pay particular notice to anyone who may be lurking. Have your keys ready, walk purposely to the vehicle, get in and immediately lock the doors, pull away as quickly as you can, and look for a tail.

When travelling

Make sure that you observe the 230 rule and always lock your doors. Whenever you're coming to a stop, whether that be a traffic light or a body in the road, always leave yourself enough room to manoeuvre past the obstacle. Never, ever, let yourself be hemmed in. In cities, try to drive in the centre lane away from the pavements. If approached by anyone tapping on a side window when you are stopped or slow moving, ignore it, act as if you can't hear it and move.

Getting out of the car

Always have a good look around you as you approach the place you are about to park. Well-lit areas where there are other people are much better places than side streets. If you use car parks, try to use ones where there are security officers. No matter where you park always have a good look around before you unlock the door to get out.

Advice for you and your Principal

If your Principal is one of the many that like to get out on their own and drive themselves, you must make sure that they are aware of carjacking and how it occurs and what they can do to prevent it.

Summary

The specialist driver will be an expert at defensive and evasive driving. He will always conduct continuation training in his work day vehicles or as similar vehicle as possible. To attempt the evasive turns requires considerable skill and their success depends on many things such as the width of the roads that the ambush is mounted, the road surface, the type of vehicle, whether it is front or rear wheel drive, auto or manual, and of course the skill of the driver. Unless you are looking after someone with considerable threats against their life then the biggest danger on the road will come from other road users. Patient defensive driving is the only weapon that you can use to protect your self. Finally do not forget that the vehicle is probably the deadliest weapon that you have on the team, just like any other weapon if it is handled incorrectly you can kill your colleagues with it but handled correctly and used as a weapon you can save lives with it.

Route Reconnaissance

The reasons for taking time to carry out route reconnaissance are many. Obviously, we want to know the way to go. We might want to know how long a move is going to take. We want to know how vulnerable we are to particular types of attack on particular routes.

Route recces are always carried out with a very low profile and as covertly as possible. Anti-surveillance drills should always be exercised to ensure that you are not being followed. Any terrorist or criminal that realises you are carrying out a recce will know the route that your principal will be taking and will have an opportunity to surprise you on it. If the move is important and considered high risk, then several different routes may be looked at.

Route Recce Cards

A route recce card of a planned route can prove invaluable. For short distances and especially in cities the linear route recce card is probably the best choice. Linear cards are very simple to produce and copies can be kept in the cars and the operations room. They are written in such a way that anyone can grab a card and follow the route. They always read from bottom to top, and even when you turn, clarity is achieved by the road always remaining straight, even if in reality you are turning left, right and about. Further clarity is achieved by placing all the driving directions on the right and all the other information on the left.

Computer Programs

The details of a computer navigation programme are very simple and each line is a single instruction. These instructions can also be printed along with the corresponding maps. Linear route recce cards and computer programmes, such as AutoRoute Express, are excellent aids to help you get to your destination, but neither should replace maps, which should also be carried. Once you have produced the recce cards then use a photocopier (colour is best) to reproduce the recces. Large prints of the recce can be placed in the ops room and A4 or A5 paper sizes can be kept in the vehicle.

In This Chapter

Understand how to carry out Route Recce's.

Know the different types

What to look for and how

The Classic Route Recce card read from bottom to top, all directions on one side with information on the other. This card is great for short runs in the city

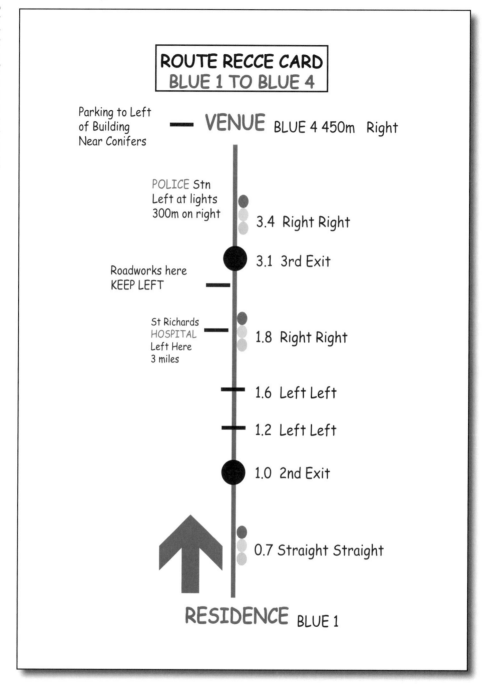

ROUTE RECCE CARD
BLUE 1 TO BLUE 4

Parking to Left
of Building
Near Conifers

— VENUE BLUE 4 450m Right

POLICE Stn
Left at lights
300m on right

3.4 Right Right

3.1 3rd Exit

Roadworks here
KEEP LEFT

St Richards
HOSPITAL
Left Here
3 miles

1.8 Right Right

1.6 Left Left

1.2 Left Left

1.0 2nd Exit

0.7 Straight Straight

RESIDENCE BLUE 1

Satellite Navigation

Before you venture out on a recce, look at a map. Get a 'feel' for the route, the general direction and the terrain. Never ever, rely on Satellite Navigation (Sat-Nav) alone. No matter how good your system is, it will let you down. You will lose a signal or the machine will freeze and need a re-boot, just when you really need it. Sat-Nav is a fantastic aid to navigation; it is great for working out alternative routes in the event of road blocks and accidents. But it should never be used on its own; always have maps of the area that you are operating in.

Choosing the right route

Whenever a road move is necessary we will take as much care as possible, not only to choose the safest route but travel on it at the right time. We need to plan for when things go wrong, and things will go wrong! Ambushes and attacks might well happen and these need to be anticipated. You also need to plan alternative routes in case of accidents or other road blocks, as well as a plan for mechanical failure.

The faster we are travelling, the more difficult it is for someone to attack us. However when we are driving on the roads we are, of course, governed by the law, the traffic flow, speed restrictions, roadworks, and many other natural hazards that will slow us down. We are far more susceptible to attack when we are slowed down or are stationary. We can be stopped by a roadblock; we can be slowed by corners and bends; and we can be stopped at junctions and lights.

Detailed route checking

Whenever possible we should carry out a detailed check of the route on which we are going to travel on. By doing so, we are aware of any hazards on the route and how long the journey will take. Just as importantly, we reduce our chances of getting lost enroute. Doing a U-turn, and having the Principal ask, "Are we lost?" Is crushingly embarrassing.

The things that we note on the recce are numerous and are mostly common sense. The use of a dictaphone can help if you are on your own. Otherwise, a second person in your vehicle taking notes is ideal. Remember to keep a low profile. Look at any feature that might slow you down or stop you, e.g. traffic lights or junctions.

High risk targets

If you are in a high risk area with a risk of being ambushed then you should take particular care to note all of the likely places that might have roadside or culvert bombs. Examples include tunnels and bridges, culverts and steep banks, etc. Snipers can hide in thick scrub and trees or any overlooking features such as hills, cliffs, or tall buildings.

Note the time

When making the actual trip with the Principal you should have a very accurate idea of how long it will take. If you are taking the Principal to an airport you must get him there not too early so he has to click his heels in the airport for hours, but not so late that check-in is just closing! By completing the recce, keeping to the speed limits and travelling at a time that enjoys similar traffic conditions, you will know when to leave the residence to arrive on time. It is best if the recces are carried out in similar traffic conditions to the actual trip. Checking a route from your hotel to the airport late on a Sunday evening is not going to give you an accurate estimate of how long the journey will take in Monday morning traffic!

An example of the information computer mapping and route finding software. These programs can save us a lot of legwork, and whilst they have their limitations they do make a good starting point to produce your own route recce card

The Boltons to London Heathrow Airport

0900	0.0	mi	Depart the Boltons on Boltons Place (North West) for 109 yds
0900	0.1	mi	Road name changes to Boltons Gardens for 98 yds
0900	0.1	mi	Keep STRAIGHT onto COLLINGHAM GARDENS for 120 yds
0901	0.2	mi	Keep STRAIGHT onto COLLINGHAM ROAD for 0.2mi
0902	0.4	mi	Turn LEFT (West) onto A4 (Cromwell Road) for 2.9mi
0907	3.3	mi	At Roundabout take the THIRD EXIT onto A4 (Great West Road) for 1.1mi
0909	4.4	mi	At EXIT 1, road name changes to M4 for 7.6mi to WEST
0915	12.0 mi		Keep LEFT onto ramp 0.3mi towards A408 Sign Heathrow Airport
0916	12.3 mi		Keep LEFT onto ramp for 174 yds towards Heathrow Airport
0916	12.4 mi		Take M4 (Left) onto local roads for 0.9mi
0917	13.3 mi		Keep STRAIGHT onto TUNNEL ROAD for 0.5mi
0918	13.8 mi		Road name changes to INNER RING EAST for 0.1mi
0918	14.0 mi		Arrive Heathrow Airport

Summary
Driving Distance: 14 miles
Trip Duration: 18 minutes

Calculate the correct distance

Set the trip meter at the start of the recce, so at any point along the route you know the distances involved. When the Principal asks you, "How much further?", A reply such as "Seven miles, and we will be there in ten minutes, Sir" is infinitely better than "Not sure, Sir, but it shouldn't be much further." By being aware of exactly how long a trip should take and the distances involved, you are in a much better position to take the correct action if something goes wrong or more simply to answer your Principal when he asks, "Have we got time to get a coffee?"

Check for communication black spots

By making regular radio checks enroute and monitoring your mobile signal strength, you will discover any black spots and poor mobile phone coverage. Communication black spots might be a favourite ambush location! You should never plan any stops for fuel or refreshments in a black spot. These areas should be marked on all maps and recce cards so that everyone knows about them.

Emergency care

Should you have an incident or accident enroute, where is the nearest hospital that takes casualties? At all times on your route know where this is. Remember that not all hospitals take casualties (although the doctors at a maternity hospital might be able to offer first aid, which is better than nothing). If your Principal or any of your team need a doctor then you will receive much better care at a hospital with an Accident and Emergency department. Accident and Emergency hospitals are normally open every day of the year.

Nearest safe havens

Police stations and military barracks make good 'safe houses' to rush the Principal should you be being chased or attacked. You should note the whereabouts of any safe refuges, on or near your route. Remember that police stations are not always open for business. Racing towards a police station that is closed is not going to make it a safe haven!

Roadworks

Anywhere that you are forced to stop could be turned into an ambush point for the terrorist or common thief. Road works, sharp bends, and temporary traffic lights are all potentially dangerous. Roadworks and cones are generally installed at night, especially on motorways. Your recce might be great today only to find ten miles of cones and a single lane motorway tomorrow morning. Do your homework and check with the highways department and motoring organisations. They will tell you if roadworks or slow moving large loads might mess up your road move.

Your destination or venue

If your destination is unknown then your recce card should note useful information about the destination or venue. For example, are the entrances gated and open? Where is the safest and or most convenient place to debus? Can the cars wait at the location?

Secondary Routes

What if your route to a venue is compromised or is just blocked by an accident. How will you get the Principal to the venue? You must have a plan and be aware of any alternative routes, how to get on them and how long this other route will take. On a detour, the first thing that your Principal will ask is, "How long with this route take?" Be professional and know the answer. Sat-Nav is great in this regard. It can re-route you and give you a new arrival time in a just a few seconds.

Refreshments on Route

A recce should give you an idea of suitable refreshment stops enroute, especially on long road moves. If you find a place that is suitable, then make a note on the recce card. Tell the Principal that the place coming up is the last place to get a good coffee for the next fifty miles. It shows the Principal that you have done your homework, and that you are professional. Never miss an opportunity to empty your bladder. You cannot concentrate on your job if you are sitting in a car with the principal and you are cross legged and cross eyed.

Places of Interest

Should the Principal have some time to kill, he may ask you to take him somewhere interesting for an hour. Where will you take him? If your route takes you past a large medieval castle on a hill, the chances are you are going to be asked, "What castle is that?" Knowing this information is much better than not knowing. If you have the time, then find out this type of information. Your Principal will thank you for it.

Summary

All advance work must be done covertly and with a very low profile. You should ensure that you are not being followed. Gather as much information as you can and use it intelligently. Computer programs and Sat-Nav are great aids but they should not replace maps entirely.

Embus and Debus Procedures

Embus and Embussing are military slang words adopted by Close Protection Officers. Essentially, the words refer to board or boarding a bus or vehicle. Similar words, debus or debussing mean alighting from (getting out of) a vehicle.

The permutations for getting a VIP from a vehicle into a venue and then back into the vehicle are enormous. These notes discuss the basics and cannot take in all the variables that may prevail such as the actual location, how close you can get to it, the presence of fans, press, public, etc. Is the VIP expected or not? Is he or she high or low profile? What is the threat level? All of these factors will affect your embus and debus drills.

Because of all the variables and more importantly, our vulnerability when we are out of the vehicles and on the pavement, we must practise our embus and debus drills so that nothing is left to chance. Looking slick and professional can actually deter an attack.

Remember that any pre-planned attack on us will involve some surveillance. If someone is watching you, then give them a show. Let them see that attacking you might end in tears for them! Even if your aim is to maintain a low profile, you should raise it a little at times of embus. You will not damage your low profile too much, because even if your profile is much higher than normal you will only ever be on the pavement for a very short time. Traditionally, there are two types of debus, called orthodox and, you've guessed it, unorthodox, so you might hear about orthodox drops or unorthodox pick-ups.

In This Chapter

How to get your Principal safely in and out of venues.

Orthodox and un-orthodox drills

Dealing with crowds

Orthodox embus and debus

Orthodox is when the Principal can embus or debus from the same side of the vehicle as the venue. In other words, he doesn't have to cross live traffic to get to the venue.

Unorthodox embus and debus

Unorthodox is when the Principal has to embus/debus on the opposite side of the vehicle to the venue and we have to cross the road to get to the venue.

Embus Basics

The vehicle should be in position before the Principal departs from the venue, but if this is a public venue the vehicles should arrive as late as possible. Especially if the cars attract undue attention by arriving too early and having to wait.

The vehicle should get as close to the exit as possible. If at all possible, embusses should be made away from the public. Back doors and car parks that are not over-looked may well be safer.

Putting the Principal into the car - Embus

The driver will throughout be looking for and mentally rehearsing an escape route should anything occur during the embus.

The driver will be in gear, engine running with the door locked. He will be continually scanning all 360 degrees, ready to unlock the doors at the very last second as the Principal approaches.

When you enter the vehicle, your backside enters the vehicle first. Once that is on the seat you can swing your legs in. If the vehicle has to move before you put your legs in, then just lifting them will ensure that you are in the vehicle and OK. Those that ignore this advice and enter a vehicle by putting one foot inside before they get on the seat will find that it is almost impossible to get in as the car leaves you behind.

Debus Basics

Stop as close as possible to the entrance and the kerb, with good 360 degree observation.

Remain in gear, and cover the brakes.

Throughout the debus, the driver will be looking for and mentally rehearsing an escape route should anything occur during the procedure.

The PES vehicle will position himself as close to the Principal's car as possible but without blocking himself in. A simple method of judging this is to get as close as you

getting the Principal out of the car - Debus

can while still being able to see the tyres of the vehicle in front. The PES wheels will point out in to the road and the car will be slightly offset giving cover to the Principal's vehicle.

The PES driver will be looking for and mentally rehearsing his 'action-on-drills' should anything occur during the procedure. The engine will be running and the vehicle in gear. leave the Principal's door open, so that you can get back in quickly if anything happens. The driver can shut the door when you are in the venue.

Remember how vulnerable you are on the street during the embus and debus. You must really be animated on the street. Do your jobs well and importantly and look as though you are doing it well. Be slick and professional and make any potential attacker who's watching you think twice before taking you on. We will now run through some of the more common scenarios that you will encounter.

One-on-one debus orthodox

You are working one-on-one and you may well be the driver too! Try to get the Principal's door directly in line with the entrance of the venue. This will keep your vulnerable pavement time to a minimum. The Principal should be briefed to remain in the vehicle until you open the door for him, ideally locking the vehicle again as you shut the door and only opening it again when you give him the okay to do so. If the venue or building is considered to be pretty safe then the Principal could enter first with the Bodyguard aware of danger from both flanks and behind. If the building could be hostile, maybe full of press, fans or demonstrators then the Bodyguard should stay very close and enter at the same time as the VIP if possible.

One-on-one embus orthodox

Leaving a secure venue, the danger is from the front so the Bodyguard would leave the building first, closely followed by the Principal. The VIP should get into the vehicle first; the Bodyguard should ensure that the Principal's door is secure. He should then get in and the vehicle should move off immediately. If the Bodyguard is also the driver, he will lock the doors with the remote, even for the short time it will take him to reach the driver's door.

You must learn the basics of the embus and debus before you can cope with crowds.

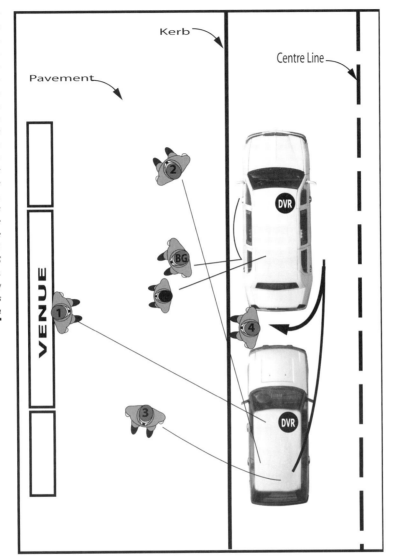

One-on-one embus and debus unorthodox

Whenever you have an unorthodox embus or debus you must consider whether it is safer for the VIP to open the door into traffic or open the door to the pavement side and walk to the rear of the car and cross the road. The actual drills for entering the building are the same for the orthodox. If you are the driver as well as the Bodyguard then ensure that you have parked somewhere safe and that you have locked and alarmed the car.

With the PES backup car; orthodox embus debus

Should the threat level require a PES then normally they will be used to provide additional cover during the debus. The embus is a complete reversal of the debus except that one of the PES (normally the team leader) will open the door just as the VIP approaches. On debus the VIP's door is left open so that should something happen quite near the car, the Bodyguard can quickly return to the car and make an escape. It is the responsibility of the driver to shut the car door when the VIP is in or very near the venue and also to stop any illegal entry into the car while the door is left open.

This UNORTHODOX drop shows the routine. But they're really are no set pieces. Just make sure the cover is on and that the Principal doesn't get run down by a car

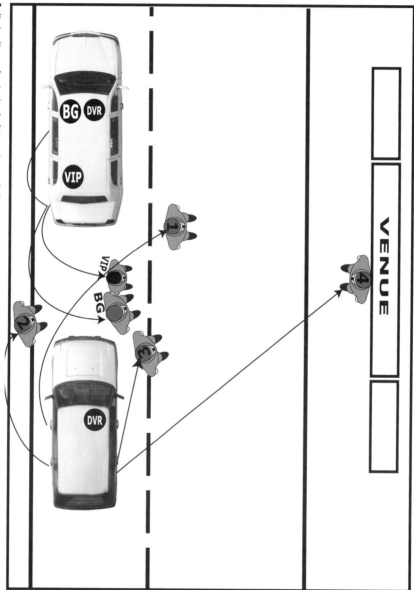

With the PES backup car; unorthodox embus debus

Again, consideration should be given as to the best side for the VIP to get out. Normally, the best option is for him to exit onto the pavement and then cross the road between his and the escort's car.

Dealing with crowds.

You may find yourself in a situation where you have to get a Principal in or out of the vehicle while the vehicle is surrounded by people. These people could be fans of the VIP if he or she is rich and famous. They might be demonstrators or they could be members of the press or paparazzi. If this is the case then you should discuss with the Principal what his priorities are because crowds, no matter who they are, should always best avoided. If you need to face the crowd then in order to move around you need to be very positive. Use your communication skills. You should be very firm, always using your voice to move people, touching them only as a last resort and even then with a positive "excuse me". Never swear or get aggressive when working with the crowds unless absolutely necessary.

Bono's Bodyguards working hard to handle the crowds during an embus

EMPICS

If you are trying to stop photographers getting pictures of your Principal then place your body between the camera and the Principal. Do not place an outstretched hand toward the camera. This can make for a very dramatic but damaging photograph, that may show your Principal in a poor light. If photographs are taken you cannot demand that the film or memory be given to you. If you are in a public place then the law in most of the Western world allows photographers to take pictures of anyone they choose. You will be breaking the law if you take film or camera memory cards from them.

If crowds are surrounding a car that you need to exit from or gain entry to, you must try and control the crowd with your voice. Fans can be told to give you some room, and photographers can be told that they will get their pictures if they move back.

This can be a very difficult position to be in if you're on your own. If you have a PES then they can, of course, clear a channel to the door of the venue or back to the vehicle for you.

With the press, unless your Principal wants to talk to them you should keep moving. If they are in your way just walk right at them. Photographers will try to move out of the way as their best pictures are obtained when they are at least a metre away. They are experts in the art of walking backwards, taking pictures as the do so. Most press photographers these days really do have to work hard to make a living. The 'press pack' seem to be getting scruffier, more aggressive, and much more determined to take risks and liberties to get the picture. You do not want to make enemies of these people and should always treat them with respect, but if you are too nice to these people they will see it as a weakness and exploit it. Always be firm and professional in your dealings with them.

Summary

Learn your drills well but remember that above all you must make the drills flexible. Throughout the embus you will be carrying out a dynamic threat assessment and the positions that you adopt will reflect this assessment. Most of the procedures will be high profile, this is a vulnerable time and you must look professional and capable throughout. If the Principal is going to be in the venue for some time you should consider the best place for the cars to park up, this is especially important if the cars are very flash and are likely to attract attention or there are parking restrictions. The last thing you need is to be explaining to the Principal that you have to wait until you can get a clamp removed or the car back from the pound.

Operations and the Operations Room

It is rare for any full-time assignment to run without an operations room. If the protection assignment is being run by a company that is providing Close Protection Officers on a sub contract basis then the operation may be controlled from the company operations room, which may be located miles from the actual operation. This is especially true when the assignment only uses one or two protection officers at any one time.

When full security teams are used, with large numbers of protection officers, then invariably there will be an operation room on site. Over the years, I have seen operations rooms set up in spare bedrooms, stables, caravans and garden sheds. Anywhere, in fact, can be used as an operations room but obviously some places are much better than others.

Where should the operations room be located?

Closed-circuit television has negated the need for ops rooms to resemble aircraft control towers with 360 degrees visibility. Cameras that can cover the whole of the site, even when it's dark; seismic detectors that let you know about every footfall on the lawn can all now be linked to a discreetly placed operations room.

When you look for somewhere to place the operations room, you should take into consideration its 24-hour function and how this might impact the Principal and his family. Especially if the operations room is situated in or very near the main house.

In This Chapter

Learn the sequence of an Op Order

How to run an operations room

Project management skills

Temporary operation rooms

Having a location to collate intelligence, brief team members, charge radios and issue instructions is vital. If you are stopping anywhere for more than a couple of hours you will always find the best place to work from and this will become your 'temporary ops room'.

TEMPORARY OPS ROOMS CAN BE SET UP ANYWHERE HORSE BOXES, CARAVANS, GARDEN SHEDS, AND A TREE-HOUSE, ARE AMONG EXAMPLES I HAVE SEEN

This might be a vehicle, a conference room in an office, or the kitchen of a residence. You probably won't even call it the 'ops room' but that is what it will become during your short stay.

Permanent operations

The Principal's residence, his office and probably his yacht will have an operations room. It is difficult to manage the day-to-day running of a large protective team without the facilities that a well-equipped operations room can offer.

The operations room becomes the hub of the whole operation where every bit of intelligence, every threat assessment is located and all security decision and instructions are issued.

In a well-equipped operations room you will find plenty of equipment and information to enable the smooth running of an assignment.

- ☑ Two-way radios and auxiliary equipment such as chargers, ear and throat microphones, etc.
- ☑ External antennas
- ☑ Computer with broadband internet access
- ☑ Landline and mobile telephone
- ☑ CCTV monitors
- ☑ Comprehensive first aid kit
- ☑ Vehicle search kit
- ☑ Gas masks
- ☑ Metal detectors
- ☑ Mail screening equipment
- ☑ Weapons and ammunition, if applicable
- ☑ The operations log

The operations room will have an operations log and all occurrences, whether routine or extraordinary, are recorded in it. Increasingly, the log is kept on a computer and if so a hard copy of the log should be printed each day and filed for reference. If you decide not to do this, I will guarantee that you will regret it. Old logs can be vital and you may need to refer to them for a number of reasons. Actual examples include, the Principal asks for the name of the visitor from XYZ Company that visited him last January; the loss adjuster wants to know who was actually on duty and where at a particular date and time or details of a suspect vehicle spotted a month ago on surveillance detection as someone thinks they have seen it again.

Computers can make our life a lot easier, but only when they are working. Unfortunately, they do stop working just when you really need them so having hard copy backups of operations logs makes good sense.

Other records and information

A busy operations room will keep a few logs and registers on the go. There will be registers to sign, so you might sign for keys, cars or radios. If a site has a lot of visitors you may have a dedicated visitor log, or maybe a contractors log to keep track of tradesmen working on site.

The operations room will have all of the necessary information and intelligence for the smooth and efficient running of the operation. This information will include heavy stuff like information on all known threats and enemies, and their methods of operation. It will have detailed maps of all the relevant locations and buildings, safe rooms etc. It will have details of route reconnaissance and local information. It will also have many lists, lists of the locations of everyone, expected visitors, personnel, house staff, vehicles, vehicles allowed on site, insured drivers, shift patterns, emergency telephone numbers, team mobile numbers, call signs, and so on.

All of this information will assist the team leader in running the protective assignment to the best of the team's ability and budget. Operations rooms are almost always run on a 24/7 basis and two team leaders each working a 12 hour shift, cover each full day of operations

Operation Orders

On operation order (op-order) is when a team leader briefs the team on all aspects of the upcoming operation. The operation order might relate to just one small part of the whole protection assignment, such as the op order you might receive prior to travelling abroad to do some advance work, or, it might, if you are in at the start of the assignment, be the order which details the whole of an assignment from start to finish.

When working `one-on-one' or if you are just part of a two or three man protection team, the need for a detailed op-order is still important. You should still compile the order even if it is just for yourself because the orders are so designed to cover most eventualities

The larger the team and the more complex the security arrangements the more important it is that a formal operation order is implemented and passed to everyone so that every person on the team knows exactly what is happening and precisely what he is doing. Many companies still use a military operation order; if they do it will look something like this:

Ground

Situation

Mission

Execution

Service Support

Command and signals

Atts and dets

These headings sometimes don't work too well when planning Close Protection operations but as many companies still use them you need to have an understanding of how it is presented.

Ground

This part of the operations order generally describes the 'ground' of that you will be working upon. That ground could be downtown Los Angeles or the Mediterranean Sea. In this part of the operation order you will be given information about routes that will be taken, maps of the general area, places of interest, as well as any venues that the Principal might be using.

Situation

This will be the main part of the order. It will specify who you're looking after, why you're looking after them, and the possible threats against them. It will list how large the team is, what equipment you have, etc.

Mission

This will outline the overall objective of the protective assignment. For instance, it might be to protect Colonel Hertz van Rental during his stay on the yacht 'Elizabeth' while in the Bay of Roses, for seven days commencing...

Execution

This will be the most detailed phase of the operation order; it will explain exactly how the mission is to be achieved. It will let everyone on the team know exactly what they're doing for the duration of the operation.

Service and support

This part of the operation order lets everyone know about the kit they've got to do the job with. This might include first aid kits, telephones, vehicles, night vision equipment, respirators, etc.

Command and signals

The command of signals part of the operations order will go into detail about radio frequencies and call signs, code-words and spot codes. All the mobile telephone numbers that you need to know will be listed here.

Atts and Dets

These are military abbreviations for attachments and detachments. We may have members of our team detached to the local police or coordinating with regular security guarding force. These would be detachments. Attachments on the other hand are people who would be attached to the team. We might have drivers with expert knowledge of the city we are in; we could have police, cooks, or interpreters involved in the operation; these are all known as attachments.

The 6Ws

Specific to Close Protection, if you base an operation order on the 6Ws, you might find this better suited to delivering a coherent and effective operation order. The sequence is as follows:

Who are we looking after?

All details of the Principal would appear under this heading – pictures and/or video of the Principal would be shown. A summary of the Principal's background and status would be explained here. A full profile of the Principal including the 7P's

When are we looking after him?

The second W deals with the dates, timings and the duration of the operation.

Why are we looking after him?

Details of a specific threat, with a general threat assessment explaining why the security is necessary.

Where are we looking after him?

Under this heading will be all of the items that were included in the 'ground@ heading of the military operation order'.

Who is doing what?

Here there will be a detailed description of everyone's duties and responsibilities at each phase of the operation. It will include everything they need to do and exactly when they will be doing it.

With what equipment and assistance?

All equipment, radios and call signs search kits, vehicles, etc. Contact numbers for Police and Ambulance, Embassy, etc.

Running operations

If you take over the running of an operation, most of the systems will already be in place and while you will want to put your personal stamp on the operation and get things running just how you like, you will be able to change things slowly as the operation progresses. In contrast, if you are lucky enough to be starting a new assignment, the amount of work that must be done before the protection can begin can be daunting. You will have to carry out:

☑ Threat assessments/profile of the Principal

☑ Build detailed 'Who's Who?' tree

☑ A plan to counter all the threats/risk

☑ Decide on minimum operator numbers and kit

☑ Test all kit, site and build an operations room

☑ Check all emergency kit, fire and first aid boxes, etc.

☑ All vehicles systematically searched and secured

☑ Security surveys of all relevant properties

☑ Local area knowledge/intelligence/routes/recces

☑ Briefings to everyone that needs to know.

A temporary operations room. Essential information is displayed on the wall. It is also a place where you can charge your radios and have a cup of tea

You will also outline 'action-on-drills' for:

☑ Successful surveillance detection

☑ Kidnap attempts

☑ Physical attacks

☑ Fire and bomb evacuation plans (they will be different)

☑ Dealing with press intrusions

New assignments

Starting a new assignment can be a challenge. If the assignment has a large team or you have more than one Principal to look after, say a whole family, the team leader needs to have some idea of project management.

Tasks-resources-schedule

In essence, you will decide on a list of things that need to be done prior to the protection operation. This list needs to be as complete as you can make it.

Once you have this list of 'tasks', you need make a list of the 'resources' that you will need to complete the tasks. Resources are manpower and equipment.

When you have lists of tasks and resources you must 'schedule' them in a logical way. A really simple example will explain how this is done. Three of our tasks concerning hire cars might be:

1. Wash hire cars

2. Collect hire cars

3. Search hire cars

When you schedule these tasks the sequence is pretty obvious. We cannot wash them before we have got them and it will probably be better to search them before we wash them.

But what if there is another task that involves the use of one of the cars? Let's say that a route recce to the airport needs doing. Maybe we can delay the washing until this has been done. It might save us washing the car unnecessarily.

If you use a computer you can use project management software that will allocate resources to all of your tasks and present them to you in various forms and charts. The best of the bunch is Microsoft Project but it is very expensive so get your Principal to treat you! If your assignment is simple or you do not have access to computers and project management software you can place your tasks and resources on a simple time-line like the one shown below.

A simple time-line, it is read from the bottom. It consists of a list of tasks with the time they should be carried out, along with who is responsible for completing it

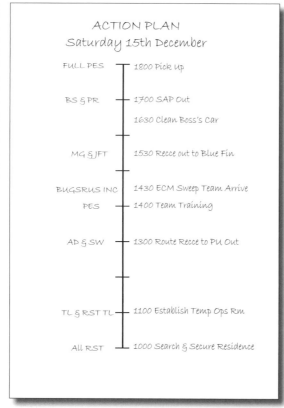

ACTION PLAN
Saturday 15th December

FULL PES — 1800 Pick Up

BS & PR — 1700 SAP Out

1630 Clean Boss's Car

MG & JFT — 1530 Recce out to Blue Fin

BUGSRUS INC — 1430 ECM Sweep Team Arrive
PES — 1400 Team Training

AD & SW — 1300 Route Recce to PU Out

TL & RST TL — 1100 Establish Temp Ops Rm

ALL RST — 1000 Search & Secure Residence

Surveillance Detection

It is a given that a period of surveillance will be carried out prior to any organised attack on you or your Principal. Your chances of surviving any attack increase dramatically if you are aware of being under surveillance. If you detect the surveillance, any intended attack on you may well be abandoned. The terrorist or criminal may move on and select a softer target. Secondly, at the very least, if you know you are under surveillance then you will be expecting something to happen, and we know that when we are expecting something, our reactions will be much better than when we are taken by surprise. If the 'enemy' is an organised terrorist group then surveillance detection may be the only way to meet the threat and survive or deter an attack.

Before you can detect that someone has you under surveillance, you must understand some basic surveillance skills. Knowing a little of how a professional surveillance operator would have you watched will not only give you an idea of what to look out for; it will enable you to use those very skills against them.

Most people's perception of a surveillance operator is someone in a tan trench coat and trilby, who will probably be carrying a copy of the Times. This couldn't be further from the truth. Terrorist and criminal organisations who carry out surveillance may be as well trained as any you will find in the secret services. They will be highly motivated and have a very healthy desire not to be caught. Surveillance operators do not conform to any specific type in regard to physical characteristics, e.g. gender, size or race. In fact, it is ideal for the surveillance team to have access to as varied a mix of operators as possible.

In This Chapter

Learn how to discover if you are under surveillance.

Understand how surveillance operators work

Surveillance Vehicles

Operators will use 'nonde' vehicles (nondescript). The car will look normal and mundane in every respect; there will be no bumper stickers or decals that might make you give it a second look. The surveillance operator will want the car to have a bit of power so will rarely use ones with particularly small engines. However, the vehicle is sometimes just used as a 'hide' with no intention of travelling anywhere. All surveillance operators are taught that two men in a car that is parked up can look very

Do not expect a 'Nonde' van to be anything other than nondescript

suspicious. Equally, everyone that is taught how to carry out anti-surveillance is told to look for two people sitting in parked cars. Surveillance can be boring and some operators do not have the discipline to follow their training. Incidentally, two people in parked cars is more common than you might think.

If we are going to be watched for any length of time then it is far more likely that the surveillance operator will use a van. The absence of windows makes this a very effective observation platform. A van can hide people and equipment in relative comfort, much better than being hidden away in the boot of a saloon car. Do not be fooled into thinking that the van is empty just because when you see it park up, the driver locks it and walks away. This, in fact, is the preferred method of delivering the nonde van onto the plot. It would be stupid and easy to spot if the driver parked up and didn't get out of the vehicle. Even the most switched off security officer might notice someone parking the vehicle and then climbing into the back!

Good surveillance vans will be equipped with 'steady pegs', which lock the suspension of the vehicle. With the steady pegs locked in place, the surveillance operator can move inside the van. Without these pegs, even the slightest movement inside some light vehicles can be spotted. Talking of movement, the operator will be equipped with a toilet in the vehicle so he can stay inside for many hours at a time. A 12 volt inverter system will be fitted so that the operator can charge radios, laptops and, if necessary, even a small fridge. The van will be soundproofed so that whispered communication with radios will not be heard from the outside. The operator may well have picture taking slots through one-way glass, or through remote parts of the exterior such as the radiator grill or bumper.

Professional surveillance operators will also use ordinary vehicles. They know that if their targets are surveillance aware, they will be looking for the surveillance 'van'. When using an ordinary car someone may well be hidden in the boot of the vehicle, manually operating the camera. The system may also be automatic or remote-controlled.

Static surveillance

The problem that terrorists or criminals have when they want to monitor our Principal's location, such as his home or office, is that these buildings are static, which means that almost all of the surveillance will have to be static too.

Mobile surveillance can be difficult to detect because of all of the movement and varying terrain. Indeed, because of the many different people you pass while on the move, it is much easier for the surveillance operative to remain undetected. This operator, though, has to be much more careful when he is carrying out static surveillance. This is because – in theory at least – he should be easier to detect as, more often than not, in order to keep a good watch on a static target he himself must remain static.

Do not think that surveillance will cease just because it gets dark. Modern cameras like this Canon with night-vision attachment can see perfectly in the dark

Before you start your surveillance detection, you must carry out a survey of the property, looking at all of the likely areas where it is possible to monitor the building. You will immediately discover areas that are primary surveillance zones. These prime zones will be a mix of areas that provide both good visibility of the Principal's building and/or provide good natural cover for the surveillance operative. Natural cover might include trees or bushes but can also be crowds of people or busy places such as cafes or car parks. Prime zones give good surveillance opportunities, with plenty of cover. It is the prime zones where we must concentrate our efforts in surveillance detection.

Secondary zones are those used by surveillance operators that do not offer such good visibility but will offer good natural cover. When the surveillance team is very conscious of not being caught, they may choose to focus all their surveillance from a secondary zone. You must look for the secondary zones and not forget to monitor these areas.

Your primary surveillance detection zone may well offer you excellent cover to carry out your surveillance detection but you should only carry out surveillance detection within the primary zone if you are 100 percent positive that you will not be compromised. You should take care to stay out of the line of sight between the zone and the residence; we can assume that almost all of the surveillance team's concentration will be towards the residence. It is far better if you can find a position that is outside of the primary zone and carry out your detection from there. You will be making every effort to blend in, but it is sensible to stay out of this line of sight.

What are you looking for?

Essentially, you are looking for the absence of the normal or the presence of the abnormal. Anyone can be a terrorist or criminal and while Hollywood casting directors will go to great lengths to ensure that every good guy looks good and every bad guy looks bad, that is not the case in real life. Terrorists or criminals look just like everyone else. Men, women, young and old, could be monitoring us. Children have also been used by different organisations as effective information gatherers.

We must look at people carefully, and then ask ourselves whether they are watching our property. You must assume that they are guilty until you can convince yourself otherwise. If you can watch someone for long enough and you are sure that they do not know you are watching them, then it will not take long for you to discover if they are up to no good.

One of the most important qualities of a surveillance operative is the ability to blend in with his or her surroundings. This of course can make it very difficult to spot that surveillance. If the people that may be watching you come from a particular ethnic group this may make it a little easier, depending of course where you are. If they are true professionals, they will dress appropriately for the area and the local population in order to blend in with the environment. Their success or failure depends entirely on their ability to fit in with their surroundings. You will not spot a good surveillance operator just because he or she is inappropriately dressed. This is a basic and easily learned skill that all good surveillance operatives are masters of. But who says you will be watched by good surveillance operatives!

Behaviour

The behaviour of the surveillance operator is the best way to spot him, whether professional or not. Look out for the way the operator walks, talks, etc. Also note their posture, their pace, their facial expressions, their moving too quickly or too slowly, outward signs of adrenalin, obvious use of covert radio or camera. All of this behaviour is easily spotted and it is here we should concentrate our attention. It will frequently be their behaviour that will let them down. Why have they been in the cafe for so long? Who is the person that keeps coming in to see them? Is that a camera they have with them? Why have they been parked up so long? Is that a radio they are using? Why are they taking notes or using a dictaphone? Are they trying too hard to blend in? Why do they keep walking up and down this road?

Equipment

The kit required for surveillance detection is minimal. However, a video camera may be essential. Modern day cameras have idiot-proof modes of operation and almost anyone can get excellent results from one. Binoculars are very useful but the best bit of kit that you can have is a notebook and pen. You can then record endless vehicle index numbers, descriptions of individual people and their behaviour patterns. This information is indispensable when you are looking for events and patterns that may point towards a surveillance operation mounted against you.

Mobile Surveillance Detection

Do not think for a moment that surveillance detection stops when we leave the premises, you will be followed from the residence or office and this can be on foot or in a car. You must remain 'surveillance aware' at all times. You need to become a people watcher, suspect everyone until they prove to you that their actions are innocent.

Aids to memory like the two shown here are only good for recalling a description at a later time such as when you are report writing. When you are on the ground you would not think 'CASBAH' just make sure that you get a good look at everybody. If you do it consciously you will not forget what they look like.

A	Age	**C**	Colour	
B	Build	**A**	Age	
C	Clothing & Footwear	**S**	Sex	
D	Distinguishing Features	**B**	Build	
E	Elevation (i.e. height)	**A**	Attire	
F	Face (shape colour etc,)	**H**	Height	
G	Gait			
H	Hair			

AIDS TO MEMORISING DETAILS OF SUSPECT SURVEILLANCE OPERATORS

Detection Methods

Simple methods are the best, when walking you can try varying your speed, moving from crowded areas to deserted ones, stopping as well as changing direction, going into places such as museums or a hotel lobby and watch who follows you in. All of these actions will make surveillance easier to spot. In a car you should still keep it simple, U turns, lane changing, varying speed and sneaking through lights just as they change to red, as well as the old twice round the roundabout trick will all make detection easier.

The very best detection method

All surveillance is designed to be 'invisible' from the targets point of view. However, if someone gets behind the surveillance team then the surveillance is much easier to detect. If surveillance on you is likely, then have a team follow you, not too closely, and if surveillance is there they have a very good chance of clocking it.

Summary

You must put yourself in the mind of the terrorist. When he carries out his surveillance, from where will it be? Find your primary and secondary zones and concentrate your effort in these areas. Never put yourself in between the surveillance operative and his target. To be good at surveillance detection you need to be good at surveillance. There are plenty of experts in this field and some excellent courses that you can attend. Once trained, many Close Protection Officers moonlight in their quieter periods as surveillance operatives.

Residence & Office Security

M ost users of Close Protection Officers are busy people. Many of them work very long hours, with some
spending much of their time in the air or on the road.
Almost all have more than one home and a surprising number
still travel to an office each day! In this chapter we will discuss the
Close Protection Officer's role in this area.

Some residences will be much more easily secured than others.
However, most Close Protection Officers will have no input at all
with regard to choice of house. Often the house will have been
purchased many years before the Close Protection Officer started
work, or their advice will not be sought during the purchase.
Except in the rarest of cases, security will hardly ever be at the top
of the wish list when your Principal is out house hunting. Security will probably be way down the bottom of his list and in many
cases security will only be considered after the purchase!

Occasions do arise where your advice is sought, especially when
choosing a short-term rent of a house, which is common if your
Principal is making a movie on location or conducting business
that requires an extended stay in another country or location.

In This Chapter

**Learn how to keep the
Principal's homes and
office safe.**

**The skills and
equipment you need
to keep premises
secure**

When choosing a property you must balance your security requirements with what the Principal requires. Invariably, the Close Protection officer will have to compromise. Your Principal may wish to be located in the city near to work. You might consider it safer to have a rural retreat. Both of these options have their merits. If your

It can be a thankless task working in the garden. But it is here where most officers will start their new career

Principal lives in the city centre, surveillance will be much easier to carry out against you because the surveillance operator will have the hustle and bustle of the city to disguise his actions. In contrast, surveillance in a small, rural community can be difficult as any strangers will find it almost impossible to go unnoticed. The city house means that roads are more congested but you normally have a lot more choice when varying the route. The rural property may not have the traffic, which, coupled with country roads, makes it easier for an ambush to be mounted against you.

The Principal's choice, hopefully based upon a bit of input from the Close Protection Officer, will no doubt be a compromise. It is rare to find a residence that is easy to defend from all types of attack, so wherever the Principal resides, the residence security team will have to work intelligently and diligently to defend it.

The Principal's residence can take many forms; the author has looked after Principal's homes as diverse as semi-detached houses to large palaces, and a permanent suite of rooms in a hotel to a large yacht that hadn't seen open water for over six years. Mostly though, the residence you will be working in will be made of bricks and mortar. This gives you the advantage of being able to surround the residence with high walls or fences and monitor comings and goings with closed circuit television.

The major disadvantage of a large static house is that your enemies will almost always know where your Principal is. They can mount sophisticated surveillance operations against you and can attack you in the building or when you enter/leave it.

To protect a residence effectively there is much that you need to know about the techniques of protection and the equipment that you will choose to assist you.

Knowing your environment

You must be familiar with the property, especially with regard to emergencies. Every-one needs to know where the fuses and consumer board are located. They must also know the whereabouts of the mains water stop cock and the key to operate it, as well as the gas tap if there is one in place. In addition, everyone must know where the safe room is, along with the nearest police station and hospital.

Surveillance detection

Nowhere more than the home and office does the security team need to set up a pro-active surveillance detection program. See the chapter of Surveillance Detection and ensure that surveillance detection is taken seriously on any residence or office that you find yourself working on.

Plans and drawings

Scale drawings of the residence can be very helpful when planning for protection. At the planning stage these maps or drawings will assist you in the following ways:

> **Working out the vulnerable points with regard to surveillance**
>
> **Formulating the best patrol routes for both day and night operations**
>
> **Working out inter-visibility for the static guarding positions, e.g. who can see what from where**
>
> **They will assist you in locating CCTV cameras and exterior lighting to best effect**
>
> **Drawings make it easier to divide a property and the garden or grounds into zones while smaller zones are effective for searches or patrols**
>
> **In an emergency such as a fire or a hostage situation a map or plan of the building can be invaluable to the police.**

Making the map

Very often you can locate some existing professionally drawn plans of the building. You can use these as the basis for your plan. Most of the western world has been mapped by aircraft or satellite and images can normally be viewed or downloaded from the Internet for a very low cost. You should, however, be mindful that your enemies have probably downloaded the same pictures!

Any plans that you do draw must be marked secret. It would be a disaster if a map showing your patrol routes, safe room, location and evacuation areas fell into the wrong hands. Once this has been completed, thry should never leave the operations room unless absolutely necessary.

Vetting the house staff

Your Principal may well have some employees that have been in his employ for many years. Ideally, even these trusted staff should be vetted on a regular basis. Police and credit agency checks should be included in the vetting procedure. Other staff, working on a short-term or contractual basis, must be fully checked out before commencing work. A system should be in place that will check with the police and quote reference agencies as well as provide proof of address. Copies of passports, visas, driving licences and work permits should be made. Personal references should be obtained and every previous employer should be contacted and asked to provide references.

> IT IS ALL TOO EASY FOR A CRIMINAL OR TERRORIST TO GET A JOB TO COLLECT INFORMATION, PLANT BUGS OR EVEN BOMBS.

In low-paid jobs such as kitchen help and cleaning staff, it is all too easy for a criminal or terrorist to get a job to collect information, plant bugs or even bombs. It is rarely left to the Close Protection Officer to hire and fire house staff but he should make sure that those responsible carry out the vetting procedures correctly.

Making the staff your friends

It is very easy to generate an 'us and them' mentality between house staff and the security team. You should avoid this at all costs. You should encourage all of the house staff to be security officers. Things like doors being left open or reporting anything that the staff thinks is suspicious can be very important information that you want to get back to you. If the staff think that you are a stuck up jobsworth, they will not bring anything to you. Furthermore, they will probably do all they can to hinder your operations and will never miss an opportunity to report back to the Principal any misdemeanour made by the security team. It is in your very best interest to foster very good relations with all of the staff.

The Operations room

All residence security operations will have an ops room of some kind. This may be a grand affair with a purpose-built CCTV monitoring suite, or it could be no more than an empty stable, where you have placed a couple of chairs and an extension lead to charge your radio. Whatever room is available it will be the hub of the security operation. Detailed information about the construction and positioning of the operations room is discussed in the 'Operations' chapter.

Hardening the perimeter

Starting from the outside and looking in, you must study the perimeter of the residence. You might be lucky and be working at a residence that has a very clearly defined perimeter; maybe it has a wall or a high fence completely surrounding the residence. Equally, you may find that the residence has no physical boundary at all and might open right up onto fields or beach.

Just because your residence is surrounded by a high fence, you can't relax and assume that the perimeter is secure. Even the highest fences can be climbed. Prisoners regularly escape over wire and only the most secure residences will have wire 25 feet high! You must look for places where the wire could be cut or climbed out of sight. Look for camera blind spots that are sections of the fence that your cameras do not cover for whatever reason. Remove anything that could be used by the criminals, such as bushes or trees that might help them breach the wire, or provide them with cover while they put you under surveillance.

All fences can be climbed, some just take longer to climb than others

Ideally, the grounds or garden should have just one main entry and exit point. This point should be controlled at all times. A system of slowing down vehicles should be used. This could be a simple chicane or tight turn, or an anti-ram ground barrier that can be lowered to allow bone-fide movement in and out, but at all other times remain locked in the up position.

Gardens and grounds

Large bushes in the garden that could help someone sneak up to the house undetected should be removed or severely pruned. Take a careful look at all trees or large shrubs that might be climbed to get over your wall or fence. Don't forget to ask for permission from the Principal or his gardener before you sharpen your machete!

The gardens should be well lit at night. The lights should be carefully positioned so that they do not assist someone breaking in by blinding the guard force. Lights should be positioned so that they shine out from the house and do not illuminate the resident security team as they patrol. Lights can be linked to infrared detectors so they are not on all of the time but ideally your perimeter should always be lit.

Patrolling the garden

Some residence gardens can be vast and require a very large team to monitor them completely. In large places, where manpower is tight or where the property has open aspects such as beaches or fields, then you must shrink the security cordon to what you can manage effectively. Make the best use of aids available such as closed circuit television, intruder alarms and guard dogs.

High or low profile

The RST has to consider what tactic to adopt with regard to profile. On some occasions it may well be prudent to have the security team adopt a very low profile and use almost covert security. This will often be because it is a sensible safety precaution or that the Principal does not want anyone to know he is resident. It is rare that a Principal's residence will ever be unguarded anyway, especially those who have some very real threats against them. However, most of the time residence security is there as a deterrent so the profile will be reasonably high. A skeleton RST should be on duty, even when the residence is empty. But it is amazing how many people leave premises under the control of just a cleaner or gardener. It's no wonder that so many are robbed while they are away or find surveillance devices when they return.

Keeping records.

There is a little paperwork that needs taking care of when running the residence security. A basic admin. setup will include the following, examples of which can be seen at the end of the book.

> **Daily Occurrence Book**
>
> **Visitors and Contractors Register**
>
> **Key Register**
>
> **Incident Reports**
>
> **Accident Book**

All of these records need to be kept for as long as practically possible. I was once asked to find the name and telephone of a carpet company that had visited a Principal "just before thanksgiving two years ago" but with that information I was able to look at the old visitors' book and impress the Principal with my 'excellent memory'. Incident and accident records have statutory times that must be kept varying from six to twenty years. You never know when these old documents will be needed so do make sure they are well filed and kept safe.

Daily occurrence book

In the operations room, the daily occurrence book will record the day-to-day goings on of the security operation, things such as who is on duty, when they go on patrol, deliveries and calls, etc. All of these will be recorded.

Visitors and contractors register

You must have a visitor handling system in place at any residence. Advise the client that he must, where possible, inform you of any visitors that he has coming and their likely time of arrival. Establish whether searches are to be carried out and what action is to be taken when unwanted visitors arrive.

Many large VIP houses are always having work done on them; workmen and people calling to give quotations will beat a steady path to the front door. Try to arrange fixed times for them to call, always check their identity, and never allow them to work alone and unsupervised. Obviously, it is always good practice – dependant upon the specific threat – to have a sweep done for surveillance devices (bugs) after the contractors have finished working.

A useful item is a simple register that records the comings and goings of all visitors or contractors to the building. This is a valuable document in the event of an emergency because it will let you know exactly who is in the building. These registers may also be used to calculate hours of work by contractors or temporary staff and ensures that you can check people's names in the book and the hours they are scheduled to work.

Key register

All house keys should be in the control of Security. Many embarrassing problems arise with locked doors and no keys. Avoid this. All keys should be recorded in a register and signed for should they be required by team members or house staff.

Restrict the issue of important keys to people who actually need them. Do not clump keys together on one bunch. Separate them and clearly mark each key (by number, not name). Imagine the panic in trying to find the garage key to rescue the boss's car from a fire, and trying to find the right key from a bunch of twenty!

Incident reports

Incidents will be recorded in the daily occurrence book. However, if a report needs to be seen by others then sending the daily occurrence book is not practical, so a separate incident report can be completed and easily passed on.

Accident records

Any accidents that happen on a residence should be diligently recorded. There are statutory periods that these records must be kept that vary from country to country.

Patrolling the building and grounds

The Residence Security Team will invariably adopt a high profile approach. This will often consist of a 24-hour presence with highly visible patrols of the garden and grounds. The aim is to leave everyone in no doubt that you have a proactive presence and breaking in would be futile. During darkness, when you have much reduced visibility, it is best to have static listening posts, which make good use of the shadows provided by the security lights. When patrolling, especially at night with their sight severely limited, the officers must use as many of their other five senses that they can. Yes, that's five more; hearing, touch, taste, smell and common!

External patrols

When patrolling, either by day or night, you need to have a plan. You might think that wandering around aimlessly is the best way to stop someone who has you under surveillance, second-guessing your patrol timings and routes. This might be true to some degree but if you do not have a plan then it is very easy to inadvertently miss areas that go unpatrolled, and if someone does have you under surveillance they will not fail to notice this flaw. When on patrol, you are constantly on the look out for any signs of intrusion. You need to pay particular attention to all ground floor doors and windows to the property as well as the property boundaries. You should ensure that anything out of the ordinary is recorded, such as sightings of dodgy vehicles, drive-bys or pedestrian walk-bys.

Patrols should always be irregular. This means you should use different times to go on patrol, and you should patrol by different routes if possible, varying the patrols' timings as much as possible. The last thing you need is having an enemy that knows there are exactly two hours between patrols and exactly where you will be at any given moment. If you can keep people guessing then you can keep them out.

Internal patrols

We may well have to patrol the inside of premises. It is rare to patrol internally if the Principal is in residence, and your patrols will be restricted to the external areas only. This is in contrast to the Principal not being on site and the building having been reopened for contractors, such as builders or maintenance staff. Then you must make sure that the building is patrolled when all contractors have left. The type of things you are looking for on your patrol are obvious but worth mentioning;

☑ All windows and doors that the contractors may have opened for access or fresh air must be secured.

☑ There are no fire hazards created and left by the contactors.

☑ All machinery is switched off and not left running unnecessarily.

The first patrol of your shift is the most important and the one that should be carried out the most thoroughly. If you do this first patrol properly you are much more likely to notice something on subsequent patrols, right in the middle of the night, that isn't right.

Emergency procedures

Procedures must be put in place to deal with emergencies that may occur at the residence. These should be written instructions that all team members can read and learn. They will include things such as the action on discovery of a suspicious package and action on discovering an intruder and immediate action if you come under attack. Everyone, of course, needs to know the evacuation procedures for a fire or bomb threat. You need to ensure that the Principal is not vulnerable to attack at the muster point. It is too easy for someone to call in a threat or set off the alarm and then lay in wait or blow up the muster point. It is for this reason that you should always try to keep the Principal's muster point different to the one that is documented.

Use of dogs

Even in today's world of high-tech gadgets and gizmos, nothing even comes close to the detecting powers of a dog's nose. Whether you are trying to detect people or explosives, the dog is still king.

Guard Dogs

The benefits of using a well-trained, patrolling guard dog are enormous. Just one dog and handler can monitor a large estate and take the place of at least six patrolling RST members. This can save a lot of money, but the downside is that the dogs need looking after every day, even when they are not working. Handlers need to be trained and the dogs need constant training if they are to remain effective.

The deterrent factor of dogs cannot be underestimated. Even the most hardened criminals or terrorists try to avoid dogs. They are either frightened of being attacked or realise that the early warning barks may well give them away.

In the UK, the Guard Dogs Act 1974, prohibits the use of guard dogs unless the dog has a handler capable of controlling the dog and the dog is under the control of the handler at all times. The dog must be secured so that he is not at liberty to go about the premises. So letting a couple of Doberman guard dogs run around the garden at day or night is strictly illegal.

Sniffer Dogs

Dogs can search almost anywhere and they are ideally suited to quickly and effectively searching property with the minimum of fuss. Because many residences are guarded 24/7 the use of the explosives detector dog is not uncommon. However, if the residence or grounds are left for any period of time then letting a sniffer dog give the premises, gardens and grounds the once over can save a lot of manpower. There are lots of specialist dog handler companies that provide dog teams on a contractual basis. You can rent them by the hour, and this is the route I recommend.

Check calls

Residence security teams should always have a check call system in place. A dedicated ops room that can receive the calls that say that you are Okay is the ideal, but a 'round robin' will suffice, that is, one assignment that calls another at a set time to let them know that all is well. Site A calls site B, then site B calls site C, and site C calls site A and the round robin is complete. A pre-planned course of action should kick in if a check call is late coming in. A small window of error should be allowed, say, just five minutes, then you need to be finding out why the call is not being made.

Duress code

Everyone must be aware of a duress code. This could be a word or phrase that means that something is wrong. Let's say, for example, that when you make the check call you always say "Site A, check call, everything OK." You duress code might be "Site A, nothing to report." This duress code tells the receiver that Site A has a problem and they are probably in trouble and the call is being listened to.

The Operations room

Depending upon the assignment, the residence that you are working in may have all purpose-built control rooms. These are, however, few and far between. More often than not, you will find yourself adapting a room in the house for this purpose. Your choice in this matter, if you have one, should be defined by the following criteria: it should be near the main house if possible, but can be placed in outhouses, barns, gatehouses, etc.

It should be positioned so that it is possible for all the hard wiring from videos, radio antennae and other equipment to be able to enter the house unobtrusively. Personnel coming in and out of the control room should not disturb the rest of the house; this would be difficult if you chose to have the control room in the attic! Control rooms can be noisy (radios, briefings, etc.) and should be positioned so as not to disturb the Principal or his family. See the chapter on Operations for information on the setup and running of the operations room.

The Main gate

The RST need to be acutely aware that they are being watched all of the time. The RST are normally the first persons that any visitor to the Principal will see; it will be the RST opening the gate and booking them in. If the visitor makes any comment to your Principal about the abrupt, or scruffy, maybe an indifferent or casual jobsworth that he met at the gate then your days are numbered. On the other hand, if the Principal is complimented by the way he was treated on arrival, this could well be your ticket out of the garden and into the PES. It's not rocket science!

Safe Room/Panic Room

In the Hollywood movie starring Jodie Foster, Panic Room showed the world the concept of having an ultra-secure area in a residence, somewhere to run should you come under attack. Within the Close Protection industry, safe rooms are not a new phenomenon. They have been used for hundreds of years. Protection Officers are always aware of their nearest bolt-hole in the event of an attack of some kind. It would be folly not to have such a place in a residence, somewhere that the family and/or the protection team can retreat during a home invasion or other terrorist threat and summon help. We call this place the 'safe room'. Think of a safe room as a secure box with just one opening. You do not just concentrate your efforts toward making the door impenetrable. All six sides of the box need to be fortified if the safe room is to be effective.

Makeshift safe rooms

When safe rooms cannot be purpose built, maybe the property does not belong to the Principal, or you are only there for a few days. You must still look for the safest room in the building, the room in which you would most likely be able to defend yourself. Ideally, this should have four brick walls and have no windows. Cellars can be turned into safe rooms quite easily, as can some bathrooms. You might add extra security to the door, or have wedges or bolts fitted. In a temporary room, you are just buying yourself a little time to summon help and await its arrival.

Purpose built safe rooms

Extreme care must be taken when using construction companies to build a safe room. Use only bone-fide, checked out companies. It could be very dangerous if information on the location and/or the construction of the safe room fell into the wrong hands. When constructing purpose-built, state-of-the-art safe rooms, the owners will often use this area to store their valuables. So if you are attacked, everything of value, which of course includes the lives of the owners and maybe the protection team, depends on the room keeping the bad guys out long enough for your response team to arrive. The purpose-built room might resemble a bank vault with yard-thick, steel-lined, concrete walls and floor, or it could be a little more subtle. Either way, when constructed it must be thought of as a six-sided box, preferably with just one very secure door. Lots of security on a door is wasted if an attacker van lifts a few floorboards and drops in on you. The door should be able to be locked very quickly, and the best way to achieve this is to have large throw bolts. Additional locks can be added, of course, but when you are in a hurry, fumbling with a key or keypad is not to be recommended. Sliding a bolt across a door is quick and simple.

Kitting out the safe room

When completing your threat assessment, you will determine how long the emergency back up, such as the police or your own response team, will take to reach your location. If you are in a remote residence, say, South Africa, then you might have to plan for a four-hour or, in the worst case, an overnight stay in the room, and the kit in the room should accommodate this length of stay. In a city such as London or New York, you would hope for a police response measured in minutes, which might mean that a lengthy stay in a safe room would not be necessary. Imagine the longest time you think you would ever be trapped in the safe room and then times that by five. So if you think that you could possibly be trapped in a safe room for twelve hours make sure that you have enough equipment to last three days. Remember, it is not only because of an intruder situation that you might use the safe room. You may well be there in the event of a nearby bomb blast that could be 'dirty' or some form of civil unrest that restricts your movement. No safe room can be designed to keep out a determined attacker, but to be 'safe' in a safe room while dying of thirst would be pretty ironic. You would ensure that the safe room contained the following equipment:

> YOU SHOULD AT ALL TIMES TRY TO RE-MAIN AS CALM AS POSSIBLE, AND REMIND YOURSELF IT IS NOT A 'PANIC' ROOM!

Communications

A panic button that is hooked up to the alarm that alerts the monitoring company or the police to a break-in is a must-have if possible. A land line and a cellular phone need to be permanently in the room. A power point should also be made available to charge the phone. A transistor radio and a television can prove invaluable, as can a can a computer, especially if it is linked to the web.

Toilet facilities

A custom-built safe room may have a toilet, but probably not. The rooms are not designed for long stays. That said, a portaloo is an excellent idea, especially if the safe room is designed to hold a lot of people, especially children.

First Aid

A comprehensive first aid kit should be in place. Included in the kit should be a supply of regular medication that your Principal or his family might take regularly. Insulin injections or an asthma inhaler are the most common form of medication, stashed in safe room medicine cabinets. You should ensure that if the Principal has any medical condition, such as angina for example, then medication is available in the safe room. If anything is going to bring on an attack of angina or asthma it's a race to lock yourself in a safe room!

Torch or lantern

Ensure these are regularly charged and checked. Power might well be cut to the room so they need to be fully charged at all times.

Food and water

Your situation and threat assessment will dictate how important this is, but even if you only ever plan to be locked in a safe room for minutes, it is a good idea to store water in the room whenever possible.

Weapons

Defensive weapons are a good idea, but if your room is safe enough, you should get into it quickly. If the door is secure, and you manage to summon help then weapons should not be needed. In a situation that warrants weapons, and where the law permits, the room might keep a shotgun, pistol, stun gun, taser or a baseball bat.

Safe room drills

Everyone must know where the safe room is and how to lock it once they are there. An evacuation practice to the room is always to be recommended especially where there are children involved. Once in the room, the Principal may or may not have members of his team with him. He must be made aware that he only comes out of the room after hearing a pre-arranged code-word or he is absolutely sure that help is at hand. It is not hard to imagine the fear one would experience being locked in a safe room. You should at all times try to remain as calm as possible, and remind yourself it is not a 'panic' room!

Incoming mail

A system for handling incoming mail must be established; ideally all the mail coming to the Principal should pass through security. If the Principal can afford it and the threat exists, invest in an X-Ray machine and screen ALL incoming mail. If no such machine is available then use your knowledge of letter bombs and use the mark 1 eyeball, but do screen ALL the incoming mail. For further information read the chapter on bomb awareness.

Household waste

All of the sensitive paper coming from the residence must be safely disposed of. Papers can be burnt but more sensibly they should be shredded. Ideally, the shredding should be done 'in house' using an on-site shredder. All refuse should be secured until the moment it is collected.

Gardens and grounds

Bushes and shrubbery near the residence should be cut right back or removed so as to make it as difficult as possible to get to the house undetected. The garden should be well lit but with the lights placed so as not to cause large shadows that an intruder could use to their advantage, Make use of infrared detectors that can turn lights on, but in large gardens be aware that birds, squirrels, cats, etc., can set these off.

Much money can be spent in a VIP's garden for perimeter protection; seismic detectors, tremblers and microphones on fences, movement detectors of all description from infrared to close circuit TV. These are all aids to the Mark One Eyeball and all rely heavily on the correct reaction from the person who receives the information from these electronic aids.

You can spend hundreds of thousands on CCTV but if the protection officer watching the monitor falls asleep, it's worth nothing!

Doors and windows

Dependant upon the threat level, doors should be strengthened and windows made of bullet-resistant glass. All windows should have curtains and these should be drawn at night. A system of verification must be used before the door of a house is opened to any visitor. This is especially important if you are working alone in a one-on-one situation. Install a video entry system, a peephole, observe through an adjacent window, but NEVER open the door to any resident without being certain of who is on the other side.

Telephones

Always advise that telephones are sited in such a position that you or the Principal cannot be observed using them through windows or doors, especially the front door. Always ensure that a list of emergency numbers is listed near the phone.

Reporting

A system of reporting must be set up, so that every operator on the ground knows who he reports directly to, and what action he is to take in event of an incident occurring.

Office Security

Your Principal will need to feel as safe at work as he does at home. Both home and work should be sanctuaries of security. Everything that has been said about residence security can be applied to office security. All of the access control, record keeping, safe room and emergency information remains the pretty much the same. If the office is co-located to the residence then of course, all of the security procedures will overlap. When the office is 'downtown' then there are other things that must be taken into consideration when conducting your threat assessment.

Routes Selection – to and from the office

Try to vary this as much as possible, but be warned that unless the risk is very high and the Principal is very concerned about that risk, then he will probably delegate the work pattern to you. If this results in pretty regular trips then you should ensure that you are very pro-active with surveillance detection procedures.

The Office building

Unless your Principal purchases his building while you are in his employ then you will probably inherit a building. Whereas a house has a limited number of family members and visitors, an officer can have hundreds or even thousands of occupants. Some of these will be known to your Principal but the majority will not. These people will include regular employees, temporary staff, clients, contractors, visitors, cleaners, and maintenance staff. A lot of care has to be given to the security of the Principal, not least because of all the people sharing the same building, any one of whom could have an ulterior motive for working there.

The Penthouse

The location of many boardroom offices is at the very top of a building. It is rare for a Principal not to want the very best office. Some of the most desirable offices will also be some of the most vulnerable to attack. Ideally, a Principal should be in a centrally located office, with no windows to the outside and serviced by its own lift. If the threat is taken very seriously then I am sure that you would be able to convince your Principal to use this dreary office with no natural light. However, the vast majority of Principals will choose the office that affords them the most status. They will also want the best view. Sometimes a compromise can be made. Offices with a view are OK if they are not overlooked and balconies and exterior access is impossible or controlled.

General security procedures and systems

The building may well be secured by a security company providing security guards. Or the guarding force may be made up of members of the residence security team. Either way you should carry out a security vulnerability survey and act on you findings. An example of a vulnerability survey.

The Close Protection Officer is frequently used as a security consultant. Sometimes this role will clash with the Close Protection duties and the officer will not have the time to effectively consult. However, being involved in all aspects of the security can be very beneficial, and there are experts that you can call in if you do not have the time. Essentially, your plan for the office security will be much the same as for the residence and will include the following:

- ☑ The production of a security plan based on the risk assessment and the manpower and equipment that you have available.
- ☑ Once implemented you should ensure that all plans are tested and revised where necessary.
- ☑ You should conduct regular reviews of all the security measures and procedures. Involve the staff in finding ways of making the systems better.
- ☑ Special contingency plans dealing with bomb threats, suspect packages and possible evacuation of the Principal should be made.
- ☑ You should liaise with the police, other emergency services and local authorities where you feel that their input will help.
- ☑ You must arrange for staff briefing and training. All staff should be encouraged to act as security deputies.

Lock Basics

As a Close Protection officer you should be knowledgeable enough to be able to give sound advice with regard to locks, alarms and access control. Often, your advice will be sought with regard to security at the Principal's home or office. I am often amazed at how little some Close Protection Officers know about basic security. You are the 'security expert' until it subsequently transpires that you didn't know some very basic security fundamentals. Then, your professionalism might be called into question. There are many different types of lock. You need a basic understanding of the different types.

Mortise Lock

A mortise fits inside a door in a recess (mortise) cut into the door edge on the outside. With this type of lock, all that can be seen from the outside is the keyhole, though some mortise locks do have a handle as well. The lock is operated by a key, which moves levers inside the lock to throw the bolt into the doorframe. Some mortise locks have only two or three levers. These locks are very easy to pick and only have a small number of key. They differ from the others in that they are normally only found on internal doors, where security is not really an issue.

Five lever locks are the lock of choice for external doors. They have thousands of different key variations and are much more difficult to pick open. Insurance company-approved five lever locks will often have a hardened plate attached to stop them being drilled open. The metal plate that the bolt shoots into when it locks is called the striking plate. It should have a box compartment to protect the bolt from an attack with a jemmy or crowbar. Most bolts are square, some have hooks but these are normally only fitted on sliding doors.

Latch Locks

Latch locks have a bolt that is spring-loaded and they do not deadlock. They should not be relied upon to provide any real security. Most of these locks have a hand or thumb key on the inside so that any intruder can break a window pane, reach in and operate the lock.

Rim Locks

A rim lock is a deadlock but rather than fit the inside of the door in a recess or mortise it is fitted on the surface. Dependent on the make, of course, they can be as strong as the very best mortise. All external locks must be able to deadlock. This means that once locked they can only be unlocked with a key. With locks, you definitely 'get what you pay for'. If it is your responsibility to specify the locks then spend as much as your budget will allow.

Hinge Bolts

Hinge bolts are metal cylinders fixed on the hinge edge of the door that fit into reinforced corresponding holes in the doorframe. When the door closes they prevent the hinge side of the door being lifted or forced. They must be fitted in pairs: one about

Many people fit good locks to a door and forget that on the hinge side there are only a few small screws. Hinge bolts stop anyone getting in by booting the hinge side of the door

six to nine inches below the top hinge; one about six to nine inches above the bottom hinge. Hinge bolts should be fitted to all exterior doors; they cost very little, are easily fitted and once fitted you can forget them. As soon as the door is closed, the hinge bolts are working. The hinge side of a door, away from all those fancy locks, is always the first side to be attacked by professionals. Hinge bolts really beef up security on this vulnerable side of the door.

Surface Bolts

Surface bolts are a good aid to security, best fitted in pairs. The top and bottom of doors use the longest screws or bolts that the staple accommodates. Fit them where they cannot easily be unlocked if a window is broken. When fitting them to gates, fit one low down as well as at the top. This stops someone just reaching over a gate to release the bolt.

A bolt that needs a key is even more secure. be careful with possible fire escapes when fitting bolts with keys

Window Security

The majority of break-ins to properties are made through windows. In addition to being a good entry point for a burglar, they also, by looking through them, give a burglar a good idea about the value of the property inside the building. Burglars generally break windows in order to open them rather than climb through them so fixed windows that don't open or locked windows are a good deterrent. Shutters or curtains that obstruct the public's view in to the building should be used, especially on all ground floor windows.

Window Locks

All windows should have a facility to lock them. Modern windows have locks that are an integral part of the window or frame. In older properties, window locks have to be added. There is a large variety of locks, designed to fit all the different types of window and frame. Every window that can be opened can be locked. Some windows can be locked when they are slightly open for ventilation purposes. Louvre's windows are rare but can still be found on some older properties. These are very vulnerable because it is easy for someone to remove the individual panes of glass and gain entry.

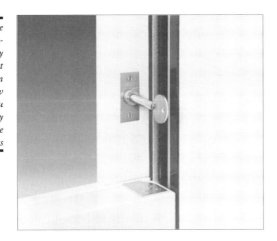

If someone breaks window glass they should still not be able to open the window because you should only use lockable window bolts

Types of Glass

Window glass will shatter into sharp jagged shards when impacted. Laminated glass has the greatest security benefit because it is difficult to break the window fitted with good locks and can prove to be a good protection from intruders. It should be remembered that while laminated glass is hard for a burglar to break it is equally as hard for you and your Principal to break out in an emergency. If an emergency exit has laminated glass, ensure that there is a tool nearby that can break the glass. Depending upon the environment bomb blast film on all windows is a sensible precaution.

Bullet Resistant Glass

Armoured glass (bullet-resistant glass) can be specified for any areas of high risks of gunshot or blast but mostly, as a Close Protection Officer, you will see it only in armoured cars.

At first glance, bullet-resistant glass looks identical to an ordinary pane of glass; it's just thicker. Also whereas an ordinary piece of glass shatters when struck by a single bullet, bullet-resistant glass is designed to withstand one or several shots at it depending on the thickness of the glass and the velocity of the bullet being fired at it. So, what gives bullet-resistant glass the ability to stop bullets?

Different manufacturers make different variations of bullet-resistant glass, but basically it's made by layering a polycarbonate material between pieces of ordinary glass in a process called lamination. This process creates a glass-like material that is thicker than normal glass. Polycarbonate is a tough transparent plastic that many know from the brand names of Tuffak or Lexan.

Bullet-resistant glass can be a quarter of an inch to over three inches in thickness. A bullet fired at a sheet of bullet-resistant glass will penetrate the outside layer of the glass, but the layered polycarbonate-glass material is able to absorb all of the bullet's energy and stop it before it exits the final layer.

Grilles and Shutters

In many circumstances, window locks provide a reasonable level of security, but in high- risk areas or high threat level security operations, windows should be enhanced by the grilles or shutters. These do not have to look unsightly and professional security companies can provide high security shutters and grilles, which will fit with the aesthetics of any building, old or modern.

Traditional Fixed Bars

Traditional steel bars that are embedded into the surrounding brickworks are very secure. However, while they might be employed to protect a very valuable and isolated window such as the basement or lavatory there are some obvious drawbacks. While they are effective at keeping people out, they'll be just as effective at keeping people in during an emergency. They are also very ugly and can make cleaning windows very difficult.

Hinged Grilles

Hinged grilles can be fitted to the inside of a window and locked in the closed position but can easily be opened in the event of an emergency, and while they are not quite as secure as the fixed steel bar they are better for this reason.

Sliding Grilles

A sliding concertina grille is similar to the old-fashioned lift gates. This type of grille is normally used to protect large areas of glass, such as patio doors and balcony windows.

Shutters

Shutters are very common in some European countries. They can provide effective security and can be opened in case of emergency. They can be as decorative as they are secure but are not suited aesthetically to all property types.

Alarms

An alarm system can provide both an effective deterrent as well as being an electric call for help when someone is trying to break in. An alarm should be looked upon as a last resort and only an addition to your good security. It should never be used as a frontline security measure.

There are three phases to a modern alarm operation:

> **1. The detectors 'detect' intruders and send signals to the control panel**
>
> **2. The panel then decides whether to activate the alarm**
>
> **3. The alarm bells sound and if programmed, messages are sent to an alarm monitoring centre that subsequently dispatches the key holder and/or the police**

To avoid false alarms it is important that everyone in the building is familiar with the alarm in use. All alarm panels take a little getting used to, and fumbling in the dark with a siren blaring and a Principal asking you what the problem is while you fumble through the user manual will not put you in a good light!

Number type keypad controls offer better security than keys and can be changed much easier. If you, as a Close Protection officer, are involved with specifying an alarm, you should ensure that the building is covered by as many zones as possible with the very minimum of two zones. This gives you or your Principal the ability to isolate zones or areas of the building: for example, you may isolate the ground floor only, leaving the Principal free to move around upstairs. Similarly, being able to alarm the whole house apart from the ops room is advantageous.

There are four types of alarm protection: external, perimeter, trap, panic.

External Alarms

External alarms are common in large houses. They aim to detect intruders before they reach the building. Detectors of varying types are located around the grounds as well as on the boundary walls and fences. The detectors might consist of infrared or microwave beams whereby a projector sends a beam of infrared light, which is invisible to the naked eye, This will be set at such a height as to be activated by a human rather than an animal. Geophones are devices that monitor vibrations; they can be installed to detect footsteps across the ground, aware that persons might jump over a fence or wall. Their sensitivity is adjusted to detect animals of a human's size.

Because of the high level of false alarms using external detectors the resulting detections from external detectors normally gets sent to the ops room, where it will be decided if the main alarm should sound. Some external detectors can be set off by wildlife such as cats, hedgehogs, foxes, squirrels and even birds, so a degree of interpretation of the detectors' signals is needed. Normal operational procedures in the event of an external detector activating would result in that sector being investigated. This might be a physical inspection by a security officer or a camera with a built-in microphone checking out the general area.

Perimeter Alarms

Perimeter alarms guard the actual perimeter of the building, i.e. doors, windows and walls. Perimeter alarms will activate before an intruder actually gets into the building because of the problems of physically getting wires back to the control room. However, modern and reliable wireless alarms make it easy to ensure that every possible entry point is alarmed.

Detectors

Magnetic Reed Contacts

Normally, doors and windows are fitted with a magnetic reed type contact; this type of switch creates an alarm when doors or windows open. These contacts switches consist of tiny magnetic reeds sealed in small glass tube; these tubes are then enclosed in a small metal or plastic case. On the door or window, one of the contacts is fitted to the frame, the other to the opening part of the door, in line with one another. The respective magnetic fields keep the reeds closed allowing the current to pass through them. With the alarm set, if the door or window is open the reeds are separated and the magnetic field is broken, thereby activating the alarm.

Traps Alarms

Traps are devices that actually catch the burglar inside the building. The following are the most common trap alarms.

Pressure Mats

A depression or 'crush mat', which is normally quite thin and plastic covered, is placed under a carpet where it cannot be seen. These traps are best positioned under vulnerable windows or doors. When the mat is trodden on, two contacts are brought together which trigger the alarm.

Vibration Detector

Vibration sensors can be used to detect intrusions in places of high risk, such as vaults, strong rooms and galleries, which are likely to attract professional thieves – thieves who might want to attack through the walls of the building. The vibrations caused by hammering or drilling register with the detector, which activates the alarm.

Break Glass Detector

These detectors are attached to glass and listen for the sound frequencies that are emitted by breaking glass. These detectors work well with breaking plate-glass but will not work with armoured wired or laminated glass. They are always worth installing into the Principal's security system.

Infrared Beams

Exactly the same as those used outside protecting the garden and grounds, infrared beams can be used indoors to protect open doors and passageways. The transmitters and receivers can be easily hidden giving effective but unobtrusive security.

An alarm panel with different zones that can be alarmed or isolated as required

Passive Infrared Detectors

These generally detect movement and are called passive because they aren't transmitting a beam and waiting to be tripped; in fact, the passive infrared doesn't transmit at all. It measures infrared energy. All living things image some degree of infrared energy. When the alarm is switched on the sensor adjusts to the level of infrared in the room. The sensors are very sensitive to increases in infrared levels and when it detects these increases, it triggers the alarm.

Ultrasonic Movement Detectors

These also detect movement, but should be avoided where possible. Ultrasonic detectors are much more prone to false alarms than passive infrared. The reason for the false alarms can be hard to nail down. They can be caused by drafts or fans and even a ringing telephone can set one off. This type of detector can give a Close Protection officer a nervous breakdown!

Other types of trap alarm can be fitted in and around the property, in particular rooms or cupboards and have switches on them. Valuable pictures can have detectors that scream if the picture is moved from a wall. Of course, safes and strong rooms can be fitted with cheap alarms used in conjunction with hidden cameras that record everything in the vicinity of the crime.

Panic Alarms

Panic buttons are permanently on and do not have to be armed like other alarms in the house. They normally consist of a switch or button that can be activated in an emergency. This button can be in a fixed position such as under someone's desk in an office or at the bedside. Panic buttons can also be wireless and can be carried on the person to all rooms of the house and even into the grounds.

The buttons are normally designed so they cannot be activated accidentally. When they are activated they may be configured to immediately sound all of the bells and sirens and inform the Central Monitoring Station. Dependent upon the situation, panic buttons can be configured just to call the police and not activate the bells and sirens.

Modern Alarm Systems

Today's alarm systems are just too good for the Close Protection Officer to ignore. The systems generally fall into three categories: the local alarm, monitored alarm and the silent alarm.

Local Alarms

Sometimes known as a 'bells only' system, the local alarm is configured to sound a bell or siren and sometimes both, but only in the locality. When the alarm is activated, the local bell or siren comes to life, sometimes in conjunction with strobe lights, which are situated outside. The bells and lights are placed so they can easily be seen by both burglar and public and thereby act as some sort of deterrent. Bells-only systems are the lowest level of alarm protection. Local alarms can benefit from a siren or bell (the louder the better) inside the property so an intruder is left in no doubt that he has triggered the alarm. If the bell or siren is loud enough, this can also have very disorientating effect upon the intruder and will make him want to leave as soon as possible.

> THE DISADVANTAGE OF LOCAL ALARMS IS THAT NO ONE TAKES MUCH NOTICE OF THEM ANY MORE.

The main disadvantage of local alarms is that no one takes much notice of them any more. The police rarely respond, if at all, and the best that can be hoped for is that the noise scares off an intruder before too much damage or theft occurs.

Monitored systems

A monitored alarm is much better than a local 'bells only' one. When the alarm sounds at the property, everything that initially happens with a 'bells only' system is the same; you can have as many bells as you like, with some very loud disorientating ones inside. The main difference is that a message is also sent to the monitoring station. The system also informs others about the activation, such as the Bodyguard or another nominated person. They may also call the police, depending upon your instructions and the level of threat to the property. Always ensure that monitoring companies are aware of any telephone number changes so they always have an up-to-date list of who to call in the event of activation.

Silent Alarms

Sometimes it might be desirable to have the alarm activated but have the bells and sirens remain silent. A panic button, for instance, that silently calls for assistance when the alarm owner comes face-to-face with an intruder might be better than all the bells and whistles activating, causing the intruder to panic and maybe do something rash. Most situations can be effectively covered with a monitored alarm, which has sirens outside along with a very loud siren inside. When the alarm is activated, the bells sound and transmit the alarm signal on a continually monitored direct private line. Should the line ever be cut or malfunction, the alarm will sound immediately.

Testing

Close Protection Officers should test the alarm or arrange for it to be tested at frequent intervals. Read the system manual and it will explain how to 'walk test' most of the detectors and test the bells and lights.

Portable Alarms

For the Close Protection officer on the move, there are some excellent portable wireless systems available; they will fit into a briefcase for travelling. They take only moments to set out and can include passive infrared detectors, door and window switches, wire-free cameras and a panic button. S systems can also incorporate fire detection. A portable system like this can be used unobtrusively in hotels – in fact, anywhere that you're Principally staying, whether it's a house or a houseboat.

A PORTABLE ALARM SYSTEM IS A MUST FOR THE TRAVELLING BODYGUARD

Arriving at a hotel, for instance, you can fit the kit to the windows and doors in a moment, attach a smoke detector to the ceiling, give the Principal a panic button, then fit an unobtrusive camera that covers the corridor and your Principal's door. After a couple of minutes of testing you can then rest assured that your Principal is safe, should a door or window open or a fire start. Also, if you see someone approach your Principal's door you are instantly alerted and can respond.

Closed Circuit Television (CCTV)

Closed circuit television is a very valuable tool in the Close Protection officer's armoury. Cameras have become smaller with more definition. In fact, cameras can be disguised to look like clocks or smoke detectors. Cameras that James Bond would be proud of, small enough to sit on top of a finger tip, can be purchased for just a few dollars. The recording systems now use disk instead of tape. The days of remembering to swap a tape every midnight are a distant memory. Modern systems can record everything from a number of cameras for weeks. The subsequent recordings are easily searched and will be encoded with the date and time.

Encoded wireless CCTV systems allow the Close Protection officer to place cameras anywhere where there is power. Some cameras can be battery powered so they can be literally placed anywhere to offer your Principal the best protection. What's more, because they are wire-free, there are no cables to run through the hotel corridor or Principal's kitchen! Permanent hard-wired systems for use at the Principal's home or office can also no be very unobtrusive and still offer the power of pan, tilt and zoom. You should be aware of the laws in the land that you are operating in; some countries have restrictions on users of CCTV who monitor public places. In the UK, if your CCTV system can monitor the public then the operators will need a licence. CCTV should never be ignored; modern systems are easy to set up and when used intelligently can be the 'extra man' that the job needs. But no matter how good the system that is purchased, it is only as good as the person looking at the pictures!

Safes and strong rooms

A Close Protection officer should be able to advise his Principal as to the correct choice of safe. Antitheft, as well as fire safes, are available but you should always advise your Principal that valuable documents and jewellery should be kept at the bank or in a safety deposit box.

Free Standing Safes

Your Principal will probably want a substantial safe that can hold a mixture of documents or bulkier valuables. The best and most substantial of free standing safes are very heavy and for this reason they normally have to be situated on the ground floor or on a reinforced floor if above ground level. Free-standing safes normally weigh in at over one ton. If they weigh less than that, they should be secured to the floor.

Wall Safes

A wall safe is set into a wall, normally replacing existing bricks. It only offers minimal protection. Securing it in a strong wall and hiding it can make for a reasonable level of protection.

Floor Safes

Floor safes need to be professionally fitted; they sit in the floor so that the lid is just below whatever is at floor level. Most floor safes are not suitable for large or bulky items as the opening is normally quite small and circular. Because the safe seat is at floor level they are not as convenient to use as a wall safe, because you must kneel down to open them. In addition to this, items that are stored in the safe normally have to be stacked on top of each other. The best safes are set into a solid block of concrete. Some less secure safes are designed to fit under wooden floorboards, where they are screwed into the joists. Either type needs to be sited near a wall so the floor covering can easily be moved to access the safe.

Strong Rooms

If money is no object then a professionally constructed strong room is the ultimate security for your Principal, especially to guard valuables that might attract professional thieves. Strong rooms have an independent alarm system and protect against fire as well as theft. Taking advice from a specialist is to be recommended when specifying a strong room.

Electronic Covert Surveillance

Electronic covert surveillance is a powerful tool in the fight against crime; it can be very effective in an office environment or a VIP's residence where theft is occurring. It offers a number of benefits to Close Protection Officers when faced with the need to identify a suspect or solve criminal acts being perpetrated against your Principal. However, the management of covert surveillance systems – whether video or audio-based – needs to be handled correctly to keep within the laws of the country. You, as a Close Protection Officer, should be able to advise your Principal on the benefits as well as the problems that might be encountered when such equipment is used.

The use of hidden cameras, as opposed to those that are overt and act as a deterrent, may initially be dismissed. The thought of using such cameras might seem like spying on staff. However, there is a role for these systems in the fight against crimes committed when your Principal suffers losses due to staff criminality. Sometimes these events can be extremely hard to pinpoint. This is because staff inevitably will know what traditional systems are

LEVELS OF HONESTY OFTEN RELATE TO LEVELS OF OPPORTUNITY. HOUSE STAFF, SUCH AS COOKS AND CLEANERS AND SECURITY GUARDS HAVE LOTS OF OPPORTUNITY TO STEAL FROM THEIR EMPLOYER.

in place, and will be able to devise ways of avoiding capture. In such situations it can be difficult, if not impossible, to identify the person responsible. Unless of course you get lucky and catch them red-handed, the probability of detection will be very low, and any staff member or contractor committing crime is of course aware of this. Very often some employees and contractors see crimes against the employer as a soft option with minimal risk. This is because they have been placed in a position of trust. Sadly, 'levels of honesty relate directly to levels of opportunity' and those persons that have the most trust often have the most opportunity.

Your Principal has every right to protect himself against such criminals, and the use of covert surveillance can swiftly solve these problems. The technology allows hidden cameras to be employed, depriving the suspect of the knowledge of what systems are in use. If, for example, a series of thefts take place from a Principal's busy kitchen, you can deploy hidden cameras – usually fitted into everyday items such as clocks, smoke detectors, box files, etc. These ascertain the identity of the criminal and may be used as evidence in any subsequent legal action or industrial tribunal hearing.

The use of covert CCTV solutions is very cost-effective, as equipment is only required as and when incidents take place. It used to be hired, but the cost of the equipment fell dramatically after the scandal in America where a child carer was accused of shaking a baby to death. At the same time in an unrelated case, film footage was shown on TV of a carer abusing children. The result of this was that thousands upon thousands bought covert cameras to spy on there nanny while they were at work. These cameras were hidden in books, clocks, cuddly toys, smoke alarms, and room lights and sockets. This demand has meant the there are many types of hidden camera available and all at very reasonable prices. If you 'Google' for 'spy camera' you will get a list of almost 300,000 returns!

The Moral dilemma

Close Protection Officers should always ensure that they consider the feelings, and the privacy, of others when using covert surveillance. Covert cameras should be used only when a serious crime occurs, such as the theft of high value items, drug-related crimes, etc. Your sole intention should be to identify a person or persons unknown, in order to take action; this might include terminating their employment, taking legal action to recover costs, or passing information on to the police to allow them to take appropriate action. There are lots legislative documents and codes of practice designed to protect the interests of innocent staff and contractors to your Principal's business premises, and these ensure that the rights of individuals are not eroded, while also allowing businesses to take necessary steps if they experience crime or unacceptable behaviour in the workplace. Much of this legislation is grey and can appear ambiguous, and Close Protection Officers/security consultants will need to consider their approach when interpreting the various documents.

Legally speaking

In essence there are no privacy laws in the UK, just a mixture of different legislation, codes and case Law. The important documents to consider before undertaking covert surveillance in the UK are the Human Rights Act and the Data Protection Act.

The Human Rights Act

This act implements the European Convention on Human Rights. Article 8 of the

Act is of particular relevance in such cases because it provides that everyone has the right to respect for their private and family life, their home and their correspondence.

This is a catch all piece of legislation that is often subjectively interpreted. However, if the criminal activity warrants covert surveillance and the potential impact has been properly considered, then the risk of a breach of the legislation is unlikely.

The Data Protection Act

This act is primarily concerned with the management and use of images after capture. In the UK there is no specific law regulating the use of CCTV at your Principal's office, or home. There are voluntary codes to help users comply with the Data Protection Act (DPA). The Code of Practice for users of CCTV and similar surveillance equipment sets out exemptions to an individual's right of access to data that is specific to them. If you set up a camera at your Principal's residence and the camera can 'see' into a public place, then Joe Public, in that space, can ask to see any video tape recording of them that you might hold. While under the DPA these individuals have the right to view any data held which relates to them and their activities. A data controller – which could be you, the Close Protection Officer, or a Police Officer if you have handed them the evidence – can withhold CCTV footage if the disclosure of the information might prejudice any investigation of a criminal act or the apprehension or prosecution of offenders. It is worthwhile noting that if you are suspicious of someone's motive in wanting to view the footage, or if allowing them access to the footage could infringe upon another's privacy, then you should consider denying them access. However, professional advice should be sought before you do so.

Covert surveillance should not be used in areas that employees, guilty or innocent, would generally expect to be private, such as toilets and private offices. However, if there is the suspicion of serious crime taking place in these private places, and the crime is grave enough for you to intend involving the police, then covert surveillance can be used in these areas. Even then, your camera placement should be considered to encroach as little as possible into the privacy of any innocent persons. Should you wish at a later date to use your footage as evidence, and you have unreasonably encroached on someone's privacy, then you may find your evidence becomes inadmissible.

Summary

Residence security can, if you let it, get boring. There is no glamour attached to walking the grounds of a large house in the rain night after night. It can be hard to stay motivated all of the time, but rest assured in the certain knowledge that the day you relax, the day that your mind is not 100 percent on your duties will probably be the day you lose your job.

Residence and office security, like so many other jobs in our industry, have to measure their success by nothing happening. That's the way it should stay. Nothing happens because you are vigilant. You're doing your job, and you won't let anything happen.

You are supposed to be a security expert, so you need to know all about security hardware such as locks, alarms and CCTV

With just a little common sense, and knowledge of the laws of your country, you will find covert surveillance can prove an excellent tool to protect your Principal against crime. However, you must though be aware, and very sure of, the legalities. Your Principal will not thank you if he takes your advice and uses covert surveillance only to find himself on the wrong end of a claim for rights infringement.

Eavesdropping Detection

I t is not the intention of this chapter to turn you into a bugging or debugging expert; however, the Bodyguard should have a working knowledge of this type of surveillance device, its capabilities and limitations.

Who's bugging who!

You, as a Close Protection Officer, may be the target of an eavesdropper hoping to get some information about your client. Your client – depending upon who they are and what they do – may be targeted for eavesdropping by any of the following:

- ☑ The Principal's business partners or associates
- ☑ The Principal's business competition
- ☑ Professional intelligence gathering agencies, police, customs
  The Principal's family, wife or husband
- ☑ Private detectives working for any of the above
- ☑ Kidnappers
- ☑ Terrorists
- ☑ Government
- ☑ Investigative Journalists

How are bugs 'planted'?

There are a number of ways that the listening device can make its way into your Principal's office or home. The most common methods are:

- ☑ Intruders, break-ins, etc.
- ☑ People posing as telephone or gas engineers, etc
- ☑ Office cleaners
- ☑ Bugs given as gifts – especially electrically operated. For example, desk lamps, radios, calculators. Other items include fountain pens, briefcases, etc.
- ☑ Areas that the Principal visits regularly can easily be bugged For example, if they often take a particular suite of rooms at the same hotel.

In This Chapter

Understand what bugs can do.

Learn how to combat their use.

How can the Bodyguard help?

The good Close Protection Officer will always be alert to surveillance and advise his Principal of the following:

- ☑ To be cautious of unsolicited gifts.
- ☑ To be aware that all conversations and negotiations can easily be recorded by surveillance equipment.
- ☑ That telephone conversations (including mobile telephones) are totally insecure.
- ☑ All the Principal's key personnel or close acquaintances should be considered potential surveillance targets. For example, Solicitors or Accountants.
- ☑ The Principal should never use other people's telephones for important calls.
- ☑ For sensitive discussions the VIP should promote the use of his own 'swept' premises for meetings
- ☑ Ensure that all the Principal's paperwork is cross-shredded.

Different types of bugs.

TELEPHONE/AUDIO. Easily fitted to a phone and can be monitored or taped.

ROOM AUDIO. Rooms can he monitored by many differing bugs such as:

ROOM BUG. (A small, battery powered bug can transmit audio up to 1000m.)

HARD WIRE MICROPHONE. The microphone may terminate at a recorder or transmitter some distance away from the target room.

RECORDING/ TRANSMITTING BRIEFCASE. Purpose built case with concealed electronics.

NORMAL TAPE RECORDER. Modern digital tape recorders are small enough to be easily concealed and used to record your Principal's conversations at meetings, etc.

INFINITY DEVICE. Used to listen to the 'room audio' via the telephone line.

INFRA RED TRANSMITTER .This transmits invisible light into an optical receiver.

MAINS MODULATION. Devices of this type will transmit the room audio to a nearby receiver.

VICTIM USER. Many items designed to look normal may transmit room audio, e.g. fountain pens, calculators, electric sockets, plugs and plug adaptors and table lights.

Are you or your Principal a potential target? If eavesdropping on anything you say, write, type, or do could increase someone else's wealth or influence, then the answer must be yes, you are a potential target.

Questions to ask yourself or the Principal about bugs

Do others seem to know about your Principal's confidential business activities or professional trade secrets? If they do then this is the most obvious indicator of covert eavesdropping activities. How have others learned about the business? If you are sure that the information has not been leaked then it would be careless not to suspect that you have been bugged. You should arrange for a professional sweep straight away.

Have you noticed strange sounds, power drops or volume changes on your phone lines? Some wire-taps can cause problems with telephone lines, especially amateur wire-tap equipment. Any noise such as static, popping, scratching, feedback, voices or hollow silences should be investigated.

Does your phone make a funny sound when it's put back on the hook? This can be caused by a device that turns your phone into a microphone, which can be listened to anywhere in the world. If you are suspicious of a phone then remove it from the socket and get it checked out.

Has your FM radio started playing up or broadcasting familiar voices? Many amateur spy devices use the same frequencies as normal music FM radio. Look for the transmissions at either end of the FM radio band, which is where they tend to be set. If the radio squeals horribly at a particular point of the tuning dial then slowly move it around the room and adjoining rooms. If the squeal gets louder and more urgent then the chances are you are stood very near to a cheap amateur bug bought from a shop.

Is the radio in the car playing up? Is it 'getting weird'? Remember that the antenna your car radio uses may be (and often is) exploited by an eavesdropper, and that such usage may interfere with radio reception (so be concerned if you automobile radio suddenly starts getting weird).

Have you or your Principal been the victim of a burglary in which little or nothing was taken? Professional surveillance operators might break into a home or office to place a bug and you might never know that they were there. If they have to break in they may well disguise the real reason by making it look like a burglary.

Have you or your Principal been given any type of electronic device such as a calculator, radio, alarm clock, or MP3 player? Spy shops are full of 'gifts' to give to the unwary. If they are electrical then they will always have the power to transmit voice, pictures or other data. Other items, such as fountain pens, have a battery hidden inside and have a limited life if they are given to the victim, who will of course not change the battery when it dies.

Do your door locks suddenly not "feel right", are they starting to get "sticky", or do they completely fail?
This can be evidence that the lock has been picked. If any lock starts playing up then immediately recommend that it gets changed. Someone may well have bypassed your lock. If it is not obvious why then the chances of the reason being surveillance are very high. Arrange for an immediate sweep of the premises. If nothing is found then maybe the lock was just failing and no one had been tampering with it. Changing it will at least stop your Principal being locked out when the lock actually fails.

Transmitters are very small and they can easily be incorporated into everyday items. If that item already has a power source like the clock and the plugs then they can transmit indefinitely

Have you noticed that the water or telephone company seem to be camped near the Principal's residence? You need to be highly suspicious of any utility vehicles in your vicinity. Call the company anonymously complaining about obstructions or other concerns or just ask outright to discover if the 'workers' are genuine. Do the vehicles have tinted windows and space where someone could hide undetected? Have they got a ladder or pipe rack on the roof, which is a great place to disguise or hide an antenna?

Have gas, telephone, plumbing, or air conditioning repair people turned up to do work when no one called them? If you fall for this one then you do not watch enough TV. Never let tradesman in if they arrive unannounced. Never leave tradesmen unattended for so much as a second even when you ordered them.

Summary

If you think the Principal may be being bugged then call in the experts; do not play around with small, hand-held 'detectors'. They just don't do the job no matter what they promise on the box. A lot of expensive equipment is needed to do the job properly, and that's just the start. Then you've got to get trained in its use. If the Principal insists that he purchases his own equipment for you to use, you should insist that he pay for your training to go with it or he'd be wasting his money.

The Security Advance Party

The Security Advance Party may find themselves working months in advance of the Principal's visit, scouting for the most secure hotels or houses to rent, planning routes and gathering local intelligence. They might also find themselves just minutes ahead of the Principal, checking routes to the Principal's destination and giving the BG real time traffic reports. They might then carry out covert searches and 'quick looks' of the venue, ensuring that all is OK before the Principal arrives.

The SAP need to be experts at maintaining a low profile, as their position frequently demands it. They need to be skilled in anti-surveillance because if they are followed, this will give vital information to the terrorist or criminal about the Principal's future movements. They should be trained in building search and be able to do this quickly and effectively, both overtly and covertly. The skill of discreetly checking out a venue, like a restaurant or bar, without letting anyone know what you're up to, while knowing that you haven't been followed, takes considerable skill and experience.

They need to have excellent communication skills as they may often liaise with others, such as hotel security or the police. They need to be completely up-to-date with the current threat assessment as this will dictate the type of 'advance' work they carry out.

Playing Leapfrog

The Security Advance Party will often travel the same route as the Principal. They will be extremely vigilant on route with regard to surveillance. Should an enemy recognise them for what they are, they could compromise the route or the venue.

In This Chapter

The duties of the SAP

RAG Zones

Search Techniques

Use of Sniffer dogs

Time and route travelled

Route recce's and time are of major importance. They must leave enough time to be able to check the route and search and secure the venue before the Principal arrives. It is better to be early than late, but not too early as it is best to travel the route as close as possible to the one to be travelled by the Principal.

Action on route

While carrying out anti-surveillance drills, you must also be monitoring the route for problems that may befall the Principal, i.e. traffic accidents, which cause tail-backs, road works, the sort of things that were not there when the recce was done. You must also remember that you should continually look for suspicious persons or vehicles. Anything noted must be relayed back to the BG or your Team Leader. IF IN DOUBT CALL IT IN.

Action at venue

At the venue, you are still as covert as possible so as not to draw undue attention to yourself or tip off an observer that your VIP is arriving. A thorough check of the outside of the venue is the first priority. Suspect packages, parked cars and sniper points must all be considered.

If you are not being covert and are carrying out thorough, overt searches such as you might for your Principal's business annual general meeting, or you are working at a property in which you are known, or owned by your Principal, etc., then the searches are going to be carried out in much more detail than is possible when you are covert.

Searching inside the venue has to be methodical and a system set up to ensure that all areas are searched and no areas missed. Do not search just the rooms that the Principal will visit. A bomb in a basement or a room above will still kill or cause mayhem. Use the RAG system, explained on the next page. Don't forget that it's not just bombs you might be looking for. Depending on your Principal, there may be people who want to bug rooms to listen to everything said.

Building searches

We cannot carry out effective searches if we are not completely aware of the main threats to the Principal. What does the enemy want to achieve? Are your enemies likely to try and kill your Principal or would they rather disrupt or embarrass? How vulnerable in that building is your Principal? The threat might be a bomb, but what is the risk? What is the likelihood of this occurring? What is the size of the likely device? Is it more likely to be a suitcase in a hotel lobby or a car bomb in an underground car park? Can your threat assessment go any way to answering these questions? Consider the structure of the building.

To make a building search assessment you need to think of what would happen if a device went off at a particular place in or near that building. That way you can prioritise your search areas. You should divide your building/area into colour-coded zones: red, amber, and green.

The RAG zones

These zones can be plotted on a plan or diagram of the building and grounds but unless you are very experienced and you know that the plans are accurate and drawn to scale, then the zones should only be 'pencilled in' until you actually visit the location. You may discover something that the map doesn't show. For example, in a green area there could be a LPG tank providing gas to the property. This area may have to be treated as a red zone to ensure that it is searched thoroughly.

The Red zone

This is the zone that depicts the actual area that the Principal will occupy, where he will be the most vulnerable, and where he is most likely to be killed or injured should there be a bomb.

The Amber zone

This covers areas adjacent to the space that the Principal occupies. The Principal is still vulnerable in these areas and if an explosion occurred there then the chance of injury or death is still high.

The Green zone

These are areas of low vulnerability, e.g. gardens and grounds some distance away. If a bomb was to explode in the green zone, the Principal may not be injured but still suffer some major disruption or at the very least, acute embarrassment.

Systematic searching

All building or room searches must be systematic, methodical and thorough. A two-person search team is better than one, but any more than two searchers in all but the largest rooms and you will get in each other's way, and the search will be less effective. Remember that just a couple of ounces of high explosives could kill or maim many people in a small room and that two ounces of explosives could be concealed almost anywhere. So look everywhere.

How to search

The first thing to do is to try to search the room from the door. Stay outside the room or, if this is not possible, only go in as far as you need to see the bulk of the room. Use your senses – have a good look around, listen for suspicious or unusual sounds. Are there any suspicious smells? When you think you have the measure of the room, you can enter and start your systematic search.

Many people have different ways of searching. It does not matter whether you search from the top down or from right to left, as long as you have a system that is designed to cover all of the areas, and that you stick to that system.

One system is to start at the entry point and move from left to right, first searching everything below your eye-line, then, before continuing, searching everything above your eye-line. What you must NOT do is to go first to the place that interests you the most, then, if there is nothing there, go to your next favourite place and so on. This does not work, as it contains no method. You will miss whole areas unless your search is systematic and methodical.

Your search might be a fingertip search or it might involve screwdrivers and mirrors. The threat assessment will determine the extent of your searching. If you are taking the place apart, make sure you have enough time to put it all together again. If speed is of the essence and your searches are for explosives, then the use of a sniffer dog can be beneficial.

When the search is finished

Once you have searched a room, you must ensure that it stays clear, so either lock it or have someone guard it. If, after you have searched the room, you are asked by the police, security, or organisers whether the room is clear, don't say YES. Never make such a bold statement such as, "This room is clear." You just state that you have "searched and found nothing".

Should anything suspicious be found then your first action should be to look after your own safety. Carry out the 4Cs. The last thing you need is for the Principal to arrive among the mayhem, so you should inform the Bodyguard or team leader ASAP.

Further duties for the SAP

The SAP will generally stay in position until the VIP arrives. Then, depending on the brief, they may either stay and provide perimeter security, backing up the PES, or they may have to get to the next venue of the VIP to start the whole procedure again.

Using explosive detector dogs

If your Principal has a threat that may involve explosive devices, then the search dog is the champion of quick and efficient searches. Despite new and ever more sophisticated technology, nothing is more mobile, versatile, reliable or discriminating than the well- trained, explosive detector dog. These dogs are an essential element in the fight against terrorism and organised crime. The dog's nose is extraordinary; I once saw a search dog in Northern Ireland find a gun that had been used to murder a woman. The gun had been buried in a ditch and undisturbed for thirty years! The dog indicated its presence as if it had buried there just the day before!

Today, there are plenty of civilian dog teams and the days of having to use moonlighting police and military dog handlers are past. If the threat to your Principal is high and he is always on the move, then having a sniffer dog permanently on the team can prove to be invaluable. If your need is less frequent then there are plenty of contract dog teams who will work on short contracts.

Dogs need handlers

It is no good just to buy the dog and hope it will work for you. These dogs need a dedicated, well-trained handler and to have continuation training on a daily basis. Years ago, I came across a Principal who had spent £2000 on a superbly trained, explosives-detector dog and gave it to his security team, just like you might give them a search mirror. They treated it as a pet and didn't know how to 'work' the dog. After a couple of months the dog was everyone's mate, and would run around when it was 'working'. In reality, however, it wasn't working at all as tests that were carried out revealed. The dog had to be sent back to be retrained. Dogs must come with trained handlers and they work better if it is the same handler each time.

Test the dog team

When using contract handlers you must test them regularly. The handlers will often carry stuff for you to hide. Be wary of a handler that doesn't want you to test them or tries to lead you too much into where you should hide the stash. A good handler and dog will welcome any opportunity to test the dog this way. Essentially it's almost impossible to hide something from a good dog.

To do this you will need to have access to some explosives or the dog's training aids. When you tell the handler that you have hidden something and you would like them to try and find it, you should see no difference in the way the handler works the dog. If you do – let's say the handler is more animated and working hard at stimulating the dog with more encouragement than usual – you should question their commitment. Note how the dog and handler work when they know something is there. This is how they should always work.

The very best way to test the dog team is to hide something and not tell the handler this is the ultimate test but it does carry some risk! You should be aware that when the dog handler sees his dog indicate the presence of explosives, the adrenalin dump from the handler will turn into hard anger when he discovers that you set him up. He will hate you for it, but at least you will know that the dog team works, even if they never work with you again!

There are plenty of dogs and handlers that just go through the motions, relying on the fact that finds of explosives are very rare and that most laymen wouldn't know if the dog is not working or not. Test your dog teams whenever you get the opportunity. If the dog handler gripes about this then change the dog team. There are plenty of good ones out there.

Different breeds of dog

The bulk of search dogs are drawn from the gun dog breeds. English Springer Spaniels and Labradors are the most popular, but some German Shepherds have been used to great effect. The German Shepherd, however, can scare people when used in public spaces. If this is not a problem then the German Shepherd can, in addition, be an effective RST member and double up as a guard dog when not employed searching buildings.

If the public are involved then it is rare to come across people who are scared of Labradors or Springers, and because of lots of exposure they will associate the dogs with either drugs or an explosives search.

Summary

The SAP team need to keep themselves on top of the threat assessments so that they know what they are looking for. They should always strive to be low profile and be able to blend into most places. They should also be skilled in both overt and covert search techniques.

The SAP duties are extremely important to any operation, even though many feel that the job lacks the 'glamour' of the BG or PES. However, it cannot be stressed enough that a vigilant SAP could easily save the life of the VIP.

Location Security

Here we discuss some of the different locations that you may have to secure. The advice given is for guidance only. Not all airports, restaurants or hotels are the same and common sense needs to be applied to secure each particular location to the best of the team's ability and budget.

Restaurants

Obviously some restaurants are much safer than others. In an ideal world, the Close Protection Officer would be able to choose the most secure restaurant but this rarely happens unless the risks are very high. More often than not the Principal will always choose the restaurant according to its reputation and the quality of food and service, rather than the security. Some Principals may be influenced in their choice of restaurant by your security recommendations but unless the threat is of a particularly high level, he will dine there and you will have to do the necessary to see that the Principal remains safe.

Prior to the Principal arriving at the restaurant, the use of an SAP is to be encouraged. They can check that the restaurant is actually open, the booking has been made, and that parking is available if necessary. They can discreetly vet the clientele already there. Most importantly, they can recommend the best seating arrangements for both the Principal and the Close Protection Officer. Then, when the head waiter later greets the Principal and leads him to a table, the Principal can be blissfully unaware that the table has been chosen for its security features rather than its outlook.

Popular restaurants require tables to be booked in advance. It might be prudent to use a false name to make the booking. If you are looking after a well-known celebrity then the only way you might get a table is to namedrop. If your Principal attracts the press and paparazzi then you should always try to book using a pseudonym. Information about where the famous are going to be is well paid for. Your secret venue will often be compromised by someone who works for the restaurant.

In This Chapter

How to best protect your Principal in hotels, restaurants and the theatre and more

In most cases, the very best seat in the house – and the one that your Principal will want to sit at – will be the worst seat with regard to his security and will probably in a lit window or worse! Be prepared to discuss this point with your Principal or compromise with him. If he insists then you must work around this. For example, if your Principal insists on sitting by a window then your compromise might be to station someone outside the window discreetly guarding it.

There may be occasions when the Close Protection Officer is invited to eat with the Principal. In this situation it is easy to forget what you are there for. This can be especially so if the meal is nice and the conversation is interesting. Do not embarrass your Principal by not eating anything or having your head on a stalk; just remain very alert while you eat the meal to any situation that may arise.

If the protection you are providing is required to be low profile, and the Principal is meeting someone else for dinner, you may well not be invited to sit down with him. In this case you should choose a position where you can keep a constant eye on your Principal as well as the restaurant entry and exit points and toilet entrance.

Ideally, a seat at the bar that gives you a good view of the restaurant is great but not always possible. You may have to sit down and eat. If you are able, you should choose a position that enables you to see the doors and most of the restaurant. As you are not with the Principal, try where possible to sit them with their back to a wall. Arrange to be one course ahead of them (miss the starter, fatty) so that you finish before him.

If the Principal leaves abruptly while you are eating your sweet, you may well be embarrassed should the waiter chase you for payment. Always try to pay by credit card and keep receipts as this makes reconciling expenses easier.

Shops, markets and department stores

When the Principal decides to go shopping, the Close Protection Officer should remain close at all times. He should enter every shop no matter how small and remain alongside them. If you have a personal escort section then they must use copious amounts of common sense when deciding to follow a Principal into a small shop, especially when trying to maintain a low profile. Six men entering a small store and only one of them purchasing something will do nothing but raise your profile.

In large department stores, the Personal Escort Section should always follow the Principal inside. Some large stores are like small towns; they have streets and lots of exits on different levels, with many people inside. So while the chance of crime can be lower because of cameras and in-store security they are certainly not crime free and the Principal still needs protecting. In training scenarios, I have frequently seen students stay outside a large shopping centre because they think that the profile will be raised too high if they enter. I have also seen their embarrassed faces an hour later when their Principal is nowhere to be seen. He left by another exit and these guys got left behind! The escort section should always enter these places and treat these stores like the small towns they are. Remember that we should never forsake security for profile unless it is absolutely necessary.

If you are trying to maintain a low profile while shopping, it is important for the Personal Escort Section to be experienced in this type of protection. Providing low profile protection can be extremely difficult to do well. If you are not careful, your attempts at maintaining a low profile you can get you into a lot of trouble; people may mistake your attempts at maintaining a low profile for those of the common shoplifter. Imagine the embarrassment as you are being questioned by store detectives and the police as your Principal walks past leaving you there at the store.

You must work hard at maintaining a low profile but not forgetting that you are still being watched by your Principal and you may be being watched by your enemies. Keeping a low profile does not mean that the protection is diminished. You must be clever enough to balance both and this is only possible with training and practise.

Theatres, Cinema and Opera

Large, luxury cinemas with private boxes are fast becoming a rarity though they are much more common in theatre and opera. Those that are still around in cinema can be very expensive but as long they are still available and your Principal agrees, then they are the way to go as far as security is concerned. Seating in the boxes can vary between around four persons up to a dozen or more. If possible, security can sit in the box as well and they are usually secured from the single exit at the rear. Private boxes will often have private lifts and additional security makes their use even more beneficial. Some boxes, however, can leave a Principal on show and some people in the stalls will be able to watch their every move – especially in the first row of the box. Check this, you might have to advise the Principal to sit further back in the box.

Large buildings with lots of people in them should always come with a health warning! Any hint of fire or emergency and the large crowds can become very dangerous. You should always know where your emergency exits are and be positioned so you can get to them quickly. Advance visits, where you can talk to the management about the building evacuation procedures and their policy on bomb threats, can enable your threat assessment to be as comprehensive as possible.

Theatre tickets are pre-bookable, and a recce to the theatre to choose the most suitable seats is the best way to obtain seats you want. If you cannot get to the theatre then the next best thing is to call them up and ask them for advice. Very often they will know what seats VIPs and their security teams use, or at the very least, they will be able to give good advice about emergency exits.

Modern cinemas can be a pain; many of them have a first-come gets best seat policy. So if you have the manpower available then getting a couple of guys at the front of the queue to secure your seats is invaluable. When you find yourself out there in cattle class or the stalls, protecting the Principal can be harder than you think. A dark room, full of members of the public can lead to some compromises. Clearly, if the threat against your Principal was very high you wouldn't be there but you still have to keep your wits about you.

I was told about a PES member that got so engrossed in a movie and didn't notice when his Principal visited the toilet – maybe the film had got to a good bit! Never become too interested in the show. Do not forget why you are there. If it's good, promise yourself you will come back when you're not working.

Don't sit the Principal in the middle of a long row; you will have problems moving out in a hurry. Essentially, you should be as near to a fire exit as you can. The very rear is more comfortable than the front.

The Principal should have at least one member of the team behind him and someone either side in a row. People may want to leave early or visit the toilet and this may involve them walking past your Principal. Just ensure you vet them well before they do.

Always take a small torch to the cinema, as well as earpieces for telephones and radios that you will want to keep on throughout the performance.

Casinos

I have read more than once that you can relax your security arrangements inside casinos. This is just not true. There are plenty of security officers and lots of cameras watching everyone, but the officers and cameras are looking after the interests of the casino owner. They are not really there for your security and cannot be relied upon to do so. There are many undesirables that frequent such establishments. When you're in the casino you should remain as close to the Principal as possible. If you are a regular visitor, you may get to know the security and the casino floor managers and this can make your job a little easier.

If your Principal is anything other than a casual gambler he may find that he goes to private gaming areas within the casino. You may or may not be invited but you should insist that you stay with him. Some card schools will not allow a non-playing third party into the room so you will have to remain outside. Just treat that room as you would a hotel or office room and ensure that anyone entering poses no threat to your Principal.

Leaving a casino is, of course, a vulnerable time and you should expect attention from criminals. Leaving in vehicles with very little exposure on pavements or car parks is the only way to do it. Use plenty of anti-surveillance and stay very much in Code Yellow.

Speaking engagements/public meetings

Your Principal might be a business person, an actor, a politician, or a priest. One thing that many Principals have in common is that they meet the public and speak to them. To do this they often have to be right there among the public or just a platform away. This can make the Close Protection Officer's job very difficult. You might be protecting a Principal at a company annual general meeting, and have hundreds of angry shareholders who think your Principal deserves to die a painful death because

Speaking in public can make your Principal vulnerable to attack. Subtle barriers and the intelligent placement of Protection Officers will negate the risks and the public will hardly notice

their shares have taken a tumble. He might be an author at a book signing, an actor at a film premier or a sports personality at a press conference. There are many reasons why your Principal might need to speak to or be among the public, and it's your job to see that he stays safe.

Depending on the situation, there may well be a few levels of security already in place, making your job a little easier. This might include police, who may or may not be armed. The building or area that you are in may well have its own security personnel. None of this security should be taken for granted, but of course it can help the overall protective effort. Your security will always be enhanced if you liaise with these people beforehand. At some events, you may not be the only protective team working that day, and you may have Close Protection Officers from different teams tripping over each other. Whilst other teams may help you secure the area, never be in any doubt that other security teams have absolutely no interest in protecting your Principal – that's what you're being paid for.

Barriers

Whenever you can employ a physical barrier you should do so. Good physical barriers include things like all raised platforms. The theory is that if all the good guys are on the platform, the height of the platform is an obstacle, and the bad guy has to overcome it to get to the good guys. The platform might be very high and physically armoured or it could be just as stage, a few feet off the ground. Either way, the obstacle may stop an attack or at least slow it down and give the security time to react.

Another physical barrier is the speaker's podium. Of course, this can be armoured as well as bristling with microphones. A good wide one will cover most of your Principals vital organs.

The physical barriers such as ropes and hurdles can be surprisingly effective at keeping a safe distance between your Principal and the crowd. At a book signing, a very wide desk that the author can sit at can maintain a safe distance between him and his fans. Strategically placed furniture and Close Protection Officers will ensure that anyone who wants to physically attack the author has to negotiate the wide desk first. This can, of course, make it a little harder on the attacker and buy the Close Protection Officer a little time to react.

Vetting the crowds

Unless your barrier is big and bullet-proof it will not stop a determined attacker. You must be constantly scanning the crowd and assessing the threat. You need to be getting the requisite eye contact and looking at people's hands. What are their eyes saying? What are they focused on? What are they holding? Are their hands in their pockets? What is in that bag? What's in the pocket? Having one or two people away from the Principal and covertly scanning the crowd provides a good chance of seeing something is amiss.

Longer range attacks

When working with crowds it is important not to get too short-sighted and completely forget about long-range attacks. If your threat assessment implies that your Principal might be at risk from a professional with a rifle, then vantage points that may be used by a sniper should be observed. In addition, you should ensure that you provide plenty of hard cover and body cover to at least make a sniper's target acquisition difficult.

Receiving lines

We have frequently seen on TV lots of people waiting in line to shake the hand of someone important. The receiving line may snake past your Principal, who remains static, or your Principal might move along a static receiving line. Very often, receiving lines are well planned in advance and you have knowledge of everyone in the line. On other occasions, however, you might not know anyone in the line. It is a good idea to have a team member moved down the line ahead of the Principal while the Bodyguard remains close to the Principal as he moves down along the line. If you have the manpower, another person can be behind the line but moving with the Principal can give heightened security without the profile being raised too high. Study the people in the line. If anyone has criminal intentions you won't have long to react, so you must be ready.

Public toilets

You and your Principal will use public toilets more than you might imagine. Toilets on aircraft, restaurants, theatre and public houses are all public. Normally toilets are the quietest part of a building and are often not covered by CCTV. Because of this they can be the favourite haunts of all types of undesirable from soliciting gays and heterosexuals, to common criminals. Whenever your Principal uses public toilets you should ensure that he or she has adequate protection.

When working with a team someone should always have responsibility for the toilets that your Principal might use. He should count people in and count them out again, so that should the Principal use the toilet he knows exactly how many people are in there. This security team member can follow the Principal into the toilets and know exactly what he might expect to find.

When working in a one-on-one situation, checking toilets can be a little more troublesome. If you are a female operative looking after a female Principal then going to the toilet together will not to raise your profile because women go to the toilet together all the time! Men do not. If two men are bursting for the toilet, the chances

Close Protection Officers can spend a lot of time pounding Hotel Corridors like this one

are that one will go first and then the other. A male Bodyguard with a male Principal may feel uncomfortable if they both use the toilet at the same time, but you just have to get over your embarrassment and go along with him. Once in the toilet, if there is no one there, then of course you can maybe give him some space. Don't stray too far. If you leave him in there, other people may enter and you will have to follow them in.

Hotels

I know Close Protection Officers who spend much of their time in hotels. The countries and cities might change regularly, but they are always pounding a hotel corridor somewhere and room service has become a way of life. Some Principals travel the world extensively. Their travel accommodation can be anything from short-term lets of large houses or even yachts, but mostly they stay in luxury hotels, that can be found in almost every country of the world, even some of the poorest.

When renting property, security is treated just like any other residence, but hotels throw up a whole load of security issues. That is because we will rarely have exclusive use of a luxury hotel. We may rent a whole floor to the hotel but it will still have lots of other guests and public areas that will require your attention. Securing a hotel is a very common task for the Close Protection team and is rather more complicated than 'sitting outside the Principal's room'. We will discuss this in more detail below.

> TREAT THE HOTEL STAFF WELL AND YOU WILL BE REWARDED. THEY CAN DO SO MUCH TO HELP YOU AND YOU NEED THEM ON YOUR SIDE

Choosing the hotel

When carrying out pre-visit advance work, you might get to choose the hotel that your Principal will stay in. However what constitutes a secure hotel, as far as you are concerned, might not meet the expectations of a Principal who may well sometimes put luxury before security, often assuming that luxury and security go together. In some hotels, this might be true but in all the others, security is a compromise and you must put measures in place so that the Principal can enjoy a luxurious and secure environment. If you do get to choose, then look for a hotel that is quieter than most. The less people around the more chance you have of noticing something not quite right. A quiet hotel can make your surveillance detection a little easier.

The hotel entrance and the outside area

Care and vigilance must be employed outside the hotel with places like adjoining buildings that might share roof space (very common in many European cities). Overlooking buildings can also be a problem as can underground car parks.
The hotel entrance is always very important. You should choose a hotel that will

enable you to have speedy embus and debus procedures and, ideally, the entrance should not be overlooked. This is easily achieved in country house hotels but city centre hotels often have entrances right there on the pavement. Experience has shown us that entering and leaving the hotel are the most dangerous times. Is the front door the safest exit? Is there a more protected exit you could use? You should have parking facilities not only for secure storage of your vehicles but somewhere to enable you to wait for your Principal prior to a road move. In city centre hotels, where parking is often at a premium, it is not uncommon to have to pay large amounts of cash to the hotel porter to ensure that your parking bays remain free.

Cooperating with the staff

Experience has shown that the best security is achieved with the full co-operation of the hotel staff, especially the Security Manager and the Hall Porter. You will not get anything from these people by demanding it. They are probably used to meeting VIPs much more important than the person you're looking after. They will have been involved with many security operations and they will understand your concerns. Working with the hotel staff is much better than trying to work against them because you will not win. These people carry much weight and authority in a hotel; you most definitely want them on your side. You get them on your side by being courteous, respectful and seeking their advice.

Most security managers understand that your only concern is the safety and security of your Principal. Very often, they will do all in their power to assist you. You must understand that the hotel security manager has to balance your requests with the safety of all the guests in the hotel and ensure that your security measures do not unduly interfere with any of the other paying guests' enjoyment of the hotel.

Hotels like having VIPs to stay as it does wonders for their business. The Close Protection Officer can easily get used to being treated like a VIP himself. Of course you can enjoy the facilities that the hotel has to offer but just don't forget your reason for your being there!

The security of the hotel itself

It is rare for you to find yourself with enough manpower to effectively secure the whole hotel, but if you are in a position to do so then do it. Essentially we secure as much as we can, concentrating of course on the bits that our Principal is occupying at the time. Have someone at each entrance, strategically placed to notice any dubious entrants; obviously, these officers must have instant communications to the BG and VIP suite. Surveillance detection zones can be established depending of course on the threats that you face.

Choosing the room

Select a suite that offers the best 'natural' security even though this often isn't the best suite in the hotel. The suite should be high enough not to be vulnerable to a brick or grenade thrown through the window. This usually means the third floor or higher but not so high that the city emergency services cannot get a ladder to you in the event of your being trapped by fire. How do you know how high they can reach? Call and ask them. Unfortunately, this rules out penthouse suites in some of the larger hotels so if your Principal insists that you stay on the hundred and twenty-first floor then make sure you study the chapter on hotel fire very carefully!

Building a good rapport with the hotel staff can secure you a good parking slot. Though in some hotels it will still cost you a small fortune

A suite at the end of a corridor is preferable because anyone approaching it needs to have a reason to do so. If there are rooms beyond yours then people will be walking past your Principal's room and this can make security less effective.

You must ensure that the suite is not overlooked by other buildings or share a balcony with another room. If this is impossible then you should take the necessary precautions and ensure that your Principal is aware of this weakness in the security perimeter. The use of curtains or blinds can help.

Securing the room

The Principal's suite should always be searched thoroughly before occupation. Make sure that once searched, no member of the hotel staff is granted access without being accompanied and monitored.

A member of the security team needs to be in the corridor 24 hours a day. This will be hard on the feet as well as the mind and wherever possible it is a good idea for these officers to have a chair. Also, if you can get away with a table which restricts the width of the corridor you will have a pretty good setup to control and monitor the access and egress from the Principal suite.

The control room

If the stay in the hotel is going to be more than one night, the team should have a control room. This should be directly opposite – or at least have a line of sight – to the Principal's room. You should arrange for all deliveries to the suite to be first delivered to the control room. If you are using a mobile alarm and CCTV system, then they can be monitored by the ops room or the guy in the corridor.

You may find that it is your personal accommodation/room that becomes the ops room. This can be through budget restraints or just the hotel room's lay out. This can be a pain at times and if you're busy it can be difficult to catch up on sleep. But at least you are always at the sharp end and always know what is going on!

Hotel fire safety precautions and procedures

"Fire!" A word that when screamed at the top of your voice can strike fear and panic into almost everyone. For there is something very primeval about fire, one of the great dual-edged swords of civilisation; when we have it under our control to warm and cook for us, we can't imagine living without it. But when fire is out of control we have every right to be very

SLOWLY WALK THE ROUTE FROM YOUR ROOMS TO THE EXITS. IMAGINE THE CORRIDOR FILLED WITH SMOKE.

scared of it. It will burn us to a crisp, or kill us with a deadly gas. It will destroy buildings with more devastation than the biggest bomb.

Whenever you stop in a hotel or other large building, with or with out your Principal, uppermost in your threat appreciation must be fire. Fire safety is your responsibility. You might be in an excuse for a hotel in some third world country with little or no fire precautions, or in a luxury hotel that you might find in London, Paris or New York. Sadly, even in developed countries, death caused by fire is one of the largest causes of accidental injury and death.

You must have a plan

You must have a plan to escape a building in the event of fire or smoke. Everyone needs to be made aware of the plan; this includes your Principal and his family. Your plan cannot be generic; it must be specific to the building you are in. You must have a plan of the hotel in your mind; you should know how many floors there are and the general layout.

Starting with your own room, is there fire-fighting equipment in the room? Is it serviceable? Check the inspection dates and the pressure gauges of extinguishers. Look for the fire instructions. Be very wary if you cannot find any! Read them. Do they make sense? Are they just a generic notice or is it specific to the hotel. Is the muster/evacuation point the best one? Look out of the window. Is this a viable way to escape? If you or your Principal jumped would you survive the fall? What obstacles are under the window? Do the windows open enough for you or your Principal to get out? If the windows won't open make a note of what you can break them with. Does your mobile phone work in the room? If it does not, can you direct dial from

In undeveloped countries a few sand buckets might be the extent of the fire fighting equipment especially at villas and hotels!

the landline in an emergency? Ensure that you know how to turn off the fan that delivers air into the room via the air conditioning. Are these vents sealable to stop smoke entering? What could you seal them with?

You need to find the two nearest fire exits from yours and the Principal's room. Use the map that most hotels will have fixed to wall inside your room. But don't take the map for granted; have a good look round for any route that you could use out of the building in an emergency.

Slowly walk the route from yours and the Principal's rooms to the exits. Imagine the corridor filled with smoke. No, go on. Really imagine it. You're probably going to be on your belly, crawling under the smoke. How are you going to find the exit? You should count the doorways and corridors and any obstacles and commit them to memory. The whole route to the exit should be walked, along corridors and downstairs. Look for any obstacles and commit the route to memory. On your route, note the nearby fire alarms and fire extinguishers or fire hoses. If there are none visible, you must call the hotel management and ask where they are. When they tell you, go and verify that the equipment is actually there and is serviceable.

Just because a door has a sign that says Fire Exit, do not assume that it is an exit. Fire exits can be vulnerable areas when it comes to theft or the illicit access of prostitutes or staff, etc. I have found many fire doors that have been locked for security reasons. do not take exits for granted. OPEN THEM. It will probably have a sign saying that it is alarmed, IGNORE THIS AND OPEN IT ANYWAY. Very often, they are not alarmed. If it turns out that they are, it doesn't matter too much. Just apologise to the security officer that comes running and explain what you are doing. Nine times out of ten, there'll be no problem. When I have done this, as soon as the security is sure that you are not a crook but a security professional doing a job then you will be okay. In fact I have struck up some good relationships with security officers and hotel managers that I have met when they have come chasing me after I had checked that fire exits really are exits.

This routine must be carried out with all the escape routes at your disposal. If your quickest and best route is blocked by fire, you need to know your secondary exit as well as the first.

If there is a hotel fire

Your first priority in the event of a fire is evacuation; you should only fight a fire that you are very confident of extinguishing. If you suspect a fire – even if you are slightly suspicious of any smell that smells even remotely like smoke – then you should call the hotel operator immediately. Give your name, room numbers, and a brief description of the situation. Your Principal should be briefed to do exactly the same but impress upon him to alert you also if you are not there with him.

If you are trapped by fire in your room

Always feel the door with the back of your hand. If the door or the knob is hot do not open it. You are trapped in the room and it may well be much safer to remain there than try and evacuate. There is plenty that you can do to increase your chances of survival in this situation.

Your first priority is to let someone know that you are in the room. Use the hotel landline or your mobile phone; ensure that the emergency services know exactly where you are. You can signal to them by hanging out a large, light-coloured item such as a towel, bedsheet or bathrobe. If there is smoke coming into your room, open the window just enough to let fresh air in and the smoke out. Do not break the window unless it is absolutely necessary because heavier smoke may begin to enter from outside and you may want to shut it later. Rip curtains down. They may catch fire from flames on the outside or hamper your exit through a window in an escape. Fill the bath with water. Get wet towels and sheets and place them all around the door or anywhere else where smoke might be entering. Remember that air-conditioning vent and remember how you decided you were going to seal it!

Check the door and walls frequently. If they are hot, throw copious amounts of water on them; use your ice bucket or kettle, or maybe fashion a bucket from a bath towel. It is imperative that you try to remove the heat from the door, floor and walls and lots of water can do this and buy you precious minutes. If smoke is still entering the room, a wet towel over your nose and mouth will help filter the smoke

Do not jump from the room unless you are sure that it is survivable and only then as a very last resort. A fall from even low heights can cause serious injury or death. Continue to protect yourself from the fire in the ways mentioned above and keep signalling from your window for help.

If you can escape from the room

If the door is not hot, get on the floor and slowly open but be ready to close it quickly should you see smoke entering your room. If you think your exit is clear then evacuation is always best. Ensure that you and the Principal stay low to avoid smoke and odourless but deadly carbon monoxide. Now you will be thankful that you have already been through the evacuation in your mind as you count the number of doors, corridors and obstacles to your exit. Proceed down the stairs as quickly as you can. Use the handrail and with luck you will reach your exit, with the warm feeling that you know it is open because you have been there before and checked. If on your way out you come across smoke in the stairwell then you should retreat and when you get to a smoke-free area you should escape, if possible, via your secondary route. If all routes out are blocked then you should retreat to the safest area that you can find and carry out the drills that are outlined in the above paragraph if you are trapped by fire in your room.

Summary

Much of the security that you provide whilst on the road will be 'off the cuff' you will make it up as you go along. This is OK and in fact it is essential for you to be able to do this. However you should never forget the importance of having a proper plan. If you can get advance work done then this is infinitely better, than 'cuffing it' even if you are an expert at improvisation.

Fire is a common killer and respects no one. Fire plans and evacuation drills must be in place for all buildings where you are going to stay. And if you are staying anywhere for any length of time then establish an intelligent surveillance detection program.

Trains Boats and Planes

Many Principals are rarely in any one place for long. A hectic business and social schedule can mean a lot of travel by different means. It isn't uncommon for a Principal to finish 'work' in London or New York and then travel thousands of miles just for a few days with his family, returning to the city just as quickly as he left. Travel can place the Protection Officer with plenty of problems to overcome; we will discuss the main forms of transport below:

Trains

It is becoming increasing rare for the rich and famous to use the train for long distance travel. Even the British Royal Train is in danger of being scrapped because it is so rarely used. However, you may well find yourself on a long distance train in Europe and America, where they are more common and because of the greater distances involved. They are more effective than those in the UK, especially those that travel through the night and offer sleeping accommodation.

When travelling by train you should always arrange in advance for seating. Some companies just issue tickets and the seats are taken on a first-come-first-served basis. This can make it difficult for a party larger than two to be seated together. If you can pre-book seats then you must do so. Whenever possible sit in a block at the end of the compartment. If money isn't a problem then book a separate compartment and guard it accordingly. Luggage on trains is much more vulnerable to theft than it is on other forms of transport and arrangements need to be made to look after it.

In This Chapter

All about travelling with your Principal and providing effective security en route

Familiarise yourself with the emergency equipment on the train. Wherever you are on the train, you should always know where your nearest emergency exit and communication cords are located. You should also know the whereabouts of fire fighting equipment and if other kits are available, such as axes and torches. When things go wrong, you do not want to waste precious time asking yourself where you saw that emergency torch!

On sleeper trains, it is important that someone remains awake at all times to guard against any opportunist thefts or attacks. If the team is big enough then it's best done in pairs as it can be extremely difficult (though not impossible!) to remain one hundred percent alert when you are dog-tired and in a warm and gently rocking carriage. If you do fall asleep, you won't be the first Close Protection Officer that has woken his Principal just as the train is pulling into a station. He won't thank you as he struggles to put his socks on while the guard is blowing his whistle and preparing to leave your destination with you still onboard!

Underground trains

Many of you will find yourself on underground trains with Principals that like them for the convenience they can offer. Depending upon which country you are in, the underground railway may well be the safest place to travel; it can also be the riskiest. Parts of the same network may well be safer than others. You need to find this information and put it to good use; the local police are a good place to start. Almost

Working the Moscow Underground is much like any other in the world

all mass transit underground trains from the London Tube and Paris Metro to Hong Kong's MTR are all very busy at rush hour. Depending on your assignment, you can use the anonymity that these crowds provide, but be warned: it can be difficult for a large team to stay together without being conspicuous, especially when the crowds are at their peak and everyone seems to be using shin kicks and elbows to get on the train.

Don't get caught out with escalators and lifts. You need to be in the same lift as your Principal. He won't appreciate spotting you just as the lift doors close, leaving you standing outside! With all those people around you must stay close, very close, or you will be separated.

When these trains are busy, there will often be standing room only. You will be invading your Principal's personal space as the train fills with even more travellers. Whether your Principal finds a seat or remains standing you should surround him and then try to give him his own little oasis of calm in the area you are providing in the middle.

Travelling with a Principal on these trains is hard work for the Close Protection Officer, and he needs to be at a very high state of awareness throughout. In all countries, some parts of the underground train network seem to be a magnet for undesirables, such as professional pickpockets, hooligans, aggressive beggars, drunks, and the mentally ill, so be prepared to meet all of them. It can be very stressful but thankfully, most underground journeys are quite short.

Boats

Close Protection Officers can find themselves on a couple of different boats, but mostly they will work on private yachts. These can be anything from a small boat with just a few berths, a galley and a crew of one or two, to very large and imposing crafts that are anything up to 500 feet long, with large crews that might include maintenance workers, catering staff and cleaners, along with the regular sailing crew. You might also find yourself on a cruise ship, where there are hundreds of both crew and passengers.

Cruise ships

These days the large cruise ship is just not exclusive enough for most of the world's super rich. Even ships with the status of the QE2 are rarely used by VIPs with Close Protection Officers. I have seen extensive writings about providing protection on these large vessels, and apart from a very few basics, providing security on a large cruise ship is best treated just like regular work. Your Principal will have a residence (cabin) that needs securing and this is best treated just as any hotel room. Visits to places on the ship, such as restaurants, the gym, swimming pool or shops can be approached just as if you were not onboard. Just as in a hotel, you would ensure that you are aware of the emergency evacuation procedures, and these may be a little more complex, involving, for example, lifeboats and life vests. Cruise ships are like a small city, in which passengers are encouraged to forget their troubles and relax, once they are onboard. It is natural for passengers on vacation to let their guard down but the Close Protection Officer must not. The large cruise ship is not the sterile environment that it might appear; crimes and accidents do happen onboard. One of the most feared sea crimes is that of a pirate attack. However, the large cruise ships are rarely targeted because it is almost impossible to board a cruise ship when it is in open water. The sides of the ship are too high and offer no easy access for pirates.

Cabin security

Always enter your Principal's cabin before he does. Check inside the bathroom and balcony area before leaving him inside. Don't assume that your cabin is as secure as a hotel. Many people have keys to your cabin and while you and the Principal are elsewhere, your Principal's cabin door may be left standing open for hours while the cleaning crews or cabin steward services the room. A cabin door's locks are often outdated and are not re-keyed as frequently as hotel rooms. Make sure your Principal uses all locks on the cabin door including the night latch. Make sure he never opens the cabin door to strangers. Just as you would in a hotel, ensure that you and your Principal protect both cabin key and cabin number. A dishonest crew or passengers will look for the opportunity to snatch a loose key or one that is left unattended. When in port, be sure to leave your key with the registration desk before disembarking. Always use the ship's safe for valuables, especially cash, jewellery and passports. Always lock your cabin door and ensure that your Principal locks his. Never leave cash in your room. Remind your Principal to do the same.

Stay in public areas

Once you are onboard and out to sea, don't assume that you are totally safe from criminal acts. While there is little danger of an outside criminal robbing or attacking you onboard ship, crimes are just as easily committed by crewmembers or by fellow passengers. Cruise lines are notorious for employing transient and seasonal employees at low wages. Because of this, turnover is high and the cruise lines often struggle to keep a ship fully staffed. This leads to just about anyone being hired when they are undermanned. While many of the crew will be hardworking and honest, you cannot assume that the ship has properly screened that nice cabin cleaner or the friendly waiter. Don't think that nice clean uniforms equates to nice, honest staff. Stay awake!

You should only stay in public areas; straying into poorly lit, private areas of the ship makes your Principal highly vulnerable. I once worked for a Principal that liked to play cards with the crew of a large cruise ship. Throughout the night, there was lots of cash, booze and undesirable-looking characters in the crew area and it was hard work looking after him in this environment.

On some large cruise ships, there are security personnel who patrol in plain clothes. You may well spot them before they notice you. If you become known to the security personnel, they can be a great help with advice and assistance.

Even if you have travelled on the same ship before, you should always attend (and get your Principal to attend) the ship's lifeboat drill. Learn the best route from your cabin to the lifeboats and fire exits, no matter where you are on board – casino, cinema, bar, etc. You should always know where the best route is to muster stations and where lifejackets are located.

Lifejackets can be stolen as cruise souvenirs. Always check to make sure there are enough life jackets in yours and your Principal's cabin. If you need more, ask your cabin steward to provide them.

Always use the handrails; decks can be slick and it takes a while to get your sea legs.

Being at sea can lure you into a false sense of security. Even though the crime incident rate is lower than on dry land, there can still be predators on board, especially sexual ones. If you are responsible for the safety of teenagers on board, then be very wary of places such as the ship's nightclubs, casinos, swimming pools and jacuzzis. These are favourite spots for those looking for a victim.

Expect to meet lots of intoxicated passengers. Food and liquor consumption peaks onboard ships and this brings out the worst in people who are not used to it. Just because passengers are dressed up to the nines doesn't mean they will act appropriately or not be overly aggressive to you or your Principal.

Being on board a cruise ship is anything but a relaxing time for the Bodyguard – not that there ever is a relaxing time!

Private yachts

Much more common than the cruise ships, the private yacht is often an item owned by the super rich users of Close Protection. Sometimes they will be moored for months and your task will more 'residence security' or you might find yourself at sea for weeks at a time.

When you are moored, your Principal will probably be using the yacht only as a floating hotel. He may well have parties and invite people onboard and use the yacht as a base for pleasure and business. Security should be a little easier than securing a hotel, especially as your boat will probably have its own secure boarding. Gangplanks should always be raised whenever possible; this will mean that it will probably be raised only late at night. If the port has strict security, then everyone, in theory, will have a reason for being there. Dock areas attract thieves and levels of honesty often relate to levels of opportunity. Suspect everyone and do not make it easy for him/her. Often, the captain will use members of the crew to carry out basic in-port security, but these guys do not make the best security officers; especially as they will, more often than not, still be carrying out their normal crew duties throughout the day and the guard duties will be unpaid extras. Clearly, we would need to question their ability and motivation in this instance. Ideally, if the port is notorious and not easily secured, then an RST should be used to keep a watch on the yacht on a 24-hour basis. Your Principal may baulk at the cost but sometimes this is an absolute necessity. Lights, cameras and an access control system will assist the RST and this will also take a lot of the pressure off of the Bodyguard, who will be able to relax a little between trips out with the Principal.

Because of the fewer crewmembers, it is easier to vet and get to know them than it could ever be on a large cruise ship. Make sure that everyone knows your function. You are responsible for security. You cannot do this to best effect if you are helping to run the yacht so make sure the captain knows that you do not work for him! Otherwise, you might find your self roped into doing things that will restrict your true function. I know of instances where there has been some resentment of security by the crew; the crew work long and hard and it appears to them that security are doing nothing all day. Your communication skills, as well as involving the crew in

Large yachts can offer a level of luxury that the large cruise ships cannot hope to surpass. Complete with a large crew they are capable of sailing anywhere in the world. Often the Principal will meet the boat after it has been positioned. Large yachts can be an attractive target to modern pirates

your emergency plans, should show them how professional you are. On a small yacht, you definitely want the crew on side. If you 'large it' and look down on them, as some prima donnas do, then at the very least you had better employ a food taster!

Pirates

Once he is at sea, the Close Protection Officer cannot afford to relax. Pirates can more easily board a yacht than they can a large cruise ship and a constant watch needs to be made in areas where there is a danger of piracy.

Modern Pirates are nothing like their swashbuckling ancestors. Today's pirate will be armed with Rocket propelled Grenades, machine guns and very fast boats

Global piracy is now one of the biggest threats to world shipping. Large cargo ships, as well as private yachts, are in danger. These threats are very real and in some areas, they easily eclipse the risk of terrorism. Somalia, which is a war-torn country in almost complete anarchy, has fast become one of the world's pirate hot spots, with hundreds of attacks in the last few years.

Today's pirates do not resemble a Hollywood-type, swashbuckling Johnny Depp. Crews are often vicious criminals, who rape, torture and murder as well as plunder. A favoured tactic of Somali pirates is to capture the vessel, along with the crew, and take it to one of their safe havens around Mogadishu. There they hold the hostages and the ship for ransoms of many hundreds of thousands of dollars.

These modern pirates travel in fast powerboats and carry machine guns and rocket-propelled grenades. It isn't enough just to avoid these pirate areas as they have now started to use 'mother ships', so they can sail right out into international waters and then launch their smaller boats when they see a target.

Know your pirates

The best defence is to know your pirates and consider avoiding the areas of highest risk. This may sound obvious but if you research the areas of highest attacks then it is possible to avoid them. Most pirates should be looked upon as armed muggers. When in pirate waters you should always ensure that someone is looking out for approaching craft. Radar will assist with some of the larger craft, but small speedboats can be upon you very quickly, and the mark one eyeball is the best defence.

Safety in numbers

Some people think that there is safety in numbers and a few yachts travelling together might deter some attackers; others think that such a policy makes for richer pickings and may make an attack more likely.

Radios and lights

If you are in an area that may have a risk of piracy, consider restricted use of VHF. However, although pirates are unlikely to have direction-finding equipment, if they hear yachts chatting to each other on VHF they will know you are around somewhere. Lights at night, both navigation lights and the use of any other lights visible from a distance, may attract pirates. Pirates are mostly low-tech opportunist muggers; if they can't see you at night then this may well save you from an attack. That said, you should be aware that it is illegal and dangerous to show no lights.

Guns – to carry weapons or not

This is another contentious issue. Most yachts probably do not carry weapons or if they do, they keep it very quiet. Should you insist your Principal carries weapons? There is no foolproof advice; there have been cases where just showing a gun to following pirates has been enough to stop an attack. In other cases, yacht crews have been killed with their own weapons.

If you do carry weapons, you have to be an expert in their use, and be capable of using them without hesitation. Shotguns are a good choice and can be very effective when repelling boarders but a heavy belt fed machine gun would be better. If this is not possible then an assault rifle would, of course, be very effective. However, it is often illegal. Whatever weapons you choose or have available, it should go without saying that everyone is familiar with them and knows the 'pirate plan'. Instinctively, you will know the best course of action to take if you are suddenly confronted by someone in a small boat, brandishing an anti-tank weapon. Fighting back while you're in a fragile boat can be the very best thing to do or the very worst. I'll leave that one to you and hope you make the right decision.

Is it legal to carry weapons?

In many countries, carrying weapons onboard can place you on the wrong side of the law. In international waters, you might be okay but you can't stay there forever and as soon as you land in a port you may well find that even if you are allowed to carry weapons onboard, there is a legal requirement to declare them. They will probably then be impounded for the duration of your stay at the port.

You must have a pirate plan

You must discuss the event of piracy with the Principal. Some Principals do not want to carry weapons and would rather allow the pirates to steal from them without resistance, hoping that this will leave them unharmed. Having a stash of cash and valuables that can be given to the robbers, separating them from the real wealth, can be a good idea. If you show the pirates a safe that has some cash, jewellery and everyone's passports, you can easily convince them that this is all the stash when, in reality, the real valuables are hidden elsewhere.

If your plan is to fight back, then make sure that the weapons are accessible and that everyone who may have to use one gets to practise using it. You should practise your anti-boarding drills as often as you can. If the crew are going to be used, ensure they practise as much as you do. When out on an empty sea, consider letting everyone get some shooting practice at a target you are towing. This can be good fun and keep everyone familiar with the weapons. Ensure that they are cleaned thoroughly after any practice; you should so this yourself. Damp sea air and weapons just do not go together, and if you do need to depend on these weapons then you want them to work and not jam after they are first used. This, of course, could be disastrous.

You are not on holiday

Working in Close Protection on boats can be great fun, but it is hard work. It can sometimes be difficult to remember that you are not on holiday. This is especially so when on the smaller boats; you will very often be roped into taking the kids snorkelling, or teaching them to dive. When you're out at sea you may well dine with the Principal and his family. On some yachts, you might find yourself surrounded by sunscreen and bikinis. You need to show professional restraint and not get involved.

I remember a guy working in the South of France, let's call him Mike, who after a party left his Principal's boat late at night to see a girl he had met earlier. She was living in a yacht moored nearby. He did not anticipate his Principal getting up so early and seeing him as he swam back to the yacht in the morning. He tried to bluff it and said that he had been for an early swim, but the Principal had seen him leave the other yacht. He was in London Heathrow and jobless by lunchtime. REMEMBER, YOU'RE NOT ON HOLIDAY. YOU'RE WORKING.

> WORKING ON A BOAT IN SUNNY CLIMATES IT IS EASY TO START ENJOYING YOURSELF. THIS IS OK JUST DON'T ENJOY YOURSELF TOO MUCH!

Aircraft

Air travel is one of the safer ways to get from A to B, and, apart from road travel, it is the most common. Your Principal can fly on a multitude of scheduled flights to and from almost anywhere in the world. There are also helicopters for shorter hops and many more of the rich and famous own their own aircraft or have time-shares in one. When your Principal travels by air, you need to know a little about air travel to ensure that there are no unpleasant surprises on route.

Private Aircraft

As far as security planning is concerned, the best and most secure air travel arrangements occur when your Principal is using a private aircraft or one of which he has exclusive use. These aircraft are smaller and most of them fly slower and lower than commercial flights, but by removing the long check-in and baggage claim times, they can prove to be quicker overall. If the aircraft belongs to the Principal and cost is not an issue then the benefits are plentiful,

> **The pilot and other crew can be vetted and checked out just like any other employee**
>
> **Queues for check-ins are avoided**
>
> **Long check-in times can be slashed**
>
> **Choice of take-off slots, which can be brought forward to or dropped back (often without penalties) if needed**
>
> **Your Principal has complete control over routes and itineraries**
>
> **Baggage weight restrictions may well be more generous (can be more restrictive if the aircraft is full)**
>
> **Getting weapons on private aircraft can be much les problematic than on public airlines. But getting them off in an alien country can be just as fraught and sometimes impossible.**

Commercial air travel

Unless your Principal is very famous and influential, you will have to check in with all the other passengers. You may often be travelling 'first' or 'business' class alongside your Principal which is great. There will be other times when your Principal leaves you and the rest of the team to cope with 'cattle' class. He will be stretching out with complimentary champagne while you will be cramped in a seat with a crying kid next to you and complimentary peanuts if you're lucky!

First class or cattle!

If your Principal is in first class and you are in economy – which is more common than you might imagine – it is unlikely that you will get to see your boss until baggage reclaim. You should always fight your corner and do your best to convince your boss that you need to be up there in first class alongside him. Cost will very often win the day though, and if the Principal feels safe in the aircraft where everyone has been searched twice, then off to cattle you will go.   This is not a disaster if the first class area is just a curtained-off area at the front of the aircraft. You can get a seat that will put you just a few feet and a shout away from your Principal. If the first class area is on another level of the aircraft, you are not going to hear a shout for assistance so you may as well just get on and watch the in-flight movie for all the good your doing. Just consider it as a positioning flight, getting you to your destination, where you can resume your Close Protection duties properly.

If members of the team are going economy while the Bodyguard and/or the Principal are in first or business, then get at least one of the team to check in very early so that you have someone airside as soon as you, and/or the Principal checks in and goes airside. Airside must be considered the safest part of the airport. So, as soon as possible, pass through the 'departures' gate to airside. In theory everyone, even the staff, will have been searched before they enter airside but don't let this fool you into relaxing, even for a moment. Airside is not the sterile area you might think. It has its dangers, with crooks, drunks and photographers, who might want to do you or your Principal harm.

Suspect everyone

It's worth noting that almost everyone who has ever hijacked an aircraft has been searched through to airside! You should be aware of suspicious activity in and around your immediate surroundings. You should also inform the proper authorities if you are concerned about an unattended item or suspicious activity in and around the area. If your Principal buys any valuables in duty free, ensure that these are packed properly into the hand luggage; do not leave them in the duty free plastic carrier bag as everyone has one of those. It goes without saying that you should never leave your or your Principal's luggage unattended even for a second, because that's all it takes to steal it or stash contraband in it.

Getting the best seats

When flights are anticipated, a must-see website is www.seatguru.com, which holds information about seating arrangements and the layout of most of the world's aircraft and airlines. Seats are colour coded and are rated with regard to size, comfort, spacing, legroom, laptop power connection, reclinability and noise, etc. Many airlines these days allow you to pre-book seats; some even let you check in 24 hours before your flight, using the internet! If your airline doesn't allow advance check-in then it will pay to be early in the check-in queue so that you can choose the best seats available at the time. This facility from seat guru will ensure that nothing is left to chance and that you can occupy the seats which allow you to do your job more effectively. It is rare for you to be unable to call the

SeatMap Key

- Good Seat
- Be Aware
- Poor Seat
- Power Port
- Exit Location
- G Galley
- L Lavatory
- C Closet

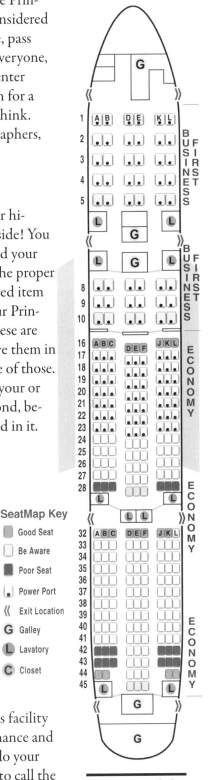

SeatGuru Aircraft Plan

airline and get the aircraft type for your flight, but even if you are unsure as to which aircraft you will be boarding till you actually get to check in, www.seatguru.com works on many mobile phones. So you can check your seat suitability right there in the check-in queue.

Don't hire cars from the airport.

If you are landing at an unfamiliar airport then it is best to use a taxi to your hotel or venue. Airports attract criminals that can spot a hire car a mile away. The criminal likes to take advantage of people when their guard is down. No matter how good you think you are, you are vulnerable if you are driving an unfamiliar car, tired after a long flight, or in another time zone in another country. You may also be on the wrong side of the road or trying to read a map. One thing is certain; you are not giving security your best attention. Especially if you are 'one-on-one.' It is much better to get away from the airport in a cab, with only security to worry about. Then you can hire a car once you are at the hotel. If you talk to the hotel in advance, then the car will be right there waiting for you. Doing it this way is much better when you need to return to the airport. Leaving the car at the hotel and hiring a cab to the airport is much safer. You are saved the hassle of the large queues, which are invariably found at the hire car returns section.

Air hijacking

Hijackings have become less common since 9/11. Governments and airlines are now applying strict security measures to all types of air travel, both domestic and international. Any hijack situation is extremely dangerous; you have the risk of being shot by the terrorists and possibly by the rescuers, so keep your head down – both physically and metaphorically. It will enhance your chances of survival.

You should never own up to being a Bodyguard. At best, you will be regarded with suspicion and you may well be looked upon as a soldier that is expendable! In a hijack situation, you are much better being the personal assistant or colleague. Whatever you choose, make sure that you and your Principal have the same story. A few do's and don'ts for hijack situations are as follows:

> **Do not assume all hijackers identify themselves at the beginning of a hijacking. Hijackers may keep an eye on passenger activity by holding one or more of their number in reserve among the ordinary passengers. So suspect everyone.**

> **Avoid making eye contact with the terrorists, especially in the first frantic minutes when the hijackers are not confident they have total control of the aircraft.**

> **You must listen very carefully to the hijackers and follow their instructions explicitly.**

If the hijackers start to collect valuables and passports, do not hide or attempt to withhold anything.

You must try to be as quiet and as inconspicuous as possible. Don't ask the terrorists for anything, not even to go to the toilet.

Don't talk to other passengers unless it is absolutely necessary. Do not give the hijackers any reason to think you are plotting something. Only speak when absolutely necessary or when spoken to by a terrorist.

Do not refuse the terrorist's offer of food, drink or tobacco, but consume them only in moderation. If you are offered an alcoholic drink, accept but do not drink it. It is much better to be sober in such a situation!

WHEN TRAVELLING ENSURE THAT YOU HAVE NO DOCUMENTS SUCH AS VISAS OR ID CARDS THAT IDENTIFY YOU AS A BODYGUARD

Try to remain as calm as possible throughout the hijacking and conserve your energy. If the situation is prolonged then try to snatch sleep when you can.

Prepare yourself psychologically for the possibility that the hijackers will, at some point, question you at gunpoint and/or under other forms or pressure.

Mentally rehearse a plausible and unremarkable account of your employment and the specific reason for your being on the aeroplane. Remember – never say the word 'Bodyguard'.

Surviving the flight in the event of an emergency

According to statistics, two-thirds of people involved in air crashes survive. As many as one-third of those who do die might have survived if they had known what to do. You and your Principal must know what to do.

Seat belts

Use your seat belt. You should wear it without exception whenever you are seated. Make sure your Principal wears his. It's not big or clever not to wear it. Turbulence can occur with little or no warning and many injuries are caused by it every year. As soon as the plane touches down, you will hear lots of seat belt clicks as the idiots unclip them. Collisions on the ground are more common than those in the air. Keep your seat belt on until the sign says you can remove it. The flight stewards have a duty to ensure that everyone has their belt on when the pilots request this. A good tip if you need to get some sleep on a flight is to put your blanket over your body, and then buckle the seat belt over the blanket. Later, during the flight, if the seat belt light comes on then the flight attendants will be able to see you are buckled up without having to wake you.

The safety demonstration

Always watch the in-flight safety demo. As you do so, mentally rehearse yourself doing the things that you are being shown. Imagine putting on the life jacket, take a moment to visualise yourself reaching under your seat and putting it on as you have been shown. Pay particular attention to the oxygen masks and how they work. Read the emergency card so you know it by heart. Know the crash position.

Check your exits

Check to see where your nearest emergency exit is and take a moment to visualise how you would get to that exit. It might be dark, the attitude of the aircraft might put the exit uphill or down. How many rows of seats are there between you and the exit? You might have to count them in the dark. You have plenty of time before take off. Visualise this now; close your eyes, and really imagine the scene. Imagine that you are in a smoke-filled aircraft, hear the screams, and count the rows to your exit. Performing it in your mind will make it so much easier to do it for real! Then do this again for your secondary exit. How many rows to that one? Let the Principal know what is going to happen. "If we need to get off in a hurry, sir, we will be using this exit, and if that is blocked we will be using that one." Some Principals will tell you that they do not want to know anything like that in advance, but you should always involve the Principal whenever you can.

Many of your passengers that survive a crash will be in shock; some will panic and not listen to any instructions that you might give them, while others will stay still as if in a trance. Because you have visualised it, you will be much more 'switched on' than most of them, even the crew, so you can get on with saving yourself and your Principal. Interviews with survivors of air crashes confirm that the common element among the overwhelming majority was that they had a specific plan of action and then when things went wrong, they followed it.

If the plane is crashing

If you are certain you are crashing then you should ensure that there is nothing in a pocket – a pen for example, can harm you. Remove spectacles and empty your bladder (You may have done so already!) This considerably reduces the chance of internal injuries. You should always travel with a personal smoke hood. If you don't have one, wet a handkerchief, headrest cover or blanket, so that if there's smoke after impact, you can hold it over your mouth. If no other liquids are handy, use your urine if you have any left. Cover your head, preferably with a pillow. Then, either cross your arms over your calves and grab your ankles or put your palms forward and cross your wrists between your head and the seat in front of you. In the latter position, it's best to slide your feet forward until they touch the seat leg or the under-seat baggage in front. In doing so, your legs are less likely to snap forward on impact. If you're lucky enough still to be alive, then the chances of you surviving are still slim until you get out of the aircraft.

As soon as the plane comes to a complete stop, undo your seat belt, get out of your seat and move quickly to the exit (How many seat rows?) If you are sitting with your Principal then take control of him and take him with you. If your Principal chose to save money by putting you in coach whilst he was in First Class then it is about now that he will start regretting this! If you can get to him to help him evacuate then do so, but the chances are you will only be able to save yourself while your Principal ponders the first principle of personal security!

Don't take anything with you; you'll need your hands free to keep your balance in the aisle as you step over bodies and luggage, or find yourself being pushed from behind by panic-stricken passengers. If the aisle is blocked, walk over the backs of the seats. Don't waste your time crawling on the floor to avoid any smoke; you'll only end up being trampled by and/or buried under all the other passengers who are suffocating. But if there is smoke, do keep your head down. You'll know you've arrived at the doors when the floor lights are red rather than white. Do not push the passengers in front of you. You won't get through any faster and this will only increase the chance of people falling and the exit becoming blocked. Once out of the aircraft, move as far away from it as possible.

Summary

Generally speaking, travel can be enjoyable, but it is a stressful time for the Close Protection Officer. You can breathe a huge sigh of relief when a particular trip is over and the Principal is back in his well-secured and monitored residence. But while travelling, you must always expect that someone is out to take advantage of your vulnerability while you're on the move. A lot of planning, coupled with good Dynamic Threat Assessment applied to every aspect of the travel should keep you and your Principal safe.

Those that have not supplied protection while on the move, often scream "Yippee!" when they learn of their first bit of travel, especially if it is to some sunny part of the world. They spend time thinking about sunglasses, tall drinks, sun-cream and the glamour of first-class travel, but the dream soon gives way to the reality, and the reality is that travel security is just damned hard work.

Walking Drills

Providing effective protection when on foot can be a difficult task. Most criminals or terrorists are going to mount an attack when the VIP and the team are at their most vulnerable. Terrorists and criminals carry out threat assessments too. If criminals are targeting your Principal, they will take note of the sophisticated security measures in place at his home and office, such as CCTV and intruder alerts, along with all of the natural security barriers that are in place, such as perimeter fences and brick walls. Naturally they will consider it makes sense to mount the attack when he is most vulnerable and when they are less likely to be caught. Even your most stupid enemy is probably going to wait until you leave all that security behind you and step onto the pavement!

Why walk anywhere?

Apart from when looking after very recluse Principals, most Close Protection Officers will spend more time on the pavement than you might imagine. It doesn't matter whether they are looking after a pop star or a president; they all spend time on the pavement. Once he's on the pavement we not only have to protect our Principal from the 'main' threat but also from anything else that happens on the street. Street crime and accidents occur almost every minute of every day in every city of the world.

High or low profile drills

High profile drills where we are acting as a deterrent are much easier to perform than low profile drills. It is much simpler to show out and look menacing than it is to blend into the background. Four or five guys or girls all wearing the same dark, similar-looking suits can easily look like a uniformed army. Most of the formations that we discuss later in this chapter are suitable for maintaining a high profile, especially when the operatives are dressed the same.

In This Chapter

How to provide effective protection whilst on foot

High and low profile walking drills

Hi profile walking drills

High profile walking drills will invariably mean that you are very close to the Principal. If you are in a populated area, your high-profile drills will attract a lot of attention. Most VIPs – unless they are very famous – can easily walk down a busy street with just one or two low-profile protection officers and be very secure while they do so. If those same officers adopt a high profile then many people on the street (which, of course, includes street criminals and other low life) would notice and be attracted to the Principal. Most Principals do not want to attract this undue attention.

Some Principals crave attention and will do anything to be noticed. Indeed, most of them would not be noticed if they went jogging in Hyde or Central Park early in the morning and took just a couple of low-profile officers to jog with them for protection. When such Principals want to be noticed and maybe photographed, then going jogging mid-morning, surrounded by guys in suits and sunglasses, should get that person the publicity they desire. However along with the good will come the bad. A team of high-profile Bodyguards will attract attention, and some of that attention may well be undesirable, so the team will need to be well-practised and effective.

If you were to sit somewhere and watch the goings on in some of the world's most expensive shopping streets, such as Rodeo Drive, Oxford Street, Champs Elysées or 5th Avenue, you wouldn't have to wait too long before you saw 'a wall of suits'. This might be six or more large and ugly Bodyguards surrounding their charge. The general public, assembled on the street, will know there is a VIP in the vicinity, although it will be difficult for them to catch a glimpse of him or her because they will be well hidden behind a wall of muscle, sunglasses and suit.

Low profile walking drills

If you show Joe Public a picture of a Principal and a Bodyguard walking down the street, Joe should ask the question, "Which one is the Bodyguard?" If your brief is to be inconspicuous and not attract any trouble then the only way you can achieve this is by maintaining a low profile.

The low profile drills are simple: we just need to provide discreet and effective protection while not attracting any undue attention. As soon as Joe Public realises what we are doing, he will notice the Principal and as soon as Joe Public notices him, so might the aforementioned street criminals and low life. It doesn't matter if you are working high or low profile, the Bodyguard will always stay very close to their Principal at all times. Standing slightly behind and to the left or right of the Principal is a high-

> YOU SHOULD NEVER SACRIFICE SECURITY FOR PROFILE. YOU HAVE TO PROVIDE JUST AS MUCH SECURITY BUT MAINTAIN A LOW PROFILE

profile drill and when a low profile is required, the Bodyguard must be up there with the Principal, walking alongside him as if he were a friend or colleague. When the Personal Escort Section is maintaining a low profile, they must act almost as if they were on a surveillance mission. They should never be too close to the Principal to be associated with him. They should always be close enough to react should a situation develop. It must always be remembered that you should never sacrifice security for profile.

It does not matter whether you are providing low or high profile protection. Your Principal will want you there immediately

EMPICS

Clearly, the further you are away from the Principal the lower the profile around him. If you are too far away to react effectively to a threat, the lack of a profile could cost you or your Principal dearly. At the very least, it might cost you your job.

So, when you are on a low-profile walking assignment, you are always trying to balance security with the profile. However, you should always be prepared to raise the profile to maintain the required amount of security if necessary. For the PES, low-profile security in each must be practised regularly if it is to be done well. To do it well is difficult because while you are providing effective protection you are also trying to do the following:

1. **Maintain a low profile with regard to Joe Public.**
2. **Give your Principal confidence by always being in the right place at the right time.**
3. **Show anyone that has you under surveillance that you are providing effective protection – so good, in fact, that you would hope to deter them.**

As you can see, these aims do have some conflict. We need to go unnoticed by some, and others need to see how professional we are, all at the same time. Inexperienced officers find it very hard to keep the profile low and the security high. But a good Close Protection Officer can easily balance the three essential requirements with practice and experience. If the low profile protection is going to fail during the gain-

A Low profile team. Only those in the know will be able to point out the close protection officers. The profile is low but the protection is in place

ing of that experience, it will do so in one of three ways:

1. **The profile will be raised higher than the Principal feels is necessary.**

2. **The Principal feels that he is vulnerable because his security is so far away and the profile is too low.**

3. **The profile has taken priority over the security.**

It is difficult, especially when you are experienced, to maintain a low profile. When you are young, keen and trying to make a good impression, it is all too easy to raise the profile and pile on the security. In some environments, your life can depend on the low profile that you present while moving around unnoticed. If your Principal has asked for a low-profile operation, your breath on his neck might displease him!

Although you are striving for a low profile, you should still ensure that you are providing effective security at the same time. If the Principal looks at or around he needs to be quickly assured that the team are with him, he will do this by trying quickly establish eye contact with a member of the team. If the Principal has too much difficulty in looking for his team, he will think that you are not there and feel vulnerable. If you make him feel vulnerable more than once then you are not going to last too long on the team.

In your quest for a low profile, you must not forget that you may be noticed by third parties. For example, imagine you are trying to keep a discreet distance from your Principal in a large department store. This could create an embarrassing situation if you are mistaken for a shoplifter. Especially if the Principal sees one of his team being questioned by the Police as he leaves the store! You won't receive any thanks from him for that. You must blend in: if you're in a shop, then shop; if you're in a bar, then drink. But do this with the knowledge that you are being watched by your Principal, Joe Public and any criminal or terrorist who might have you under surveillance.

Foot formations

The foot formations are only for high-profile protection. When you are keeping a low profile, we do not use formations at all. Instead, we have a fluid cordon around the Principal. The area that we occupy will dictate where the cordon is wide or closed up. When there are lots of people around, then PES will close up on the Principal but

> FOOT FORMATIONS MUST NOT BE RIGIDLY ADOPTED. SOME OFFER BETTER PROTECTION THAN OTHERS BUT NOT IN ALL ENVIRONMENTS. OTHERS PRESENT A LOWER PROFILE. YOU SHOULD ALWAYS ADAPT THE FORMATION TO YOUR SURROUNDINGS

the profile will remain low *because* of all the other people around you. In a quieter and less populated area, it may be necessary to open the court considerably in order to maintain the low profile. But, of course, not so far that they cannot quickly respond to a situation that might develop.

Walking One on One

Behind and slightly to the right (figure walking 1) if you are right handed and to the left if you are left handed. But this is a high profile position. If you can offer better protection from somewhere else then get there.

Walking 1

Two Person Formation

Figure '*Walking 2*' shows one extra officer the team on the left has the extra member slightly further back this doubles the protection but because he is further away the profile doesn't go up too much. The example on the right shows the third person ahead of the Principal this offers yet more protection especially on the street where it always pays to have someone in front of the Principal. When someone does go in front ensure that they go on the opposite side to the Bodyguard. The Principal can obstruct the Bodyguards view, the second officer will easily compensate for this blind spot.

Walking 2

Three person Formations

Three people can provide very good protection in the figure '*Walking 3*' the team on the left walking down the page have opted to lower the profile by moving ahead

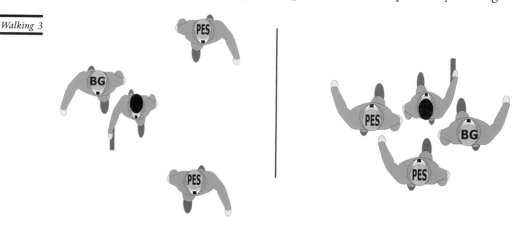

Walking 3

and behind the Principal. In the same diagram the team on the right walking up the page adopt a classic formation. The profile is high but the protection is very good. The more people that you put around the Principal the more that everyone needs to concentrate because the protection officers restrict each others view. Everyone's area of responsibility is pretty obvious and 'tail end Charlie' will spend a lot of time looking behind him.

Five Person Formations

The two most common formations are 'one on one' and the 'full team'. The full team is traditionally includes a four person PES and the Bodyguard. The classic five person formation is the 'Open Box' The name aptly describes the formation except when this formation is actually used on the street the box would rarely look like the one shown, especially as this formation is often used when someone wishes to maintain a low profile. When the box is 'open' the distances between the protection officers will vary according to the Dynamic Threat Assessment. If the threats are low and the Principal wants a low profile then the team could even be on the opposite side of the

Students practising an 'open box' formation, moments before they are attacked.

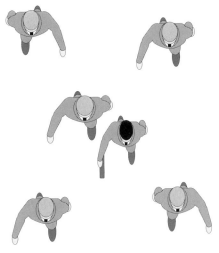

road. The box just provides a fluid cordon of protection that is always surrounding the Principal. When the risk assessment dictates, for example if the Principal walks from a quiet almost unpopulated area into a busy shopping area the box may well close up. If the risk increases then the team may adopt a 'Closed Box' This is where the box is shut up tight. All the protection officers within arms reach of the Principal. The closed box formation offers good protection but the profile is very high and it is uncomfortable for everyone, especially the Principal.

A Closed Box formation

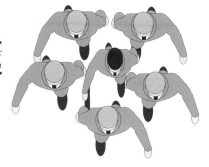

Who Controls the Formation

The short answer is everybody. I know of teams that have covert hand signals that the Bodyguard will give to the team, these signals are for such things as 'close up' and 'go left' etc. This 'signalling' is actually mentioned in the UK security Industry core specification but this is total rubbish. If a team member needs telling then he needs to find another job. A good Close Protection Officer does not need a hand signal he will already be in the best position, reading the situation, performing his own Dynamic Threat Assessments as the drill progresses. He will always be in the right position at the right time.

Look at the numbers of the PES and you will see that their position changes

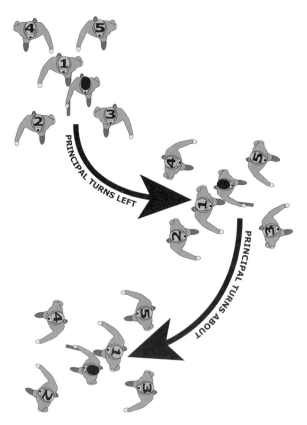

Changing Direction

Remember that the escort section are providing a fluid cordon of protection. If the Principal changes direction this is not followed by everybody on the team shuffling around to get back to their position. If you are the tail end charlie and the Principal turns 180 degrees then you are now on the point.

Areas of Responsibility

It cannot be stressed highly enough that you need to concentrate on your area of responsibility Too often you see team members in training looking everywhere except where they should be.

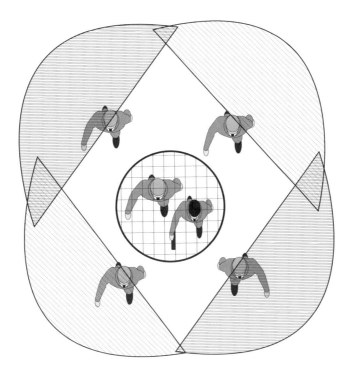

Jogging

If you can convince your Principal that the best jogging is to be had in the gym on a treadmill, then all well and good, but if your Principal prefers wide open spaces or the open road then this will make it slightly more difficult for you. Generally a Principal doesn't employ us to tell him what he *cannot* do. We can advise him that due to the current level of threat, he may well be advised to stay inside. If he chooses to ignore this advice then make sure you follow some sensible precautions.

Ideally, we will want to know the exact route the Principal will take. However, this is not always possible, especially when the Principal chooses to run cross-country or just to run as he feels. He may start out wanting to run just three miles but if the mood takes him, he may turn that three miles into ten. You would hope that every member of his Close Protection team would be fit enough to able to stay with him, and your Principal would not be the first to try and make a point by outrunning his Bodyguards!

It is always better to have one or two protection officers very close to the Principal at all times during the run. Some Principals will want to run on their own and not want to hear the heavy footfalls and breathing of their protection team. If this is the case, then the protection officers can run a little ahead and a little behind the Principal, so giving him the space he requires. If there is only one protection officer and you cannot run right next to the Principal then you should choose to run behind him. Do not run in front of the Principal. You are much more likely to twist an ankle or break a leg while turning round to monitor his progress. You should always use a backup vehicle whenever possible. This vehicle will be invaluable should the Principal injure himself while running or if you come under any form of attack. In the event of a long cross-country run, then the use of mountain bikes is recommended. A couple of Close Protection Officers on mountain bikes can follow the Principal, the theory being that should something happen, the bikes should give them a speedy reaction and they should, again in theory at least, be less tired than the running Principal. That said, if the gradients are particularly steep then the cyclists may find that they lag well behind the Principal, who powers away from them!

Summary

Walking drills can be a pretty straight forward affair, especially on short known moves such as from an arrivals lounge at an airport to a waiting car. However if the Principal is not sticking to a plan such as when he is just shopping and going nowhere specific then you will have your work cut out. Forget the ball room dancing that they teach at some training establishments, there is no one formation that should not be adapted for your environment.

Your formations will always be subject to your Dynamic Threat Assessment. Remember that you should never sacrifice security for profile no matter how low your Principal wants to maintain it, if it is too low and you are too far away you may as well not be there at all.

Using Weapons

Y ou'll soon find that there are few places in the world where you can legally carry a concealed weapon. In the USA, rules vary from state to state with different licensing, training courses and permits required. Moreover, unless you are a permanent resident, getting the permits is almost impossible. Russia and most of Europe have stringent gun laws. Any civilian Bodyguard who tells you he routinely carries a weapon in Europe is probably lying or doing so illegally. Over 90 percent of Close Protection Officers working in cities outside war zones are doing so without carrying a gun.

On rare occasions and in certain countries, e.g. war zones, such as Iraq and Afghanistan, the situation may well require the Close Protection Officer to be armed. Any bone fide company is not going to give this position to someone who has just done a week's introduction to firearms. The job is going to be offered to an ex-soldier or policeman, with years of experience, rather than just a few hours!

You may have noticed on websites and in brochures that the companies that train with weapons frequently wear dark glasses and show people with their faces blacked out so they can't be recognised. (Walter Mitty comes to mind!) They tend to base their whole course around guns and dark glasses. These courses, if they are run safely with good instructors, can be great fun but they are not going to get you a job in armed assignments with a good company.

In This Chapter

Learn about weapon selection

How to give bodycover with a weapon

How and where to carry the weapon

Working on armed assignments

If you want these armed assignments then you are going to have to work hard and put in a lot of time on the range to gain the considerable experience required. That said, many military people outside of the infantry do not have the necessary experience with small arms and these people must receive their training elsewhere.

You cannot learn weapon handling from a book; if you wish to learn to use weapons then you need to enrol yourself on a course that will teach you the basics. Then you must practise those basics by joining a club of some kind until they become instinctive. This might take four weekends or four months but if you practise, practise, and practise, you will become proficient, and by proficient I mean safe. That is, safe to train in pressure situations and to take your skills to the next level. Once the basics have been learned and committed to muscle memory, and all the basic drills have become instinctive then the student can be instructed in the techniques that can be employed by the Close Protection Officer.

I have trained hundreds of students to use weapons in a Close Protection environment. Some take to it like a duck to water while others take longer and some people just do not have the ability to handle weapons proficiently. Basic safety on a particular weapon can be learned in a long weekend but this does not commit anything to muscle memory. What's more, after a few weeks away from the range, a student will be back to total beginner status. A week is not a long time in a firearms environment, nor is three weeks, but it is rare to find a course that will last this long. I would certainly not employ anyone who had to routinely carry weapons if he had only done a course on the subject. There are too many people out there that have lived with a weapon for years in the military or the police to make me choose a new guy over them. If you are offered a job with weapons and you do have limited weapons experience then you really ought to question the motives of your employer.

These pages on weapons will not deal with basic weapon handling. We will discuss only those aspects of weapon handling and shooting that can be employed successfully by the protection professional who is already an experienced weapon handler. That said, my fear of lawyers means that I cannot write about weapons without first discussing 'basic weapon safety' and only if you are an expert in this area should you skip ahead to weapon selection before reading these basic safety rules.

Weapon selection

Most people have an opinion on which is the best weapon for CP. Some opinions are good, based upon practical experience in the field. Others are ill thought out, uninformed guesses. Your choice of handgun may well be made for you; the weapons might be there on the job. You may have to compromise. If you have a choice, it would be wise if working as part of a team that you all choose weapons that will use the same ammunition; if everyone has the same ammunition it is just one thing less to worry about.

Basic Firearm Safety Rules

1. Handle all firearms as if they were loaded! 'Unloaded' firearms kill people every day.

2. Never forget that a gun has the potential to produce serious injury or death in a single instant of carelessness. Make safe gun-handling a habit to be followed at all times. After you have determined that a gun is unloaded, continue to handle it as though it were loaded.

3. Always keep your firearm pointed in a safe direction! In selecting a safe direction, you must also take into consideration that a bullet can ricochet or glance off any object it strikes and that bullets can penetrate walls, ceilings, floors and windows. Remember: you should never point a gun (whether loaded or unloaded) at another person or at yourself.

4. Keep your finger out of the gun's trigger guard and off the trigger until you have aligned the gun's sights on a safe target and you have made the decision to fire! By keeping your finger completely outside the trigger guard until you are aimed at the target, you are guaranteed that any shots you fire will go safely in the direction of your intended target.

5. Always be certain that your target and the surrounding area are safe before firing! Remember that a bullet can travel as much as several miles, so you should be certain of what your bullet could strike before you pull the trigger.

6. Whenever you handle a firearm, the first thing you should do (while keeping it pointed in a safe direction with your finger outside the trigger guard) is to open the action to determine whether or not the firearm is loaded!

7. If you do not know the proper way to open the action of a particular firearm then do not handle it. Ask someone who does. I have seen people make real fools of themselves just because they were too embarrassed to ask about an unfamiliar weapon. Do not experiment. Thoroughly read the instruction manual or get a thorough brief from someone who knows the firearm.

8. Never use any firearm unless you completely understand its operation and safety features. Do not assume that one weapon will operate in just the same way as another. Some weapons might look very similar but operate in very different ways.

9. Before firing your weapon in training, you should routinely ensure that your firearm is in good working order and that the barrel is clear of dirt and obstructions! Any obstruction that prevents the bullet from moving easily down the barrel can cause pressure to build up in the weapon. A small bit of mud, gun grease, excess lubricating oil or rust can cause pressure to build up to the point where the barrel bulges or bursts upon firing, resulting in a damaged gun and serious bodily injury to the shooter or those around him.

10. Only use ammunition recommended by the firearm manufacturer and always be certain that the ammunition matches the calibre of your weapon!

11. Quality ear and eye protection should always be worn when shooting in training. Continual exposure to the noise of gunfire can permanently damage your hearing if protection is not worn. Shooting glasses, preferably with side panels, help to guard against eye injuries from ejected cases, and the splash back of pebbles and fragments from butts or targets.

12. All firearms should be stored unloaded and secure in a safe storage case, inaccessible to children and untrained adults The transportation of firearms is regulated by laws. Always transport your firearm in a safe, unloaded condition and in accordance with applicable laws.

13. Always remember that no set of rules can cover all possible situations. The safe and rational use of a firearm depends on the common sense and proper training of the user. Always follow safety rules and think before using any firearm.

Reliability

Do not take reliability for granted as some weapons are better than others, and if the gun does not consistently launch its projectile then why have the hassle of carrying it? Ask other people or use your own experience. In our industry, weapons can get a lot of abuse and very little real use. One weapon can be very reliable with one type of ammunition and terrible with another. Speak to dealers or manufacturers and ask what ammunition they recommend. Then use this as your starting point in your reliability range testing. It should have a simple design with rugged construction from quality materials. Good designs do not change, and the old favourites like the Browning Hi-Power have hardly changed in 50 years. They haven't changed for the simple reason that they work.

Ergonomics and fitness

The weapon should fit your hand. You should be able to load, unload, clear stoppages and operate it easily and safely. I have seen many people use weapons that are far too large for their hands. Similarly, if you have hands like dinner plates you shouldn't opt for a very compact weapon as you will always be fumbling for the safety or screaming as you lose your fingertips on the range! There is an old saying that a hit with a small .22 beats a miss with a large .44. How the gun fits in your hand is a critical component of your ability to hit a target reliably, especially under stress. That large squeeze-cocker beast might look good on your hip, but it won't look good on the floor when you drop it while trying to draw! You must also consider how the weapon is going to be carried. Is it going to live in a vehicle glove compartment? Or are you going to conceal it on your waistband? The answers to these questions will assist you in choosing a weapon with the right ergonomics.

The control of the recoil of the gun is vital to the Close Protection Officer; the poorer the grip the more recoil, and the less accuracy beyond the first shot. In fact, if the weapon does not fit your hand, accuracy will be probably be lost on the first shot under duress. Some modern high capacity weapons frequently need hands like shovels for a proper fit.

Most modern weapons made in the last 50 years are well made and very reliable. It is folly to choose one that doesn't quite fit when there is so much choice. Fitting isn't difficult; just pick it up and see if it fits your hand and feels balanced. If it is too big or unbalanced you will not be accurate. You will also be at risk of dropping it and you will make it easier for it to be taken from you. Don't accept any compromise. IT MUST FIT PERFECTLY. Your favourite weapon must be the one that fits. Making weapons bigger to fit is rarely a problem because bigger grips can replace the originals, but if you have small hands there is sometimes nothing to do except choose another weapon even though the one you want is nice and shiny and would look good on your hip.

Accuracy

You must prove the weapon to be consistently accurate with the ammunition you are going to carry on a daily basis. When you are training and not under duress you should be able to consistently get quick acquisition head shots on a target from 25 to 30 yards. Don't be quick to blame the accuracy of the modern handgun. I have frequently been handed a weapon to check because the owner thought it defective or inaccurate. Very often the only thing defective was the person who gave it to me. Becoming accurate is not like riding a bike: you will eventually lose the ability. The more you practise the better you get. An old saying I know, but true nevertheless.

Magazines

High-capacity magazines that protrude from the weapon are to be avoided if possible. It is much better to have a magazine that fits the weapon correctly. This way you are much less likely to snag the magazine or have misfed rounds.

Ease of Loading

The weapon should be quick and easily loaded. Most combat weapons are easy to reload but some are easier than others. If you are in a fire fight, with all of them being pressure tested on the range during training, you will welcome the weapon that is easily reloaded while you are loaded with adrenaline.

Targeting

The sights should be of a design that doesn't snag clothing but does provide fast sight acquisition. It is rare for a Close Protection Officer to take traditional aimed shots but when he does, it is good for him to have sights, with quick sight acquisition.

Ammunition

Ammunition must be readily available. Don't assume that just because ·40 ammunition is in abundance at your gun club that you can find this ammunition everywhere. Of course it's up to you to check for availability in your theatre of operations. Remember that you will need to test your weapon/bullet combination and have enough ammunition for he job in hand. You must also be able to rotate the worn, often loaded and unloaded ammo.

It might be better, given a particular area or country, that you choose another gauge of ammunition to suit what is commonplace in that country. Whatever weapon and ammunition combination that you choose, make sure that you use them together in all of your training.

Stopping power

A knowledgeable guy and enthusiast called Evan Marshal has compiled the world's largest collection of statistics on handgun ammunition effectiveness. You can see some of his work by visiting www.StoppingPower.net. On this site he states that the three most important components of 'stopping power' are:

1. **Bullet placement**
2. **Bullet placement**
3. **Bullet placement**

This is true of course. A well-placed shot from an air pistol can stop anyone. But this is only of any use if we have time to think about the placement and can aim to get it there. As a Close Protection Officer you will more than likely be under stress and reacting to a situation that gives you no time to think about bullet placement. It follows then that the ideal bullet will stop someone no matter where you hit them!

The revolver versus the semi-auto

Revolvers are easier to operate, especially loading and unloading; they are considered safer and easier for users with limited training. They only carry around six shots whereas the autoloader can hold as many as 15 or more. This may not be the disadvantage that you initially think; statistics show that most protection officers won't fire a shot in anger but even when they do the average number of shots fired will be less than six. If you are in a situation that requires lots of bullets then you will be better off with an autoloader. Some people swear by 'speed loaders', which can load all six chambers of a revolver in double quick time. However, if you are in a stressful situation and in need of bullets quickly, then you will need an autoloader, which offers not only more bullets per reload but much quicker reloads. Spare ammunition is more easily carried for the autoloader, as magazines are much flatter then a speedloader

Revolvers can be fired double-action, which is intrinsically safe, but a double-action trigger is harder to learn and not as quick to fire when you're are in a retaliatory situation. Autoloaders have the advantage that they can be double action, single action, or double action just on the first round.

Revolvers mostly do not have a safety catch; this can be an advantage or a disadvantage depending upon your circumstances.

Most revolvers are chunkier and harder to conceal and carry whereas autoloaders tend to be of a flatter shape and can be concealed much easier. Because revolvers do not have a magazine in the grip, they can be made to fit small hands by the use of interchangeable grip stocks.

Revolvers do not need a sold grip or stance to push back against in order to operate the reload; they will still fire if under duress you have a bent wrist or a loose grip. Some autoloaders will not.

If your assignment requires you to load and unload your weapon regularly, then revolvers are much 'kinder' to ammunition than autoloaders. This is especially true of that top round in the autoloader's magazine that keeps on being pushed in and then dragged out of the breech.

Revolvers do not suffer from any autoload problems; they will never fail to cycle the next round as unlike the autoloader they do not have a feed ramp.

Unlike autoloaders, revolvers do not depend on ammunition to generate the minimum recoil energy to cycle the next round into the breach. The bullet is already there! This means that a .357 Magnum revolver, for example, can fire anything from the lightest .38 special target load to virtually any .357 Magnum loading. Depending upon your environment this ability may be very important.

Particular weapons.

You could write a book or two on the merits and disadvantages of particular weapons – and people have done so. Most people will have a certain allegiance to the weapon that they did most of their training with. Others will have had recommendations from colleagues. It doesn't matter which weapon you choose as long as its fits most of the selection criteria outlined above.

Advances in the gunsmith's art have come on in leaps and bounds over the past 20 years. Weapon safety is better than ever and we now have plastic weapons that outperform gun metal, but whether it's just a case of 'sticking with what you know' or just being traditionalists, many Close Protection Officers, if given the choice, will choose one of the following handguns:

Browning Hi-Power (P35)

My favourite handgun is the Browning Hi-Power. This really is one of the most notable handguns of the last century for a number of reasons. It was the maker's John

M. Browning's (a legendary American gun designer) last pistol design. It was the first to introduce the high capacity, double-column magazine.

It is one of the most-used military service pistols of all time. In fact, during World War II, the Hi-Power, also known as the P-35, saw service not only with a number of the allied forces but was also used by the German military! The fact that the Hi-Power remains in production today without major changes says a lot about the soundness of its basic design and the following it has. Made in Belgium, it is a product of that country's huge arms company Fabrique Nationale, often referred to as FN.

Perhaps the pistol's unique feature was its 13-round, double-column magazine. It was Browning's intention to retain a single-column magazine because he was concerned about the reliability of the double-column type. It was an FN designer who decided to use the double-stack magazine. The amount that the higher-capacity magazine adds to the width of the grip is surprisingly small but those with very small hands will not like it. The Hi-Power has enjoyed good civilian sales worldwide thanks to its cartridge, reliability and high-capacity magazine.

When I see the latest sales brochures from different manufacturers and the excellent advances in weapon makers' art, I am sometimes tempted to stray but never do. Maybe I'm a little old fashioned, or maybe it's just a case of sticking with what you know, and I really do know this handgun. Over the years, I have put tens of thousands of rounds down the range with this weapon and they just keep going.

SIGARMS P229 SAS

This weapon is designed specifically for the concealed carry and over 90 per cent of the carrying that the Close Protection Officer performs will be concealed.

SIGARMS describe this weapon 'the ultimate in concealed carry performance'. It has had a radical dehorning process resulting in an ultra smooth, snag-free profile, which makes it ideal for concealed carry. Each pistol utilises the new DAK™ trigger system and features a smooth, dehorned, stainless steel slide with front SIGLITE® Night Sight and a contrast rear sight over a lightweight, black, hard-anodized alloy frame with rounded trigger guard and dust cover. A superb choice.

A Table full of CZ75's These weapons were used 'out of the box' to train students and worked flawlessly for many thousands of rounds. The weapon in the foreground is the instructors H&K

CZ 75

The CZ 75 is in some quarters regarded as one of the world's greatest 9mm pistols. It features an aluminium alloy frame, a decocker, a firing-pin block and an M3 rail for tactical lights and/or laser sights. More than 60 countries use the CZ 75 in an official capacity. It is one of the best 'out of the box' weapons that I have ever used.

In training, we have used brand new CZs straight from the box and then used them almost continually on the range for months on end. They shoot straight; the ease of use gives new students confidence. It has great safety with regular three-dot sights and weighs around 27 ounces. The double-action trigger pulls a smooth 12 pounds and in-single-action mode it has a pull of around half that.

These days there are lots of fancier pistols – polymer this and composite that – but you really can't go wrong by choosing the CZ.

Hundreds of weapons

The Browning and the CZ75 are just two of literally hundreds of pistols that can be used for Close Protection. There are many reasons for using any weapon but particularly because of personal preference or a friend's recommendation. All weapons, but especially pistols, have ardent fans or detractors who will sing the praise or slate a particular model. One thing is for sure; it's rare that someone will spend a small fortune on a side arm and then admit to you that it's a piece of shit. Whenever you ask for advice about weapons, be careful whom you ask. Often, the 'information' that you will be given could well be measured and intelligent – then again it may not!

Only dummies don't practise!

Once you have a firearm, the very next and most important purchase that you must make is some good quality dummy ammunition. You must practise filling magazines, loading, unloading, making ready, and changing magazines and so on. It's not fun and it can be boring, but you must be disciplined and practise regularly. If you can train with a team mate then you can make it a little more fun by introducing a competitive element to the training.

AFTER WORKING WITH THOUSANDS OF STUDENTS ON THE RANGES WITHOUT DOUBT THE MOST DANGEROUS WERE THOSE WITH A BIT OF WEAPONS EXPERIENCE WHO THOUGHT THEY KNEW IT ALL!

On the range, it is amazing to see the mistakes that people make with weapons, even when they are not under any stress and with weapons they are supposedly familiar or they have owned for ages. Not seating a magazine correctly is a classic handling error and will lead to the weapon stopping, fumbling with top slides and safety catches. If people are making errors on the ranges when not under duress then they should definitely not be placed into a position where there reactions might mean the difference between life and death. Practise your handling over and over again. Strip it, assemble it, strip it again. Everything about the weapon must be committed to muscle memory. It must become instinctive, you must be able to do it in your sleep.

Concealed carry

Unless you are operating in a war zone or working in the military or the police, then any weapons that you do carry will be concealed. Concealed carry permits can be impossible to obtain in some countries and many Bodyguards routinely break the law by carrying. I remember a story about a team whose Principal insisted that one of them carry a concealed weapon – 'the team gun'. In the country they were in it was

Inside Belt Holsters are good for concealment but can be a pain, literally, if you need to be sitting down. They are easily removed and can be placed strategically in a vehicle for quick access. But remember once out of the belt you will need two hands to draw it

illegal for non-residents to carry weapons of any kind. The consequences if they were caught would be very serious. They would argue every morning about whose turn it was to carry the weapon. It was a great lump of gunmetal, a .44 Desert Eagle without a holster, which they had to tuck into their waistband. They were in a hot country and the weapon could never have been described as being in concealed carry.

There is always a compromise to be made; if the weapon is very well hidden, it will probably not give speedy access. If it is strapped to your leg and tied down like Billy the Kid then you get super fast access but no concealment.

Belt holsters

There are lots of different types of belt holsters that will allow a concealed carry as long as you have a jacket or shirt to conceal it. The belt holster comes in two main styles: inside-the-waistband and outside-the-waistband. Inside-the-waistband hol-

A .45 in a belt holster. This type holster can help to smooth out the bulk of the weapon but if anyone looks hard enough they will probably see it

sters are a bit more concealable with just the pistol grip showing. Because the belt and your waistband goes around the outside of the holster, the gun is pressed closer to and often 'into' the body and is much harder to spot if someone is interested enough to be looking. The trade off is that these carrying systems can be much more uncomfortable than outside-the-waistband holsters.

With outside-the-waistband holsters there is more choice as more manufacturers make them. The belt worn usually always has to be wide, so as to stabilise the holster, especially when using heavy weapons with high-capacity magazines. If the belt is too narrow it has to be particularly tight which can prove to be uncomfortable.

Paddle holsters

These have a large area of leather or nylon that tucks into the waistband. It does not need a belt but you are advised to wear one for security. The only real benefit is if you are on an assignment in which you have to keep removing the weapon throughout your day. Removing a paddle holster is much easier then unthreading a belt. Some people I know swear by paddle holsters, but I don't trust them; they can easily ride up out of the waistband, especially when in vehicles and that embarrassing noise of gunmetal on tarmac would be too much to bear. I feel much safer when a weapon is physically attached by a belt. I know that some paddle holsters have belt holes but that defeats the object. It's not a true paddle if it's attached to a belt.

Holsters are made with different degrees of rake. Rake is the angle that the holster sits on the belt and presents the stock to you. If you hold a pistol in your gun hand, keep your wrist straight and locked and slowly sweep your hand along your waist. You will notice that the barrel points forward when it is forward of the hip joint and points to the rear when it goes behind your hip joint. When you stop level with the hip joint, the pistol is pointing straight (vertically) down. The farther you go from your

Paddle Holster for those that need to know the weapon is a Heckler and Koch P7M8.

hip joint, the greater the angle off the vertical. Decide where on the belt you want to wear your holster and then the rake that you need will become apparent.

The most common concealment holsters tilt the muzzle of the gun to the rear. These holsters are designed to be worn behind the hip of the gun hand side. They are quick to access and do a good job of hiding the weapon. I have seen people who like to

Most shoulder holsters require the strong hand to come across the body. This make the draw and target acquisition much slower

holster the weapon on the opposite side as they prefer to cross draw. Concealed cross draws are definitely slower and it can look like a Spaghetti Western whenever hands hover in anticipation!

Shoulder holsters

Shoulder rigs look cool and that's why they are common for TV cops. Everyone should have a picture of themselves wearing one, but that's all! Shoulder holsters

Cross draws are very easy to block if they are recognised early

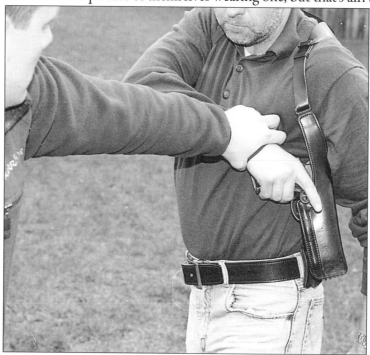

carry all types of weapons in all positions; upright, upside down, and everywhere in between but they all have the disadvantages of a cross draw, which is slow, easily seen and can be blocked at close range. They are also easily spotted and difficult to reach in a hurry. Don't waste your money on a shoulder holster. Just borrow one for the photograph and then give it back!

Bumbags/fannypacks

There is nothing wrong with putting a gun in a bag. If you are a girl, or a guy in touch with his feminine side, than you can carry a weapon in a handbag. You could carry it in a supermarket carrier bag. You could carry it in a bag marked 'this is a gun' and it would probably still be less conspicuous than if you carried it in a bum bag. Anyone with any experience who sees a Close Protection Officer with a bumbag will assume that you are carrying. So much so, that if you want to convince people that your security team are armed. then just let a couple of them wear bumbags! All these bags/pack have all the disadvantages of the cross draw in that some are quicker to get into than others. Some are very well designed, while others are terrible and require two hands at draw time. There may be occasions where they serve a purpose, but they are not usually recommended.

In-car holsters

Most holsters, irrespective of whether they are in or outside the waistband are uncomfortable to wear when driving. Lots of people that are in and out of cars all day like to use a paddle holster so they can easily remove the weapon, complete with holster, and place it within reach in the car. This is wrong. If the paddle holster is not in your waistband, then it becomes a two-handed operation to remove the weapon from the holster. I have had people argue that this only takes a second or so longer. I disagree. If I am in a position to need to draw weapons, then I want every single second to do so.

My favourite place for a weapon in a car is just under my right thigh and not in a holster at all; it's on my strong hand side, I know exactly where it is because I can feel it. I can reach it with one hand in the blink of an eye. It is easy to lift one cheek of your backside and replace the weapon into a belt holster before you get out of the car. Just don't forget.

Door pockets are also a good place as long as you secure the weapon so the only time they move is when you reach for them. If you are going to use a holster in a car, have it fixed so that it is a one-handed movement to draw it. You can buy holsters especially for wearing in vehicles that attach to the front of your belt by the buckle; these are best avoided as they are just not practical.

Never put a weapon in the glovebox. If you do not need a weapon and just want to store it for a journey then it should be locked in the boot/trunk. If you think you might need the weapon then the last place you want it in an emergency is in the glovebox. Put it where you can reach it instantly with your gun hand, as long as Joe Public can't spot it as he walks by or overtakes in a truck. Then you are fulfilling the function of 'concealed carry'.

The Stance

A lot has been made of stance; people have written whole books on the evolution of shooting stances. As a Close Protection Officer you do not have to worry about it because you won't use one! The word 'stance' by definition also means 'static', which is, of course, not what we want to be if you are ever a target. Stances are fine for the range when you are standing and shooting at cardboard targets that are not shooting back. If two words were ever made to go together it is 'fire' and 'movement'. Stances and movement just don't go together.

Target Shooting using the Weaver or Modified Weaver. This is great for scoring points on the range but you are not going to adopt this stance in the real world

The Real World

We have an advantage now because we have lots of footage of real gunfights and do not have to rely on testimony or eyewitnesses. These days we have cameras everywhere and thousands of towns and cities are completely covered by video. The police, military and civilians regularly carry cameras. There are hundreds of videos and photographs of people reacting under fire and returning fire. These videos are from war zones and police situations from all over the world. The most common position (not a static stance) seen on these videos is probably the most instinctive – it is the crouch. This entails bending your knees and leaning forward as far as possible while keeping the head up. These pictures show police officers who have probably trained for years using, say, a weaver stance with two hands on the weapon, and the first sound of gunfire they are in a crouch and moving and shooting with one hand, things that may never have been practised on a range. A terrorist intent on hurting you is not thinking about how he is standing, he is thinking about hurting you or your Principal. If you stop and think about how best to stand, even for a particle of a second, you may end up wishing that you were firing a second earlier, even if it was only in the bad guy's general direction.

> IF TWO WORDS WERE EVER MADE TO GO TOGETHER IT IS 'FIRE' AND 'MOVEMENT'. STANCES AND MOVEMENT MAKES NO SENSE AT ALL AND WE WILL BE MOVING!

Stances are for target shooting. They assist you in maintaining a good weapon platform, especially when shooting at targets that are over four yards away. Isosceles, and its variants, Weaver, and modified Weaver and others all have their fans and detractors. Most people I have seen over the years use a sort of Weaver-type position. It does allow for good target acquisition and allows you to quickly drop down into a kneeling position as well as engage targets to the left and right an in front. However the targets I am talking about are paper or cardboard. One thing that almost all stances have in common is that they employ two hands on the weapon.

One Hand or Two?

If you have time to stand, get two hands on the weapon, bring it up to the eye and take careful aim. You have to do this before you can effect an escape from the danger to your Principal. Then you're okay. Take aim, using you sights, and hit the target. The chances are, you are never going to be in this situation. You are going to be reacting to the sound or sight of a gun or maybe the threat of a knife. Because your reaction time is not on your side and speed is everything, you will need to get the weapon

Two hands are better than one. You should train to shoot with one hand three times as much as you train with both.

out and make a noise with it, hoping to ruin your opponent's aim. If that first, quick shot can also be accurate, this is going to greatly increase your chances of survival. So you must train to be prepared for such situations.

Most of your training should be carried out using just one hand. As a Close Protection Officer, your weak hand may well be doing other things, as we will discuss later. Two hands will always mean greater accuracy, especially after the first shot when you have to handle the weapon recoil. We should always train for the worst option, so if we do most of our training with one hand and in a situation we get to use two hands then this is a bonus. It follows that if we always train with two hands and a situation occurs where we are forced to use one hand then this is not good.

The Draw

We can safely say that 99 times out of 100 when we need a weapon quickly, we will be reacting to something and the weapon will not be in our hand but in a holster. In other words, someone may well already have the drop on us. Because of this need for

You should practice drawing from real world situations. If you spend a lot of time sat on a chair in a hotel corridor then make sure that you practice drawing from that position

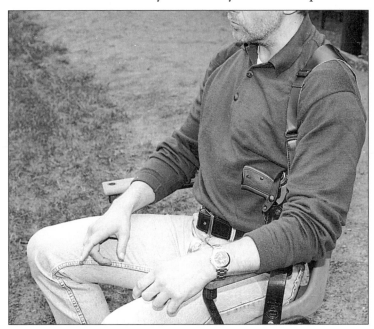

speed this must take precedence over all aspects apart from safety.

When we draw, we need to have the sharp end of the weapon pointing in the direction of the 'reason for drawing' as soon as possible. This is why cross draws are not recommended. In a cross draw, when the weapon is clear of the leather, it is still at least 90 degrees off target. Compare this to a strong hand, straight draw and the weapon can be making a noise the second it clears leather and the rounds are travel-

> When learning a new drill remember that
> Slow is Smooth and Smooth is Fast

ling in the right direction, especially when the body is tilted back into the 'short draw', which in America is known as the 'speed rock'. The combination of your wrist bringing the barrel up on to target as soon as the barrel clears leather, and pushing the hips forward and leaning back brings the weapon trajectory up very quickly so that the round can hit someone in the 'centre-of-mass'.

Getting slick

Draws must be practised repeatedly. To become proficient, you must practise drawing from a variety of positions. Many people only practise drawing their weapon, while standing in a very strong position such as the Weaver. You must condition yourself to draw quickly and smoothly from a variety of different positions, such as when you're sitting in an armchair or in a vehicle, as well as when you're walking or running. Drawing a weapon is an emergency drill and must be practised regularly. I have known people that have been embarrassed about practising basic weapon skills. Weapon handling skills do require practise; it is not something that you learn and don't have to worry about again. I don't apologise for reminding you yet again that our gun fights are going to be reactionary. Speed is everything.

Bodycover and the short draw

Practise each draw slowly at first. Make sure you have a good grip on the weapon, a grip that you are not going to have to adjust before you squeeze the trigger. Take the safety off as soon as it's safe to do so, and get the weapon pointing in the right direction. For many years we received laughter from our students when we told them

Practising the short draw. If you do not rock back at the same time as the draw valuable time is lost bring the weapon up to the target

'slow is smooth and smooth is fast' but the message is clear. When you are training, do it right. Perform it nice and slow and keep it as smooth as you can. With practice and while keeping it smooth, the speed will come, but you have to be prepared to put the time in at first, and then keep it slick by plenty of continuous training.

The Short Draw whilst providing Bodycover. Notice the instructors hand, ready to grab the 'Principal'. If he falls off of the BG's Back this could be very dangerous.

Weapons and Bodycover

When someone is 100 percent safe and well drilled in the basics when stationary, the training that is specifically for Close Protection can commence. Firstly, people need to be taken from the comfort zone of a static, strong-standing position. Other body positions, kneeling, sitting and lying should be introduced. Weapons should always start in leather, and every drill should incorporate a draw. This can be very dangerous because loaded and ready weapons in holsters are inherently dangerous, even with some of the modern two and three point safety systems built in. The student needs excellent concentration and safety awareness is needed at all times, even when put under stress. When standing and drawing from the hip, most of the body is already behind the weapon, which is, of course, where you want to be. Drawing a weapon when sitting or lying means some of your body will be in front of the weapon when it is drawn and before it can be brought to bear on the target. Sometimes, even experienced shooters shoot themselves. When they do so, it's normally a result of complacency or stress. Shooting yourself is not to be recommended. If you don't die at the time, you could die of embarrassment later!

Providing bodycover should initially be taught without weapons and certainly not with live ammunition until the student is proficient at providing the cover. It might seem a bit silly at first but no one was ever shot with an index finger.

Target Acquisition

It does no harm for the Close Protection Officer to learn about carefully aiming a weapon and trying to be as accurate as possible. In fact it is great fun on the range to

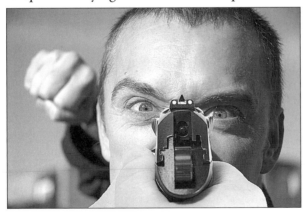

Shooting needs to be as instinctive as pointing rather than using the sights of the weapon

compete with each other on accuracy. Nevertheless history has shown us that it is highly unlikely that a Bodyguard will be in position with the time to take carefully aimed shots. We are just not given the time to place the fore-sight between rear-sight and then place this on to the target. Furthermore to aim traditionally we would need to close our weak eye to facilitate getting this sight picture.

You need to become proficient at point shooting, you do this by keeping both eyes open and pointing the weapon where you want the bullet to hit. You would normally shoot at the centre of mass for no other reason that it is a bigger target. It is impressive how accurate this method can be. As soon as the weapon clears the leather and the barrel is pointing toward the target, as your arm points toward the target at punching speed the trigger finger should already be working.

This classic picture showing Jack Ruby killing Lee Harvey Oswald shows the detectives 'wow' factor. Everything just happens so fast they have no time to react. But the whole sequence was recorded and Ruby had approached with an outstretched gun hand. Had the detectives been in code yellow and looking they would have seen him and would have had time to react.

EMPICS

Summary

If you are going to be employed to carry a weapon you should impress upon your employer the need to practice. If you can get him to pay for range time and ammunition even better. One thing is for sure, you cannot rely on the skills you learned with a weapon years ago to help you win a fire-fight to day. If you are in a situation where there is even a remote chance that you will need to draw your weapon you must ensure that you are well practised in its use. Remember that fit is more important than anything else, if the gun doesn't fit then you wont hit a thing with it even if you do manage not to drop it. Try as many weapons as you can before committing yourself to an expensive purchase. When you are on the range practice a lot with one hand shooting, and draw the weapon from situations you may find yourself in like sat in a car or on a stool. Practise firing as soon as the weapon has cleared leather, do not wait to aim, keep both eyes open and shoot the centre of mass.

Unarmed Defence of the Principal

M ost books about Close Protection have a chapter or two on unarmed combat. Some spend as much as a dozen paragraphs teaching the reader how to disarm an assailant with a knife or a gun. Information that could save your life if only you could remember it at the time! Unarmed combat, much like bodycover or building search, is a practical subject that just cannot be learned from a book alone. Some muscle memory just has to be involved. You can learn a lot from a book, but do not expect to learn practical things by theory alone; these things must be physically practised.

There are whole libraries of books written about unarmed combat, self protection, street survival and martial arts. One of my friends wrote most of them! His name is Geoff Thompson, a prolific writer who has amassed a vast knowledge of many fight disciplines and has been fortunate (or unfortunate!) enough to be able to test much of his theory in a real arena. None of his books are specific to Close Protection; they centre on self protection and work as a door supervisor. A quick look at www.geoffthompson. com will lead you to some of Geoff's titles such as:

> **Real Punching**
> **Real Kicking**
> **Dead or Alive**
> **Fear – the friend of exceptional people**
> **The Fence**
> **The Three Second Fighter**

All of these books are required reading and you will be able to take much from them that you will be able to use in your career as a Close Protection Officer.

In This Chapter

How to defend our Principal without weapons

Defence against a gun

Buying time to escape

Martial Arts

Over the years I have met some excellent Close Protection Officers, who were also superb martial artists. Equally, I have known many very professional Close Protection Officers who did not practise martial arts at all. But I must say that of all the idiots and least professional officers I have ever come across in the industry, almost all of them purported to be martial arts experts, and it was this 'expertise' that pushed them towards the Close Protection industry.

Almost all martial arts are said to develop the mind as well as the body and your technique, so why have I met so many people who were black belts, but only at their own discipline and on their own mat? Off the mat they were arrogant, looked down on others, and spent much of their time looking in the mirror, believing the art they practised was superior to all others. There is no place for this type of attitude in Close Protection. The team is everything and there is no room in it for the large egos that some black belts in martial arts bring along with them.

When martial arts are practised for the right reasons they can be very beneficial to the Close Protection Officer; they are a great motivator to stay fit. There is a grading system, giving measured goals to maintain enthusiasm, interest and the desire to continue. They can give the officer excellent reactions. There is not one system that is to be recommended above all others. There are some systems that really are only any good for a Japanese battlefield six hundred years ago. On the other hand, there are some modern systems, less than twenty years old, which are much more effective in today's street battle. These new systems of self defence steal little bits of what works from many of the old arts and have rolled them into modern systems to beat the enemy of today. Today's enemy, of course, is much less honourable than those Japanese warriors of another time.

The British Combat Association

This organisation was founded by Peter Consterdine and Geoff Thompson in the early 1990s. These two guys were the pioneers of a form of self protection that actually works on the street. In the years before the association was formed, they independently looked at self protection from every aspect. They studied fear control and used very realistic (animal day) training sessions to test their theories. They also practised on the odd idiot or two who caused trouble at the clubs, where they worked as doormen. Peter and Geoff between them have about 16 or 17 dan grades and are experts at a number of different fighting systems. They are formidable fighters, yet at these seminars the one thing that is emphasised more that any other is avoidance. You cannot lose a fight that you are not in, and by not being in it you have won. This is true for everyone, but for the Close Protection Officer it is fundamental and forms the basis of his function.

Avoidance is everything.

Question anyone in the street and they will tell you that they do all they can to avoid a violent conflict. However do they really? No, the vast majority do not. They might think of their personal security once or twice a day but that is about it. When something happens they are normally taken by surprise, which means that they are reacting slower and without thought.

To defend yourself or your Principal with your fist, feet, head or a handgun requires you to be in a conflict situation. Unlike most members of the public, the professional Close Protection Officer will spend every waking moment, using considerable experience and skill to avoid any form of confrontation. When you are working as a doorman in a club, avoidance can be difficult; trouble knows where you are and comes looking for you. When working as a Close Protection Officer, you know where the trouble might be and you avoid it. Nevertheless, we have to accept that what we are trying so hard to avoid may sometimes confront us. Being professional, this will not be a surprise, but sometimes avoidance is impossible and the only way out is to go through the threat and take it head on.

Hit and run

It is better to make a good run than a bad stand. Avoidance and escape should always be your first priority. However if it comes down to it you may well have to fight to defend yourself and your Principal. Even in the middle of conflict you should be looking for the way out. Experience has shown countless thousands of times that the best way to win is to leave the fighting at the first opportunity. Your definition of win may be to win the fight, extract revenge or teach a lesson. But the real winner is the person that does just enough to make his escape and, as the old cliché says, 'lives to fight another day'.

Buying the time.

The usual reason for a Bodyguard to involve himself in conflict is to buy the time needed to escape with his Principal or for the escort section to assist him. You can buy this time with a punch, kick, slap, headbutt or any other technique that you consider will work for you. What will work for you is what you have practised.

Two professional Bodyguards practising their unarmed combat pause to pose for the camera!

Many martial art 'experts' can, in the heat of the battle, experience what Peter Consterdine and Geoff Thompson called a 'log-jam of technique' and what I call 'analysis paralysis'. They know so many techniques and they use fractions of a second to decide which is the best technique to employ in the given situation. A fraction of a second can decide the outcome of the conflict. If you know just one or two methods of attack, and these are range dependent, say, a right hook for close encounters and a powerful front kick for when they are a bit further away, you are not going to waste any time deciding which to use.

Punching to buy time is just like any other 'action on drill'; you must commit it to muscle memory. Because the professional works hard at not being taken by surprise, then an aggressive pre-emptive strike, handing all the disadvantages of surprise to your attacker, can be very effective. Action will beat reaction every time. So you must do things that make them react. As soon as it is you doing the acting, the chances of you and your Principal surviving the attack are considerably greater.

IF YOU KNOW TEN WAYS TO COUNTER-STRIKE AN OPPONENT YOU MIGHT WASTE VALUABLE BITS OF A SECOND DECIDING ON THE BEST OPTION TO USE. WE CALL HIS IS ANALYSIS PARALYSIS.

You do not have to study martial arts to learn how to punch and kick, but you do need to be shown how to do so to the best effect. The techniques cannot be taught entirely from a book, but the aforementioned books about kicking and punching by Geoff Thompson are a good start. A coach or a club is the only way to bring the basics off the page and translate this into power when hitting the bag or your assailant. The couple of techniques that you learn must be practised over and over again. I know Protection Officers that will practise throwing their favourite right-cross 2500 times a month. They will practise it close up, they will practise closing down distance before delivering it, they will practise it from moving behind their Principal, they will practise on a target that appears from behind, they will practise delivering it from a sitting position. These people take pads and mitts everywhere and never miss the opportunity for practice.

Not only is this right-cross practised physically all of the time, generating fantastic muscle memory and power, but it is also practised and rehearsed mentally. The professional officer will deliver his devastating right-cross to any person in any given situation. He will line it up perfectly, he will let it go with no tell tale signs or warnings, he will follow it through with his bodyweight. These mental rehearsals are extremely effective in developing technique and should not be underestimated.

Johnny Wilkinson was one of the best ever kickers of a rugby ball the world had ever seen. He was famous for the drop goal in the last minute of extra time in the World Cup final. Wilkinson didn't get this good by accident; his practice sessions are legendary within the sport. All rugby fans know the stories about how he arrives at the training ground hours before any one else and then stays behind when they all go home. In the World Cup final, the stadium held their breath as England and Australia traded point for point. At full time, both teams were exhausted but they had drawn and had to face a further 20 minutes of extra time. While all the players took a few minutes to rest and gather themselves, Wilkinson went to the other end of the pitch and did some kicking practice! Practice makes perfect, we all know the saying, but it is discipline that makes us practise something over and over again.

In a conflict situation, you would be very lucky if things happened exactly as you planned them. They would probably not. Every situation will be different, every opponent or attacker will be different, and while you will try to train for every eventuality, the chances are that things will not go to plan. There can be no predetermined procedures to fit all circumstances. This makes it all the more important that you master your basic punching and kicking techniques, so as to be able to improvise the best attack possible. An American president once said, "In preparing for battle, I have found that the plans are useless, but the planning is indispensable."

Aggression is everything

You do not have to show the almost obsessive practice behaviour displayed by Johnny Wilkinson, but if you only practise your punching and kicking a tenth as much as he did then you would become a very accomplished kicker. All that practice will give you both power and speed; this, coupled with aggression, will help you win the day.

The aggression you employ must be overwhelming; it must be dispassionate, and unemotional, it must instil instant terror and anxiety in your attacker, forcing him to react rather than act. Your punches and/or kicks do not have to be technically perfect, but if you deliver them with immense, calculated aggression the effects can be devastating.

Defence against a gun

After careful consideration before writing this chapter I would like to offer you the following rules of self defence when confronted with a gun.

> **Rule 1: Be somewhere else**
>
> **Rule 2: Have something bulletproof between you and the gun**
>
> **Rule 3: Watch fewer movies**
>
> **Rule 4: Don't break Rule 1**

Being somewhere else

This is absolutely the best defence against any type of handgun. All of our prior preparation and planning is designed to keep us away from someone with a gun. When this is impossible we will hopefully be able to bring Rule 2 into play.

Have something bulletproof between you and the gun

If we are in an environment where weapons may be in evidence, or if the threat against us is such that there is a risk of our attackers having weapons, then we would be stupid not to use some ballistic material in the shape of a vest or a car between us and the threat. When we do find ourselves in abuse of rules one and two then I hope that you have observed Rule 3.

Watch fewer movies

Hollywood has always been a big fan of handguns and trick shooting, from the cowboy Roy Rogers through Clint Eastwood's Dirty Harry and any number of James Bonds. Because of hundreds of movies like these there are millions of people who have the wrong idea about handguns. They may think that it is easy to take a weapon off someone before they can squeeze the trigger. Or that it is possible to (intentionally) shoot someone in the hand at 100 yards.

The real world

The reality is that if someone is already holding a gun and close enough, then the odds are stacked heavily against you, even if you are a 'weapon disarming' expert. Even if that person is a complete novice and has never fired a gun before, the chances of you not getting shot are pretty slim. In addition, if that person knows anything at all about weapon retention your chances of disarming them drop to almost zero.

Surviving the handgun attack

Of course, it is not impossible to survive a handgun threat in real life; people do it all the time. Survival depends on quite a few factors:

The gunman's intention

What is the intention of the gunman? Does he want to kill or kidnap? If the intent is to kill then you or your Principal might be hit before you even know you are under attack. On the other hand, if the intention is to kidnap then the weapon will be there as a compliance tool as well as a defensive tool should you or the Principal resist. You should be aware that even if the intention is to kidnap the Principal, the Bodyguard will probably be shot. This is for two reasons; the first and most obvious is that you are a threat to their plans. Secondly, by shooting you, the weapon will have a much greater compliance effect on the Principal.

How much distance

The amount of distance between you and the attacker is everything. Anyone who has worked with handguns knows how inaccurate they can be. If there is a distance of more than 15 metres it is highly likely that a moving target will be missed. Running away in a crouched, unpredictable zig-zag and you will be even harder to hit.

How much training the attacker has received

Considerable training is needed to be able to use a handgun at any distance other than very close range. I have seen people use a pistol at the range when they were used to shooting rifles. They look amazed at their first target of twenty metres, seeing none or just one or two holes out of ten hit the target! OK, it's not long before it becomes ten out of ten, but to get ten out of ten in a good small group of holes takes considerable practice at twenty metres.

Even if your attacker is ex-special forces or has been well trained, he will still have adrenalin and, if he is using a handgun, it will take a cool customer to hit a moving target over any great distance. If the attacker has you at close range and has had weapon retention training then this is going to be much more difficult to get the drop on him.

How much training you have received

If you have trained and practised disarming techniques then, of course, your chances of survival are much higher. Knowing what to do with a weapon if you do take it off of someone is important too. You will be much better prepared if you know how to use the weapon as well as take it off of someone.

Beating the draw

Weapons are rarely carried openly up until the moment of use. They are always coming from somewhere; a bag, a shoulder rig, a hip holster and overcoat pocket. When training you should always practise countering the draw from different carry positions. These sessions with your training partners can get very competitive and aggressive and this is to be encouraged; the lessons learned in these sessions will give you a very good idea about what is possible to achieve and what isn't.

Grabbing the gun

In the event of you disarming the attacker, then all your actions should follow the basic premise: manoeuvre your body out of the way while simultaneously taking hold of the weapon. It goes without saying that once you take hold you must never let go; now, your life literally depends upon your strength and aggression. You will, without anyone having to remind you, focus all your attention on the muzzle of the weapon and where it is pointing. Of course, twisting it so that it is pointing towards your attacker is desirable. But your aim is to rip it from the hand of the gunman, causing him as much pain as possible during the process. If this becomes a wrestling match then the chances of being shot as you roll around the floor are high. You need to use the leverage of the weapon and work against the joints; you need to work fast with lots of aggression. You must train with you partners and find what works for you. For the training to be any good it must be realistic, you and your training partner must assume a life or death attitude and really go for it. Be prepared to stop as soon as your partner shouts, as it is very easy to break digits. Wearing a thin pair of leather gloves can protect your hands from being ripped open by the weapon sights and other protrusions.

Stopping the weapon from firing

Handguns are mechanical. IN THEORY, there are many things you can do to stop the weapon firing. Some semi-automatic weapons will stop working if the top-slide is held back slightly, but others won't. The attacker may intend to use a revolver. He can be prevented from firing it if you can hold the hammer back or get a pinkie in front of it. If the hammer isn't back then just hold the chamber to stop it rotating as the trigger is squeezed and this will prevent it firing. Other weapons have two or three point safety systems and by partially releasing the attacker's grip on a part of the weapon you can stop it working. If the safety catch is enabled or if you can enable it in your struggle, then this might well stop it working. All of these techniques require you to have a hand or two on the weapon, and if you have a hand on the weapon then do not bother with any of the above. Take the weapon from the attacker as this is the only guaranteed way to render the weapon safe.

When you have the weapon

The very best thing to do with a weapon that you have successfully taken off someone is to club them with it hard and more than once. Most handguns, being a good heavy blunt instrument, make for good impact weapons. Then, get some space between you and them, cock or re-cock the weapon and take control of the situation.

Summary

If you are a martial art expert then that is excellent. The dedication and discipline that you displayed to become an expert weighs heavily in your favour. You should continue to train with the techniques that you know will work. Keep things simple. Remember the technique log-jam. If you do not have any combat training, then you need to get some – you need to learn to punch and kick. You need to be able to do this instinctively and with power.

The expert and the novice need to ensure that they work with aggression. Aggression is everything, you must train with this. You cannot just practise your techniques and hope that the situation you later find yourself in will provide you with the aggression. In conflict you only get out what you put in. Speed and aggression will always win, even if your technique is less than perfect. However, perfect technique delivered with speed and aggression is unbeatable.

Unarmed and up against someone with a gun is to be avoided at all costs. If you can't avoid such situations then make sure you use plenty of armour. If you are going to try and disarm an attacker, then do so with massive amounts of aggression, keep your body out of the line of fire and get hold of the weapon. Your action forces reaction and if everything goes to plan action always beats reaction.

Looking After Children

Plenty of Close Protection Officers at some time in their career will have the job of looking after a minor. Those of you that think this sounds like an easy task probably don't have any children of your own! There are of course exceptions and I am sure that there are few rich kids out there that are a pleasure to look after. It's just that I haven't found any!

Many of the rich and famous users of Close Protection Officers take their children's security as paramount. The Principals know that criminals or terrorists could harm or kidnap their children because of who they are. This is why plenty of Bodyguards can be seen on the 'school run' and some of these find themselves staying at the school all day rather than just dropping the children off. Some schools make it easy to stay, but I have come across schools that insist that the Bodyguard leave the school grounds. Then protection has to be carried out from the outside with the Bodyguard hoping he is not going to be mistaken for a pervert!

Age makes a difference

Very young children, say from 4 to 11, are particularly easy to look after. They tend to do as they are asked, when they are asked, and without question. Any older than this and some children become quite independent and often resent your presence, especially if their friends do not have Close Protection Officers. Most of these kids will move from school and then on to college. Colleges are notoriously hard to secure, but more about that later.

In This Chapter

How to look after Children.

School Runs and Living in.

Collection Passwords

Criminal record checks

Employers of Close Protection Officers in the United Kingdom may want to get an enhanced disclosure from the Criminal Records Bureau for any of the officers that are working with their children on a regular basis. In addition to all of the regular criminal record checks that a standard disclosure requires, an enhanced disclosure may contain 'non conviction' information, which a chief constable may choose to disclose if he feels that this might be relevant. For example, an individual may have a 'clean record' but he may have been accused of molestation twice; for one reason or another it might never have got to court. The Chief Constable in this instance has the right to include this information on an enhanced disclosure. This information will of course be most welcome if you are employing someone to look after children.

Role model.

Close Protection Officers can often become popular with the youngsters that they look after. The resulting influence that the Close Protection Officer can have over the children is considerable.

You should be aware that much of what you say may well get reported back to the child's parents. It can sometimes be very difficult to please both the parents and the child. Doing exactly as the parents want is the correct way to progress, but it can make your relationship with the child difficult, which in turn can hamper your protective arrangements. You should always try to find a little compromise and keep both the children and parents happy but always remember who pays your wages.

Some children have been known to blackmail their Bodyguards, constantly threatening to tell 'Dad' what you did or you didn't do, said or didn't say. They will sometimes even threaten to make things up, just to get their own way. Other children can be a delight to look after and there are many children in between these two extremes.

Looking after children at school

You might find that you only have to drop off and pick up the child from school. If this is the case it can be difficult to vary your routine that much. Yes, you can leave early, but any attacker will know that you are going to end up at the school sooner or later. And of course your pickups at the end of the school day will almost always be at the same time.

Never, ever, be late when picking up the child. Always arrive early and be very proactive with your anti-surveillance drills. You need to instruct the teachers in writing that barring an emergency of some kind, you and you alone are the only person apart from the parents that will collect the child. Give the teachers/head your mobile telephone number so that if you are ever late (don't be!), they can call you. Explain that anyone picking up in your absence will use a password.

Prearrange a password that can be used by a colleague if the worst happens and you cannot be there to collect the child. Don't expect the school to carry out your instructions; test the system. Just because you sent a letter to the head last term giving your phone number and new password doesn't mean to say that your instruction will be carried out. You must expect them to be lax about this. Very often, they will not take the child's security as seriously as you will, especially at busy times such as the end of the school day when they have lots of children and parents to deal with.

Once a code or term has been decided upon, you should arrange for a colleague to collect the child, get him or her to give the wrong code and then see what happens. If he or she causes alarm, they can quickly 'remember' the correct password, but if the child is handed over to a stranger with the wrong password or no password at all, then this needs to be addressed immediately. Arrange a face-to-face meeting with the head teacher and explain the importance you place on your security arrangements.

> **ARRANGE A FACE-TO-FACE MEETING WITH THE HEAD TEACHER AND EXPLAIN THE IMPORTANCE YOU PLACE ON YOUR SECURITY ARRANGEMENTS.**

Get assurances that they will not let this happen again. Follow your meeting with a letter they gained, using your mobile telephone number and the password. It is rare for a school to mess up twice and you can rest assured that the child will never be handed over to someone who does not have the correct password.

Living in

Some boarding schools and colleges, especially those that are used to accommodating the children of the rich and famous, often make arrangements for the accompanying, live-in security team. Depending upon the threats that exist and the vulnerability of the child or young adult, you will have to choose between a high or low profile, or you may choose to vary the profile by maintaining a low profile while on campus and a high profile when the Principal goes 'downtown'. A low profile is much more conducive to the Principal/student's learning and I would suggest that only in extreme cases such as the very highest profile children would you expect to offer high profile protection to a student while actually on campus. British royal princes and princesses have invariably used a low profile while on campus with a heavier, higher profile security team working outside.

To maintain a low profile while on campus, it does help if the Close Protection team members looked like they should be there as either tutors or students. Some of you might fit in well to a college environment although I'm guessing that many of you will not!

If your Principal is staying in the halls of residence then this can be treated just like a hotel room and secured accordingly. There are plenty of single sex halls of residence and this, of course, will affect who can be on the team. A male Principal will require an all-male protection team for the halls of residence at least.

The best way of securing students is to give them some responsibility; at the very least they should be letting you know what their itinerary will be, and where you could best protect them from. It is rare for a protection team or Bodyguard to actually attend a class with the Principal. Looking after the security of the room or building that the Principal is located in is normally all that is required. A panic button that can alert you immediately the Principal needs some assistance is an excellent idea and the Principal should be encouraged to carry one of these at all times. Furthermore, the Principal should be encouraged to carry a mobile phone at all times. The Bodyguard's mobile phone number should be entered into the Principal's speed dial. You should suggest that the best speed dial to use is number 9. This gives the Principal numbers 1 to 8 for personal numbers and once that you explain to him that number 9 is the first number of the emergency services, 911 or 999, and that the first number he/she means he/she got a call you, they will always remember that you are there on number 9

Summary

Looking after children can be demanding but it can also be fun. Some children are very vulnerable and security should be taken very seriously. Always check that schools follow your instructions. Encourage youngsters to take some responsibility for their security. Teach them about personal security, paying particular reference to the first Principle. Don't forget who pays your bills. While you have got to keep the child happy you must also fulfil your obligation to the parent who is paying you.

Protocol

P rotocol (or lack of it) is the single most common reason for a Bodyguard to lose his job. Of all the Bodyguards that are dismissed from employment, probably as many as 80 percent are sacked not because the job is coming to an end, or they are no good with a weapon, or their driving skills are rusty. They are sacked for lack of protocol.

Realistically then, if you value your job, you need to master protocol more than any other subject. Some of you may find that the subject comes easy; others will find it difficult or maybe never master it .The subject is not one you can learn totally out of a book. You will learn the finer points as you go along, but learn it you must or you will not last two minutes in the industry.

When we talk about protocol as a Bodyguard, we are not just talking about its dictionary definition, e.g. knowing when to bow or which way we pass the port at a banquet, and although these things are not excluded from Bodyguard protocol, many things are included that you would not normally associate with the word protocol.

There are four areas of protocol in which officers slip up and, surprisingly, it is not because of some obscure Japanese or Arab custom. Essentially, they let themselves down with the most basic mistakes that they should have learned on their mother's knee! Most of these faux pas will come under one of the four headings of **DRESS, HYGIENE, HABITS,** AND **BEHAVIOUR.**

In This Chapter

Understand why protocol is so important.

Find out what wil get you instantly dismissed

How not to embarras your Principal

Understand the difference between a soup and a dessert spoon!

A Definition of Protocol

> ## Conducting yourself in a manner synonymous with the Principal and the situations that you may find yourself in.

What does synonymous mean?

Generally, it means we should look similar to the Principal. This is particularly important if you are striving to maintain a low profile. If you and your Principal were on the golf course together, you would not look out of place. You should not look like you were there to protect or rob someone or collect a debt. You must look as though you're there to play golf.

If you are being employed as an 'ugly' – by that I mean that you are just there to look horrible and menacing, with a high profile – then you may not want to be synonymous with your Principal. The heavy gold chains and teeth, leather jacket and studded gloves may well be the right thing to wear and that, together with an angry, growling presence might be the best protocol that you have to offer. But most protection officers, who are providing a professional and low profile, need to be synonymous.

Dress

Appearance is an extremely important part of Close Protection; it is probably the first thing that will get you hired or fired.

If you are dressed immaculately, you will appear to exude confidence and strength. People will assume that you have the knowledge and ability to take care of yourself. They assume this solely from your appearance. Therefore, it is clear that dress can play an important part in your role as a Bodyguard.

Obviously, the most important part of your clothing is the suit. It should be made of at least 50 percent wool. Suits that are 100 percent wool look good and are great for the winter but are too warm for the summer months. Do not wear polyester suits, they crease easily and look awful.

The colour of the suit is important. You should choose a solid colour; you do not need pinstripes or chequered patterns. Light navy blue and grey are considered conservative. Dark suits exude authority although they should be chosen wisely. Reserve your black suit for funerals or being a nightclub bouncer or better still do not wear black at all.

You should choose a shirt with a traditional stiff collar, nothing too fancy. You do not want studs or button down collars. If you lose a stud or button, you will look scruffy all day. Light pastel shirts are okay up until about 6pm, thereafter shirts should be white. If you know that your itinerary is going to give you no time to change your shirt, then wear white. You should show about half an inch of cuff through your suit. If you are wearing a double cuff then plain style cuff links are fine. If you have single cuffs do not wear cufflinks, even if the shirt has holes for them, as it looks stupid; cufflinks are for double cuffs only.

Making a good first impression. Clean and smart with good eye contact and oozing Professionalism. Anything less and you will not give the Principal the confidence he needs to have in you

Your tie should be silk. It should be a darker colour than your shirt; the knot should be of medium size but this size should match the collar. With a standard traditional collar, a Windsor knot looks best. The width of the tie should be on a par with the width of the lapels on your suit.

YOU NEED TO WEAR BELT AND BRACES; belts are a necessity for clipping radios or weapons to; braces will keep your trousers up with all the items you've got on your belt.

BLACK SHOES WILL GO WITH ANY COLOUR SUIT. Brown shoes go with nothing! Lace-up shoes are preferable to buckles or slip-ons that have a habit of coming off, just as you need them. Whatever the shoe it must be highly polished at all times. Many people judge others by the state of their footwear. Ensure that anyone gets only a good impression from your conservative, black, laced up footwear. In summer or in hotter climates then take your lead from what the Principal is wearing. Tevas or leather sandals may well be synonymous.

SOCKS, WHEN WORN WITH A SUIT, SHOULD BE DARK IN COLOUR and should match the suit. They must reach over the calf so that when sitting with legs crossed you are not showing a disgusting pink hairy leg to your Principal.

YOU CAN ALWAYS DRESS DOWN BUT IT'S HARD TO DRESS UP. Imagine you are smartly dressed for a dinner party to which you thought you were escorting the Principal. It turns out to be an informal BBQ in someone's backyard and your Principal is wearing jeans. In your suit, you can go some way to lowering your profile and feeling less uncomfortable by removing your jacket and tie, even rolling your shirtsleeves up. If the position was reversed, however, i.e. you thought you were going to a BBQ and ended up at a dinner party in a check shirt and jeans, there is little you can do to rectify the situation. Again, it should be emphasised that dressing down is easier than dressing up.

> TWO GOLDEN RULES ABOUT DRESS
> NEVER OVER-DRESS THE PRINCIPAL
> ITS EASIER TO DRESS DOWN, SO DRESS UP.

DO NOT WEAR JEWELLERY Men can get away with wearing a wedding band and a gold watch but that's about it. Do not wear chains, earrings, nose rings, signet and sovereign rings. That is, of course, unless you're looking after someone who wears all of this jewellery and then you will try to be synonymous. Ladies should only wear wedding bands and stud earrings.

NEVER OVER OR UNDER DRESS THE PRINCIPAL. Always try to anticipate how the Principal is going to be dressed. You do not want to be significantly scruffier or smarter. Remember, we want to be synonymous. Imagine your embarrassment if you were wearing your most expensive suit, your gold cufflinks and silk tie and your boss was dressed in jeans. If the person who your Principal is meeting shook your hand first, thinking you were the Principal, there would be embarrassment all round. You just don't need it. Be synonymous.

DO NOT WEAR YOUR TROUSERS TOO SHORT. They should just touch your shoes, breaking the crease a little. Make sure that all your clothes fit; a tight collar will ruin your day, too short a pair of trousers will not make you look very professional

ALWAYS TRY TO AVOID TAKING OFF YOUR JACKET. If you have to, make sure that your shirt is long-sleeved, pressed and no weapons or tattoos can be seen. Depending on your Principal, you may have to invest in some other types of clothing such as dinner jackets or sports jackets. Get them fitted properly and err on the side of conservative.

Women have to take many of the same points on board as mentioned above, and in some cases it is extremely important that they do not overdress their female Principals or they are definitely in with a chance of instant dismissal. Women are advised to dress smartly but conservatively and not wear anything that will restrict them from doing their job, such as high heels and tight skirts and also keep jewellery to a minimum. If your Principal is at a different black tie event each evening, then the male protection officer can get away by wearing the same dinner suit and no one would notice, but women wearing the same dress would be noticed immediately. Women do need to pack many more clothes than men to maintain a low profile.

Dress codes when working overseas have to be learned. In certain scenarios, 'dressing up' will consist of wearing a white pair of shorts, a polo shirt, and white training shoes, whereas other countries will have strict rules on dress and you will have to keep most of your body covered. Just be synonymous with the Principal and you should be fine.

Hygiene

WE HAVE ALL MET SOMEONE WHO STINKS OF BODY ODOUR. If it's a friend or colleague we can tell them (politely). If it's your Principal then you might have to put up with it. If it's you, then rest assured if you were working with me I would tell you about it!

Often, when you smell body odour on a person, the smell is from their clothes rather than them. They think they can sweat into a suit all day for several days and it won't smell! It doesn't matter how much you shower: if your clothes stink, then so do you. Avoid body odour at all costs. Shower as much as possible and launder your clothes regularly. If you smell and you share a car with the Principal, don't expect to keep your job too long. When the Principal gets a whiff, you will probably get the sack. It being a hot day, or if you have been in a car all day is no excuse. There are no excuses. Just stay clean. If a member of your team stinks, don't just call him silly names behind his back. Tell him to sort it out.

TEETH SHOULD BE WHITE; BREATH SHOULD BE FRESH. Close Protectionn and halitosis are not good companions. There is nothing worse than garlic breath and sweat and it never ceases to amaze me how many times that I smell this stuff while I'm at work. If you are working tomorrow, DON'T EAT GARLIC TODAY. In confined spaces, such as vehicles and lifts, your Principal will not like it, nor will the team members that weren't out with you last night and can smell it. If the Principal finds it particularly offensive, he might take a dislike to you and that can make your curry very expensive. Especially if you find yourself out of work because of it.

Your hair should be tidy and synonymous. If you are looking after a rock star then a ponytail might be synonymous, but your ponytail will not fit with the majority of business people. Whatever hairstyle you adopt, keep it in good condition. If you Principal sits behind you in the vehicle he might not enjoy watching your dandruff fall into his motorcar! Fingernails should be clipped and clean. All this stuff is what our mums taught us when we were very young, so why are there so many dirty operatives out there?

It may be good for your heart but it is not condusive to keeping your job. Do not eat garlic when you are at work

Wear odourless deodorant whenever possible. If you use scent or aftershave ensure it is not overpowering. We don't want to make our Principal's eyes water when getting into a car with us. Some aftershaves are more repulsive than garlic, especially if too much has been used.

I apologise right now to all those people that bought this book only to be told stuff about basic personal hygiene that you have known all your life. But I had to include it because there are still some of you that whiff and maybe you haven't yet worked out why!

Habits

Everyone has habits. We are talking about the bad ones that if we are caught in the act does not show us in a good light.

SMOKING. Never do it, even if the Principal smokes, never do it. If asked, do not lie to the Principal and say you do not smoke. If you do, he may just see you lighting up one day. The best policy is NEVER to smoke on duty. Many companies that employ Bodyguards do not allow any smoking while working. The smell clings to your hair and clothes, it is offensive to others, and it looks unprofessional. You might be able to guard the Principal's car and have a cigarette at the same time, but to anyone watching you it looks like you're just having a smoke break.

An unshaven smoker will not last long in the industry

NOSE PICKING. This does seem to be the national pastime. Stop at any set of traffic lights; look right, look left and someone will be picking their nose. Be conscious of the fact and don't do it. If you must, use a handkerchief. Most people find nose picking distasteful.

BALL REARRANGING. Gentlemen – leave yourselves alone.

GUM CHEWING. Don't do it. It looks bad, can sound terrible and pollutes the western world! You do not need gum to concentrate, despite what some people might insist. The sight of a three or four protection officers chewing is not pretty and oozes cowboy. Professional Protection Officers do not blow bubbles!

BAD LANGUAGE. Some people need to kick the bad language habit. No one likes bad language and if your Principal hears it, or worse still, his children, then you may well be looking for another job. Ban all bad language while working. If it is allowed when out of earshot of those that might be offended, it is only a matter of time before someone makes a mistake and uses bad language where they shouldn't. Some protection officers that come straight from the Armed Forces swear continually and it can take a while for them to get out of the habit and extend their vocabulary.

LOOKING BORED. Nothing looks worse to the Principal than bored looking security officers. How can you be bored if you're doing your job properly? You should always look animated and look as though you are doing your job.

Curb these bad habits; a reference from a previous employer will not help you if it states that you were sacked for continually playing with yourself!

Behaviour

Always be on your best behaviour. The one time you chat to a waitress, the Principal will notice you and think that you are not doing your job. The opposite sex can be a big distraction and it has been the downfall of many a good Bodyguard. I recall an incident in the South of France when an experienced Bodyguard, someone who should have known better, left his yacht and his Principal, while in the small hours, to visit a pretty thing that that was moored thirty yards away. What he did not expect on his return was to find his Principal on deck when he dived in from the other yacht and began his swim home. The Principal didn't believe his story about an early morning fitness swim and she dismissed him on deck there and then. A summer's work gone, and a reputation damaged all for the sake of a couple of hours in the sack. Don' play where you are paid!

Never let the Principal see you behaving badly. Horseplay and raucous laughter from an operations room might appear to the Principal if he hears it as in discipline. Some examples include down-loading porn, inappropriate emails, sexism, using the Princ pal's telephones, etc. These are all examples of bad behaviour that can get you fired

Timings

It goes without saying that you should never keep the Principle waiting. Nothing is more guaranteed to make her think you are unprofessional than being late.

Form of Address

Ensure that you address the Principle correctly. If a specific title is required then use it. There is no room for the "I don't call anyone Sir" mentality. Forms of address are numerous. You might work for a doctor, a captain or Your Royal Highness. Nevertheless, the Principal might insist on being called by a first name, but even if everyone else on a team uses a first name you should only do so when invited to. Meanwhile, in the absence of a title, the Sir or Ma'am will suffice.

Personal Opinions

Do not express your personal opinion – especially on subjects such as politics or religion. If you are asked directly what you feel about a particular subject or situation then you may feel the need to answer, but not having any strong views on any subject will stand you in good stead.

Confidentiality

You will often be in a situation where you learn things that are very 'gossipworthy' but however much you are tempted, anything you learn must remain with you. There are occasions where your confidentiality can be tested in the extreme. I have been involved in situations where the wife of your Principal is insisting that you tell her if your Principal has seen his mistress! You must tread carefully in situations like this. If you simply refuse outright to say anything then the wife may well arrange for you to be dismissed. However, if you tell her anything then you will be dismissed. You will have to use all of your communication skills to explain your confidentially policy!

If any information leaks from the team and the Principal or the team think that you are responsible, you will be history very quickly. Be a rock, your Principal must be able to trust you.

Familiarity

Even if your Principal is very relaxed or insists that you call him by his first name, you should still strive to not become over familiar. Getting too close to the Principal or any member of her family or house staff will almost always end in your dismissal. You might well be treated like one of the family, but you should take a reality check often. You are hired help, you are not family, and you are there to do a job.

Forms of Address

The following are some examples of the way you would address titled people from different parts of high society in the United Kingdom. We have given how the person would be introduced followed by how they should be addressed. I am sure that not to many of you will be looking after the Queen of England but we will start by learning how to address her and go on from there. Very often it can happen that your Principal whilst not having any formal title or form of address can meet people that do. Knowing the correct form of address will show your Principal how professional you are.

The Royal Family

The Queen

Introduced as: "Her Majesty the Queen."

Addressed as: A ruling monarch would always address you first. When replying, first use [May it please] "Your Majesty", thereafter, as "Ma'am."

The Duke of Edinburgh

Introduced as: "His Royal Highness, Prince Philip, The Duke of Edinburgh."

Addressed as: "Your Royal Highness, at first, thereafter, as "Sir."

The Prince of Wales

Introduced as: "His Royal Highness, Prince Charles, the Prince of Wales."

Addressed as: "Your Royal Highness", at first, thereafter, as "Sir."

Royal Princes

Introduced as: "His Royal Highness, The Prince Edward."; "His Royal Highness, Prince Michael of Kent."

Note that only the children of monarchs are the Prince, the Princess.

Addressed as: "Your Royal Highness", at first, thereafter, as "Sir".

A Royal Princess

Introduced as: "Her Royal Highness, the Princess of Wales."

Addressed as: "[May it please] Your Majesty", thereafter, as "Ma'am".

A Royal Duke

Introduced as: "His Royal Highness, the Duke of Kent".

Addressed as: "Your Royal Highness", at first, thereafter, as "Sir".

A Royal Duchess

Introduced as: "Her Royal Highness, the Duchess of York".

Addressed as: "Your Royal Highness", at first, thereafter, as "Ma'am".

The Clergy

The Church of England

Archbishop

Introduced as: "[His Grace] The Archbishop of...".

IF YOU ARE EVER STUCK FOR A NAME THEN SIR OR
MAAM WILL NEVER GET YOU INTO ANY TROUBLE

Addressed as: "Your Grace", or "Archbishop".

Bishop

Introduced as: [His Lordship],"Bishop Smith of Oxford".

Addressed as: "My Lord", or "Bishop".

Dean

Introduced as: "The Dean of Epsom".

Addressed as: "Mr Dean", or "Dean".

Vicar or Rector

Introduced as: "Mr Jones".

Addressed as: "Mr Jones", or "Vicar" or "Rector".

The Roman Catholic Church.

The Pope

Introduced as: "His Holiness Pope Benedict XVI ", or "His Holiness the Pope".

Addressed as: "Your Holiness".

Cardinal

Introduced as: "His Eminence Cardinal Smith", or "Cardinal Smith".

Addressed as: "Your Eminence", or "Cardinal Smith".

Muslims

How you address the Imam or prayer leader of a mosque depends on whether he is a member of the Sunni or Shiah sects.

Sunni.   Introduced as: "Sheikh Muliammed Haleem".
Addressed as: "Sheikh Haleem."

Shiah.

Introduced as: "The Most Revd Iman of the Mosque of Central Bradford".

Addressed as: "Iman Fagih, Hadji Fagih", or "Mr Fagih".

The term Hadji is a title used by any Muslim who has made a pilgrimage to Mecca.

Hindus

Two of the more common Hindu titles are "Swami" (used by religious teachers) and Pandit (a title assumed by some Brahmins members of the highest, priestly caste).

Note the use of the suffix 'ji', added as a sign of respect.

Introduced and addressed as: "Swami" / "Panditji".

Sikhs

Every Sikh temple has a granthi (reader), who is addressed by the title "Bhai" (brother). Note the use of "ji" or "Saheb", as a sign of respect.

Introduced as: "Bhai Santokh Singh".

Addressed as; "Bliaiji", or "Bhai Saheb".

The Peerage and non-hereditary titles

Duke

Introduced as: "[His Grace], "The Duke of Nowt".

Addressed as: "Duke".

Duchess.

Introduced as: "[Her Grace], The Duchess of Nowt".

Addressed as: "Duchess".

Widower of a Duke (dowager duchess)

Introduced as "The Duchess of Nowt".

Addressed as: "Duchess".

Younger son of a duke

Introduced as and addressed as: "Lord George".

Wife of the younger son, of a duke.

Introduced as: "Lady George Pangbourne".

Addressed as: "Lady George"

Don't beat yourself up by committing all of these to memory. If, for example, you are working with a marquess then you will probably be told how to address him. But if you don't know, or simply can't remember, then just fall back on Sir and you will not be being disrespectful.

Working with Arabs

It is rare to work in Europe as a Bodyguard for any length of time and not carry out some work looking after Arabs. It was a very busy time for the Close Protection industry when the new Arab oil millionaires arrived in Europe. Many of these new mega-rich families had their first few years in the West surrounded by Bodyguards. These were heady days, and it seemed there was no limit on their spending power. I recall a Bodyguard finishing a three month summer in France, being given a Rangerover car as a thank you. This gift equated to around three years pay for the average worker at the time! Expensive gifts like this were almost commonplace, and it seemed that you couldn't call yourself a BG until you had a kilo of gold in the shape of a Rolex on your arm, a gift from some grateful sheik.

By the mid 1990's many of these big spenders had all but disappeared. They are still around now but the vast majority are more careful with their money. They employ middle-men who screw down costs and the end of assignment gifts are now much smaller; with many middle-men getting much richer! Arabs can be very demanding to work for but the extra money always compensated for this. Working with Arabs can be very rewarding and not just financially, but you must understand a little about them and their culture.

Should you find yourself working for Arabs then start the job cautiously and find out as much as you can from other team members about the do's and don'ts concerning the Arab family. It's very easy to offend without even knowing it and lose your job before you've even started!

The Arab world presently consists of the following countries:

The Democratic and Popular Republic of Algeria

The State of Bahrain

The Republic of Dujbouti

The Arab Republic of Egypt

The Arab Republic of Iraq

The Hashemite Kingdom of Jordan

The State of Kuwait

The Republic of Lebanon

The Socialist Peoples Libyian Arab Jamahihiya

The Islamic Republic of Mauritiania

> **The Royal Kingdom of Morocco**
>
> **The Sultanate of Oman**
>
> **The State of Qatar**
>
> **The Kingdom of Saudi Arabia**
>
> **The Somali Democratic Republic (Somalia)**
>
> **The Republic of Sudan**
>
> **The Syrian Arab Republic**
>
> **The Republic of Tunisia**
>
> **The United Arab Emirates**
>
> **The Yemen Arab Republic**
>
> **The Peoples Democratic Republic of Yemen.**

The area covered by these countries is three times that of Europe and the total population is over 200 million.

The mixture of races, which includes Berbers, Negroes, Kurds and others, ensures there are a variety of cultures and civilisations. There are, however, two common bands: members of the Arab League and, most importantly, Islam, the Muslim religion.

Islam influences virtually every aspect of life in the Arab world. Its authority varies between countries – it is probably at its strictest in Saudi Arabia – but everywhere abuse of the religion will not be tolerated.

The Arab culture and its conventions – based on their rich philosophy, history, language, nomadic heritage and religion – are often confusing to us. Yet an understanding of them can mean the difference between keeping our job and losing it.

Dress

In an Arab country, appearance is highly important as it can reveal one's status. It is advisable for Westerners to wear suits and ties for all types of business. Safari suits are acceptable at informal occasions and a minimum of long trousers and long-shirt sleeves for general wear. Women's skirts should reach below the knee (if in Saudi Arabia below the ankle) with blouses and sleeves that cover the elbow. Women should definitely not wear trousers.

When in an Arab country, even on days off when you are not working, you are expected to respect but not imitate the Arab way of life. In Oman, for example, it is against the law for a non-Arab to wear Arab dress and nowhere is it acceptable for non-Muslim Westerners to carry prayer beads. When entering some houses and buildings, shoes should be removed.

Touch and sole

Arabs consider our reluctance to make bodily contact to be cold and aloof. In general, they are warm and sociable, sensitive by nature, and with a very good and sometimes teasing sense of humour.

Shaking hands is mandatory, but as a Bodyguard you must wait for the hand to be offered. They often maintain their grip on your hand to establish friendship; you should not try to withdraw your hand until it is released.

Arab friends will embrace each other warmly and kiss cheeks. This custom would probably never be extended to you as a Bodyguard no matter how long you had worked for them.

None of the above relates to Arab women WHO MUST NOT BE TOUCHED UNDER ANY CIRCUMSTANCES. While we are working, we should not even attempt to establish eye contact with Arab women (or young girls). If this does happen, then drop the head slightly and lose the eye contact. Should you be observed looking into the eye of someone's wife or daughter then your job will most definitely be on the line.

The left hand is considered unclean by Arabs and is reserved strictly for personal hygiene. It is NEVER used for touching food, drink, cigarettes or people.

The sole of the foot should never be pointed towards another person as this is considered extremely rude and insulting. Always keep the soles of your feet on the floor.

Whistling in public is considered bad manners in some Arab countries.

Important dates

The Muslim calendar loses eleven days each year and is based on physical sighting of the moon, so dates do vary from one country to another. The following are approximate months for important Muslim festivals:

February – one day: Lailat Al-lsra wa Al-Mi'rat (the Prophet's night journey to heaven).

April – Three days: Id Al-Fitr (end of Ramadan).

June – Four days: Id Al-Adka (pilgrimage to Mecca).

July – One day: Al Hijra (Islamic New Year).

September – One day: Milad al-Nab (the Prophet's birthday).

Always the ninth month of the Muslim calender: Ramadan – the month of refraining from eating, drinking and smoking between sunrise and sunset.

If you are working for an Arab during Ramadan you should not be seen eating, drinking or smoking during the day.

A brief introduction to Islam

Arabs can trace their history to over 3000 BC. The word 'Arab' comes from the Semitic word meaning 'desert dweller'. Muhammad, the founder of Islam, was born in Mecca, in what is now Saudi Arabia, around AD 571. He was a member of the powerful Quraish tribe.

At the age of forty he recognised himself as the Prophet and vigorously propagated the religion of Islam. His divine revelations were preserved in the sacred scripture, the Koran (Qur'an). The Koran is believed to contain everything that has happened and will happen in the universe. When God spoke to Muhammad in the Arab tongue, this was and is considered the Holy language. The book is written in a powerful and poetic way and is the basis of Arab eloquence, a quality much admired in the Arab world.

Millions of Muslims pray to Mecca five times a day, and do so in shops, offices, streets and wherever they happen to be. All try to make the pilgrimage to the Holy City at least once in their lifetime. God's will was revealed to Muhammad at Mecca and Medina. Entry to both these cities is forbidden to non-Muslims.

Some countries allow non-Muslims to enter Mosques. Shoes must be removed and women must wear head scarves.

Men must cover their body from the navel to the knees.

Women must cover their whole body except the face, hands and feet while inside and must cover most of the face when going outside or meeting with adult males outside their own close relatives. Some Islamic jurists allow the face to remain uncovered.

Muslims are not allowed to wear dress that is symbolic of other religions.

Muslims do not eat pork or animal fat. Muslims buy their meat from special butchers (Halal Meat).

All kinds of alcoholic drinks are prohibited.

Lawful things are called Halal and prohibited things are called Haram in Islamic Law.

Mealtime Etiquette

More and more Close Protection officers find themselves in situations that are alien to them; the most common situation is the formal dinner. Very often in this situation the Close Protection officer is required to maintain a low profile while enjoying a meal with his Principal and other guests. The pomp and etiquette that can surround such an occasion can be a minefield for those of you who don't know your dessert from your soup spoon.

If you aren't used to formal dining then it would be much better for you to provide the low profile protection without actually sitting down to the meal. Unfortunately, in many cases this can prove impossible without the cooperation of the host. When you do have to sit down to a formal dinner, you will do well to remember to check which dress code is required. Invariably, formal dinners will require a necktie though this is not always the case. Never guess, always ask or read the invitation carefully.

Seating Arrangements

Always check the seating plan. If you can have a say in the matter choose your seat or table for no other reason than to provide the best security for your Principal. Look at all the possible security scenarios and choose the best table that you can. Be aware that at some fund raising dinners the person sat next to your Principal or at the table opposite is only there because of the amount of money paid for the seat. Often these people have not been vetted in any way.

It's not enough just to be at the next table; your position at the table is important. You need to have an unobstructed view of your Principal and his surroundings. If, because of the low profile that you have adopted, the other people sitting at your table are unaware of your security responsibilities, then once seated you should begin conversation with your dinner partners on both your right and your left.

When sat at the table, do sit straight but not stiffly. Leaning slightly against the back of the chair, slouching and slumping are not acceptable, nor is tilting your chair back. The best thing to do with your hands when you are not eating is to keep them on your lap. It is perfectly acceptable to wrest your hands and wrists on the table when you are eating, but we all know the rule about elbows.

Napkin Etiquette

If the dinner is not too formal then you should put your napkin on your lap as soon as you are seated. Contrary to some Hollywood films, napkins are never placed in shirt collars to act as a bib! If the dinner is very formal you would leave your napkin alone until the host puts the napkin on their lap.

When to Start Eating

Generally speaking, you do not want to be the first one to eat no matter how hungry you are! If you are at a large banquet type table, then generally your host will probably ask you to start before everyone has their food. If you at a smaller table with, say, six to twelve people at it, you wait until all the guests at your table have been served.

Which Utensil to use first

Generally speaking, most tables are set so the cutlery is arranged in the order of its use, starting from the outside in. There are two distinctly different ways of using a

knife and fork properly. In Europe, generally speaking, the knife is held in the right hand and the fork in the left. The prongs of the fork face down when the food is cut; the food remains on the fork in the left hand with the prongs down as it is brought to the mouth. In America, the starting positions are the same with the fork in the left hand and the knife in the right. However, once the food has been cut, the knife is placed flat on the plate and the fork is taken by the right hand and turned with the prongs facing up. It is then placed into the mouth using the right hand.

Bread and Butter

The biggest etiquette mistake people make with a simple bread roll is to use a small spreading knife to cut the bread. You should always break the bread with your fingers the small knife provided is for spreading butter only. Do not butter the whole roll or slice of bread at once. Tear off a small piece and butter this only.

How to Eat

Most of us know how to eat; we do it every day. Indeed, most of our eating is done in an informal situation and with common foods that we know how to eat. However, there are a few foods that might get us into trouble if we don't know how to eat them properly:

Artichokes

If you've never eaten artichokes before, then do watch how other people eat them. Essentially though, you tear off a leaf, dip it briefly in the accompanying vinaigrette or sauce, and put it through your teeth to remove the soft edible part. Discard the thin inner leaves. Cut out the centre and you will be left with a heart, which is delicious. Eat the heart with a knife and fork.

Avocados

Avocados are very often served in their skin and just halved; you may pick up the avocado and, while holding it in one hand, you scoop out the contents with the fork.

Caviar

You may be lucky enough (or unlucky enough depending on your point of view) to be served caviar. Very often, this will be served in a small bowl with its own spoon. To make canapé, you make small amounts of minced onion lemon slices and toast. As it is passed, you assemble it with your knife, pick it up and eat it with your hand.

Shellfish

Shellfish can be both noisy and messy to eat so it should be avoided if possible. However, if shellfish is forced upon you then again you should try to take your lead from someone else – watch how they tackle the crab, lobster or clams. You should know that you are allowed to hold the shells with one hand while spearing the meat with a fork. Never eat clams that are not fully open, and never noisily suck juice from shells no matter how delicious!

Meat and Poultry

For chicken and turkey ribs and chops, you should always eat as much as you can, using a knife and fork. Only if it is an informal meal should you pick up a bone with your fingers to finish it.

Snails

If you are served snails, you will more than likely be given a pair of tongs to hold the snail and a small pick to remove the flesh. Very often served with garlic you may eat all the garlic sauce from the shell on to the bread that is usually served with it.

Soup

The soup spoon should be held in your right hand with your thumb on top. Spurn it slightly away from you and fill it by moving it away from you across the surface of the soup. Then sip the soup without making any noise from the side of the spoon, not the point. To get the very last of the soup, tip the soup dish away from you and scoop it up with your spoon.

Spaghetti

Though you may be skilled at eating spaghetti, it is very easy to make a fool of yourself and get sauce on your chin, your shirt and your tie! Take just a few strands onto your fork and twirl them against the edge of your plate to roll up the spaghetti. If the spoon is served, put the tines of the fork into the spoon and twirl away. If you find that you have dangling ends of spaghetti, either suck them quietly and slowly into your mouth or just bite them off and hope they fall back onto your plate and not your lap.

Summary

Many of the skills in this chapter we learned at our mothers knee and I hope that most people didn't really learn too much from the hygiene and habits chapters. You should be aware that protocol can be a minefield in different countries. Essentially exercising good protocol means not embarrassing yourself or your Principal. You must do your homework when visiting other countries with different cultures as it is here that it is easier to mess up.

Radios and Voice Procedure

Good communications are vitally important to a protection operation. Anyone on the team must be able to pass on information quickly and precisely. Likewise, his fellow operators must be able to hear and understand exactly what is said and meant. The preferred communication tools on protection operations are a combination of the two-way radio (walkie-talkie) and the ubiquitous mobile phone. Both of these items of communication have their good and bad points.

Mobile Telephones

Close Protection Officers should have a 'work phone'. A work phone is either a separate phone or SIM card used exclusively for use when at work. The telephone number of this mobile phone is given to everyone on the team – the Principal, the Principal's family, in fact anyone who may need it. Your work phone should have all the numbers needed for that job in the memory of the phone for quick access (at the very minimum, all the team members that you might conceivably need to call or text). The use of a belt clip or lanyard is advised to avoid loss of the phone and information that it contains. Your SIM card should always be password protected. Remember not to store any number/name combinations on the phone that could cause you problems if the phone was lost.

The main benefit of a phone over the two-way radio is one of distance. Calls can be made to the other side of the world with ease and can be almost immediate. Even the best two-way radios have a range of just a few kilometres.

In This Chapter

How to use radios.

Correct voice procedure

Covert Radios, Spot Codes and Pro-words

Mobile telephones have been made much more effective since they have had the ability to send and receive text messages. Detailed messages can now be sent to anyone anywhere in the world, even if the recipient is out of range at the time of transmission. As soon as the phone comes back into the coverage area the text message will be delivered. Texts can be sent to 'distribution lists' so that many people can get the same message at the same time. This is an excellent way to circulate information quickly and effectively.

Mobile phones are now so common throughout most of the world that their use will attract little or no interest, which is good if you are trying to maintain a low profile. A two-way radio always raises the profile if it is not used covertly.

The Two-way radio

The main benefit of using two-way radios is that one person can communicate with everyone (within range) at the same time. The mobile telephone cannot compete with the immediacy of the radio. In times of crisis it is infinitely better to be able to scream for help into a radio just by pushing the PTT (push to talk) button, rather than dial an individual mobile telephone or compose a text message!

Two-way radios are half-duplex, which means that they can carry information in both directions, but not at the same time. This restriction means that only one person

can speak at any one time. Full-duplex radios (which can carry information in both directions at once, just like a mobile phone) are available but not in common use. Very often it is 'desirable' that only one person can speak at any one time!

Good radio equipment is essential and can easily pay for itself over a short space of time. Poor equipment will always let you down when you least expect, and can ruin whole operations. Motorola's equipment is used more than any other. It isn't cheap, but has proved itself time and time again. Many operators invest in Motorola accessories, such as headsets and covert microphones. They are almost certain of the fact that for any job they take on, Motorola's equipment will be available and, even in the unlikely event of another type of radio being used, there will be adapters, which enable the use of their equipment. If you are not partial to other people's ear wax then you might invest in some Motorola equipment of your own!

Security on the Air

Radio communications are not secure. RADIO COMMUNICATIONS ARE NOT SECURE. I meant to repeat it; because it's very important! All radio transmissions can be easily intercepted and there's not a lot we can do about it. For this reason, we must always assume that someone is listening to everything we say. So in order not to let the listener know what we're up to, we will use prearranged code words and phrases, we won't talk in 'clear'. By this, I mean mentioning town names or person's names over the air. We will change frequencies frequently, and only use the radios when absolutely necessary. If you have sensitive information and you have to talk in clear to make yourself understood then this information is better sent using a mobile telephone, which is more secure.

Covert Body Communication Equipment

Body communications equipment must be small enough to be concealed naturally under the clothing of the operator. Motorola make a number of different packages that will satisfy the requirements of any team, from simple kits that look just like a

Ear Mikes come in two versions wired like this one or wireless. Both types lower the profile but the wired system is more robust and is not as reliant on batteries

mobile phone earpiece, to sophisticated wireless equipment that costs many hundreds of pounds.

Voice Procedure

When using a two-way radio, speak clearly into the microphone, holding it about two inches from your mouth, speak slowly and deliberately, be short and to the point.

Call Signs

A call sign is used to identify each person on the net. These are normally made up of letters and numbers or a mixture of both, i.e. X-Ray, Lima One. (XL1)

The Control Room in this example is '0' (zero) The Bodyguards call-sign is XL1 (X-Ray Lima One) The PES TL is XL2 and so on.

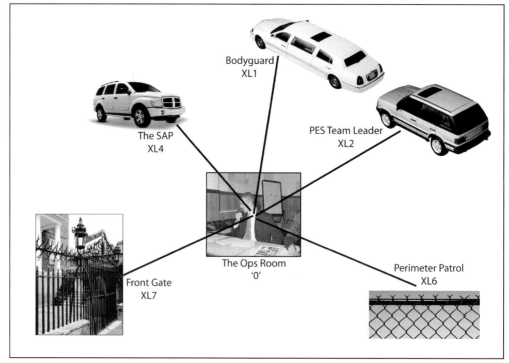

Bodyguard
XL1

The SAP
XL4

PES Team Leader
XL2

The Ops Room
'0'

Front Gate
XL7

Perimeter Patrol
XL6

Pro-words

Pro-words are easily pronounceable words or phrases, which are used to convey an exact meaning. Their use enables one word or phrase to be used in place of a complete sentence. Please see below for pro-words plus their meanings.

ACKNOWLEDGE Instructions to a C/S to acknowledge a message which has just been transmitted.

CORRECT You are correct.

FIGURES Used before groups of figures sent, except in the case of grid references. In that case you would use the pro-word GRID.

HELLO Used as an initial introduction.

I SPELL Used when spelling out a word or letter using the phonetic alphabet.

OUT This is the end of my transmission to you.

OUT TO YOU This is the end of my transmission to you; no reply is expected and a call to another call sign follows immediately.

OVER This is the end of my transmission; a reply or acknowledgement is required.

ROGER I have received and understood your last transmission.

SEND Send your offered message.

WAIT I must pause for up to ten seconds. No other call sign is to transmit during this period.

WAIT OUT Your transmission is received; a further transmission on the same subject will follow later.

WILCO Message received and understood and will be complied with.

WRONG What has been said is wrong; the correct version is...

Some Example Transmissions
You should notice that when you make the initial transmission, that is the only time that you would not use your own call sign before speaking. Before you send any message, you give your call sign, not the one you're speaking to. This is made perfectly clear in the following examples, The first example is a radio check initiated bt control to XL1 and the second is a short exchange between XL4 and XL2

CONTROL *"Hello, X-Ray, Lima One, This is control, Over."*

XL1 *"X-Ray, Lima One, Send, Over."*

CONTROL *"Control, Please call me when complete, Over."*

XL1 *"X-Ray, Lima One, Wilco, Out."*

XL4 *"Hello X-Ray, Lima Two, This is X-Ray, Lima Four, Over."*

XL2 *"X-Ray, Lima Two, Send, Over."*

XL4 *"X-Ray, Lima Four, Send ETA for this location, Over."*

XL2 *"XL Figures, One, Four, Zero, Zero, Hours, Over."*

XL4 *"X-Ray, Lima Four, Roger, Out."*

Spot Codes and Code-words

Whenever we operate in the same location for any length of time, we use spot codes on our maps for specific locations, such as road names or junctions, etc. We also use identity codes for all members of the team, as well as other individuals, male and female. This also applies to the Principal's vehicles and associated buildings such as the residence or office. By

SPOT CODES AND CODE-WORDS ARE GOOD FOR
THREE 'TY'S BREVITY, CLARITY AND SECURITY

using code words, not only are we maintaining our security over the airwaves when using the radio, it is also much quicker to use simple code words to communicate something to the rest of your team.

It's easy to see now that by using these codes, not only can we keep our radio messages short and sweet we can also keep them as secret as possible. However, one of the main advantages of using code words and spot codes is for clarity.

Let's say that you are on the radio to your operations room to tell them that you have finished searching the venue and that you are standing by to receive your Principal. Which of these would be better to say over the radio?

Hello Control, this is alpha 1; "We've finished the search of the venue it is now secure we will stay and wait for the Principal. Over.

Or this:

Hello Control, this is alpha 1; Gone Blue at Romeo 4, Over.

Although spots and code words may seem a lot to learn they will prove invaluable and you will find you'll soon be using them as part of your everyday speech.

Yes, if someone listened to your radio communications for any length of time it wouldn't be too difficult to crack your code words. Our uses of code words are used to make it difficult for any casual listener to understand what we're doing. By changing the words regularly and keeping radio traffic to the bare minimum we can keep our operations as secret as possible.

The phonetic alphabet

Always ensure your message is clear. It may on occasion be necessary to use the phonetic alphabet to spell out words or letters. Don't say the letter 'C' if people on the end of a static crackly transmission might mistake your 'C' for a B, D, E, G T or a V and, if they are American, a Z. If they do you could you could end up looking a proper 'C '

The Phonetic Alphabet

Alpha	November
Bravo	Oscar
Charlie	Papa
Delta	Quebec
Echo	Romeo
Foxtrot	Sierra
Golf	Tango
Hotel	Uniform
India	Victor
Juliet	Whisky
Kilo	X-Ray
Lima	Yankee
Mike	Zulu

Radio Ten Codes

Many police and security companies/agencies use the American Ten Codes or variations of them. Originally developed to improve communication confidentiality they are now commonly used by CB users and radio hams all over the world and just used as brevity codes. They do vary; those shown on the next page are taken from a recent operation order in Chicago and are pretty much standard.

10-1 = Receiving poorly

10-2 = Receiving well

10-3 = Repeat

10-4 = Message received

10-5 = Relay message to _____

10-6 = Busy, please stand by

10-7 = Out of service, leaving the air

10-8 = In service, subject to call

10-9 = Repeat message

10-10 = Transmission completed, standing by

10-11 = Talking too rapidly

10-12 = Visitors present/will use landline

10-13 = Advise weather/road conditions

10-16 = Make pick up at _____

10-17 = Urgent business

10-18 = Anything for us?

10-19 = Nothing for you, return to base

10-20 = My location is _____

10-21 = Call by telephone

10-22 = Report in person to

10-23 = Stand by

10-24 = Completed last assignment

10-25 = Can you contact _____

10-26 = Disregard last information

10-27 = I am moving to channel _____

10-28 = Identify your station

10-29 = Time is up for contact

10-30 = Ready for assignment

10-32 = I will give you a radio check

10-33 = Emergency traffic

10-34 = Trouble at this station

10-35 = Confidential information

10-36 = Correct time is

10-37 = Wrecker needed at

10-38 = Ambulance needed at

10-39 = Your message delivered

10-41 = Please turn to channel

10-42 = Traffic accident at

10-43 = Traffic tie up at

10-44 = I have a message for you

10-45 = All units within range please report

10-50 = Break channel

10-60 = What is next message number?

10-62 = Unable to copy, use phone

10-63 = Net directed to

10-64 = Net clear

10-65 = Awaiting your next message/assignment

10-67 = All units comply

10-70 = Fire at _____

10-71 = Proceed with transmission in sequence

10-77 = Negative contact

10-81 = Reserve hotel room for _____

10-82 = Reserve room for _____

10-84 = My telephone number is _____

10-85 = My address is _____

10-91 = Talk closer to the microphone

10-93 = Check my frequency on this channel

10-94 = Please give me a long count (1-10)

10-99 = Mission completed, all units secure

10-200 = Police needed at _____

Summary

Two way radios always raise the profile when they are raised to the mouth. If profile is important then use ear pieces. In the confines of a vehicle you do not have to raise the radio to your mouth and raise the profile, talk with the radio on your lap and you will transmit. Voice procedure will change between companies and countries, it does not matter what you use as long as everyone knows the procedure and it is designed around brevity and clarity. Remember that radios are not secure, never talk in 'clear'. Your radio is capable of setting off a bomb so always turn it off if you are near anything suspicious.

The Opposite Sex

Years ago, long before political correctness was an issue. It would be said by many Bodyguards that you could only make it is as a Bodyguard if you had TESTICLES. If any women present took offence they could infer to the acronym below, but this was really a tongue in cheek way of saying that Close Protection was a male only profession.

T eamwork
E nthusiasm
S tamina
T enacity
I niative
C ourage
L oyalty
E xpertise
S ense of humour

Women are now an integral part of the industry and as more and more women now become Close Protection Officers, they are taking many jobs that used to be the sole preserve of men.

Some of the traditional problems that men faced, when they were looking after women, now apply equally to women who look after men. This chapter is about working with or for someone of the opposite sex. Nevertheless, there are many more men who look after women than vice-versa so much of this information is directed in that way.

In This Chapter

Working with a
Principal or colleagues
of the opposite sex.

Differences between men and women

Apart from the obvious physical difference, we are often told that there are some other mental and emotional and intuitive differences between men and women. Generally, it is thought that women tend to be more personal than men. They are also often perceived to make less effort to keep there emotions in check, and let others know what they are feeling. This generalisation can be quite wrong. Especially when we are talking about women who have 'testicles' and women who are at the top of their professions and use Close Protection or are Close Protection Officers. Successful women at the very top of their professions may well display fewer differences, if any, than their male counterparts.

Women protection officers who have tried to use their 'charms' on male clients have become spectacularly unemployed. As have many male Close Protection Officers who have discovered that the lady client they initially thought would be a pushover, turns out to be a hard taskmaster and displays more 'balls' than they do!

Women's intuition. A sixth sense?

A study at the 2005 Edinburgh International Science Festival concluded that women may not be as intuitive as they think they are. The study consisted of entirely an online simple experiment where participants were asked to look at ten pairs of photographs. One of the smiles in each pair was a fake, the other a genuine smile. The study found that men were as good and sometimes better at spotting the fake smile. (I took the test and they all looked fake to me!)

When similar tests are taken in real life and in real time, where body language can be studied and voices analysed, women have often shown themselves to have the edge over men, especially when detecting lying or abnormal behaviour. In my experience, women's intuition has always paid dividends. If a woman that you are looking after, or one of your women colleagues for that matter, has a 'feel' for something about a person or a situation, it may well pay to take them seriously.

Difficult situations

Obvious situations do arise when a Close Protection Officer of the opposite sex to their client is at a disadvantage. Toilets and changing rooms and men's clubs are obvious examples where problems may occur. If you are in a one-on-one protection role then most situations like this are compromises. If the threat to your client is so high that using the toilet alone is dangerous, then why haven't you got same sex back up? And why are you in the area where using toilets might be dangerous? The compromise in this instance is that even though you cannot go in without raising your profile somewhat, you are aware of who has gone into the toilets since you arrived. You count them in and count them out, so when your Principal has to use them, you are at least aware if they are empty or not. Experience will let you know what is an over-long time to spend in the toilet and if they overstay you will have to use your ingenuity to check them out.

Mixed sex Bodyguards and clients can come across problems when clothes shopping, especially when changing rooms are gender divided. If you are trying to maintain a low profile then trying to look like all the other bored spouses waiting to be asked "Does my backside look big in this?" is probably you best bet. Stay as close as you can so that you can hear any call for assistance.

Getting into trouble

Some people, men or women, can be communicative. They wear their heart on their sleeve and appear to be friendlier than similar clients or work colleagues. Misreading personal traits such as touching, hugging and smiling, to be intimate actions or a 'come on' may well be disastrous. Male and female Close Protection Officers should especially heed the age old saying: "Don't play where you're paid".

Summary

A career in Close Protection used to be an exclusively male environment this is now not the case. This has nothing to do with political correctness, women have always been capable, but more to do with the rise of women in general. It is now more common to find women at the helm of large companies, or self-made millionaire entrepreneurs at the top of rich lists. It is just natural progression that women should enter the industry and do well within it. The problem is, that the career does not appeal to many women which is why there is always a shortage of well trained women Close Protection Officers.

Women students on a close protection course

The Press and The Paparazzi

If you look after a Principal that is constantly chased by the press and paparazzi then this can really hamper your security function. A determined press pack will camp outside houses and offices, they will follow you long distances in vehicles or on foot. In their eagerness to take photographs they may well place you and your Principal in danger. You only have to think about the unfortunate death of Princess Diana to realise just how much danger.

In This Chapter

The best way to handle the press.

Ho not to 'gift' them with pictures that will embarrass your Principal

A few years ago, every newspaper had its own staff of photographers but these days this is not the case. Most of the photographers that you see on the street are freelancers. They sell their photos to the major agencies, which syndicate and then sell the

Putting a hand out toward the camera is 'gift' for the photographer because it always makes a dramatic photograph. The Bodyguard in this picture is far too professional to make this mistake and is only in this pose for demo purposes

rights of the photographs around the world. This syndication can earn a photographer massive amounts for 'the' photo, but the downside of all this is that not many photographers get paid a wage any more; they are paid only when they take a picture that is worth selling. It follows that these photographers are very eager to get the

Figure Press2

Pitt Bodyguard Manhandles Photographer

A Bodyguard for Brad Pitt and Angelina Jolie manhandled a British photographer as he tried to take their picture at a hotel in western India, an incident caught on video by an Indian television station.

Pitt and Jolie are in India to shoot scenes for a movie about the life of the slain journalist Daniel Pearl.

The celebrity couple have been holed up at the city's Le Meridian hotel since arriving last week, presumably trying to avoid the horde of photographers, reporters and cameramen camped outside.

On Saturday afternoon, when Pitt and Jolie tried to leave the hotel, one of their security guards caught a British photographer trying to take their photo, grabbing the man by his neck and verbally abusing him.

A video of the incident was broadcast on India's CNN-IBN news channel, and the Hindustan Times newspaper identified the photographer as Sam Relph of Barcroft Media.

The newspaper reported that the security guard had shouted at photographers to stop shooting the couple and moved for Relph when he refused to put down his camera.

The Times quoted Relph as saying: "I couldn't breathe. He had his fingers on my windpipe and he knew what he was doing."

---

photograph. This makes them more aggressive when things aren't going their way, and more determined to take risks and liberties to get the picture. Increasingly, it would seem that when these photographers do earn money they do not spend it on soap! More than once in recent years I have heard the paparazzi pack referred to as 'the great unwashed'.

No matter how rude they are, nor how much they push and shove or shout and scream at you, you should always remain the consummate professional, smile and call them Sir or Madam. Never touch or attempt to touch the photographer's equipment. If your brief is to try to stop pictures being taken of your Principal then you can place your body between the lens and your Principal, making sure that when you do you keep a smile on your face. As soon as you put your hand up to the lens, you give the photographer a dramatic picture with great perspective of your hand looking very large and menacing. This picture, coupled with a few lines about your Principal's 'aggressive minders' can give the press a better story than the one they came for.

Over the years, I have seen many such stories that have only been possible because of a lack of professionalism shown by the Close Protection Officer. What would have been a fairly ordinary photo of a Principal getting in a car or leaving an airport, turns into an ugly scene in which the Bodyguard is the story. Almost spookily, as I'm writing this paragraph, I have received an email from my news clipping service. The clipping is shown in figure Press 2

The pictures accompanying this article showed a large Bodyguard wearing an England rugby shirt and with his hands around the throat of a photographer. Realising that there are two sides to every story, I cannot be sure what prompted such action by the Bodyguard. But to manhandle a member of the press in front of his colleagues will result in derogatory stories and photographs making the front pages. Actions like this in full public view reflect upon the Principal and if you attract negative publicity for your Principal you are very likely to quickly lose your job.

On many occasions when dealing with the press you will get some pushing and shoving. The photographers do not want to be pushing and shoving, they want to be taking photographs and more often than not, they soon sort themselves out, knowing that the best pictures they can take are almost always going to be from at least a metre or more away. Some photographers may be rude or aggressive, just to provoke some reaction. Do not give them what they want, keep smiling and use your communication skills. If you must walk through them, politely ask them to move. "Excuse me", "Make way, please" will more often than not get you some space. If you are going from a to b, let's say from your car to a restaurant, don't stop among a pack of photographers. Keep moving. Photographers are experts at walking backwards while taking their photographs.

As hard as it may sometimes seem, try not to make an enemy of the press. Always be pleasant and helpful as well as firm but courteous. Always remember to take the lead from your Principal. He or she may want to pose for a few photographs. In this situation make sure that you remain in control. If they are crowding or jostling for space, tell the photographers firmly but politely that if they don't give you some space you won't give them any photographs.

Summary
Working with the press can be a challenge but as long as you remain a smiling professional your dealings with them, while always unpleasant, may be a little more tolerable. Do not give them a story where none exists by displaying bad behaviour in front of them

Fitness for the Bodyguard

I was reading a Bodyguard manual recently and noted that physical fitness was not mentioned at all in the text. However, the manual contained a picture of the author, which made it clear that he had no interest in physical fitness. Or maybe the author just took it as a given that anyone wanting to become a Bodyguard would be fit. Let me be clear; an unfit Bodyguard is a liability, not only to himself but also to other members of his team, and, of course, to his Principal. It can be difficult to find the required amount of time needed to maintain your fitness when working long hours, especially in a stressful environment, with a demanding shift pattern.

Note that I said difficult; it is not impossible. No one is so busy that their day cannot include a half-hour maintenance fitness session. Prime Ministers and Presidents find time for it, and so should you. A fit protection officer will have more self-confidence and this confidence will ooze for others to see. He/she will look the part, and will instil confidence in others. What message does an unfit, overweight Bodyguard convey? It screams words and phrases like 'lack of self-discipline', 'unprofessional', 'slob' and 'incapable'. Who would trust their security to an ill-disciplined, overweight, unprofessional, incapable slob?

In This Chapter

Why you need to be fit

How to get fit for purpose

Why you should be fit

A fit Close Protection Officer will be much more able to deal with stressful situations than will his unfit counterpart. The effects of adrenalin on the unfit are catastrophic; they will be drained of energy very quickly, and just when a quick decision needs to be made, fatigue will hinder choosing the right course of action. Bodyguards need to be fit. Full stop.

If this is you then you will not be taken seriously in this industry. Bodyguards must be fit not fat.

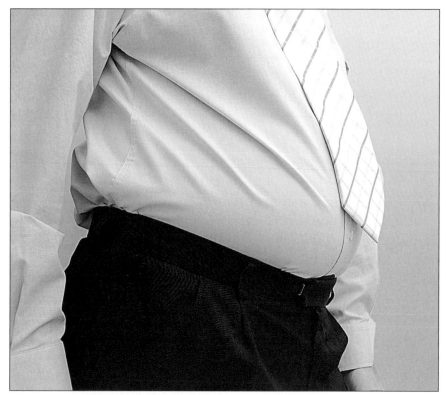

What type of training should you do?

There are three types of exercise that the Close Protection Officer will undertake on a regular basis. A brief description of these exercise types is given below.

Aerobic exercise

Aerobic means 'with oxygen'. Aerobic exercise is any large muscle activity that you can sustain for two to three minutes or longer, because exercising for prolonged periods requires a source of oxygen and its delivery to the muscles. Because aerobic exercise requires oxygen from the air to get to your muscles, the exercise can continue only when a source of oxygen is available. Your heart and lungs work together to supply oxygen to tissues in your body. Aerobic exercise forces the lungs and heart to work harder and, in so doing, strengthens and conditions them.

Aerobic activities include running, walking, swimming and cycling. A typical session lasts 20 to 60 minutes. Spending three hours each week doing some form of aerobic exercise will strengthen your heart and make it more efficient. It will also increase the ability of your muscles to use oxygen. Aerobic exercise must form the base of your fitness. It will help you physically by making you more alert, and assist you in getting rid of stress. The chemicals that are released by stress will harm you if you do not lose them.

Most Close Protection Officers will choose running because it takes the least time to get the most benefit and the equipment needed will be minimal. Good shoes are a must, especially if you are a heavy person or you are running on the roads. But that's it. You can run in almost any type of shorts or track suit.

Anaerobic exercise

Anaerobic means 'without oxygen'. An anaerobic exercise is any exercise that requires short bursts of power, such as all-out sprinting with your Principal on your back, or

Training like this stresses both your body and your mind. Preparing you for when you may be carrying your Principal to safety

very heavy weightlifting. The ability to perform this type of exercise is dependent on energy sources stored in your muscles. Because this energy supply is very limited, anaerobic exercise can be sustained only for very short periods of time.

Take, for example, an anaerobic exercise such as sprinting, or a hill carry. After about a minute, you begin gasping for air and feel a burning sensation in your lungs -- your body is screaming for you to stop exercising. During this type of workout, the point at which your oxygen supply runs out and you slip into using stored energy is called your anaerobic threshold. If you're not very fit, your body is not very efficient at taking in oxygen, and you hit your anaerobic threshold while exercising at very low levels of intensity. That means that any mismatch between oxygen demands and your ability to supply oxygen is met by anaerobic sources, but only until they run out. In our industry this may well be at a very crucial moment, and one on which lives may depend. As you become more physically fit, you are able to go further faster and yet still supply oxygen to your muscles, with less need to use limited amounts of stored energy. So, you can see that we do need to train in this area.

Anaerobic training is mostly an exercise of the mind. It's digging in and finding that little bit more to go a little bit faster or further. You should do a minimum of one, but a maximum of just two hard anaerobic sessions a week. Any more than two sessions a week will be detrimental to your fitness and will probably lead to muscles breaking down rather than being made stronger, and you should remember that the heart is muscle! When things go wrong and you need to run for cover while carrying your Principal, you will be thankful for having a high anaerobic threshold.

Resistance/strength

Resistance exercise – also called strength training – increases muscle strength and mass, bone strength and your body's metabolism. You can carry out resistance exercise to such a degree that you are exercising aerobically or even anaerobically. It can

also improve your body image and make you look the part when it comes to your appearance as a Close Protection Officer.

Callisthenics, free weights and weight machines are the most common forms of resistance training. Callisthenics, such as push-ups and sit-ups, use your own body weight as the resistance force. When using free weights, bars and dumbbells stacked with weight plates, you are responsible for the lifting of the weight, determining and controlling your body position through the range of motion. If you use weight machines, the machines allow you to lift plates, but the machine dictates the movement that you perform. Most weight trainers will argue about the best way of training: by determining how much weight and how often. However, in general, the best way to build strength is to lift weights in three sets of eight to ten repetitions. Lifting a lighter weight more times (repetitions) will build endurance and tone. Get three people in a gym that are used to using free weights and each will have an opinion about a particular exercise for a specific muscle group. Some will be better than others, but time will let you know what suits you. A typical resistance session lasts about 45 minutes.

> THERE IS NO ROOM '*USED TO*' WITH REGARD TO YOUR FITNESS. I *USED TO* BE FIT, I *USED TO* RUN MARATHONS, I *USED TO* BENCH PRESS 1000LB. YOUR BODY DOESN'T CARE WHAT YOU USED TO DO. ITS WHAT YOU DID YESTERDAY AND WHAT YOU DO TODAY THAT COUNTS

You should aim to do two or three weight training sessions per week. After a few weeks, you may notice an increase in the strength and size of the exercised muscles. These increases come from the enhancement of various chemical processes in the muscle cells. After four months of training, your body shape and the size of your muscles can be considerably improved. This beneficial effect on your body composition has another side effect; because muscles burn more calories than fat, a greater muscle mass will increase your metabolic rate. You will therefore burn more calories and reduce fat tissue. This will please many calorie-challenged Close Protection Officers.

Fitting the exercise into your busy day

You realistically need to find an hour and a quarter each day. This will give you enough time to warm up, work out, cool down and shower. Choose the most consistent part of your day. If you always start work at different times and always have time in the evenings then it may suit you to exercise after work. Most people will probably start work at the same time each day and their finish time will be different. If this is the case then morning exercise before work is the best way to be consistent. Try to exercise every day bar one, alternating hard days with easy days and very hard days with very easy days. On a very easy day, your session might only consist of a walk. But if you commit yourself to exercising every day you are much less likely to have a day off just because you don't feel like it. Consistency is the key to your fitness. Fitness is about today. Statements like "I used to be super-fit", or "I used to train every day" mean nothing. Your fitness is about today, not yesterday. You must treat your fitness like a tyre with a slow puncture; no matter how hard you blow it up, you must keep topping it up. When the tyre is flat, it's flat. How hard it was a fortnight before means nothing. Experts agree that you lose fitness at twice the speed you gain it so keep topping your fitness up or you will lose it.

Living out of a suitcase

It can sometimes be hard to find the time to exercise when you are on the road with the Principal, living out of a suitcase, moving from hotel to hotel. That said, with a little planning you can keep up with your fitness regime. Many hotels these days have a gym; some of these are large, airy affairs with a steam room and plenty of equipment, while others consist of a smelly basement room, an old 'stairmaster', and a couple of dumbbells. In between these two extremes there are plenty of hotels that are more than sufficient for what we need.

If there is no gym then we can make use of the road or the stairs for some aerobic exercise and use our own bodyweight for some resistance and strength work, such as push-ups and sit-ups. You need only minimal equipment to keep your fitness ticking over and, additionally, it will only take up a small amount of space in your suitcase.

You do not need the Gym to stay fit when on the road. Use the road to run on and your hotel floor to push away from

So if you are heading some place where there is no gym, think about taking a basic bit of kit with you to stay on top of your fitness. Always remember to take some running shoes and suitable running kit. A stability (Swiss) ball is perfect to carry out core exercises and you can also use it as a bench and seat for upper body exercises. It is compact when deflated and the few minutes that it takes to inflate can be effective as a short cardiovascular workout! A skipping rope and an exercise mat are easily fitted into a suitcase, as is a chin-up bar.

Rest is good for you

It is a common myth that training improvements only occur when you are actually exercising. In fact, fitness gains occur while you are resting. Within reason, rest is very good for your training regime. If you have been training hard and your Principal is nipping away on a three-day business trip, you may find that you will be working harder than normal anyway, so it does no harm to knock the training on the head for a few days. A short rest will work wonders for your fitness, but if that three-day break turns into a three-week break, your fitness will disappear faster than you can imagine. The road back to fitness will be hard, you will be cursing yourself for letting it go during and after each session. So use rest intelligently but do not let too much air out of the tyre!

Notebooks and Reporting

All Close Protection Officers should carry a notebook. By that, I mean a small pocketable notebook, much as you see police officers use. I know pen and paper is considered low-tech, but they work. Dictaphones are great, but the tape will be full when you need it most. It can be difficult to archive and review old notes and even if your batteries have not expired just as you really need them, you will eventually inadvertently record over important stuff.

Pocket Digital Assistants (PDA), such as the IPAQ and the Palm, are very good. You can synchronise your desktop computer with them so that you have all your information to hand. You can even write on them just like the old pen and paper. They will sort your notes into date and priority or subject order, and you can even add voice recordings. Some of these PDAs will even let you take pictures, which, as we know, can be worth a thousand words. They will also crash when you least expect them to, reboot themselves and wipe every bit of information that you've ever stored. They will die on you if they see as much as a single rain droplet, and drop them and you risk losing everything. But that's OK because you've take the necessary precaution of backing up every day! Like you've got the time! Get used to using a pen and paper and save yourself all of the techno headaches that have befallen the author.

In This Chapter

See why a notebook can save your life or make sure that you get paid for all work you do.

Use a good quality notebook that will last

Your notebook forms the basis on which reports, investigations, and any subsequent actions are based. To this end, special attention must be given to the maintenance and use of the notebook. A police officer has a set of rules which he keeps in his notebook and these have evolved by experience. We would do well to copy them.

Many police prosecution cases have been lost in court due to a badly maintained notebook and the defence attorney will frequently attempt to challenge the validity of entries. Apart from production in court as evidence, a well-kept notebook is an aid to efficiency. The ideal notebook should be a suitable size to fit in a pocket, have stiff, waterproof outer covers, and have ruled pages that are sequentially numbered.

The reasons for keeping a notebook

The use of the notebook includes the following items:

A record of all duty hours

If you are paid hourly or daily then you must keep track of all the hours that you work. When filling in a time sheet it can be hard to remember exactly how many hours you worked four Wednesdays ago.

A record of any special instructions

We are often given instructions that require us to remember telephone or car registration numbers. Always having a notebook handy makes it the ideal place to store this information and then retrieve it when necessary.

A record of any significant incidents

From time to time, you may have to report on specific incidents such as traffic accidents ,attempted break-ins or possible surveillance operations etc. Your notebook is the ideal place to record this information because you ALWAYS have it with you.

A record of things that may be forgotten

If we see suspects' cars or people when carrying out surveillance detection, and are looking for patterns, we need somewhere to record the details. When we see a similar car again, we can check in our notebook to see if it is the vehicle we have recorded already.

Evidence in court proceedings

Whether you like it or not, after any major incident the chance that you might have to attend court proceedings is high. Your notebook is an excellent aide memoire, which will assist you in recalling the facts of the incident.

Rules for keeping a notebook

☑ All entries must be in chronological order

☑ No gaps should be left between entries.

☑ A thick line should be drawn across the page after a day's work.

☑ A minimum daily entry will be made to show hours of work.

☑ Make all entries legible and in ink.

☑ Do not enter frivolities or personal notes, eg. shopping lists. Your notebook could be an exhibit in a court case.

☑ Make entries at the time of an incident or as soon as practicable afterwards.

☑ Do not erase any entries. If an alteration is necessary line out the entry with a single line so that it may still be read and initialled.

☑ Do not remove pages.

☑ Do not make rough notes on the covers.

Use of notebooks in Court

If a Protection Officer is required to give evidence in court he should attempt to do so without recourse to his notebook. If he does need to refresh his memory or quote an entry, he must first seek the approval of the court. Having done so and produced his notebook, he should then be prepared for the other parties to ask to see it. This they may do, but only the relevant entries (this is where a properly maintained notebook is invaluable). He

I HAVE WITNESSED THE LOOK OF HORROR ON STUDENT BODYGUARD'S FACES WHEN GIVEN A .5MM PENCIL RATHER THAN THE 9MM PISTOL THAT THEY THOUGHT THEY WOULD BE USING

may be cross-examined on the entry. In a decision in the Queen's Bench Division, March 1983 by Mr Justice McNeill, it was ruled that police and security officers may be cross-examined on the contents of their notebook when they have consulted it BEFORE giving evidence, even though it had not been used in the witness box. All entries should be contemporaneous, that is, made at the time, but it is obvious that sometimes this is not possible, i.e. during a chase or violent arrest. They should then be made afterwards as soon as is practical.

Joint entries

Where two or more Protection Officers have been involved in an incident, and acting in unison, they may compile their notes jointly, unless one has different recollections of what was said, heard, or done. He then records it as he recollects it.

Reports and Report Writing

Reports are submitted so that higher levels of management within the company that you are contracted to – or your Principal if directly employed – may be advised of matters on which they may be required to make decisions. Many Close Protection Officers never expect to be writing reports. However, it is common for things to be 'put in writing' and you may well find yourself writing quite a few, especially if you are employed in more regular security situations such as RST.

Guide to report writing

The following guidelines and example will ensure that any reports you do write are legible, concise, and factual. Writing a report need not be a daunting task. Indeed, if a few basic rules are followed, the report almost writes itself. The rules to remember are:

☑ Write a HEADING to show what the report is about.

☑ Put the DATE of the incident.

☑ Put the TIME of the incident.

☑ Put WHO the report is for.

☑ REFER to any notes made at the time.

☑ In the body of the report:

☑ State FACTS, not opinions.

☑ Use CLEAR, PLAIN English.

☑ Include NAMES of any persons involved and details of any WITNESSES.

At the end of this book you will find an example of a report. Handwritten reports are common. If you do not have a computer and printing facilities then reports will almost always be written in long hand and if your handwriting is neat enough may be passed straight to the client. Most people will want the report to be typed so that it looks more professional.

Summary

I have witnessed the look of horror on student Bodyguard's faces when they are given a .5mm pencil rather than the 9mm pistol that they thought they would be using on the course. We have already learned that communication skills is one of the most important skills that we can possess and notebook keeping and report writing are part of those skills. If your writing is illegible the you really should work on it, you wont need to write too much but when you do its important.

The Bodyguard
and The Law

The laws of countries are always changing. Old laws are reformed and new laws brought into force. Lawmaking can be a slow process, but the laws mentioned here could have changed completely by the time you read this. One incident, a knee jerk reaction by the government, and laws can be rushed through Parliament in weeks rather than years. It is up to you to remain up-to-date.

Laws throughout the world can appear to be very similar but that is often not the case. For example, if you were to look at your rights to 'self-defence' in almost all of Europe, Australia, New Zealand the USA and South Africa, the laws look almost identical. But in fact, they aren't. The Italian Parliament has passed legislation allowing people to shoot robbers in self-defence. Italian law permits the use of guns and knives by people in homes or workplaces to protect lives or belongings. This law was passed in 2006 and could be rescinded at any time if things worsen rather than improve. In the UK, you could use a knife but only if its use constitutes the minimum force required.

In This Chapter

Understand the law as it affects you when working as a Close Protection Officer

LAWS CHANGE; MAKE SURE YOU UP-TO-DATE AND FAMILIAR WITH THE LAW IN THE COUNTRY YOU ARE WORKING IN; ESPECIALLY IN THE AREAS OF SELF DEFENCE, THE USE OF FORCE, AND WEAPONS.

English Law

You will notice that this chapter heading refers to English law rather than British. That's because even within a country like the UK, different regions can have different laws. Some Scottish laws and legal procedures are very different from those in England. Wales generally shares the same laws as England but in 2006 they gained independent lawmaking powers, so it could well have different common, civil and criminal laws to the rest of the UK.

If the laws between England and the rest of the UK can be so very different, imagine how laws might differ between countries that have entirely different cultures, such as France, Saudi Arabia and China. As a Close Protection Officer, you cannot offer ignorance of a law as a defence in any country. It's up to you to ensure that wherever you carry out your Close Protection duties, no matter how important your VIP, that you stay within the law. It will be you who pays the price if you don't!

Firstly, remember you are not a police officer. You have limited powers and under no circumstances should you ever try to exceed your authority. When dealing with the public at your place of work you may well come across photographers, press reporters, house staff or just Joe Public on the pavement, but during this interaction you must work within the law at all times. Dealings with the police are mostly to be avoided if possible. The police can sometimes be jealous of the protection professional and have an irresistible urge to arrest them when given the opportunity.

Common, Civil and Criminal Law.

The laws in the UK, as in any other country, can be complex. In some countries, they might be less complex and in some even more so. In England and Wales you must be aware of different types of laws. If we are over-zealous in our duties we might easily break those laws. Should that happen, the best scenario might be one in which we lose our job and therefore our income; the other scenario might be one in which we lost our liberty.

Civil Law

Civil Law is the part of the law that deals with matters of the state such as Common Law, Private law and Municipal law. It is utilised by individuals such as you, your Principal, or organisations like the security company you might be working for. Your Principal's organisation also use Civil Law. When people or organisations use Civil Law, it normally results in restitution and compensation payments. The libel and slander cases we often see on our TV screens are Civil Law cases. In the United Kingdom, a civilian Close Protection Officer cannot arrest someone for committing a civil offence. This shouldn't really pose a problem as the last thing that the Close Protection Officer wants to do is to arrest someone anyway. However trespass, which is something that the Close Protection Officer will come across quite often, is a civil offence, so the officer needs to know how to deal with trespassers without breaking the law.

Dealing with trespassers

'The act of being upon, or entering, the land or premises without the right to be there'

Let us assume that you are patrolling the grounds of your Principal's residence and you come across someone unknown to you standing on the lawn. If you are sure that they shouldn't be there then they are trespassing, even if they have done so unknowingly. If the trespasser refuses a polite request to leave the premises, then the law allows you to use the minimum amount of force that is necessary to physically remove the person from the premises.

You cannot arrest and detain a trespasser because the act of trespassing in the UK is a civil offence. If, however, you have reasonable grounds for assuming that the trespasser is only on the property to commit a crime, and if that crime is an arrestable offence, then the trespasser can be arrested. You will learn later about arrestable offences.

Common Law

Common Law is the unwritten law of England and Wales. Common Law has developed over many years and is based on decisions that are made by the courts, as opposed to the written legislation put in place by Parliament. Decisions made by judges and juries set a precedent for future cases. We have rights of self defence under Common Law.

Self defence and reasonable force

Under the law, you are entitled to use reasonable force to protect yourself, another person or your property. You are also entitled to prevent crime or to help legally arrest a criminal. So, in the UK at least, the Close Protection Officer is catered for in the self defence laws, because 'self defence' can involve someone other than yourself, e.g. your Principal or your family.

The force that you can use has to be reasonable, but what you consider reasonable to use in any situation will depend on the circumstances and the threat you are facing. Broadly, the laws says that for force to be reasonable it must be absolutely 'necessary' and 'in proportion'. The problem with the word reasonable is that what seems reasonable to you in the heat of the moment has to seem reasonable to a jury of your peers, whose only experience of self-defence might have occurred in a school playground when they were seven-years-old.

Yes, it is can be necessary and reasonable to carry out a pre-emptive strike and do this in self-defence, as long as you are entirely sure that you are acting in self-defence. You do not have to wait to be hit. To quote my old friend Peter Consterdine, "Blocking is Bollocks." The last thing you want to be doing is waiting until you are trying to block things that are incoming. Be first. First is best, as long as you are in fear of your safety and acting in self-defence then you are not breaking the law. However, if your response is out of proportion to the violence offered, then your claim of self-defence will evaporate very quickly.

There is very little difference between acting in self-defence, which is within the law, and breaking the law. If it is judged that your response was out of proportion, then you are breaking the law. You must be seen to use the minimum force necessary. Imagine you are completely unarmed and are attacked by someone with a baseball bat. If you pick up a chair to defend yourself then your action might well be judged to be in proportion. However, if you manage to get the bat off the person then now you are armed and the assailant is not. If you now proceed to beat him with his own bat, which many would deem as reasonable, the law will probably not see it as such and you will be prosecuted for assault.

The law does not allow you to retaliate against a criminal. Punishing criminals is a matter for the courts, and you must not take the law into your own hands by trying to punish an offender yourself. There have been plenty of cases when householders or occupiers of private property have been prosecuted for acts of violence committed against intruders.

A claim of self-defence, especially one involving a pre-emptive strike, is much more likely to be believed by a jury if immediately after that strike you left the scene in fear of your safety. This is good news for Close Protection Officers because it is exactly what we should strive to do. If we find ourselves in fear of our safety, very often our best defence is a very hard and extremely aggressive pre-emptive strike followed by an extremely fast ACE.

Criminal Law

Criminal Law is concerned only with illegal acts committed against individuals, property or society as a whole. Criminal Law uses the power that Parliament has given the courts to seek punishment for these offences, Persons guilty of breaking Criminal Law face punishment and rehabilitation.

Offences and their detection

Let us start examining offences and their detection by making sure that we understand the terms used to describe offences we are most likely to come across while working in CP. Then we can progress to look at ways in which we can detect that an offence has occurred. There are many criminal offences on the statute book. In this section, we shall explore several you are most likely to come across:

1. Theft

The offence of theft is committed by a person who; dishonestly appropriates property belonging to another with the intention of permanently depriving the other of it.

2. Robbery

A person is guilty of robbery when he steals, and immediately before or at the time of doing so and in order to steal, uses force on any person or puts any person or seeks to put any person in fear of being subjected to force (Theft Act, 1968 Section 8.)

3. Burglary

The offence of burglary is committed by a person who enters a building, or part of a building, as a trespasser with intent to:

- ☑ Steal anything therein
- ☑ Inflict grievous bodily harm on any person therein
- ☑ Rape any person therein
- ☑ Unlawfully damage the building or anything therein

(Theft Act, 1968, Section 9).

Having entered any building or part of a building as a trespasser, a person is also guilty of burglary if he:

- ☑ Steals or attempts to steal anything therein
- ☑ Inflicts or attempts to inflict grievous bodily harm on any person therein

4. Aggravated Burglary

The offence of aggravated burglary is committed when a person commits burglary and at the time has with him:

- ☑ Any firearm
- ☑ Imitation firearm
- ☑ Any weapon of offence
- ☑ Any explosive

5. Criminal Damage

Criminal Damage occurs when a person without lawful excuse destroys or damages property belonging to another intending to damage or destroy such property or is reckless as to whether such property would be destroyed or damaged.

6. Criminal Damage – endangering life

Involves the person damaging or destroying his own or another's property with the intention of endangering the life of another. He would also be guilty of this offence if the person causing the damage was reckless as to whether the life of another was endangered by his actions.

The threat of Criminal Damage or Criminal Damage endangering life is also an offence.

7. Criminal Damage

This offence covers the circumstances where a person possesses tools, etc, for use by himself or another in causing Criminal Damage. Arson, deliberately setting fire to property, is now defined as Criminal Damage. Similarly, if by setting fire to property the person puts others' lives at risk, he would be guilty of Criminal Damage endangering life.

8. Assault

The range is very wide and covers anything from the threat of violence to grievous bodily harm.

Burden of Proof

It is important for you to understand one other important principle of British law.

The burden of proof in our legal system lies with the prosecution. It is their responsibility to gather and present sufficient evidence to prove beyond reasonable doubt that the person is guilty as charged.

Powers of arrest

Being a Close Protection Officer does not give you any specific powers of arrest. The only power that you have is the same as those of any other member of the general public – in other words, private citizen's power of arrest. This power of arrest is bestowed under the Police and Criminal Evidence Act, 1984. The act is more commonly referred to as PACE. Before discussing the actual sections of the act, it would be advisable to look at what it means to arrest somebody.

An arrest is the taking or restraining of a person from his or her liberty in order that he or she shall be forthcoming to answer an alleged crime or offence.

More specifically, under Section 24 (sub sections 4 and 5), of the Act it states:

Any person may arrest without warrant:

- ☑ Anyone who is in the act of committing an arrestable offence
- ☑ Anyone whom he/she has reasonable grounds for suspecting to be committing such an offence

There are other acts which also confer powers of arrest and they are as follows:

- ☑ Vagrancy Act 1824
- ☑ Criminal Law Act 1967
- ☑ Theft Act 1968

There is a power of arrest under Section 5 of the Vagrancy Act 1824, which states:

ANY PERSON MAY ARREST WITHOUT WARRANT A PERSON FOUND COMMITTING AN OFFENCE UNDER THIS ACT.

Arrestable offences

PACE defines arrestable offences as: Any offence in which the sentence is fixed by law. This includes life imprisonment.

Of offences for which a person aged over 21 may be sentenced to prison for five years or more (PACE, section 24 (1)

(Section 24 paragraph 4) 'Any person may arrest without warrant anyone who is in the act of committing an arrestable offence, or anyone whom he has reasonable grounds for suspecting to be committing such an offence'.

(Section 24 paragraph 5) 'Where an arrestable offence has been committed, any person may arrest without warrant anyone who is guilty of the offence or anyone whom he has reasonable grounds for suspecting to be guilty of it'.

Two examples to consider are:

1. While working on a Residence Security Team you notice that one of the house staff is loading meat from the kitchen into her car and you are sure that she is stealing it. As you reasonably suspicious that person is committing theft?

2. Let's say that you noted it but didn't arrest her, and very shortly after, the cook says that a large amount of meat has been stolen from the cold store. When the person returns, you can effect an arrest.

Both of the above examples have good grounds for arrest because:

☑ An arrestable offence has been committed (theft)

☑ You have good reason to believe that the person is guilty of that offence

It is not always necessary for you to actually see the offender commit the act of theft as long as you know that the offence has been, or is being committed.

Arrest procedure

Once you have deprived someone of their liberty, having told them, for example, "You're not going anywhere until the police arrive", you have effectively arrested them. You might not think you have; you may not have formally put a hand on their shoulder and said, "I arrest you". But you have arrested them all the same. Just by not allowing someone to leave a room means they are arrested. Even if you tell them they are free to go at any time but have your biggest, ugliest and most menacing team members standing by the door preventing them from leaving, you have arrested them whether you wanted to or not.

Many difficulties surrounding arrests exist, including possible dangers for you as a Protection Officer. If you do not follow the correct procedure or rely on inaccurate information, you might be sued for wrongful arrest. The penalties for wrongful arrest can be quite severe. It is therefore advisable that an arrest should be made only if there is absolutely no alternative. If the conditions are such that there is time for the police to be summoned, then do so, and allow them to effect the arrest. It is worth remembering that once you have arrested someone you also take full responsibility for their safety and welfare; if they come to any harm while under arrest, it is the arresting officers that may well learn what it is like to be arrested! Therefore, if you are forced to arrest someone, it should be done with the minimum of fuss and commotion. Always ensure that the person being arrested understands:

☑ Who you are

☑ That they are being arrested

☑ What they are being arrested for

Forget the TV cops; it is perfectly adequate to use words such as, "I am John Smith of XYZ Security. I am arresting you for theft."

Use of a caution

Section 10 of PACE states that 'a person must be cautioned before questions are put to him to obtain evidence that may be given in court'.

It is not necessary for you to make a formal caution in your role as Protection Officer. If the person makes any form of reply, make notes of anything that is said and report it to the police. Above all, do not attempt to interrogate the individual. Anything they say in answer to your questions will be inadmissible anyway. The suspect should be handed over to the police at the earliest opportunity. Let them do what they are paid for. You just give the full details to assist the prosecution. Hopefully, they will then plead guilty and you won't have to attend court.

You may find yourself in a situation where your Principal wants you to investigate a crime before there is any police involvement. This may involve you questioning the person you have arrested. If you are going to a question an arrested person in England or Wales you must give them a caution. Ideally, you would record the time in your notebook that you used to give him the caution and include the names of any witnesses to the caution. The caution that is used in the United Kingdom at present is worded as follows;

"You do not have to say anything. But it may harm your defence if you do not mention when questioned something which you later rely on in court. Anything you do say may be given in evidence."

Procedure following arrest

Once you have detained someone it is essential that they are treated properly and professionally.

That is to say that they should be:

- ☑ Able to exercise their right to make a telephone call, to contact someone outside
- ☑ Must be accompanied at all times
- ☑ Segregated from all other people (particularly witnesses or other suspects)
- ☑ Continually observed to prevent either accident or self-inflicted injury
- ☑ Escorted to the toilet to ensure that they do not attempt to escape or dispose of evidence

A male Protection Officer should never be alone with a female prisoner. Ideally, a female CPO or a female member of the house staff should stay with the prisoner. Similarly, a male prisoner should not be left alone with a female Close Protection Officer. If this is not possible then you must ensure that a colleague or other person remains with you and the prisoner at all times to make it easier to deny any dishonest accusations.

A Protection Officer does not have the right to search the baggage or person of someone they have arrested and detained. Unless, of course, there are reasonable grounds to believe that the person has a weapon, with which he may injure himself or others.

By following this procedure you will be able to counter any subsequent accusations of impropriety. Having ensured that the arrested person is being dealt with correctly you must then hand him/her over to the police giving all relevant information and evidence.

The Use of Force

The Criminal Law Act 1967, Section 3 (1) states:

'Any person may use such force as is reasonable in the circumstances in the prevention of crime or in effecting or assisting in the lawful arrest of suspected offenders or persons at large'. The word reasonable is again used and the same rules apply as for self-defence. If someone resists arrest your response must be reasonable and proportionate.

summary

It is a mistake to think even for a second that because of the job that you do you are above the law. There are policemen out there who will enjoy arresting you. Especially if they feel you are acting above your station in life or earning more money than they are! Do not give them the excuse, you should always act well within the law, do not let anyone such as a team leader or a Principal to push you into breaking the law, it will be you that is punished if you are caught so it must be your decision.

Computer Security

A Close Protection Officer, try as he might, cannot escape the computer revolution. Computers are everywhere. No one writes reports long hand any more, most reports never see an envelope and no one has to lick a stamp. If the report needs to be somewhere it's rare that it can't get there electronically. Who wants to wait two or three days for information sent by courier or Royal Mail when that same information can be sent and received within seconds and be more secure on its journey?

A team leader will need access to information about the assignment such as emergency procedures, staff rotas, staff contact information, threat assessments, vehicle allocation and payroll. This and much more will very often be kept on a computer and most likely, this will be a laptop. This machine will probably take care of all communications whether they are email, fax or, more commonly, voice. The Principal may well have a portable computer and have desktop machines at home and at the office.

Basic Computer Security

It would be fair to say that a working Close Protection Officer just would not have the time to become a computer security expert; there are people that dedicate their lives to that and are still always one step behind the cyber criminals. However, the Close Protection Officer should have a good grasp of computer security for his own use and be able to recognise when to call in an expert.

To be proficient at basic computer security requires us to understand a little about the following subjects:

1. Physical security of the computer
2. Network security
3. Viruses
4. Secure email
5. Backing up data
6. Physical Security

If someone gets physical access to a computer, he or she can

In This Chapter

Understand basic computer security

Give sensible advice to your Principal

Protect the teams email

easily gain access to the information stored on the computer. If you leave a laptop in your car or on a bus like Scotland Yard and the Secret Service seem to have a habit of doing – then the information on that computer will be compromised. Even if the computer is password protected there are other methods that even those with little knowledge of computers can use. Most computers can be started without the use of passwords: there are 'rescue disks' designed for just that purpose. However just simply removing the hard drive from a computer and placing it in another will negate the need for a password and give full access to the hard drive

Securing the Hardware

Keep any computers which have sensitive information away from the general public. Don't think that you will last long in your new security job if you 'lose' a computer. When they're not with you, keep them locked away.

There are specialist devices available for attaching computers to desks, or for locking computer cases closed. These are great and can deter the opportunist. Just remember that you also need to prevent an intruder from actually reaching the computer in the first place – information can be stolen without moving the computer itself.

Physical Security of Networks

Very often, whenever there are a group of computers in your ops room, or the Principal's home or office, you can bet they are networked together. Networks are convenient and allow different computers to share things like internet connections or printers, etc.

If the network is not secure, it can let intruders join it. Once on the network, they can move around the whole computer network, stealing sensitive information from any or all of the computers that are linked. The links can be physical, i.e. hard-wired. They can also be wireless. Imagine someone three hundred metres away from your Principal's home reading every email he or she writes!

In big business, the computers which store the sensitive information are often kept in a specially cooled and guarded computer room, in a secured building.

Power Supply

There are two issues with power supply. One is the matter of power smoothing, preventing sudden surges or drops in supply, and the other is supply itself. Blackouts and brownouts can cause the computers to suddenly shut down, losing any information stored only on the computer's short-term memory (RAM). Sudden surges or drops in supply can cause physical damage to computer components.

In many developed countries, power smoothing is hardly ever needed, but when the Close Protection Officers finds himself in less developed parts, power cuts and surges may happen hourly. You will need a UPS (uninterruptible power supply) and as most of these have smoothing built in, they will protect your computer and the information on it.

A UPS (uninterruptible power supply) is used to protect against sudden loss of power. It's something of a misnomer as it doesn't itself provide power – it's essentially a large battery that charges itself from the power main. The computers are plugged into the UPS and if the mains power cuts out the UPS provides enough power for the computers to shut themselves down and save all their information.

Most UPSs will signal the computer when the main power cuts out. Get your local computer expert to ensure that yours does (preferably before you buy it), and ensure that your computer is set up to respond to that signal.

Network Access

Network access, such as internet access, tends to be at the mercy of large organisations, which run the local internet 'backbones' (the main routes). Even if you buy your connection through a small provider, their own connection is usually with one of the larger organisations. When working in some countries, finding a reliable network access supplier can be difficult. The reliability of your local providers can be vital to the success of your operation if it relies on timely and accurate information to be sent and received.

Network Security

If your computer is not connected to any other computers and doesn't have a modem, the only way anyone can access your computer's information is by physically coming to the computer and sitting at it. So securing the room will secure the computer.

As soon as your computer is connected to another computer, you add the possibility that someone using the other computer can access your computer's information.

If your network (your connected computers) consists only of computers in the same building, you can still secure the network by securing the rooms in which the other computers are located. An example of this would be two computers sharing the same files and printer, but not having a modem and not being connected to any other computers.

However, it's wise to learn about other ways to secure a network of connected computers, in case you add something later. Networks have a tendency to grow. If you have a network, an intruder who gains access to one computer has at least some access to all of them.

The Locked Front Door

As soon as your network connects to somewhere outside your building, you need the virtual equivalent of a locked front door. If you don't have that, all the information you have on your computers is vulnerable to anyone who wants to gain access.

Like real doors, virtual doors come in a wide variety of types, security levels, and expense.

The simplest (but not the safest) way to secure your network is to keep 'moving' if you're connected to the internet through a modem and have a 'dynamic IP address' (ask your service provider), your address keeps changing. If your address keeps changing and you're never on the internet for very long, it's very hard for someone to deliberately intrude on you. However, if someone is determined to snoop on you or your Principal, he or she will, so you need to take the security a step further than just moving.

As soon as you have a stable address and a permanent (broadband) connection, you lose the 'obscurity' advantage that a dynamic IP and sporadic connection provides. You must install a real 'front door'.

Passwords

The most basic lock for your front door is a password. Ensure that every computer on your network requires a password before anyone from the network can read your information or write to your hard drive. If a password isn't required, there is no front door at all. If you're not sure how to setup passwords on a network then I strongly recommend you get hold of a computer expert, or at least a very good manual.

Changing forgotten passwords isn't easy, however. It's better not to forget them in the first place. If your system has a 'master password' that has access to everything, make sure two people on your protection team know that password. If there's only one, what happens when that person is on a day off or unobtainable?

Passwords are only as secure as they are difficult to guess – if your password is your name, for instance, or the word 'password', it's like putting a lock on the front door and never bothering to actually lock it.

There are many ways of ensuring a password is difficult to guess – here are a few of them:

☑ Don't use words less than eight characters long

☑ Include both uPpeR & lOwEr case letters, numbers and punctuation marks

☑ Don't use old military regimental numbers

☑ Don't use anything which can be guessed by someone who knows you or has your information, e.g. names of family, pets, licence numbers, passport numbers, phone numbers or similar, street address (current or past!), or words which are visible from your desk (like the brand of the monitor)

☑ Don't use legitimate words in any language, brand names or logos

☑ Don't use the same password on two or more computers, or the same one you had last year!

Remember that ANY password can be figured out in time, and if someone guesses one of your passwords they might try the same thing for another computer

Suggestions for good passwords include:

Something you'll recognise.

A line from a book or a line of poetry – and use the third letter of each word. Include punctuation (but not spaces)

A really, REALLY bad misspelling of a word

Two words from different languages stuck together with punctuation marks. Good examples:

Iam#6of8 (I'm the 6th of 8 children)

iC@nTgn0$ (I can't get no satisfaction)

You must think up your own. For passwords, the weirder and more idiosyncratic the better.

Permissions

Passwords usually come with usernames. A good username and password system will enable you to set up several roles for your computers. Each role will need different types of access; it will use different programmes and different data.

If an intruder guesses or finds out one person's username and password, they will have access to any programmes or data to which that person usually has access. For this reason, you might like to limit what each person is allowed to access.

Most computer systems have something in place, which does this. Under most systems, it's called 'permissions'. Your computer manual or local expert can help you set it up on your computers. Give each person only what they need to do their jobs; no more, no less. Why give someone the ability to copy files if they won't ever have the need to do so?

Firewalls

Firewalls hide your computer network from the outside world and vet all traffic in and out. None of your computers should be able to access the internet or be accessed from the internet without going through the firewall. Firewalls, whether software or hardware, do require setting up correctly. If this is down to you, consult an expert or get a good manual.

Viruses

Computer viruses are hostile programs written to create havoc and mayhem. They can corrupt your computer, making all that information that you stored about that new CP Job unobtainable, or they might send porno images to all your friends or your Principal! They can only do damage if you, or some programme acting on your behalf, actually runs the virus programme. You would be absolutely safe from viruses if you never ran any programs. But this would make computers pretty useless.

To be reasonably safe, be very careful what programmes you run. Buy or download programmes from trusted sources, use an up-to-date virus checking programme regularly, and definitely before running any newly installed programmes.

Don't think that standard programs are safe. Microsoft Office documents can have mini-programmes embedded in them, called 'macros'. These mini-programmes can spread a virus. Someone sending you a CV for the best BG in the west might be a competitor, sending you a virus that will ruin your business. Or the virus could send vital information on your Principal to a terrorist organisation.

Virus Checkers

Many companies make programmes you can use to search your computer and locate or remove viruses from the computer. They can scan the existing files, and scan files as they are added to your computer – most do both.

These programmes are only as good as their virus definition databases and you must update this regularly. This invariably means subscribing to a service. Be aware that there is always a lag period during which your computer is vulnerable to any new virus. The period consists of:

    1. The time between when the virus is released, and when it is first noticed and reported.

2. The time between when it is reported, and when detection and repair software is made to remove or negate it.

3. The time between when the software is created, and when you download it to your hard drive and run it to find/remove the virus.

Remember you're only protected after the third stage; it could be hours, days or weeks from stage one to three!

Securing your Email

For obvious reasons, Close Protection Officers need secure email. It could be disastrous if details of operational emails were intercepted. All operational emails should be encrypted so that if they are intercepted or copied en route then they will not be able to be read.

Encryption

Encryption is the process of changing text so that it is no longer easy to read.

Commercial encryption uses methods which are very secure. Almost all modern encryption methods rely on a key – a particular number or string of characters, which are used to encrypt, decrypt, or both.

To illustrate how encryption systems work we will use some examples. Let's say that an advance party in one country is communicating with its operations room in another. To ensure that their communications are secure, they could use private key encryption or public key encryption. Each of these systems is discussed below, as are their limitations.

Private Key Encryption

Private key encryption is the standard form. Both ops room and advance party share an encryption key, and the encryption key is also the one used to decrypt the message. The difficulty is sharing the key before you start encrypting the message – how do you safely transmit it?

Many private key encryption methods use public key encryption to transmit the private key for each data transfer session.

If the ops room and advance party want to use private key encryption to share a secret message, they would each use a copy of the same key. The advance party writes its message to the ops room and uses its shared private key to encrypt the message. The message is then sent to ops room. The ops room uses its copy of the private key to decrypt the message.

Private key encryption is like making copies of a key. Anyone with a copy can open the lock. In the case of the advance party and the ops room, the keys would be guarded closely because the messages can be both encrypted and decrypted.

Public Key Encryption

Public key encryption uses two keys – one to encrypt and one to decrypt. The sender asks the receiver for the encryption key, encrypts the message, and sends the encrypted message to the receiver. Only the receiver can then decrypt the message. Even the sender cannot read the encrypted message.

When the advance party wants to share a secret with the ops room using public key encryption, they first ask the ops room for their public key. Next, the advance party uses the ops room's public key to encrypt the message. In public key encryption, only the ops rooms' private key can unlock the message encrypted with their public key. The advance party sends their message to the ops room. The ops room uses their private key to decrypt the advance party message.

The things that make public key encryption work is that the ops room very closely guards the private key and freely distributes the public key. The ops staff knows that it will unlock any message encrypted with its public key.

Limitations of Encryption

Cryptanalysis, or the process of attempting to read the encrypted message without the key, is very much easier with modern computers than it has ever been. Modern computers are fast and powerful enough to allow for 'brute force' methods of cryptanalysis. They use every possible key in turn until the 'plain text' version of the message is found.

Obviously, the longer the key, the longer it takes to use the brute force method of cryptanalysis – but it also makes the process of encrypting and decrypting the message slower. Key length is very important to the security of the encryption method - but the 'safe' key length goes up with the amount of security required.

Encryption doesn't necessarily make your data secure. Not using encryption, however, means that any data in transit is as easy to read as the contents of a postcard sent in regular mail. Encryption at least ensures that anyone who does read your messages has worked hard at it.

Backing up your Computer

All the information you keep on your computer is stored on a hard drive. The important thing to know about hard drives is that they have moving parts, and like all things which move, those parts will eventually wear out. The hard disk on yours or your Principal's computer will fail – it's just a matter of time.

But disk failure should not be the only reason to keep a copy of your important and/

or sensitive data somewhere else – your computer may be in a fire or a flood. A thief might steal the computer. Lightning might strike it. You or someone might make a mistake and wipe out your database. If you haven't got a copy then this might hamper your long term employment prospects!

So we ALWAYS back up the data. But where do we store it? We can store it on another hard drive (don't forget what I said about hard drives) or on removable media, such as disks or tape. None of these are any safer than your hard drive and they will all fail at some time. But having a copy or backup in two places is much safer than one. Having it in three places is even safer. Backups should be stored off site; if the ops room burns down the back-ups won't burn with the original data.

Backup Media

There's a bewildering variety of things you can backup onto. There are floppy disks, tapes, removable hard disks, rewritable DVD-ROMs, and the very popular USB key ring flash memory storage.You can even back your data onto most MP3 music players.

Your backup media (the thing you back up on to) will probably come with software which will ask which files you want to back up, and will copy them onto the backup media for you. their are programs that can automate this process so that you do not forget.

Backup Strategies

With as much data as is stored on a modern computer system, how do you decide what to backup? Should you just put the entire system on a DVD or tape and be done with it? There are several problems with putting your entire system on a backup, not least of which is the cost of tapes and CDs. Also, the time to perform a backup is increased when the entire system is stored. If backing up is quick and painless we will do it more often, right?

As long as you have the original CDs for your software, there is no need to include the programmes themselves in backups. For example, your operating system and word processor shouldn't be backed up. The data files, however, cannot be recreated so you should include them in backups.

Back up everything you need and back it up often. It really depends on your computer usage, but an hourly backup or a monthly one could be reasonable depending on the type of data you are securing.

Verify your backup. You must check the integrity of the backups.

Summary

Computers are now everywhere, most people communicate by using them on a daily basis. If you are not computer savvy then you should get yourself on a course. It is unlikely that your Principal will ask you to secure the computer network at his office. However you should have a basic undserstanding of how to keep your own data safe

Your computer system is only as strong as its weakest part. A determined intruder will keep looking until they find vulnerability. Security through obscurity is weak. A hidden thing is more secure than a highly visible one, but don't trust hiding on its own to protect your data.

The Risk of Fire

While working in Close Protection, no matter what the level of threat, one of the most dangerous threats will be that of fire. It's amazing that people can call themselves protection professionals despite never having had any fire training, never having used a fire extinguisher and possessing no knowledge about even the basics.

The Close Protection Officer should ensure that anywhere the Principal is in residence is adequately protected against fire. That means that there is a means of escape from all locations, smoke alarms are fitted and that equipment (the right equipment) is available to fight the fire.

This may be relatively straightforward at the Principal's residence or on his boat. When you are working in hotels or restaurants, however, it is up to you to check escape routes and equipment.

The difference between a first-class protection officer and an average one more often than not is that the 'good guy' has, and is constantly developing, powers of observation. That is, he notices things which have a bearing on his duties, such as potential fire hazards and the like. He has a sense of suspicion; he is curious and wants to know what is going on. Who is in? Who is out? Are there contractors at the residence? He is not afraid to challenge the obvious and politely enquire. As a professional Close Protection Officer, vigilance is essential at ALL times.

REMEMBER:

- ☑ Fire respects nothing.
- ☑ It leaves people HOMELESS and you JOBLESS
- ☑ It DESTROYS, it MAIMS and, it KILLS.

The nature of fire

Before you use any fire fighting equipment it is essential that you understand the three elements that create fire. REMEMBER: Remove any of the three elements and fire cannot start or continue to burn. Let's look at the three factors separately:

In This Chapter

Fire is a big killer You need to know how to prevent it and fight it

Heat

Heat can come from many sources:

Discarded cigarettes

Sparks from welding equipment

Electrical faults

The Sun

A house fire can cause more injury, death and damage than a well placed bomb. Fire drills must be practised, and equipment kept serviceable at all times

Fuel

Fuel can be described as anything that burns. This can be divided into:

SOLIDS: wood, cloth, paper, etc.

LIQUIDS: petrol, paint, oil, etc.

GASSES: acetylene, coal, gas, etc.

Most of the articles and materials we use in daily life will burn.

Oxygen

Freely available all over our planet! Not just in those metal cylinders found in hospitals and welding shops but in the air that gives us life. The same air we breathe in order to keep alive will sustain fire that so often destroys life.

This can be explained by performing the following simple experiment. Consider a lighted candle (we have heat from the match, fuel from the wick and wax and, of course, oxygen in the air). The candle is covered with a jar and a few seconds later the flame flickers and goes out. The same thing would happen if the heat or the fuel had been removed.

Your Actions on finding a fire

All fire fighting equipment is designed to attack one or more of the three elements, e.g. a water extinguisher reduces and removes the heat source and puts the fire out.

The following rule of thumb should assist a CPO to remember what has to be done:

F   **Find**

I   **Inform**

R   **Restrict**

E   **Extinguish**

Find

Very often, something else finds the fire for us. Heat sensors or smoke detectors do nothing other than detect the presence of smoke or fire. However. the Close Protection Officer or Residential Security Team member, using their senses of sight and smell, may well also detect a fire. You need not necessarily see the fire. A fire can be detected by smell (smoke) or by heat. It goes without saying that once a fire is found, any action taken should be immediate and extremely positive.

BY REMOVING ANY ONE OF THE THREE ELEMENTS YOU
CAN PUT THE FIRE OUT

Inform

Sound the alarm. Get people out of the building, and call the Emergency Services, giving as much relevant information as possible. Make sure you know the address and the best way for the fire tenders to approach.

Restrict

Restrict access Do not allow anyone back in until you are absolutely sure that it is safe.

Extinguish

Only if it is safe to do so. Try to contain the fire. Close doors and windows and remove any flammable materials; extinguish the fire. Do not activate the extinguisher until you are close to the fire. Use the right kind of extinguisher.

Types of Fire

In the UK there are four classifications of fire. They are as follows:

Class A

TEXTILES – Wood, paper, cardboard, cloth, etc.

Class B
LIQUIDS – Petrol, oil, paint, wax, etc.

Class C
GASES – Acetylene, hydrogen, propane, butane, etc.

Class D
METAL – Magnesium, aluminium, etc.

Fire Fighting Equipment

The type of fire fighting equipment used, whether portable or automatic, depends upon the category of fire that is being fought. It is essential that you get to know and fully understand the fire fighting qualities and potential of all the equipment at your location. Very often in some hotels extinguishers are none existent or are so well hidden, they may as well not be there. Find them before you need them!

Each type of fire requires its own particular means of extinguishing. It can be extremely dangerous to use the wrong type of equipment.

The Class C type of fire is dangerous and at NO TIME should you attempt to extinguish it. This type of fire must be left to the experts.

Class D is the most dangerous of all fires and NO attempts should be made to put it out. Call the experts immediately.

Hand operated extinguishers

There are a few simple rules to remember when using these extinguishers. All are fairly simple to operate and are effective if used according to the maker's instructions.

☑ You must READ the labels and LEARN the required method of operation. Remember also which type of extinguisher is to be used on which particular kind of fire.

☑ The following tips should be remembered:

☑ Gas extinguishers, particularly Carbon Dioxide (CO_2), become freezing cold when used – DO NOT hold the metal casing as your hand as it could become blistered or stuck to it.

☑ Water and gas extinguishers are most effective when aimed at the BASE of a fire.

☑ Foam extinguishers are used to lay a blanket of foam OVER burning liquid. The foam should be aimed at the far side of the fire and allowed to spread across the burning surface.

☑ The simple bucket of water is still a useful item if you do not have immediate access to an extinguisher.

☑ Buckets of SAND are also simple and effective when used to dam the flow of a spilt liquid. Be prepared.

Specialised Equipment

At this point, it might be helpful to consider some of the fire fighting equipment used in specialised installations, e.g. computer rooms, photographic laboratories.

CO2 Flooding system.

Most of these have a built-in system that uses a gas (Halon or CO2). It smothers the fire automatically by removing the air (oxygen) without causing secondary damage. In rooms with such installations all persons in the area must leave immediately activation occurs, as they are in danger of being suffocated. Nobody should attempt to enter such a room or area if the alarm has been activated. All such installations have signs warning personnel what action to take in the event of fire. Your principal may well have this type of flooding system in strong-rooms and computer rooms as they can extinguish a fire with the minimum amount of damage.

Sprinkler systems

Sprinkler systems are used in a variety of buildings where Class A items such as clothes, furniture, paper, etc. are stored or manufactured.

The system is activated directly by the heat of a fire. The 'head' releases water to dowse the flames. You should check the pressure gauges and valves controlling the sprinkler system. The valves are generally locked in the OPEN position. Once activated, this system can only be closed down manually. The position of the stop value will often be indicated by a notice adjacent to the door giving access to the valve.

Dry and wet riser systems.

Many large premises such as residential apartments, hotels and office buildings have a riser system installed to enable the emergency services to get large amounts of water to any part of the building without laying hoses up several flights of stairs. The only difference between one system and the other is:

- ☑ The DRY riser system pipe work remains empty until filled with water by the Emergency Services pumps.
- ☑ The WET riser, as the name implies, is kept filled with water ready for instant use by the Emergency services at the floor required.

Foam flooding

Another item for the Emergency Service's use is the foam flooding system found at places such as boiler rooms or flammable liquid stores. This system allows foam to be pumped inside without the need to enter the room. This system also has an inlet valve placed in an external wall, which is covered by a panel and indicated by a notice. It is essential that access to such valves is always available. Never allow vehicles to park or goods to be stacked so as to obstruct access to them.

Smoke and fire-check doors

In many public buildings and office blocks, fire and smoke check doors are held in the open position. When the fire alarm is activated, the doors automatically close. They do not lock, only close. It is a vital part of a Close Protection Officer's job to ensure that all fire/smoke check doors are unobstructed.

Fire blankets

The Fire Blanket (found in most kitchens) is used to smother a fire, e.g. a blazing chip pan. The blanket is thrown completely over the pan in order to prevent air from reaching the flames (removing oxygen). This blanket can also be used if a person is on fire. He should be laid on the floor and the flames quickly smothered with a blanket.

Car Fires

Always carry a fire extinguisher in a car. Try to have one fitted unobtrusively in the passenger compartment for quick access but if this isn't possible, having one in the boot/trunk is better than none at all. Make sure that the extinguisher is designed to be used in vehicle fires!

Summary

Over the years, I have been amazed to discover that quite a number of Close Protection Officers have absolutely no knowledge about fire and fire safety. Often they assume that this kind of stuff is for the lowly uniformed security officer, and not the Close Protection Officer.

The professional is well aware that a fire in the dead of night might well be the deadliest foe that he will ever meet. He will always be aware of specific hazards; he will know all of the escape routes in EVERY BUILDING he works in; he will pay attention to the positioning and serviceability of all fire fighting equipment around him and know how to use it. He will take it upon himself to ensure that all his principals' house staff are aware of fire hazards and fire fighting equipment, especially ensuring that kitchen and cleaning staff are made well aware and practiced whenever possible in the use of fire blankets and extinguishers.

The UK Security Industry Authority

I n the 1990's the British Government decided that it would licence the whole of the security Industry. They formed the Security Industry Authority (SIA) as part of the new Security Industry Act 2001. This was in an era when the government of the time was trying to regulate (and tax) as much of any industry that they could. The regulation bandwagon gathered speed when The Association of Chief Police Officers (ACPO) reported that the security industry had many criminals working within it and said that if everyone in the industry was vetted and licensed then this would make things much better. I thought it funny at the time, as the police themselves are vetted and licensed and barely a week would pass in any police HQ without another prosecution or allegation of criminal activities by the police. Police were being accused and convicted, of assaulting, raping and stealing on a scale that seemed unprecedented. In fact it was only a tiny minority of crooked police that giving the whole of the police a bad name. This was in fact the same for the security industry; a very small minority bought the whole industry into the spotlight. When the figures on criminals in the industry were calculated they included in their figures bouncers and car clampers who had a notorious record of criminality within their ranks.

In This Chapter

We show you the 15 mandatory sessions you must complete if you want a UK Close Protection Licence.

At that time there were many criminals and ex-criminals working as bouncers and car clampers and including these professions in the "security Industry" did taint the whole industry, when in fact the rest of the security industry which included over 100,000 security officers and 1000s of Close Protection officers probably employed fewer criminals the UK police! But regulation was going to happen no matter what and it finally started to roll out in 2003.

In the manned guarding industry, licensing was costing the security industry money, every security officer needed a licence that was costing them almost a week's wages (more tax!) the security companies were told that the industry training qualification that their trainers held needed to be changed and everyone groaned, more expense. But it was not long before the main benefit of licensing started to become apparent. The training that the officers needed was developed to a good standard and the professionalism within the guarding industry began to rise.

The SIA used the manned guarding model and applied it to Close Protection officers. They had industry experts develop the core competency. When a candidate passes the course based upon this, and can prove that he or she does not have a criminal record they can then apply for a licence to operate. The course is a minimum of 150 hours guided learning, as well as having a qualification in First Aid.

To specify a minimum of 150 hours was commendable but the testing procedure leaves a lot to be desired. Probably with costs and convenience in mind, almost all of the 'awarding bodies' have opted for a multiple choice examination that with a pass marks of only seventy per cent. This makes it much too easy for the students to pass and does make a mockery of the whole licensing process. If the licence is to be held in any regard it should be earned rather than given away. The tests I have seen really do insult the intelligence , but this effectively means that if you can afford the course fee you can become a Close Protection Officer.

The SIA core competency specification detailed the required training programme in fifteen areas. The following sessions are taken directly from the SIA Specification for Core Competency Training and Qualifications for Close Protection Officers Remember that this really is a minimum training requirement; too many courses are designed around these fifteen sessions with the aim of passing the awarding bodies tick test. Rather than teaching Close Protection to higher standard than the authorities require. That's the problem with 'minimum standards', people will reach them and go no further. If you are serious about a career in Close Protection then you need to be sure that your training provider is not just going through the motions for you to just pass the test after you have passed them your money.

Session 1: Introduction to the Roles and Responsibilities of the Close Protection Operative

Aim:

To introduce and explain the roles and responsibilities of the close protection operative.

To introduce and explain the roles and responsibilities of the close protection team.

Objectives:

By the end of this session trainees will be able to:

- Explain the purpose and diversity of the close protection sector
- Give examples of notable close protection incidents; successes and failures
- Explain the difference between a client and a principal within the role of close protection
- Explain the different roles within a close protection team
- Explain the roles a close protection operative may undertake whilst working alone
- State the professional attributes of an effective close protection operative
- Explain the range of equipment available to the close protection operative
- Explain the purpose of close protection training and licensing.
- State why it is necessary for a close protection operative to be responsible for their own continual professional development (CPD)
- Give examples of the different types of people to whom close protection operatives
- are required to provide personal protection and describe the different tasks
- involved
- Explain the need for a close protection operative to be flexible and act in a
- professional manner during an assignment.
- Explain how working alone affects how a close protection operative carries out his/her role

Session 2: Threat and Risk Assessment

Aim:

To understand the importance of threat assessment and risk management

To produce a risk assessment

Objectives:

- By the end of this session trainees will be able to:
- Explain what is meant by threat assessment and risk management and understand the relationship
- Explain the main threats to a principal within a close protection context.
- Explain why it is necessary to conduct threat assessment and risk assessment on
- people and venues
- Describe threat and risk assessment techniques used concerning people and venues
- Understand the process for carrying out threat assessment and risk management when a principal is arriving and leaving a destination
- Explain the need for on-going assessment, response and contingency plans
- Describe how close protection operatives gather operational intelligence within the UK
- Understand the factors to be taken into account in assessing risks
- Describe the various threat levels
- Carry out and produce a risk assessment/audit

Session 3: Surveillance Awareness

Aim:

To have a basic understanding of surveillance, counter-surveillance and anti surveillance methods

Objectives:

By the end of this session trainees will be able to:

- Describe the range of unwanted attention e.g. criminals, media, followers, stalkers, fixated persons
- Describe a range of basic surveillance techniques
- Describe a range of anti-surveillance techniques
- Explain the various technical aids that may be deployed by people or groups to assist them in surveillance
- Explain what actions can be taken to counter unwanted surveillance

Session 4: Operational Planning

Aim:

To discuss and demonstrate operational planning

Objectives:

By the end of this session trainees will be able to:

- Explain operational planning
- Explain how important threat assessment and risk assessment is in operational planning
- Design an operational plan to include risk assessment factors
- Explain the importance of time management and resource allocation
- Explain liaison with other agencies

Session 5: Law and Legislation

Aim:

To explain and discuss the legislation which impacts on a close protection operative

Objectives:

By the end of the session trainees will be able to:

- Explain the parts of civil and criminal law that have an impact on the role of a close
- protection operative, in particular the Human Rights Act, the Data Protection Act and the Health and Safety Act
- Identify key areas of the Misuse of Drugs Act of 1971 and the Public Entertainment
- Licence (Drugs Misuse) Act 1997 which relate to close protection activities
- Describe the relationship that close protection operatives must have with official agencies and how to work with them

Session 6: Interpersonal Skills

Aim:

To discuss the importance of interpersonal skills within a close protection environment

Objectives:

By the end of the session trainees will be able to:

- Explain the need for effective interpersonal skills
- Explain the range of interpersonal skills needed within the role of a close protection operative
- Explain the importance of briefing and de-briefing
- Explain effective negotiation skills
- Explain the importance of effective communication with principals, clients and others involved in close protection operations
- Explain the need to be properly assertive
- Explain the importance that protocol has in close protection

Session 7: Close Protection Teamwork

Aim:

To discuss the importance of teamwork within close protection

To conduct an operational briefing

Objectives:

By the end of the session trainees will be able to:

- Describe the attributes of an effective team
- Explain the importance of knowing and using other team members' abilities and skills
- Explain the importance of personal and team preparation
- State the importance of standard operating procedures (SOPs)
- Describe the importance of effective communication within the close protection team
- Explain the structure and purpose of operational briefings and de-briefings

Session 8: Reconnaissance

Aim:

To discuss the purpose of and carry out reconnaissance

Objectives:

By the end of the session trainees will be able to:

- Explain the purpose of reconnaissance
- Describe issues to be considered when conducting a reconnaissance
- Describe the role of a security advance party
- Conduct a reconnaissance
- Describe the difference between a covert and overt reconnaissance

Session 9: Close Protection Foot Techniques

Aim:

To discuss and demonstrate close protection foot techniques

Objectives:

- By the end of the session trainees will be able to:
- Explain the role of a close protection operative on foot and as a personal escort
- Explain the roles within a close protection team whilst on foot
- Explain the role of a team leader
- Explain the need for flexibility whilst on foot
- Explain the range of communication techniques to be used whilst on foot
- Demonstrate a range of close protection foot formations
- Demonstrate effective body protection of a principal
- Demonstrate foot evacuation of protected person(s)

Session 10: Route Selection

Aim:

To understand the need for and process of route selection

Objectives:

By the end of the session trainees will be able to:

- Explain the need for route selection and planning
- Explain the need for assessing risks associated with selecting routes and what factors must be taken into account
- List the considerations when selecting modes of transport
- Explain the relationship between route selection and methods of transport
- Demonstrate the ability to read and interpret a range of maps
- Describe the range of technological tools used in route planning
- Explain environmental factors to be considered when planning and timing a route
- Describe a range of factors that may impact on operational planning e.g. timetables, festival days
- Produce a primary and secondary route plan

Session 11: Use of Close Protection Vehicle Techniques

Aim:

 To discuss the use of vehicles in close protection procedures and associated techniques

Objectives:

By the end of the session trainees will be able to:

- Explain the need for vehicle security and precautions taken to maintain this security
- Describe the risk assessment implications with regards to the use of vehicles
- Explain the need for alternative transport plans
- Describe the variety of vehicle and driving arrangements and how this impacts on
- the role of the close protection operative and team; i.e. chauffeurs, self-drive,
- people accompanying the principal
- Demonstrate how to embark and disembark from a vehicle in a variety of scenarios
- Explain the legal obligations close protection must undertake regarding the use of vehicles

Session 12: Search Procedures

Aim:

To discuss and demonstrate search procedures within close protection operations

Objectives:

By the end of the session trainees will be able to:

- Explain the procedures for and implications of searching buildings, vehicles, open venues, people
- Demonstrate basic search techniques
- Explain the law in relation to search and control of access
- State the importance of post search security
- Describe the use of technology available to assist search
- Describe how to deal with unauthorised / dangerous objects

Session 13: Incidents and Dilemmas

Aim:

To discuss how to deal with incidents and dilemmas within close protection

Objectives:

By the end of the session trainees will be able to:

- Describe typical incidents that may arise during close protection operations
- Describe examples of dilemmas that a close protection operatives may encounter
- Explain how effective communication within a close protection team is necessary when dealing with incidents and dilemmas
- Explain the personal responsibility of a close protection operative when dealing with incidents and dilemmas
- Explain the implications of relevant legislation on close protection when dealing with incidents and dilemmas

Session 14: Venue-Based Security

Aim:

To discuss venue-based security operations

Objectives:

By the end of the session trainees will be able to:

- Describe the range of venue-based security operations e.g. homes, business premises, hotels, show venues
- Describe the relationships between mobile and static CP operations within venue based security
- Describe the role of a security advance party
- Explain the importance of effective handovers and briefings
- Identify common factors that may influence operational plans at various sites
- Explain the need to cooperate with hosts, staff and other key individuals at sites
- Explain the use of the range of communication equipment and other technology that may be used in venue-based close protection
- Describe a range of common contingencies that may be employed in venue-based
- close protection operations e.g. alarms, safe rooms, evacuation contingencies
- Describe a range of common countermeasures that may be employed in venue based
- close protection operations e.g. patrolling, access control

Session 15: Communication and Conflict Management Skills

In line with other SIA qualifications for licensing, the SIA requires all security operatives who interact with the general public to be trained in communication and conflict management skills. For the purposes of this qualification close protection operatives should have the same knowledge and understanding of communication and conflict management skills as other security operatives but will be trained using practical scenarios relevant to close protection.

Licensed close protection operatives will also be licensed to work as security guards and door supervisors. When deployed in other security roles the same principles of communication and conflict management will apply but the context and environment may differ. Close protection operatives should be made aware of the need to become familiar with the likely conflict situations that may occur in different security roles

Training in communication and conflict management skills should be tailored to the context of close protection. Awarding bodies should ensure that the training syllabus includes relevant practical scenario situations in both the training syllabus and the assessment processes

Aim:

To develop knowledge and skills in communication and conflict management

Objectives:

By the end of the session trainees will be able to:

- Describe a range of potential conflict situations within close protection
- Describe how to assess the level of threat posed in a conflict situation
- Recognise human responses to emotional and threatening situations
- Identify the conditions and behaviours that trigger or inhibit an angry response in people
- Explain the basic elements of communication
- Explain the importance of non-verbal communication when dealing with emotionally charged situations
- Explain the importance of adopting an appropriate initial response
- Identify the most common situations where there is a risk of escalation into violence
- Demonstrate an understanding of the attitude/behaviour cycle and how to prevent escalation
- Explain a range of techniques to diffuse and eliminate conflict situations
- Explain an escalation in risk and how to manage anger and aggression
- Explain the difference between assertion and aggression
- Describe the effects of stress within close protection
- Explain the use of appropriate physical techniques for dealing with conflict
- Choose the most appropriate responses to a situation involving potential conflict

A Note about session 15 Conflict Management

In the UK, when the Security Industry Authority was writing the core competency for training and qualifications of Close Protection officers they insisted that one of the modules that must be taught and tested would be conflict management. They had also sensibly added to this module to the core competency specifications of bouncers, security officers and wheel clampers.

This was "new" for the Close Protection and industry. The authority insisted that all the UK Close Protection instructors would need to attend a conflict management instructor's course before they could continue to teach Close Protection. Jobs for the boys!

The issues that were raised by many in the UK industry were twofold, firstly the subject of conflict management was not the new to the Close Protection industry, in fact it had been taught for many years. Secondly the conflict management course that the security industry inflicted on the industry had nothing to do with Close Protection it was the same module that was designed for the door staff and was based almost solely on confrontation.

The Close Protection officer is never telling drunks that they can't enter a venue because they are wearing Nike training shoes, and then dealing with the aftermath that such an instruction can attract. To work conflict management training must be specific to the environment that you are working in and it is hoped that any provider of such training would modify the conflict management module to suit the subject.

The vast majority of conflict management training centres on two areas, communication skills and threat assessment. Close Protection officers are experts in both of these areas. The Security Industry Authority module for conflict management covers areas such as 'signalling non-aggression' and 'defusing and calming situations' this is fine in a bouncer or retail security officer situation, but not necessarily so for Close Protection. Signalling non-aggression can sometimes be the opposite of what a situation requires to ensure the safety of your principal. Furthermore, it is rare for the Close Protection officer and his principal to stay and defuse or calm situations because always the first priority of the bodyguard is to remove the principal from the conflict.

All of the Close Protection officer's day is taken up with conflict avoidance. Conflict *management* is for those occupations such as door staff and security officers whose working day is filled with conflict arising from members of the public. The well-trained and experienced Close Protection officer will avoid, confront and manage conflict using all the skills at his disposal. There are specialist schools that teach conflict management along with physical intervention to a much higher level than the security industry authority asked for and any Close Protection officer could learn a lot by attending one of these courses.

Forms and Checklists

Bomb Threat Checklist

This form should be kept on a clipboard right next to the ops room telephone.

TELEPHONE BOMB THREAT CHECKLIST

This checklist is designed to help you to deal with a telephoned bomb threat effectively and to record the necessary information. <u>Record the call if possible</u>

QUESTIONS TO ASK THE CALLER

When is the bomb going to explode?

Where is the bomb right now?

What does it look like?

What kind of bomb is it?

What will make it explode?

Did you place the bomb?

Why?

What is your name?

What is your address?

Where are you calling from?

AFTER THE CALL

Exact Time of the Call	Date

The Callers Voice

Calm	☐	Crying	☐	Deep	☐
Angry	☐	Normal	☐	Ragged	☐
Excited	☐	Distinct	☐	Clearing Throat	☐
Slow	☐	Slurred	☐	Deep Breathing	☐
Rapid	☐	Nasal	☐	Cracked Voice	☐
Soft	☐	Stutter	☐	Disguised	☐
Loud	☐	Lisp	☐	Accent	☐
Laughter	☐	Raspy	☐	Familiar	☐

Background Sounds

Street Noise	☐	Machinery	☐	Animal Noises	☐
Crockery	☐	Voices	☐	PA System	☐
Music	☐	Static	☐	Other	☐

TELEPHONE BOMB THREAT CHECKLIST

In This Chapter

Examples of the forms and checklists used by Close Protection Officers on a daily basis

Security Vulnerability Survey

A survey form like this, used at the Principal's offices and residences, should ensure that you get all the information you need.

SECURITY VULNERABILITY SURVEY	
Building Name	**Date of Survey**
Name of Security Surveyor	**No of Occupants**
Building Perimeter	
Type of Construction	
Number of Entrances & Exits	
Is all Access & Egress monitored? How?	
Describe Perimeter Fences	
Are Perimeter Fences Adequate?	
Height of Windows from Ground. How are they Protected	
Roof access from adjacent buildings? Roof Openings? Are they secured?	
Who occupies adjacent property? Any threats arising from this?	
Vehicles	
Where are employees parking	
What security is in place at the car park	
Is there under building parking? Who's offices are above?	
Are guards involved in the car park control	
Lighting	
Is the perimeter lighting adequate?	
Are faults or bulb-outs reported?	
Locks And Alarms	
Are keys controlled and stored safely?	
Are cameras properly placed?	
Are more cameras needed? Where?	
Is the alarm serviced?	
Who is the locksmith for the building?	
Are key combinations changed regularly?	
What is the lost-key- policy?	
Is the Alarm line monitored? Who by?	
Are CCTV pictures recorded? Digital or Analogue? Is the quality of recording acceptable?	
Is the fire system serviced regularly?	
Are the evacuation plans sound?	
Is the muster area suitable?	

Excel Protection Security Survey

Security Vulnerability Survey - Page 2

SECURITY VULNERABILITY SURVEY	
The Guarding Company	
Name of the Guarding Company	
Are they a registered Company?	
Are all the staff trained and licensed?	
Are the guards adequately supervised?	
Are their patrols recorded on a computer?	
Has the company got adequate insurance in place?	
Can the CP team trust this company?	
Name the security supervisor?	
Employer, Visitor and Contractor Controls	
Are all visitors and contractors recorded?	
Are all visitors and contractors escorted?	
Are they issued with passes? Do the passes expire?	
General Comments	
Include here any information about the security of the building that may impact on the safety and security of the principal.	

Excel Protection Security Survey

Incident Report

Incidents need to be recorded, they may be serious such as reporting suspicious activity with regard to surveillance or it may be more mundane.

Incident Report				
To	Mr. Tom Fitzgerald	From	Mr Michael P. Lord	Date: 31 Dec 2006

SUBJECT: Theft from House Kitchens

On 30 December 2006 at 2210 hrs I was on duty at the rear of the residence, as part of the RST, when I noticed that Mr Anthony Wong, a member of the house staff, was placing a large case of wine in the boot of his private car.

I asked Mr Wong if he had permission to remove the wine from the kitchens and he said he did. He left the residence with the wine in his car at 2230 hrs.

At 2340 hrs, I spoke to the kitchen manager, Mrs S Robinson, as she was leaving the residence. I asked her if Mr Wong had permission to remove wine from the premises. She told me that he did not.
I told her that I had seen him take 12 bottles earlier in the evening.

Mrs Robinson asked that I prepare this report for the morning and that she would carry out a stock check.

M P Lord
CPO

Daily Occurrence Book

This book records everything that you do. Every phone call, every patrol and any occurrence no matter how seemingly insignificant is recorded in this document which will be located in the ops room or the RST base.

Daily Occurrences Book · The Boltons

A new sheet per shift

SIGNING ON

Date:	Time	All Equipment & keys checked	Print Name		Sig: Don't sign until you've checked! List any comments on the 1st line of the Occurrences section
Date:	Time	All Equipment & keys checked	Print Name		Sig: Don't sign until you've checked! List any comments on the 1st line of the Occurrences section

CHECK CALLS

0600☐	0700☐	0800☐	0900☐	1000☐	1100☐	1200☐	1300☐	1400☐	1500☐	1600☐	1700☐
1800☐	1900☐	2000☐	2100☐	2200☐	2300☐	2400☐	0100☐	0200☐	0300☐	0400☐	0500☐
0600☐	0700☐	0800☐	0900☐	1000☐	1100☐	1200☐	1300☐	1400☐	1500☐	1600☐	1700☐

PATROLS

Time Out	Time Return	Comments,

OCCURRENCES

Time & Initials after each entry

Key Register

All keys need to be accounted for. a key register leaves you in no doubt who has keys, when they went out an if they have been returned,

KEY ISSUE

No 10 THE BOLTONS

Key Issue					Key Return			
Date	Time	Key Description	Person Receiving	Signature	Returned by	Date	Time	Signature
4 Jan 07	0805	Stable Block	Colin Brady	*(signature)*	SARAH	4/1	1035	*(signature)*
4-1-07	0915	Swimming Pool	SARAH Thompson	*(signature)*				
4/1/07	1000	CLEANERS	JOHN PLUMBR	*(signature)*				

Visitor/Contractor Record

Whenever visitors and contractors enter premises their arrival and departure times alongside the reason for their visit.

Visitor Record — **The Boltons**

Date	Pass No	Full Name	Company	Visiting who	Car Index	Time In	Signature	Time out	RST Initials

Principal Questionnaire

You may have a Principal that will fill a form like this himself and if so this is ideal. However, more often than not the Bodyguard will fill this himself as he comes by the information, I have seen forms that ask the Principal about his vices such as gambling and taking mistresses! You will get to discover this information very quickly but it is probably not wise to ask these embarrassing questions directly.

PRINCIPAL QUESTIONNAIRE

Personal Details

Name:		Date of Birth
Addressed as:		Blood Group

Current Residence/s

Relevant Medical Details

Family Members at Residence

1	2
3	4
5	6

Staff at Residence

1	Job?
2	Job?
3	Job?
4	Job?

Threats and Enemies

Details of previous threats or attacks

What person or group poses a threat if any?

Lifestyle

What Activities do you carry out regularly and where, such as dining out, golf etc

Why did your last bodyguard leave?

Convoys

Anything that can ease the administration headache of convoys has got to be a good thing. This simple sheet will let you know who is in each vehicle the convoy position and call sign.

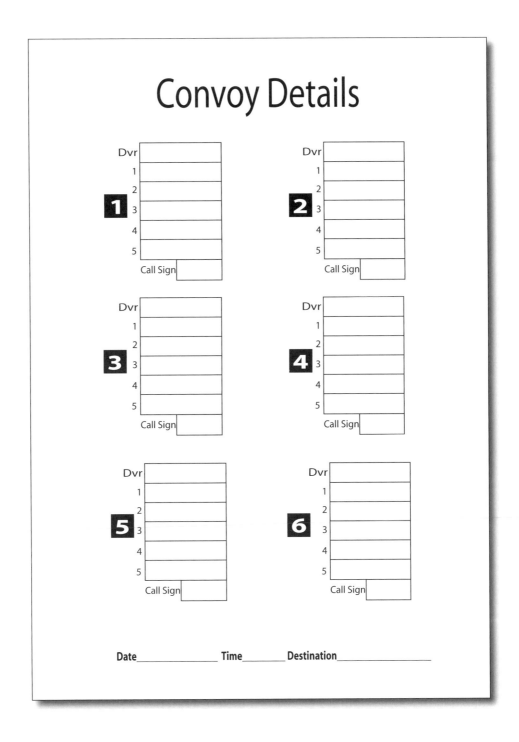

Hotel Check-List

This form can be used by the SAP, if you have used a hotel before then file the check-list so that it can be used at a later date.

HOTEL CHECK-LIST

Hotel Details		
Hotel Name:		Tel:
Address		
		Email:

Check In and Out

Check in Date	Time	Check Out Date	Time

Booking Details

Room No	Location	Room No	Location
Room No	Location	Room No	Location
Room No	Location	Room No	Location
Room No	Location	Room No	Location
Reservations made by		When	

Ops Room Location

Restaurants

Name	Open/close `
Name	Open/close `

Facilities

Medical Facilities ☐   Business Centre ☐   Gymnasium ☐   Pool ☐   Shops ☐   Laundry ☐

Hotel Staff

Manager	Name	Tel ext
Security Manager	Name	Tel ext
Head Porter	Name	Tel ext
Doorman	Name	Tel ext

Security

Security Officers Yes ☐ No ☐ Numbers and duty times

Parking

Adequate parking? Secure? Where?

Any Other Information

City Information Form

If your Principal travels to different cities then these info forms can be a great help. If you file them you can quickly build up a very useful database.

CITY INFO

Basic Details	
City Name	Country
Language Spoken	Currency
Airport Name	Distance to City Centre

Principal's Contacts in City	
Name	Tel No
Name	Tel No
Name	Tel No

Emergencies	
Police/Fire:	Embassy Tel:
Nearest Hospital	
Doctor or Pharmacy	

City Threats or Danger	
Criminal	
Terrorist	
Other	

Useful Numbers	
Favourite Hotel	Tel No
Favourite Restaurant	Tel No
Car Hire	Tel No
Search Dog Handler	Tel No
Translator	Tel No
Local Security Company	Tel No

Any Other Info

Restaurant Check-List

If your Principal uses the same restaurants all of the time then a list like this will not be of much use, but if he travels to new restaurants then this form can be used. After travel these can be filed with the the city info files and they will save a bit of leg work when you return to the city.

RESTAURANT CHECKLIST

Restaurant Details		
Restaurant Name:		Tel:
Address		
		Email:
Cuisine Type:		
Manager:		Head Waiter:
Dress Code?		Seating Capacity

Booking Time		
Date	Time	For How Many
Reservations made by:		When
Name of person who took booking:		
Booked in the name of:		
Is the BG/Team Eating?		Estimated customers in at this time

Other Facilities
Secure Parking
Room for Team to Wait

Any Other Information

Air Travel Checklist

Stick baggage receipts on the back of this checklist. Colour coded luggage tags will assist you in loading and unloading vehicles and ensuring that all luggage is accounted for. You might choose purple for the Principal with different colours for others in his party and CP the team. This makes things much easier at baggage reclaim.

AIR TRAVEL CHECKLIST

Departure Details

Airport Name	Airport Code
Airline Name:	Flight No

TERMINAL NUMBER	DATE	TIME
Latest Check-in Time	Earliest Check-in Time	
Aircraft Type:	No of Seats Booked	
Express Check in:	Preferred Seating	
Stopovers?	Flight Origin	

Alternative Airport in case of cancellation:

No of items luggage checked?

Telephone Numbers

Airline numbers	
Airport Police	
Airport Emergency Medical	
VIP Lounges	

Arrival Details

Airport Name	Airport Code
Arrival Time	Car Hire

Any Other Information

Notes

Notes

This book has a companion web site which can be found at:

www.bodyguards-bible.com

Owners of this book have exclusive 'members only' access to this web site. The members only section of the site has additional information about training to become a bodyguard, getting work, working overseas, and much more. All of the forms that you have seen in the book can be down-loaded along with much more information about our industry. You will find this web site to be a very useful resource in your career as a Close Protection Officer.